AF893172

CHRYSLER

OUTBOARD SERVICE HANDBOOK

25 to 140 hp • 1966-1979

ERIC JORGENSEN
Editor

JEFF ROBINSON
Publisher

CLYMER PUBLICATIONS

World's largest publisher of books devoted exclusively to automobiles and motorcycles.

12860 MUSCATINE STREET • P.O. BOX 20 • ARLETA, CALIFORNIA 91331

Copyright © 1975, 1977 Clymer Publications

All rights reserved. No part of this publication may be reproduced, stored in a retrieval system, or transmitted, in any form or by any means, electronic, mechanical, photocopying, recording or otherwise, without the prior written permission of Clymer Publications.

FIRST EDITION
First Printing July, 1975

SECOND EDITION
Revised by Ray Hoy to include 1976-1977 models
First Printing September, 1977

THIRD EDITION
Updated to include 1978-1979 models
First Printing January, 1979
Second Printing August, 1979

Printed in U.S.A.

ISBN: 0-89287-183-0

Technical assistance by

Joe Esse, Sportsmen's Outboard Motor Service, San Francisco, California

CONTENTS

CHRYSLER

OUTBOARD SERVICE HANDBOOK

25 to 135 hp • 1966-1977

CHAPTER ONE

GENERAL INFORMATION

This book provides service information and procedures for all 1966-1979 Chrysler outboard motors from 25 hp to 140 hp.

MANUAL ORGANIZATION

Chrysler outboard models from 1966 through 1975 are covered in Chapters One through Six in the main body of this book. The Supplement at the back of this book covers 1976 and later models.

The chapter headings of the Supplement section correspond with the chapter headings in the main body. Only changes affecting the 1976 and later models appear in the supplemental chapters. Otherwise, service and repair procedures are the same as for earlier models.

This chapter provides general information and specifications applicable to all 1966-1975 models. Refer to the Supplement section for 1976 and later models. See **Table 1** for general specifications for all models by horsepower and model number.

Chapters Two through Five provide specific procedures for complete engine tune-up, disassembly, repair, and reassembly in easy-to-follow, step-by-step form.

If a procedure is impractical for the owner/mechanic, it is so indicated. Such operations are usually more economically and quickly performed by an authorized service center.

Some procedures specify special tools. In all cases, the tools are illustrated in actual use or alone. A well-equipped mechanic may be able to substitute other similar tools that are on hand or fabricate new ones.

The Appendix contains wiring diagrams for all models with electric ignition including those with Magnapower Capacitive Discharge (CD) ignition systems.

GENERAL SERVICE HINTS

Observing the following general hints and practices will save time, effort, frustration, and possibly help avoid a costly mistake.

Disconnect the battery ground cable before working near electrical connections and before disconnecting wires. But, never run the engine with the battery disconnected; the alternator or other electrical parts could be seriously damaged.

Tag all similar internal parts for location and mark all mating parts for position. Record number and thickness of any shims as they are removed. Small parts such as bolts can be identified by placing them in plastic sandwich bags and sealing and labeling the bags with masking tape.

Protect finished surfaces from physical damage or corrosion. Keep gasoline off painted surfaces.

Frozen or very tight bolts and screws can often be loosened by soaking with penetrating oil, then sharply striking the bolt head a few times with a hammer and punch (or screwdriver for screws). Avoid heat, unless absolutely necessary, since it may melt, warp, or remove the temper from many parts.

Avoid flames or sparks when working near a charging battery or flammable liquids.

No parts, except those assembled with a press fit, require unusual force during assembly. If a part is hard to remove or install, find out why before proceeding.

Cover all openings after removing parts to keep dirt, small tools, etc., from falling in.

When assembling 2 parts, start all fasteners, then tighten evenly.

Read each procedure in its entirety while looking at the actual parts before beginning. Many procedures are complicated and errors can be disastrous. When you thoroughly understand what is to be done, follow the procedure step-by-step.

PERIODIC SERVICE AND PREVENTIVE MAINTENANCE HINTS

1. Perform the following steps if motor is used in salt water.

   a. Tilt the engine out of water when not in use.
   b. Periodically run engine in fresh water to flush out salt deposits that form in the cooling system.

   NOTE: *An adapter for flushing engine with a garden hose is available from an authorized dealer.*

   c. Hose down outside of engine with fresh water and apply wax to protect the exterior finish.
   d. Periodically remove propeller and apply a lubricant to the propeller shaft.

   NOTE: *If paint is chipped on propeller, apply touch-up paint to avoid metal corrosion.*

2. Perform the following checks and services to prolong life and performance of all outboard motors.

   a. Use type of fuel, oil, and grease specified by the manufacturer.
   b. Maintain correct fuel/oil ratio.
   c. Never run outboard motor out of water or test tank.
   d. Do not overrev engines with clutch in the NEUTRAL position. Speed control should never be advanced beyond START position.
   e. Check drain, and replace gear lube in gear housing at proper intervals.
   f. Properly prepare motor for off season storage.
   g. Check propeller shaft seals after every year's use or immediately after contact with monofilament fishing line, or similar foreign objects.
   h. Never use electric starter continuously for more than 15 seconds without allowing at least 3 minutes for starter to cool.
   i. Shift gears rapidly at the proper engine speed. Do not ease gears. This causes excessive wear to the gears and clutch.
   j. Check all items subject to normal wear (water pump impeller, breaker points, spark plugs, starter ropes, starter pawls, shear pins, and items of a similar nature) at least once every season.
   k. Do not tip motor upside down or store in an inverted position or corrosion in crankcase will result.
   l. Perform tune-up at the beginning of each season. Periodically clean, inspect, and adjust the carburetor.
   m. Never exceed recommended rpm range.
   n. Adequately protect motor against excessive spray and backwash. Spray or backwash may cause premature corrosion.

3. Perform the following steps prior to long periods of disuse or off season storage.
   a. If engine has been used in salt water, completely flush as previously described.
   b. Run engine to operating temperature.
   c. With gearshift in NEUTRAL, run engine at fast idle. Remove fuel line from engine and quickly inject rust preventive oil in air intakes for 10-20 seconds or until the engine dies.
   d. Remove motor from test tank or boat and crank engine through a few times to remove water from cooling system.
   e. Drain fuel tank, lines, and carburetor.
   f. Remove spark plugs and squirt 1 or 2 ounces of engine oil into cylinders and crank engine through a few times to distribute oil. Replace spark plugs.
   g. Drain and refill the gear housing with new grease.
   h. Lubricate all miscellaneous moving parts.
   i. Remove propeller and lubricate propeller shaft. Reinstall propeller.
   j. Clean and wax exterior of the motor.
   k. Store engine upright in a well ventilated, clean, dry environment.

SPARK PLUGS

Using the proper spark plug in a 2-cycle engine is very important. Improper spark plugs can cause serious motor damage through preignition and piston burning as well as severe degradation of motor performance. Upon removal, proper examination of spark plugs can also give clues to improper motor adjustment, motor use and possible future malfunctions. The following steps describe how to interpret spark plug conditions and probable causes for abnormal indications. **Table 2** lists spark plug recommendations according to motor horsepower and heat range.

Standard Battery and Magneto Ignition

1. Spark plugs that are too hot will have a white or light grey insulator. The insulators may have a blistered appearance. Electrodes may erode prematurely and have a blue color. Possible causes, other than incorrect spark plug, could be the following.
   a. Carburetion too lean (main jet)
   b. Ignition timing over advanced
   c. Sticking piston rings
   d. Wide open throttle rpm too low (lugging engine)
   e. Reduced water flow (restricted water passages or bad water pump)
2. Normal spark plugs will have a light tan insulator with few deposits present. Electrodes will not be burned or eroded.
3. Spark plugs that are too cold will have a wet black appearance. Possible causes other than incorrect spark plugs could be the following.
   a. Prolonged trolling operation
   b. Carburetor idle adjustment too rich
   c. Improper fuel/oil ratio (excessive oil or poor mixing)
   d. Worn or defective breaker points
   e. Blocked passages or blocked check valves in the fuel recycling system
4. If plugs foul, use hotter spark plugs. If preignition or burnt pistons are experienced, use a colder spark plug.

Magnapower (Capacitive Discharge) Ignition

The surface gap spark plugs used with the Magnapower ignition systems have no true heat range, however all factors listed under standard ignition that cause spark plug fouling also apply to the Magnapower ignition systems. See Table 2 for spark plug recommendations.

FUEL MIXING

Perform the following steps while mixing fuel to prevent possible fuel contamination and improper mixing. Refer to **Table 3** for recommended fuel and **Table 4** for mixing ratios.

1. Ensure fuel tank is clean and area around filler is free from dust and dirt.
2. If possible, strain all fuel through a clean filter to remove dirt or residue.
3. Pour one gallon of fresh gasoline into an empty tank.

4. Add proper amount of recommended oil.
5. Add the balance of gasoline and thoroughly mix the fuel.

CAUTION

Always use the exact amount of oil recommended. Too little oil will cause serious motor damage, and too much oil can severely foul the motor.

PROPELLER INTERCHANGEABILITY

The proper propeller for the boat and motor combination is very important. Consider the type of use the boat and motor are typically subjected to and refer to **Table 5** for the proper propeller needed.

TIGHTENING TORQUE

Many fasteners must be tightened a specific amount as measured by a torque wrench. Tightening to proper torque can prevent damage to fasteners and warpage of expensive parts like the cylinder head. **Tables 6 through 8** provide torque values for fasteners used on 25-135 hp engines.

Table 1 GENERAL SPECIFICATIONS

Model	hp	rpm	Bore and Stroke Inches	Displace-ment Cu. In.	Com-pression PSI	Spark Plug Type	Spark Plug (Gap) Inches	Breaker Point Gap Inches	Timing @ WOT*	Gear Ratio
250 Series	25	5,000	2-13/16 x 2.300	28.57	95-105	L4J	0.030	0.020	NA	14-21
300 Series	30	5,000	2-13/16 x 2.414	29.99	125-135	L4J	0.030	0.020	NA	13-26
35500 Series	35	4,500	3 x 2.540	35.90	95-105	J4J	0.030	0.020	32° BTDC†	13-21
35600, 35700, 3500, 350 Series	35	4,750	3 x 2.540	35.90	95-105	J4J	0.030	0.020	32° BTDC†	13-21
45500 Series	45	4,750	3-1/8 x 2.75	42.18	130-140	AC-M42K	0.030	0.020	32° BTDC†	13-21
45600, 45700 Series 4501, 4503, 4502, 4504, 4521, 4523, 4522, 4524, 4531, 4533, 4532, 4534, 4541, 4543, 4542, 4544, 4551, 4553, 4552, 4554	45	4,750	3-1/8 x 2.75	42.18	130-140	L4J	0.030	0.020	32° BTDC†	13-21
4561, 4563, 4562, 4564, 4571, 4573, 4572, 4574	45	4,750	3-1/8 x 2.75	42.18	130-140	L4J	0.030	0.015	32° BTDC†	13-21
450, 451, 452, 453, 454, 455 Series 4505, 4506, 4525, 4527, 4526, 4528, 4535, 4537, 4536, 4538, 4545, 4555, 4546, 4556	45	4,750	3-1/8 x 2.75	42.18	115-125	L4J	0.030	0.020	32° BTDC†	13-21
456, 457, 458, 459 Series 4565, 4575, 4566, 4576	45	4,750	3-1/8 x 2.75	42.18	115-125	L4J	0.030	0.015	32° BTDC†	13-21
464HA	45	4,750	3-1/8 x 2.75	42.18	185-195	L4J	0.030	0.020	32° BTDC†	13-21
468HA, 469HA	45	4,750	3-1/8 x 2.75	42.18	150-160	UL18V	NA	0.015	32° BTDC†	13-21
50500, 50600 Series	50	4,750	3-3/16 x 2.80	44.70	130-140	AC-M42K	0.030	0.020	32° BTDC†	13-21
554, 555, 5540, 5550, 55720, 55730 Series	55	5,250	3-3/16 x 2.80	44.70	145-155	L4J	0.030	0.020	32° BTDC†	13-21
556, 557, 5560, 5570, 55760, 55770 Series	55	5,250	3-3/16 x 2.80	44.70	145-155	L4J	0.030	0.015	32° BTDC†	13-21

*WOT - Wide open throttle. †BTDC - Before top dead center.

Model	hp	rpm	Bore and Stroke Inches	Displacement Cu. In.	Compression PSI	Spark Plug Type	Spark Plug (Gap) Inches	Breaker Point Gap Inches	Timing @ WOT*	Gear Ratio
558, 5580, 5590	55	5,250	3-3/16 x 2.80	44.70	145-155	UL18V	NA	0.015	32° BTDC†	13-21
551 Series	55	5,250	3-3/16 x 2.80	44.70	145-155	L4J	0.030	0.015	32° BTDC†	15-26
600 Series	60	5,250	3-3/8 x 2.80	49.90	150-160	UL18V	NA	Breakerless	32° BTDC†	13-21
700, 7000 Series	70	4,750	3-5/16 x 2.80	72.39	130-140	L20V	NA	0.014	32° BTDC†	15-26
75600, 75700 Series	75	4,750	3-5/16 x 2.80	72.39	130-140	J4J	0.030	0.015	32° BTDC†	16-25
7500 Series	75	4,750	3-5/16 x 2.80	72.39	130-140	L20V	NA	0.014	32° BTDC†	16-25
750 Series	75	4,750	3-5/16 x 2.80	72.39	145-155	L20V	NA	0.014	32° BTDC†	15-30
80500 Series	80	4,750	3-1/8 x 2.75	84.36	115-125	J4J	0.030	0.020	34° BTDC†	16-25
850, 8560, 8570 Series	85	5,000	3-5/16 x 2.80	72.39	145-155	L20V	NA	0.014	32° BTDC†	15-26
900 Series	90	5,000	3-5/16 x 2.80	72.39	155-165	L20V	NA	0.014	32° BTDC†	15-30
105600, 150700	105	5,000	3-5/16 x 2.80	96.55	130-140	J4J	0.030	0.015	32° BTDC†	16-25
10560, 10570, 1050 Series	105	5,000	3-5/16 x 2.80	96.55	130-140	L20V	NA	0.010	32° BTDC†	15-26
10580, 1058 Series	105	5,000	3-5/16 x 2.80	96.55	130-140	L20V	NA	0.010	32° BTDC†	15-14
1206, 1207 Series (except HF and BF)	120	5,250	3-5/16 x 2.80	96.55	145-155	L20V	NA	0.010	34° BTDC†	15-26
1206 HF/BF, 1207 HF/BF	120	5,250	3-5/16 x 2.80	96.55	145-155	L20V	NA	0.010	32° BTDC†	15-26
1208 Series	120	5,250	3-5/16 x 2.80	96.55	145-155	L20V	NA	0.010	34° BTDC†	15-14
1306, 1307 Series	130	5,250	3-5/16 x 2.80	96.55	155-165	L20V	NA	0.010	34° BTDC†	15-26
1356, 1357 Series	135	5,000	3-3/8 x 2.80	99.80	155-165	L20V	NA	0.010	32° BTDC†	15-26

*WOT - Wide open throttle. †BTDC - Before top dead center.

Table 2 RECOMMENDED SPARK PLUGS

	Champion	Champion Substitute	AC	AC Substitute	Autolite	Bosch
25 through 55 hp						
Standard ignition						
Hotter range	L-5	L-6G	M43FF	—	AE3	W225T1
Standard	L-4J	L-4G	M42FF	—	AE2	W240T1
Colder range	L-77J	—	M41FF	—	—	W260T1
45-55 CD ignition						
Standard	UL-18V	UL-77V	—	—	—	—
*Fouling Replacement	L-77J	L-62R, L-2G	M41FF	—	—	W260T1
Emergency Replacement	L-4J	L-4G	M42FF	—	AE2	W240T1
70-150 CD ignition						
Standard	L-20V	L-19V, L-77V	V40FFM	V40FF, V40FFS	AEKO	WET1
*Fouling Replacement	L-77J	L-62R, L-2G	M41FF	—	—	W260T1
Emergency Replacement	L-4J	—	M42FF	—	AE2	W240T1

*Plugs may be used to replace UL-18V or L-20V plugs if fouling persists. Plugs are to be used only if all other fouling causes have been eliminated.

Table 3 RECOMMENDED GASOLINE

Preferred	Acceptable	Do Not Use
Low-lead automobile gas.	Leaded regular grade automobile gas.	Low octane white gas (lamp fuel).
Light aircraft gas (87 octane—low lead).	Premium grade automobile gas (no phosphorus).	Non-leaded motor fuel containing phosphorous.
	Automobile gas (85 octane minimum).	Any fuel not intended for use in modern automotive engines.

Table 4 FUEL RATIO CONVERSION

Ratio	Gasoline Quantity	Oil Quantity		
1/2 pt. per gal. 16 : 1 or 6% oil	1 gallon — 3.8 liters	1/2 pint	8 oz.	.236 liters
	6 gallons (5 Imp. gal.) — 23 liters	3 pints	48 oz.	1.419 liters
	12 gallons (10 Imp. gal.) — 46 liters	6 pints	96 oz.	2.836 liters
1/3 pt. per gal. 24 : 1 or 4% oil	1 gallon — 3.8 liters	1/3 pint	5.3 oz.	.158 liters
	6 gallons (5 Imp. gal.) — 23 liters	2 pints	32 oz.	.946 liters
	12 gallons (10 Imp. gal.) — 46 liters	4 pints	64 oz.	1.892 liters
1/6 pt. per gal. 50 : 1 or 2% oil	1 gallon — 3.8 liters	1/6 pint	2.6 oz.	.079 liters
	6 gallons (5 Imp. gal.) — 23 liters	1 pint	16 oz.	.473 liters
	12 gallons (10 Imp. gal.) — 46 liters	2 pints	32 oz.	.946 liters

Table 5 PROPELLER INTERCHANGEABILITY

Horsepower	Standard Prop	High-Speed Light Load Applications	General Heavy Duty Load Applications	Extra Heavy Load Applications
25	P346	P461	P346	P102
30	P273	P273	P273	P287
35	P287	P293	P278 P287	P278
45	P293	P273	P287 P293	P278
55	P293	P273	P287 P278 P293	P287 P278
70	P389	P439	P438 P439 P389	P391
85	P389	P372	P438 P439 P389	P391
105	P372	P383	P439 P440	P389 P438
120	P372	P383	P439 P440 P372	P389 P438
130	P372	P404 P383	P439 P440 P372	P389

Table 6 TIGHTENING TORQUES

Horsepower	25		30	
Cylinder head	225 in.-lb.	260 kg-cm	225 in.-lb.	260 kg-cm
Flywheel nut	45 ft.-lb.	6.2 kg-m	45 ft.-lb.	6.2 kg-m
Main bearing bolts	160 in.-lb.	185 kg-cm	160 in.-lb.	185 kg-cm
Connecting rod screws	170 in.-lb.	195 kg-cm	170 in.-lb.	195 kg-cm
Stern bracket pivot bolt	160 in.-lb.	185 kg-cm	160 in.-lb.	185 kg-cm
Exhaust port cover	70 in.-lb.	80 kg-cm	70 in.-lb.	80 kg-cm
Transfer port cover	70 in.-lb.	80 kg-cm	70 in.-lb.	80 kg-cm

1

Table 7 TIGHTENING TORQUES

Horsepower		35, 45, 50, 55		60		70, 75, 85, 90	
Cylinder	3/8-16 bolts	270 in.-lb.	310 kg-cm			270 in.-lb.	310 kg-cm
Head	5/16-18 bolts			225 in.-lb.	260 kg-cm	225 in.-lb.	260 kg-cm
Flywheel		80 ft.-lb.	11 kg-m	90 ft.-lb.	12.50 kg-m	90 ft.-lb.	12.5 kg-m
Main bearing bolts		270 in.-lb.	310 kg-cm	270 in.-lb.	310 kg-cm	270 in.-lb.	310 kg-cm
Connecting rod screws		170 in.-lb.	195 kg-cm	275 in.-lb.	317 kg-cm	170 in.-lb.	195 kg-cm
King pin nut		90 ft.-lb. Stake 3 times	12.5 kg-m	50 ft.-lb.	6.9 kg-m	—	—
Distributor shaft nut		—	—	—	—	60 in.-lb.	69 kg-cm
Nose cone nut (racing engines)		—	—	—	—	—	—
Drive shaft nut (racing engines)		—	—	—	—	—	—
Propeller shaft nut (racing engines)		—	—	—	—	—	—

Horsepower		105, 120, 130, 135		135, 150 (Racing)	
Cylinder	3/8-16 bolts	270 in.-lb.	310 kg-cm		
Head	5/16-18 bolts	225 in.-lb.	260 kg-cm	225 in.-lb.	260 kg-cm
Flywheel		90 ft.-lb.	12.5 kg-m	90 ft.-lb.	12.5 kg-m
Main bearing bolts		270 in.-lb.	310 kg-cm	270 in.-lb.	310 kg-cm
Connecting rod screws		170 in.-lb.	195 kg-cm	170 in.-lb.	195 kg-cm
King pin nut		—	—	—	—
Distributor shaft nut		60 in.-lb.	69 kg-cm	60 in.-lb.	69 kg-cm
Nose cone nut (racing engines)		325 in.-lb.	370 kg-cm	325 in.-lb.	370 kg-cm
Drive shaft nut (racing engines)		50 ft.-lb.	6.9 kg-m	50 ft.-lb.	6.9 kg-m
Propeller shaft nut (racing engines)		50 ft.-lb.	6.9 kg-m	50 ft.-lb.	6.9 kg-m

Table 8 TORQUE FOR STANDARD HARDWARE

Screw Size	Torque (in.-lb.)	Torque (kg-cm)	Screw Size	Torque (in.-lb.)	Torque (kg-cm)
10 - 24	30	35	5/16 - 18	160	185
10 - 32	35	40	3/8 - 16	270	310
12 - 24	45	52	Gear housing plug	90-115	100-130
1/4 - 20	70	80	Spark plug 14mm	120-180	140-205

CHAPTER TWO

TROUBLESHOOTING

Troubleshooting can be a relatively simple matter if it is done logically. The first step in any troubleshooting procedure must be defining the symptoms as closely as possible. Subsequent steps involve testing and analyzing areas which could cause the symptoms. A haphazard approach may eventually find the trouble, but in terms of wasted time and unnecessary parts replacement, it can be very costly.

This chapter describes how a 2-cycle engine works. An understanding of this will help you analyze troubles logically. In addition, this chapter includes tool recommendations. Finally, the chapter includes suggestions for finding specific troubles with a minimum of effort.

TOOLS

Emergency Tool Kit

A number of troubles can be fixed quickly at sea if you have the proper tools with you. **Figure 1** shows a good emergency tool kit. When you buy wrenches, make sure that you include at least one wrench to fit every nut and bolt on the engine. Several combination screwdrivers like the one shown are available. Of course, you can always buy separate ones. Keep the tools in a small pouch or tool box. Keep the tools well oiled to prevent rust, and never remove the tool kit from the boat; you'll probably leave it ashore when you need it most.

Shop Tools

To properly service your outboard, you will need a good assortment of ordinary hand tools. As a minimum:

a. Combination wrenches
b. Socket wrenches
c. Plastic mallet
d. Small hammer
e. Snap ring pliers
f. Gas pliers
g. Vise Grip pliers
h. Phillips screwdrivers
i. Common screwdrivers
j. Feeler gauges
k. Spark plug gauge
l. Spark plug wrench

Special tools necessary are illustrated in the chapters in which they are used.

ENGINE PRINCIPLES

Figures 2 through 5 illustrate operation of the 2-stroke engine. During this discussion, assume that the crankshaft is rotating counter-

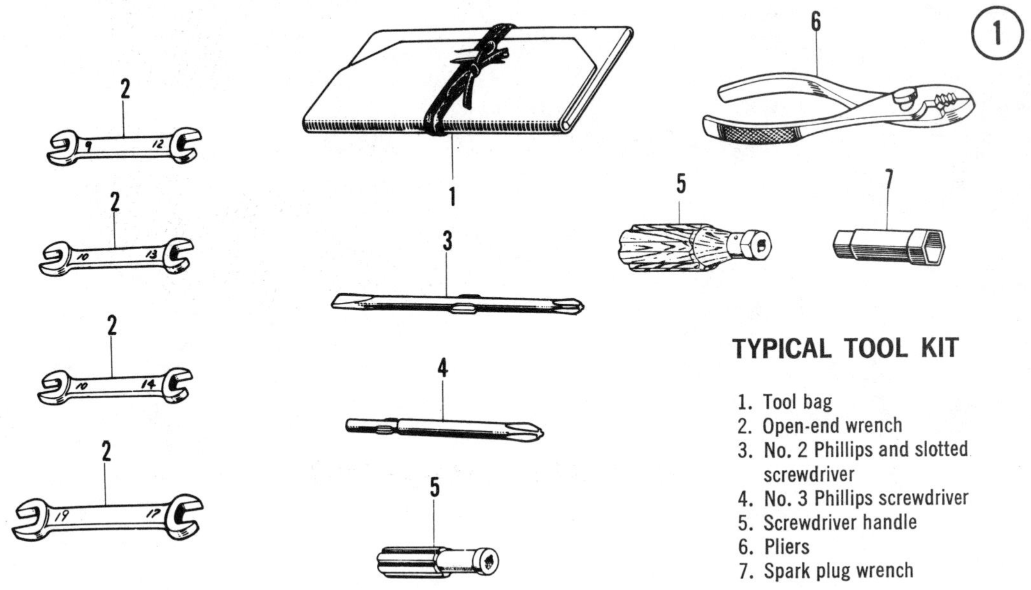

TYPICAL TOOL KIT

1. Tool bag
2. Open-end wrench
3. No. 2 Phillips and slotted screwdriver
4. No. 3 Phillips screwdriver
5. Screwdriver handle
6. Pliers
7. Spark plug wrench

clockwise. In **Figure 2**, as the piston travels downward, a scavenging port (A) between the crankcase and the cylinder is uncovered. The exhaust gases, which are under pressure, leave the cylinder through the exhaust port (B), which is also opened by the downward movement of the piston. A fresh fuel/air charge, which has previously been compressed slightly, travels from the crankcase (C) to the cylinder through the scavenging port (A) as the port opens. Since the incoming charge is under pressure, it rushes into the cylinder quickly and helps to expel the exhaust gases from the previous cycle.

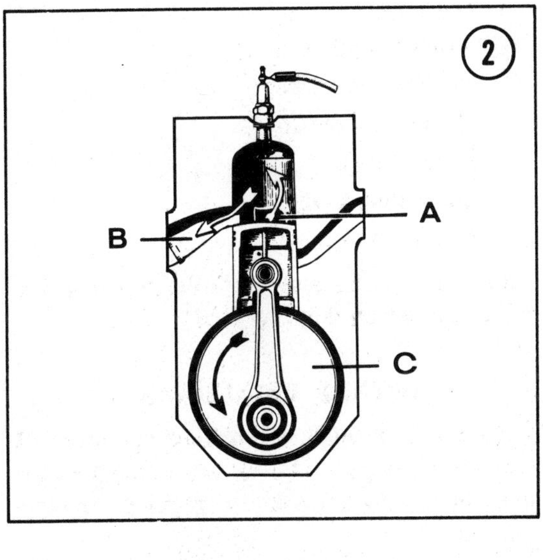

Figure 3 illustrates the next phase of the cycle. As the crankshaft continues to rotate, the piston moves upward, closing the exhaust and scavenging ports. As the piston continues upward, the air/fuel mixture in the cylinder is compressed. Notice also that a low pressure area is created in the crankcase at the same time. Further upward movement of the piston uncovers the intake port (D). A fresh fuel/air charge is then drawn into the crankcase through the intake port because of the low pressure created by the upward piston movement.

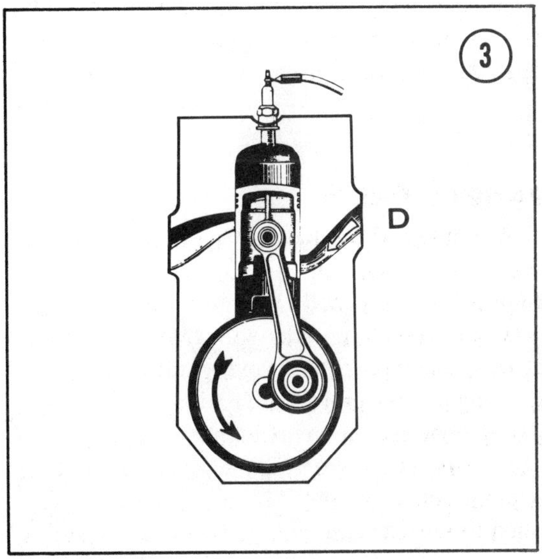

The third phase is shown in **Figure 4**. As the piston approaches top dead center, the spark plug fires, igniting the compressed mixture. The piston is then driven downward by the expanding gases.

4

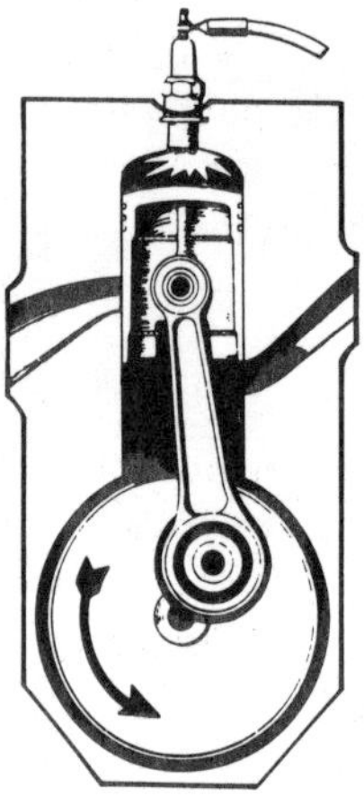

When the top of the piston uncovers the exhaust port, the fourth phase begins, as shown in **Figure 5**. The exhaust gases leave the cylinder through the exhaust port. As the piston continues downward, the intake port is closed and the mixture in the crankcase is compressed in preparation for the next cycle.

5

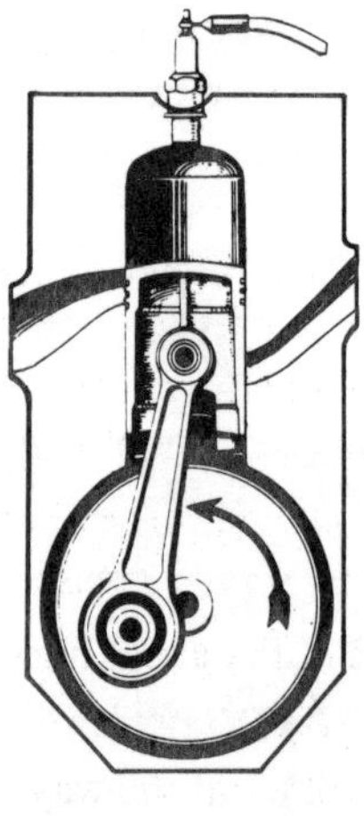

It can be seen from the foregoing discussion that every downward stroke of the piston is a power stroke.

ENGINE LUBRICATION

A conventional 2-stroke engine cannot receive its lubrication from an oil supply in the crankcase. Oil splash in the crankcase would be carried into the cylinders with the fuel/air charge, resulting in high oil consumption and spark plug fouling. In order to lubricate a 2-stroke engine, the oil must be mixed directly with the gasoline in a prescribed ratio.

Diagnosing motor trouble is relatively simple if you use orderly procedures and keep a few basic principles in mind.

Never assume anything. Don't overlook the obvious. If the motor suddenly quits, check the easiest, most accessible problem spots first. Is there gasoline in the tank? Is the gas petcock on? Has a spark plug wire fallen off?

If nothing obvious turns up in a cursory check, look a little further. Learning to recognize and describe symptoms will make repairs easier for you or a mechanic at the shop. Describe problems accurately and fully. Saying that "it won't run" isn't the same as saying "it quit at high speed and wouldn't start," or that "it sat in my garage for 3 months and then wouldn't start."

Gather as many symptoms together as possible to aid in diagnosis. Note whether the engine lost power gradually or all at once, what color smoke (if any) came from the exhausts, and so on. Remember that the more complicated a motor is, the easier it is to troubleshoot because symptoms point to specific problems.

You don't need fancy equipment or complicated test gear to determine whether repairs can be attempted at home. A few simple checks could save a large repair bill and time lost while the motor sits in a dealer's service department. On the other hand, be realistic and don't attempt repairs beyond your abilities. Service departments tend to charge heavily for putting together a disassembled engine that may have been abused. Some won't even take on such a job—so use common sense; don't go in over your head.

OPERATING REQUIREMENTS

An engine needs 3 basics to run properly: correct gas/air mixture, compression, and a spark at the right time. If one or more are missing, the engine won't run. The electrical system is the weakest link of the 3 basics. More problems result from electrical breakdowns than from any other source. Keep that in mind before you begin tampering with carburetor components and the like.

If a motor has been sitting for any length of time and refuses to start, check the gasoline delivery system. This includes the tank, fuel petcocks, lines, and the carburetor. Rust may have formed in the tank, obstructing fuel flow. Gasoline deposits may have gummed up carburetor jets and air passages. Gasoline tends to lose its potency after standing for long periods. Condensation may contaminate it with water. Drain old gas and try starting with a fresh tankful.

Compression, or the lack of it, usually enters the picture only in the case of older motors. Worn or broken pistons, rings, and cylinder bores could prevent starting. Generally, a gradual power loss and harder and harder starting will be readily apparent in this case.

STARTING DIFFICULTIES

Check gas flow first. Remove the gas cap and look into the tank. If gas is present, pull off a fuel line at the carburetor and see if gas flows freely. If none comes out, the fuel tap may be shut off, blocked by rust or foreign matter, or the fuel line may be stopped up or kinked. If the carburetor is getting fuel, turn to the electrical system next.

On electric start models, check that the battery is charged by turning on running lights. Refer to your owner's manual for starting procedures with a dead battery. Have the battery recharged if necessary.

Pull off a spark plug cap, remove the spark plug, and reconnect the cap. Lay the plug against the cylinder head so its base makes a good connection, and turn the engine over with the starter cord. A fat, blue spark should jump across the electrodes. If there is no spark, or only a weak one, there is electrical system trouble. Check for a defective plug by replacing it with a known good one. Don't assume a plug is good just because it's new.

If the plug is good, but there's still no spark, backtrack through the system. If the contact at the end of the spark plug wire can be exposed, hold it about 1/8 in. from the head and turn the engine over to check for a spark. Remember to hold the wire only by its insulation to avoid a nasty shock. If the plug wires are dirty, greasy, or wet, wrap a rag around them so you don't get shocked. If you do feel a shock or see sparks along the wire, clean or replace the wire and/or its connections.

If there's no spark at the plug wire, look for loose connections at the coil and battery. If all seems in order there, check next for oily or dirty contact points. Clean points with electrical contact cleaner, or a strip of paper.

Note that spark plugs of the incorrect heat range (too cold) may cause hard starting. Set gaps to specifications.

If a healthy spark occurs at the right time, and there is adequate gas flow to the carburetor, check the carburetor itself. Make sure all jets and air passages are clean, check float level, and adjust if necessary. Shake the float to check for gasoline inside it, and replace or repair as indicated. Check that the carburetors are mounted snugly, and no air is leaking past the manifold. Check for a clogged air filter.

Compression may be checked at sea by pulling the starter cord and noting that an adequate resistance is felt, or by removing a spark plug, placing a finger over the plug hole and feeling for pressure.

An accurate compression check gives a good idea of the condition of the basic working parts of the engine. To perform this test, you need a compression gauge. The motor should be warm.

1. Remove the plug on the cylinder to be tested and clean out any dirt or grease.

2. Insert the tip of the gauge into the hole, making sure it is seated correctly.

3. Open the throttle all the way and make sure the chokes on the carburetors are open.

4. Crank the engine several times and record the highest pressure reading on the gauge. Run the test on each of the cylinders.

POOR IDLING

Poor idling may be caused by incorrect carburetor adjustment, incorrect timing, or ignition system defects. Check the gas cap vent for an obstruction.

MISFIRING

Misfiring can be caused by a weak spark or dirty plugs. Check for fuel contamination. Run the machine at night or in a darkened garage to check for spark leaks along the plug wires and under the spark plug cap. If misfiring occurs only at certain throttle settings, clean the carburetor as described elsewhere in this book. Misfiring under heavy load, as when accelerating, is usually caused by bad spark plugs.

FLAT SPOTS

If the engine seems to die momentarily when the throttle is opened and then recovers, check for a dirty main jet in the carburetor, water in the fuel, or an excessively lean mixture.

POWER LOSS

Poor condition of rings, pistons, or cylinders will cause a lack of power and speed.

OVERHEATING

If the engine seems to run too hot all the time, be sure you are not idling it for long periods. Make sure the cooling water intake is not blocked. Remove and clean the water pump. Spark plugs of the wrong heat range can burn pistons. An excessively lean gas mixture may cause overheating. Broken or worn piston rings can allow compression gases to leak past them, thus heating heads and cylinders excessively. Check oil level and use the proper grade lubricants.

ENGINE NOISES

Experience is needed to diagnose accurately in this area. Noises are hard to differentiate and harder yet to describe. Deep knocking noises usually mean main bearing failure. A slapping noise generally comes from loose pistons. A light knocking noise during acceleration may be a bad connecting rod bearing. Pinging, which sounds like marbles being shaken in a tin can, is caused by ignition advanced too far or gasoline with too low an octane rating. Pinging should be corrected immediately or damage to pistons will result. Compression leaks at the head-cylinder joint will sound like a rapid on-and-off squeal.

PISTON SEIZURE

Piston seizure is caused by incorrect piston clearances when fitted, fitting rings with improper end gap, too thin an oil being used, incorrect spark plug heat range, or incorrect ignition timing. Overheating from any cause may result in seizure.

EXCESSIVE VIBRATION

Excessive vibration may be caused by loose motor mounts, worn engine or gear housing bearings, broken or loose parts, or a generally poor running engine.

CHAPTER THREE

OUTBOARD MOTORS (25 AND 30 HP)

3

This chapter covers the tune-up, repair, and disassembly of all 25 and 30 hp outboard motors. **Table 1** provides general specifications. **Table 2** provides tightening torque for fasteners. Both tables are at the end of the chapter.

TUNE-UP

Checking Compression

Engine must be cool before performing this procedure.

1. Remove spark plugs from cylinder head.
2. Hold throttle wide open.
3. Connect compression gauges following manufacturer's instructions.
4. Crank engine over rapidly for 5-10 revolutions. Compression of each cylinder should be within the following specifications.

   a. 25 hp 95-100 psi
   b. 30 hp 125-135 psi

Torquing Cylinder Head

Loosen each bolt, then torque bolt to 225 in-lb. Follow sequence shown in **Figure 1**.

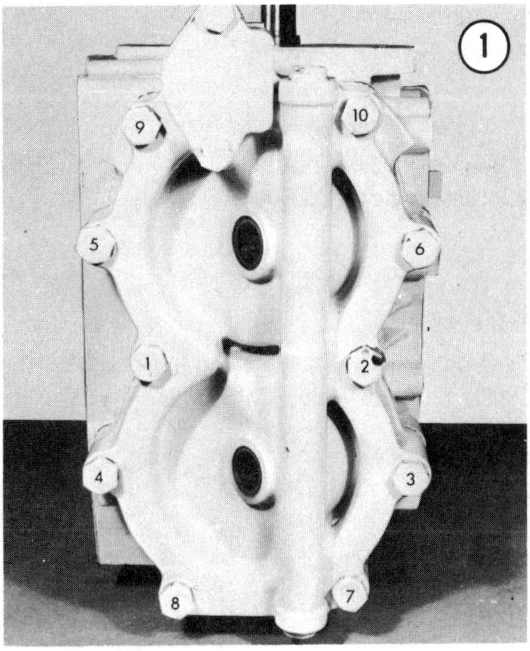

CAUTION

Do not over torque cylinder head bolts. The cylinder bores or head my be distorted. Do not under torque or the cylinder gasket may leak.

Spark Plugs

1. Remove spark plugs with 13/16 in. box-end wrench or socket.
2. Inspect plug condition. Clean or replace plugs if necessary.

3. Check electrode gap on plugs with wire type feeler gauge. Before setting spark plug gap, file center electrode flat. Adjust to 0.030 in. by bending ground (side) electrode.

4. Install plugs and torque to 120-180 in.-lb.

Breaker Point

1. Remove flywheel as described later.

2. Check breaker points for burning or pitting. Clean or replace if necessary. See replacement procedure under *Magneto* later in this chapter.

3. Squeeze cam wiper felt. If it appears to be dry, work a small amount of Rykon 2EP or equivalent cam lube into the felt. Work the grease in thoroughly by rubbing the felt between your fingertips.

> NOTE: *Rykon 2EP is supplied with new breaker points. If unattainable, ask the dealer about equivalent cam lubricant.*

> CAUTION
> *Do not over-grease the felt. Excessive grease may work between the points and lead to ignition failure.*

4. Install knock-off nut on crankshaft. Turn crankshaft clockwise until breaker point follower arm is approximately 10° past point at which breaker points are fully open. Once correct adjustment point is found, mark position on cam for adjusting other breaker point.

5. Adjust breaker point opening to 0.020 in.

6. After setting points, rotate engine 2 revolutions and recheck breaker point gap.

7. Install flywheel.

Throttle Pick-up Point Adjustment

1. Disconnect throttle link at magneto control lever. Do not disconnect throttle link at throttle cam or throttle cam may be distorted.

2. Loosen stop nut on eccentric screw which secures nylon roller to throttle arm. Tighten stop nut just enough to take up clearance between eccentric screw, roller, throttle arm, and nut.

3. Set throttle pick-up mark on throttle cam in the approximate area where contact with the roller will occur.

4. Rotate eccentric screw counterclockwise until roller is at maximum distance from pick-up point mark on throttle cam.

5. Rotate eccentric screw counterclockwise until roller just contacts pick-up mark on throttle cam. Rotate throttle cam so that pick-up mark on cam moves up and away from roller. Rotate throttle cam back to contact roller, if pick-up mark is not centered in relationship to throttle cam, and readjust by turning eccentric screw.

6. Tighten nut on eccentric screw being certain not to rotate eccentric screw.

7. Insert paper lightly between cam and roller from top side and then from bottom side, noting gap between edge of paper and mark on throttle cam. If gaps are equal, mark on cam is at center of contact with roller. See **Figure 2**.

2

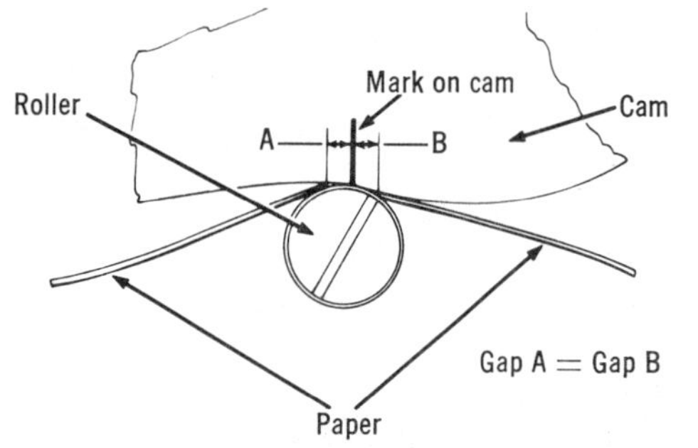

8. Connect throttle link and rotate magneto until nylon throttle stop on stator ring is against cylinder. Check to see if wide-open throttle (WOT) mark on cam is at center of contact on nylon roller. Remove throttle link from magneto control lever, loosen jam nut, then turn end of link to lengthen or shorten link until above condition is met. Tighten stop nut on link.

9. When magneto is at WOT and WOT mark on cam is at center of contact of roller, throttle shutter should be horizontal. If this is not the case, pick-up point is incorrect–repeat Steps 1 through 8.

10. On hand-start models, adjust screw in throttle stop on steering handle shaft so that set screw contacts wall of steering handle at same time WOT stop on magneto contacts cylinder.

Adjusting Carburetor

NOTE: *A tachometer is required for this procedure. If one is not available, have the adjustment performed by an authorized service center.*

1. Turn idle adjustment screw clockwise until it seats lightly in carburetor. See **Figure 3**. Do not force idle adjustment screw or the tip will be damaged.

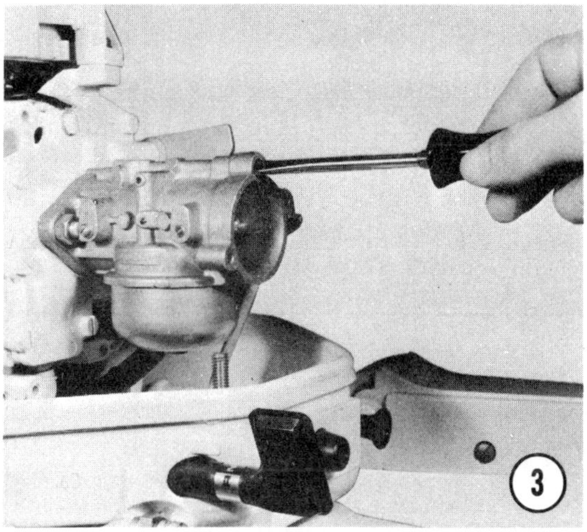

3

2. Turn idle adjustment screw 1¼ turns counterclockwise. Shift engine to NEUTRAL and turn twist grip throttle to START position.

3. Start motor, then turn twist grip to SHIFT position. Shift into FORWARD gear and warm up engine at about 2,000 rpm.

4. Turn twist grip throttle clockwise to lowest reliable throttle setting.

5. Switch tachometer to 0-1,000 rpm scale so that small fluctuations in engine speed can be detected.

6. Slowly turn carburetor idle adjustment screw clockwise—pausing for 10 seconds after each ⅛ turn. Adjust throttle as necessary to keep engine from exceeding 900 rpm. Continue turning idle adjustment screw ⅛ turn at a time until tachometer shows that engine speed is peaked and is decreasing. Note position of screw slot and amount speed decreased.

7. Slowly turn idle adjustment screw counterclockwise until engine speed has peaked and decreased to the same level as obtained in Step 6. Note position of screw slot.

8. Set idle adjustment screw at point midway between positions noted in Steps 6 and 7.

9. Suddenly open throttle fully and note engine behavior. If engine dies with a "pop," it is too lean (correct by turning idle adjustment screw counterclockwise). If engine stumbles before accelerating, it is too rich (correct by turning idle adjustment screw counterclockwise). If engine hesitates but cause cannot be determined, turn idle adjustment screw ⅛ in. in either direction and note whether or not performance improves. If performance does not change, continue turning screw ⅛ turn in same direction until there is a difference in performance.

10. On hand start models, adjust idle stop screw (starboard side of steering handle) until engine idles at 750 ± 50 rpm in FORWARD gear. See **Figure 4**.

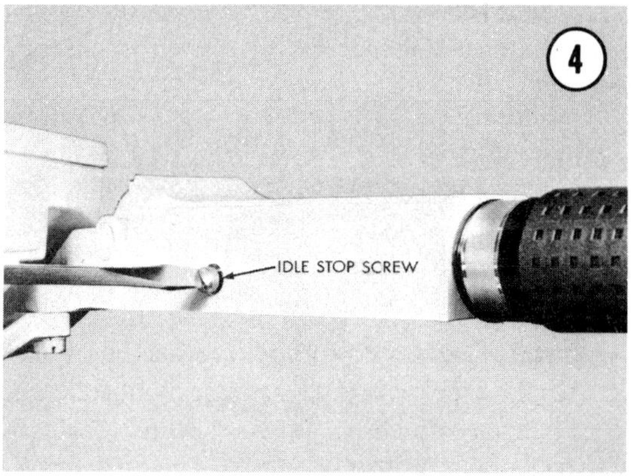

4

11. On electric start models, adjust idle stop screw (on exhaust port cover) until engine idles at 750 ± 50 rpm in FORWARD gear (**Figure 5**).

Adjusting Choke (Electric Start Models)

1. Loosen screw securing solenoid plunger to choke lever.

2. Slip a piece of paper approximately ½ in. wide into carburetor air horn.

3. While holding choke lever in closed position, push on solenoid plunger (not plunger rod) until it bottoms in solenoid. Tighten screws on choke lever swivel.

4. Pull paper from closed shutter. If there is more than a slight drag, readjust solenoid as outlined in Step 3.

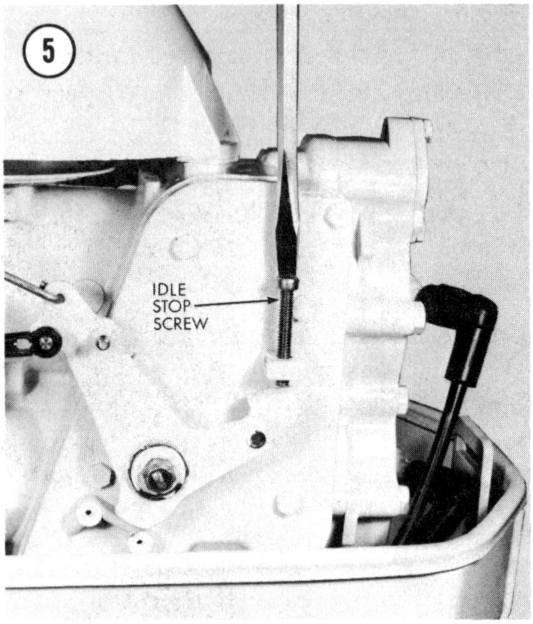

Checking Lower Unit Grease

1. With engine in running position, remove plug from GREASE FILL hole of lower gear housing. Allow a small amount of grease to flow from the FILL hole.

NOTE: *Do not check gear housing grease immediately after running engine. Allow engine to stand in the running position for at least 2 hours before checking gear grease. If water is present in lower unit, this time will allow water to settle to the bottom of lower unit.*

2. If no water is present, screw FILL plug back in 2 turns. Remove VENT plug and washer. Remove FILL plug and washer. Quickly insert nozzle of gear lube tube in FILL hole and add gear lube until it appears at VENT hole. Reinstall VENT plug and nyltite washer. Remove nozzle of gear lube tube and install FILL plug and nyltite washer.
3. If water is present, take the motor to your dealer. Have him pressure test lower unit to determine where water leakage occurs.

FLYWHEEL

1. Remove complete manual starter. See *Manual Starter*.
2. Remove flywheel nut. Insert a large screwdriver between flywheel teeth and brace screwdriver against starter mounting boss on crankcase cover.
3. Screw knock-off nut (Special Tool T2910) on crankshaft until nut is flush with end of crankshaft or approximately ⅛ in. from the top of the flywheel.
4. Position magneto stator so gaps are fore and aft. Insert flywheel wedge (Special Tool T2989 or equivalent) in stator gap. Pry flywheel up while striking flywheel nut with 16 oz. hammer as shown in **Figure 6**. Bounce hammer off nut to give a ringing blow.

CAUTION
Pry only in stator gap or stator rim may break. Never strike nut when not prying upward or crankshaft may bind in bearings. Do not strike nut with excessive force.

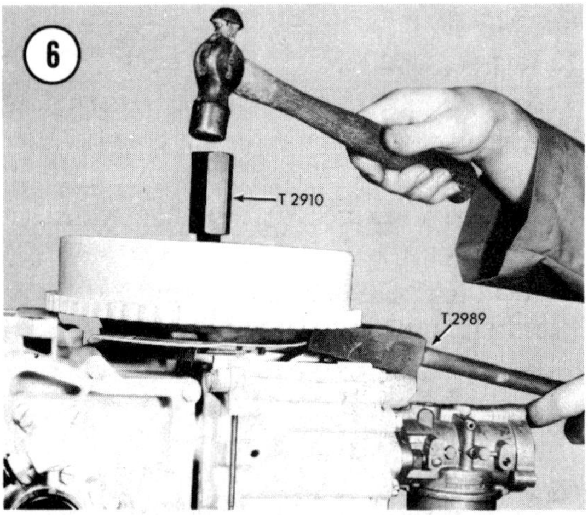

5. Carefully inspect the flywheel for cracks and breaks.

WARNING
Cracked or chipped flywheels must be replaced. At high engine rpm, a damaged flywheel may fly apart throwing shrapnel over a large area.

6. Inspect tapered bore of flywheel for fretting or working. If there is evidence of either condition or if engine has had 25 or more hours of operation, lap the flywheel bore, described later.
7. Install Woodruff key, flywheel, emergency starter collar, and nut. Torque nut to 45 ft.-lb.

Lapping Flywheel

1. Remove Woodruff key from crankshaft.
2. Apply light coating of valve grinding compound to tapered portion of crankshaft.
3. Install flywheel on crankshaft and rotate flywheel gently back and forth about ¼ turn—do not spin flywheel completely around crankshaft.
4. Rotate the flywheel 90° and repeat the above operation.
5. Remove flywheel, wipe compound off crankshaft and flywheel. Taper in bore of flywheel should have a minimum of 90% surface contact with taper on crankshaft.
6. Thoroughly clean compound from flywheel, crankshaft, and keyways.

MAGNETO

Stator Plate Removal/Installation

1. Disconnect the spark plug lead wires from the spark plugs.
2. Remove flywheel as described earlier.
3. Remove stator screw holding ground lead from crankcase cover on the starboard side of the engine.
4. Pull the wires from the shorting switch on the support plate.
5. Remove 3 screws holding magneto stator to stator ring. See **Figure 7**.

6. Lift stator and free wires from slot in stator ring.
7. Installation is the reverse of these steps.

Breaker Point Replacement

1. Remove flywheel as described earlier.
2. Remove 2 screws holding breaker point to stator plate as shown in **Figure 8**.

3. Disconnect wires from breaker point.
4. Remove breaker point from stator.
5. Installation is the reverse of these steps. Adjust breaker points as outlined under *Tune-up*.

Condenser Replacement

1. Remove flywheel as described earlier.
2. Remove condenser lead from breaker point terminal block.
3. Remove screw retaining condenser to stator plate. See **Figure 9**.

4. Remove condenser.
5. Installation is the reverse of these steps.

Coil Replacement

1. Remove flywheel as described earlier.
2. Disconnect coil lead wire from terminal block at breaker point. See **Figure 10**.

3. Disconnect coil lead wire from breaker point. See Figures 8 and 10.
4. Straighten bottom lamination on coil. See **Figure 11**.

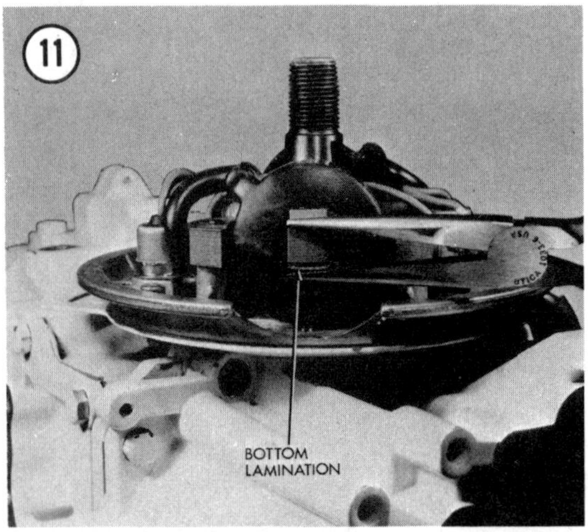

5. Remove stator from stator ring.
6. Pry lip of coil wedge spring up from coil laminations as shown in Figure 11.
7. Pull coil from laminations. Work plug lead through grommet as slack is needed. Note routing of plug lead for reference during installation.
8. Remove sparkie cover and sparkie spring from end of lead. See **Figure 12**.

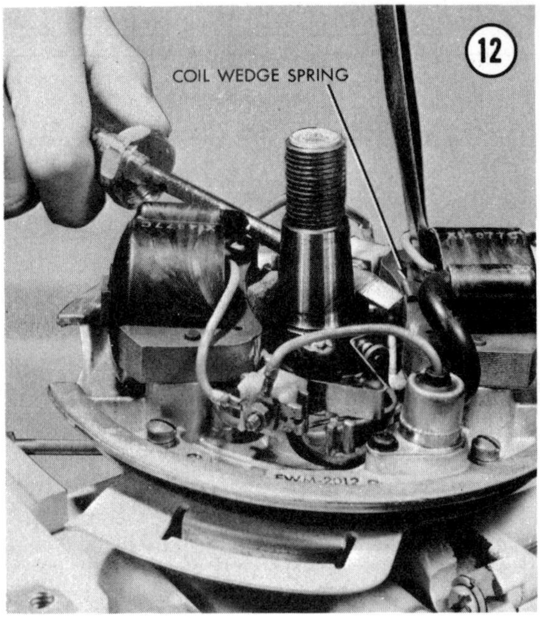

9. Pull spark plug lead through stator plate and remove coil assembly.
10. Position new coil in front of laminations so that spark plug lead enters coil at the upper left, toward the center of magneto. See Figure 10.
11. Place coil wedge spring in coil with small lip of spring facing top of laminations.
12. Install coil with wedge spring halfway on laminations. Route spark plug lead wire as originally installed.
13. Press coil on laminations until wedge spring snaps into place at rear of coil. Snap lip of spring over front edge of coil. Bend bottom lamination over rear of coil. See Figure 11.
14. Connect coil ground wire (located at bottom of coil) to breaker point mounting screw.
15. Connect wire from top of coil to insulated terminal on breaker point. See Figure 10.
16. Install sparkie spring and cover on spark plug lead. Be sure sparkie spring makes contact with wire inside insulation. See **Figure 13**.
17. Install stator.

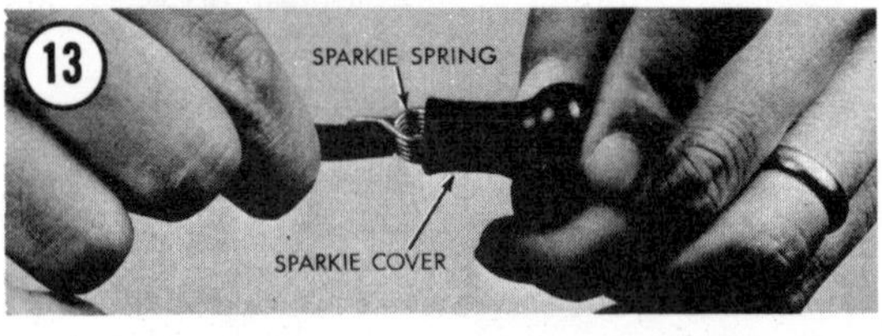

FUEL SYSTEM

Carburetor Removal

1. On hand start models, remove retainer, washer, and choke rod from choke lever (**Figure 14**).

2. On electric start models, loosen screw securing choke solenoid rod to choke lever. Slide rod from choke lever. See **Figure 15**.

3. Using hose clamp pliers, slide fuel line clamp down fuel line about one inch. Pull fuel line from carburetor.

CAUTION

Do not use hose clamp pliers to pull hose off fittings; pliers can puncture the hose.

4. Remove 2 nuts securing the carburetor to adapter flange. Remove carburetor and gasket.

5. Remove eccentric screw, nylon roller, and stop nut from throttle lever.

Carburetor Installation

1. Install carburetor gasket on carburetor adapter flange.

2. Install carburetor and secure with 2 nuts.

3. Install fuel hose on carburetor fitting. Secure with clamp.

4. Install eccentric screw and roller on throttle lever and secure with stop nut. Adjust throttle pickup point as outlined under *Tune-up*.

5. On manual start models, use washer and retainer to secure choke rod to choke lever. See Figure 14.

6. On electric start models, insert choke solenoid rod in swivel on choke lever. See Figure 15. Adjust choke as outlined under *Tune-up*.

Carburetor Disassembly

1. Remove carburetor from engine.

2. Remove 2 screws that fasten throttle shutter to shaft as shown in **Figure 16**.

3. Move shutter to horizontal position and gently pull it from shaft.

4. Remove throttle shutter.

5. Disconnect throttle return spring.

6. Remove screw retaining end of throttle shaft.

7. Pull throttle shaft from carburetor body.

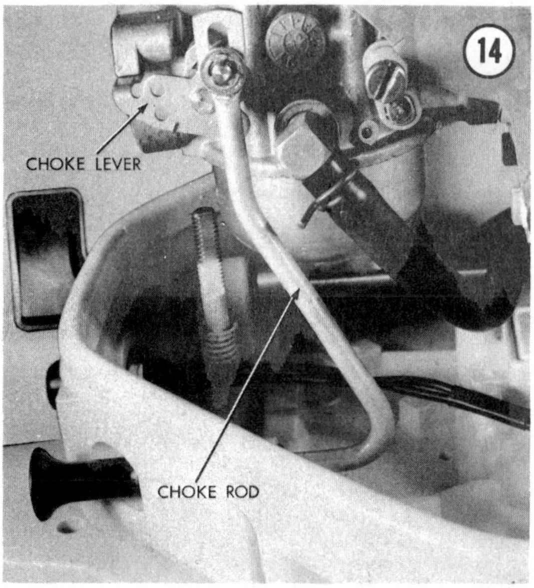

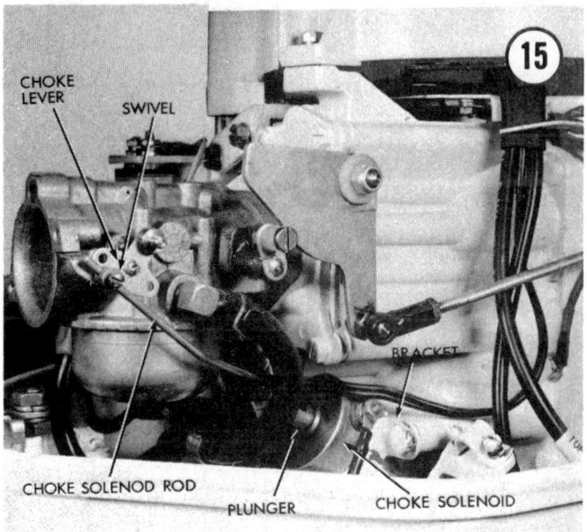

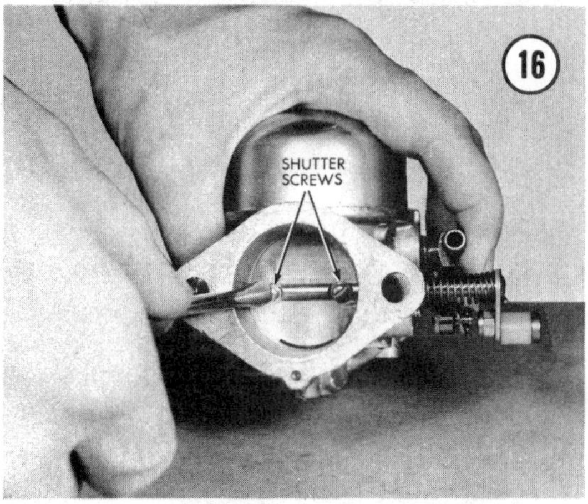

8. Remove 2 screws fastening choke shutter to choke shaft.
9. Pull shutter from shaft.
10. Unhook choke shaft spring from pin on carburetor. Remove shaft, choke relief valve, and valve spring.
11. Remove idle adjustment needle and spring.
12. Examine tapered portion of needle. If deep grooves are present, replace screw.
13. Remove screw holding fuel bowl on carburetor. Remove fuel bowl and gasket from carburetor.
14. Unscrew main fuel jet, shown in **Figure 17**.

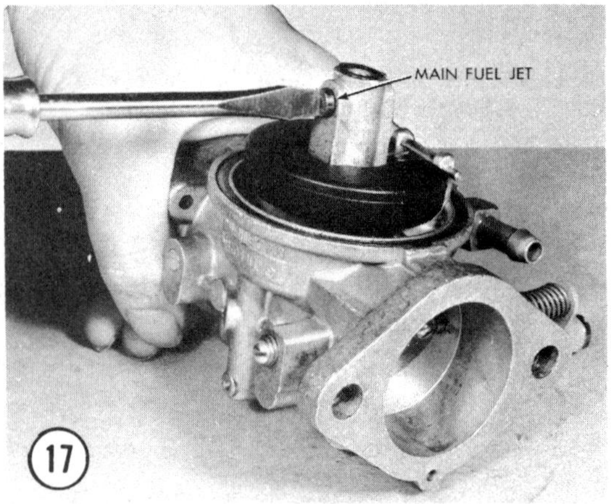

17

15. Drive out float lever pin.
16. Lift float from fuel bowl.
17. Remove inlet needle as shown in **Figure 18**.
18. Unscrew inlet needle seat.

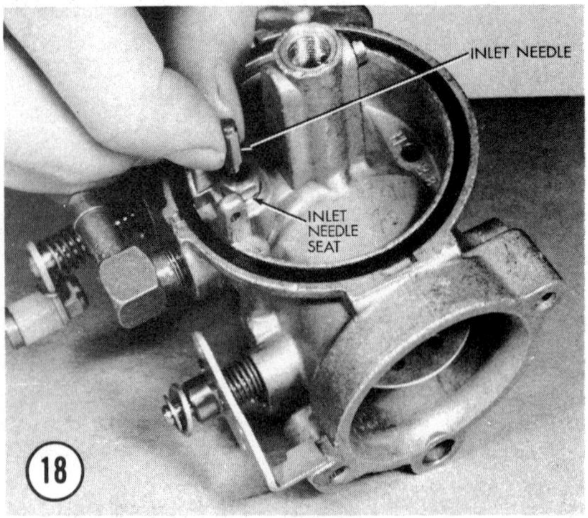

18

Carburetor Assembly

Assembly is the reverse of disassembly. Keep the following points in mind.

1. Note grooves at one end of float lever pin. Insert pin, grooveless end first, in carburetor from side shown in **Figure 19**. Grooved end should be flush with end of pivot hole.

19

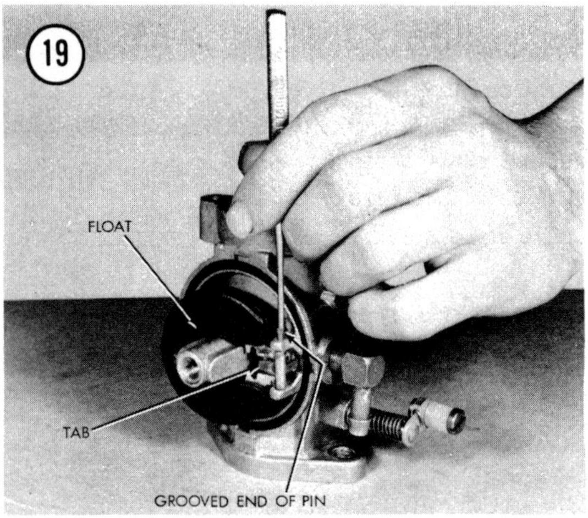

2. Hold fuel bowl upside down and check height of float. Top of float must be parallel with top of fuel bowl. To adjust float height, bend metal tab that bears on inlet needle being careful not to force needle into seat.
3. Position relief valve vertically in carburetor with pivots up and open part of pivots toward float bowl.
4. Place choke shaft spring on choke shaft so that loop is toward the lever.
5. Insert choke shaft in carburetor far enough to enter first pivot of relief valve.
6. Position relief valve spring between relief valve pivots so that spring ends straddle relief valve. Push shaft completely in and hook end of choke shaft spring on pin on carburetor body.
7. Position shaft so that side which is recessed for screw heads points away from float bowl.
8. Lift end of relief valve spring that points away from float bowl, push it until it points toward float bowl. Insert choke shutter in choke shutter shaft.
9. Hold shutter up enough to rotate relief valve more than 180° from shutter. Push shutter back down so that it holds relief valve at 180°.

10. Push loop of choke shaft spring until it snaps into place on shaft lever.

11. Secure choke shutter with 2 screws.

12. Hook small loop end of throttle return spring over pin on carburetor. Hook other end over throttle lever.

13. Rotate throttle shaft ¾ of a turn counterclockwise (looking at throttle lever side of carburetor).

14. Note that edge of shutter is chamfered. Stand carburetor on bench with mounting flange end up. Insert throttle shutter in shaft slot with cut-out down and chamfered edge away from float bowl. See **Figure 20**.

20

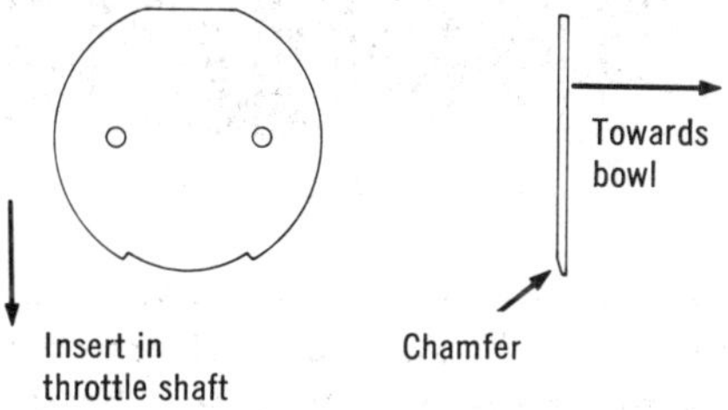

15. Gently close throttle shutter. Fasten throttle shutter to shaft with 2 screws.

16. Slowly open and close shutter. Shutter must not stick or bind at any point.

17. Install carburetor on engine.

18. Thread idle adjustment screw and spring into carburetor until needle seats lightly in bore. Do not force adjustment screw or tapered portion of needle will be damaged.

19. Adjust carburetor, outlined under *Tune-up*.

Sediment Bowl and Filter Removal/Installation

1. Loosen screw on plastic sediment bowl and remove bowl. See **Figure 21**.

2. Remove filter (screen).

3. Remove rubber gasket from fuel pump body.

4. Slide hose clamp from fuel line fitting with hose clamp pliers. Remove fuel line.

21

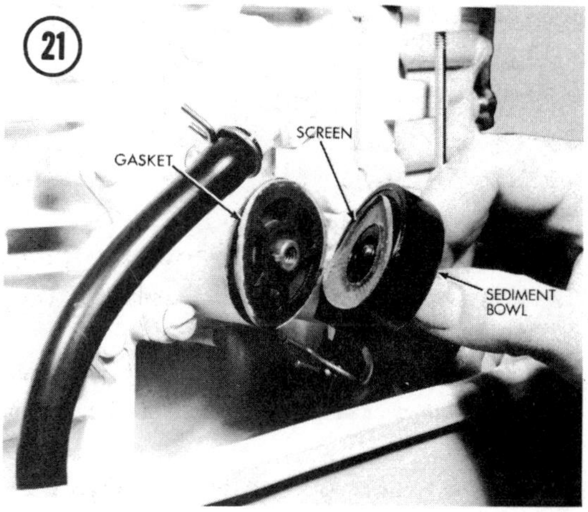

CAUTION

Do not use hose clamp pliers to pull hose off fittings; pliers can puncture the hose.

5. Position screen in sediment bowl with bent edges toward fuel pump body.

6. Position rubber gasket on fuel pump body; align slot in gasket over fuel pump key.

7. Secure the sediment bowl to the pump with knurled screw.

8. Connect hose and secure with clamp.

Fuel Pump Removal/Installation

1. Remove fuel lines from pump body and sediment bowl.

2. Remove 6 screws securing pump body to transfer port cover. If necessary, pry between upper screw holes where gasket is recessed.

3. Installation is the reverse of these steps. Use new gasket on pump body.

Fuel Pump Diaphragm Removal/Installation

1. Remove fuel pump body.

2. Remove gasket and diaphragm from fuel pump body.

3. Installation is the reverse of these steps. See **Figure 22**.

Fuel Pump Valve Removal/Installation

1. Remove fuel pump diaphragm.

2. Remove 2 screws and lift out central valve.

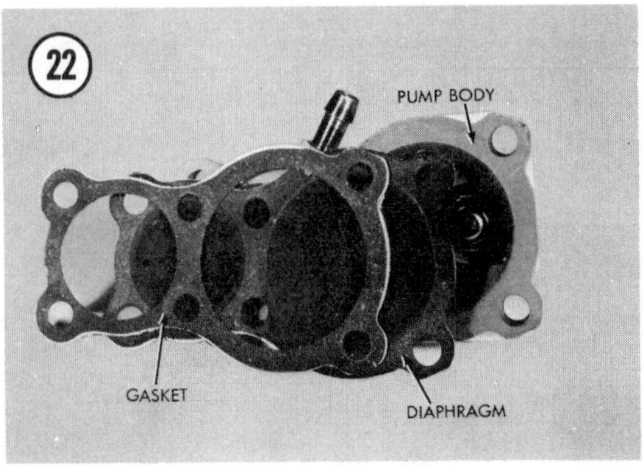

3. Install valve and gasket with concave side facing engine. See **Figure 23**.

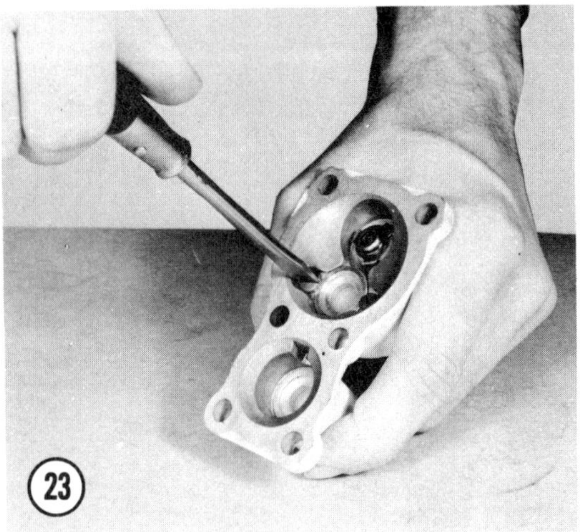

4. Secure valve with 2 screws.
5. Install fuel pump diaphragm.

Prime Bulb Removal/Installation

1. Dip prime bulb portion of fuel line in hot water (180-200°F) for a few minutes until hose becomes soft and pliable.
2. Pull hose and ferrule from adapter on each end of prime bulb.
3. Installation is the reverse of these steps.

GEAR HOUSING (25 HP)

Lower Unit Removal

1. Remove motor leg covers.
2. Loosen jam nut, shown in **Figure 24**.

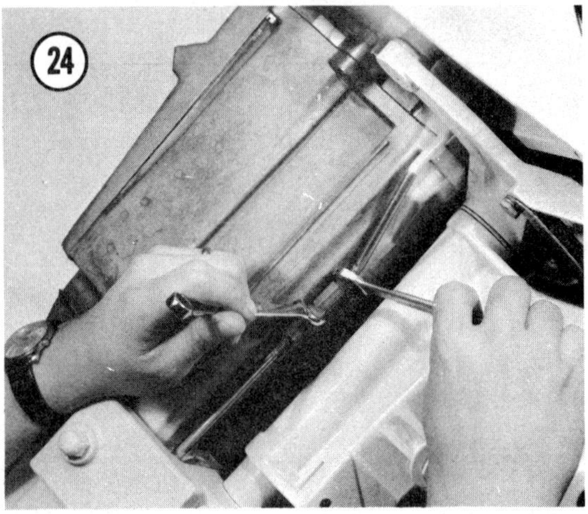

3. Shift engine into reverse gear. Turn coupling clockwise until lower shift rod separates from upper.
4. Remove 4 hex head bolts securing upper gear housing to motor leg (motor leg extension on long shaft models).
5. Pull lower unit from motor leg.

Lower Unit Installation

1. Thread lower shift rod in shift cam until it bottoms. With lower unit in reverse gear, back shift rod out until bend in rod centers over front starboard water pump mounting screw. See **Figure 25**.

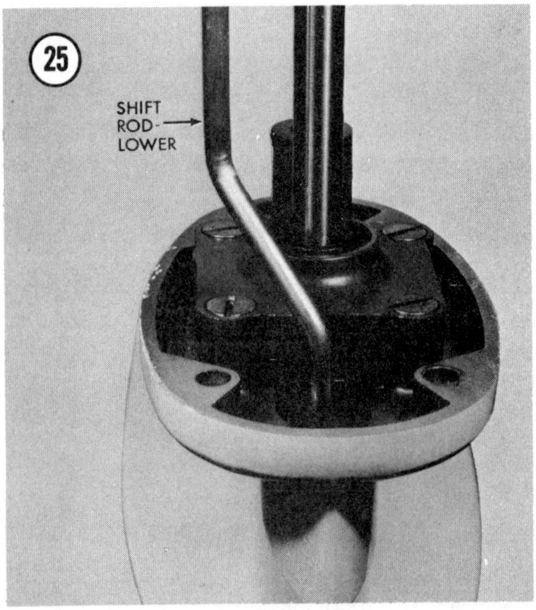

2. Have dealer pressure test gear housing to ensure that there are no leaks.

3. Slide lower unit into place on motor leg. Water line must seat in water pump seal and lower shift rod must align with hole in front of motor leg.

4. Apply anti-seize compound to drive shaft splines. Push lower unit up until drive shaft contacts crankshaft. Align drive shaft splines with crankshaft splines. Push lower unit up until it bottoms against motor leg.

5. Secure lower unit to motor leg with 4 hex head bolts.

6. Shift lower unit into NEUTRAL.

7. Thread coupler onto upper shift rod until lower end of coupler will engage lower shift rod.

> NOTE: *Upper shift rod must be up as far as possible to obtain enough thread engagement between coupler and lower shift rod for shift adjustment.*

8. Thread coupler onto shift rods until shift knob on support plate centers in NEUTRAL (knob vertical).

9. Tighten jam nut against coupler.

10. Install motor leg covers.

Lower Gearshift Rod Removal/Installation

1. Remove lower unit from engine.

2. Remove shift rod by turning counterclockwise until rod threads out of shift cam.

3. Pull shift rod out slowly to prevent cutting shift rod seal.

4. Installation is the reverse of these steps.

WATER PUMP (25 HP)

Removal/Disassembly

1. Remove lower unit.

2. Remove flat head screws holding water pump body to upper gear housing.

3. Slide water pump body up and off drive shaft.

4. Remove impeller by sliding it off drive shaft.

5. Remove impeller drive pin from drive shaft.

6. Remove water pump plate.

Assembly/Installation

1. Install water pump back plate.

2. Install impeller in water pump body. Slotted end of impeller bushing must face back plate.

3. Slide water pump body assembly down drive shaft and line up slot of impeller with drive pin in drive shaft.

4. Apply anti-seize compound to water pump body screws and secure water pump body to upper gear housing.

5. Install lower unit.

Inlet Water Line Seal Replacement

1. Remove lower unit.

2. Depress tabs on seal and pull seal from water pump body.

3. Installation is the reverse of these steps.

Water Pump Drive Shaft Seal Replacement

1. Remove lower unit.

2. Remove water pump body.

3. Pry seal out of pump body bore using a screwdriver. See **Figure 26**.

> CAUTION
> *Use care when removing seal with screwdriver to prevent scratching the seal bore.*

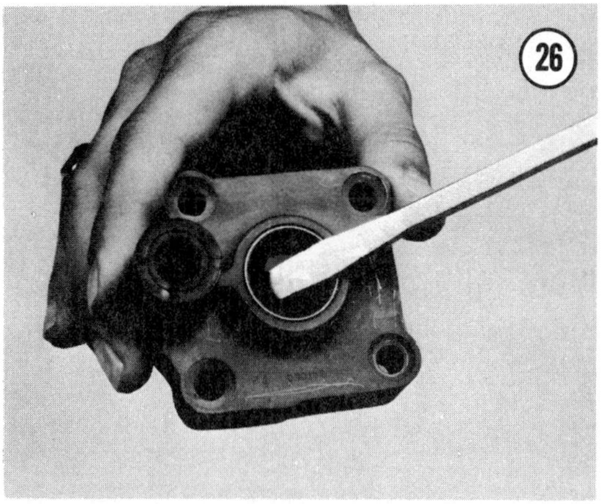

26

4. Apply grease to lips of new seal. Place seal on seal installer (Special Tool T2907) with sealing lip spring toward shoulder of tool.

5. Position seal and tool in pump body bore as shown in **Figure 27**. Press seal in bore until it contacts bottom of bore.

6. Remove tool and install pump body.

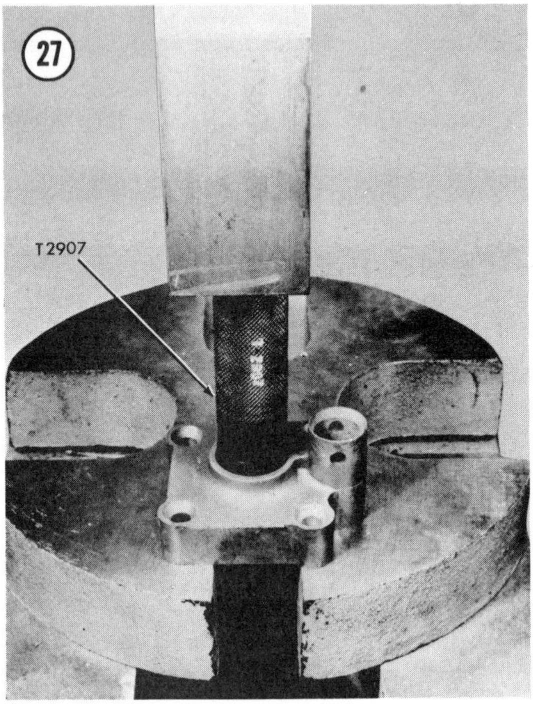

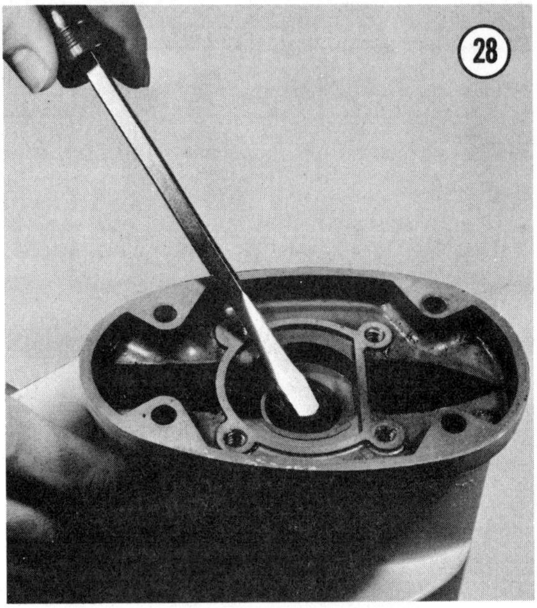

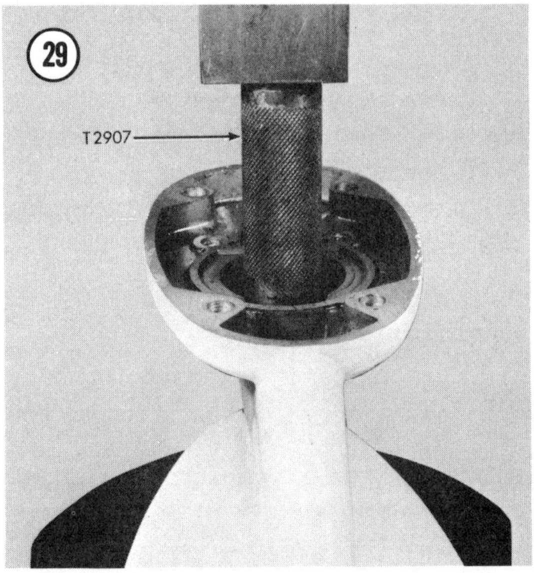

DRIVE SHAFT SEAL (25 HP)

Removal

1. Remove lower unit.
2. Remove water pump.
3. Pull drive shaft out of lower unit.
4. Pry seal out of bore in upper gear housing with screwdriver as shown in **Figure 28**.

CAUTION

Use care when removing the seal with screwdriver to prevent scratching the seal bore.

Installation

1. Apply grease to seål lips.
2. Place seal on installation tool (Special Tool T2907) so that seal lip with garter spring is against shoulder of tool.
3. Position seal and tool in bore of upper gear housing, as shown in **Figure 29**, and press seal in until it contacts bottom of bore.
4. Remove tool and install drive shaft in lower unit.
5. Install water pump.
6. Install lower unit.

PROPELLER SHAFT BEARING CAGE (25 HP)

Removal

1. Remove propeller and drain gear housing grease from lower unit.

2. Remove weed guard retaining ring with screwdriver as shown in **Figure 30**.

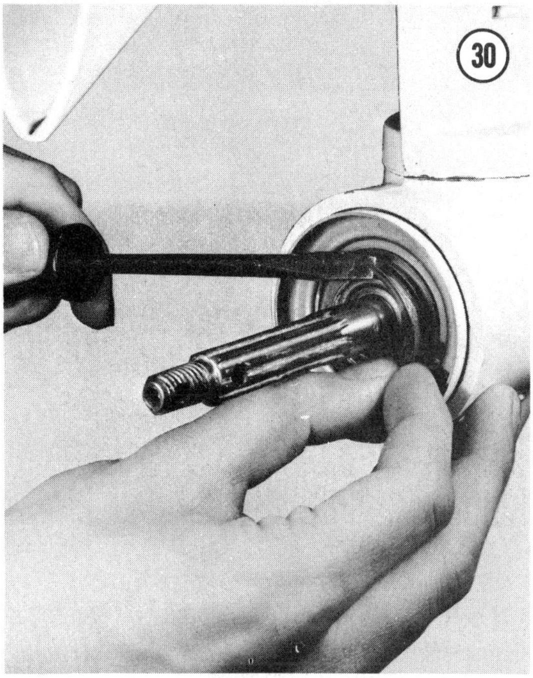

3. Remove weed guard.

4. Remove bearing cage retaining ring with snap ring pliers as shown in **Figure 31**.

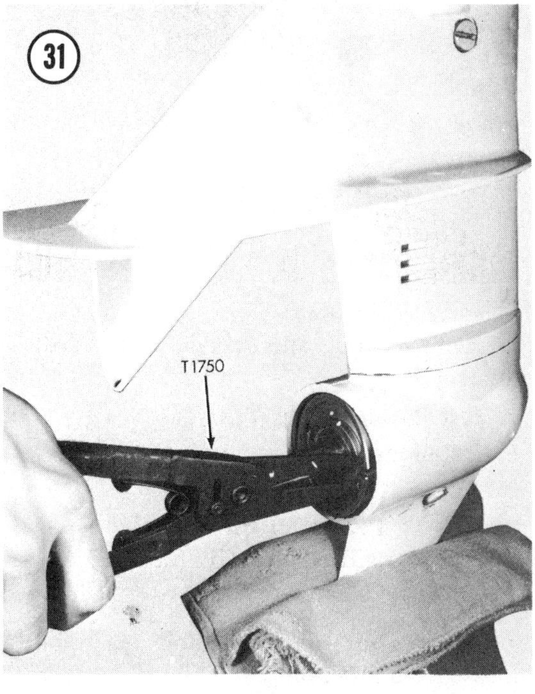

5. Install bearing cage puller (Special Tool T8948) and two ¼-20 x 7 in. screws as shown in **Figure 32**.

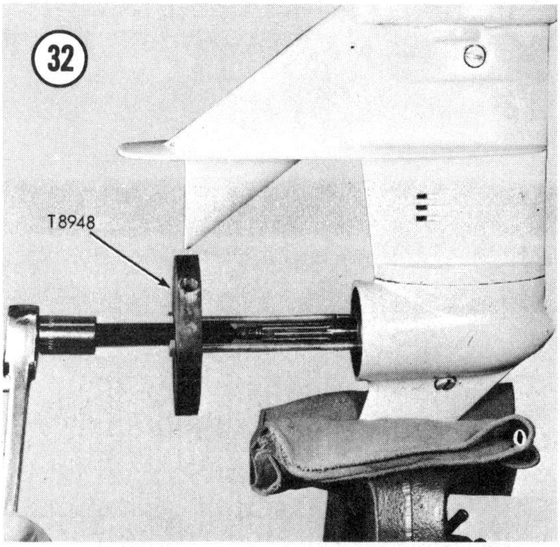

6. Remove bearing cage from propeller shaft.

7. Remove bearing cage seal from groove in bearing cage.

Installation

1. Install bearing cage seal in groove. Apply grease to bearing cage seal and between lips of propeller shaft seal.

2. Check propeller shaft for any nicks or burrs that might damage the propeller shaft seal; remove them with a file or emery cloth.

3. Slide bearing cage assembly on propeller shaft. Press bearing cage in gear housing until it bottoms.

4. Install bearing cage retaining ring.

> NOTE: *Install retaining ring with flat side facing bearing cage.*

5. Install the weed guard and secure with the retaining ring.

6. Have dealer pressure test gear housing.

7. Fill lower unit with Chrysler Outboard Gear Lube.

PROPELLER SHAFT SEAL (25 HP)

Removal

1. Remove propeller shaft bearing cage.

3

2. Drive seal away from bearing in cage with a punch and hammer.

Installation

1. Press seal in bearing cage bore using seal installer (Special Tool T2907). Install with garter spring "in" toward gears of lower gear housing.
2. Apply grease on sealing lips and on O-ring seal around bearing cage.
3. Install bearing cage.

UPPER GEAR HOUSING (25 HP)

Removal

1. Remove lower unit.
2. Remove water pump.
3. Remove impeller drive pin and pull drive shaft from lower unit.
4. Remove lower gearshift rod.
5. Remove gear housing bolt located on front lower side of gear housing.
6. Remove propeller shaft bearing cage.
7. Remove nut inside lower gear housing just behind rear bevel gear.
8. Separate upper gear housing from lower gear housing.

Installation

1. Clean and remove any oily film from gasket surfaces on both gear housings.
2. Apply sealant on both sides of gear housing gasket. Place gasket on lower gear housing.
3. Assemble upper gear housing on lower. See **Figure 33**.
4. Install nut on upper gear housing stud inside lower gear housing.
5. Apply sealant under head of gear housing bolt before installing on upper gear housing. Torque bolt to 160 in.-lb.
6. Install lower gearshift rod.
7. Install drive shaft in lower unit.
8. Install propeller shaft bearing cage.
9. Install water pump.
10. Install lower unit.

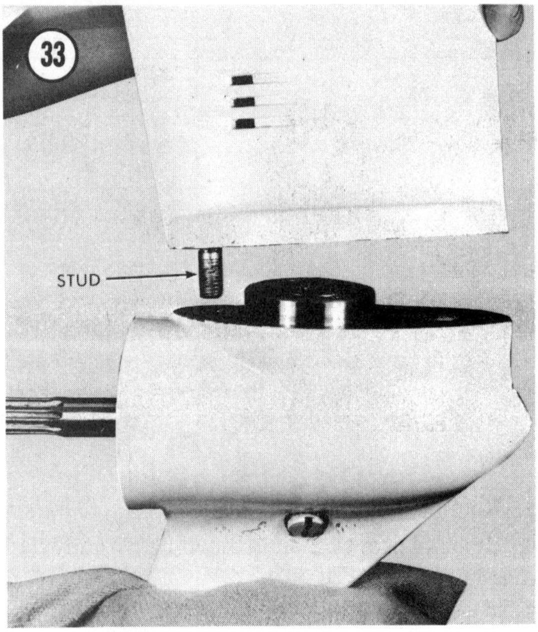

SHIFT ROD SEAL (25 HP)

Removal

1. Remove upper gear housing.
2. Pry seal from gear housing with a small blade screwdriver.

Installation

1. Apply Loctite "H" to outer diameter of seal.
2. Install seal on installer (Special Tool T8957) with raised bead on seal against shoulder of tool.
3. Press seal in bore of upper gear housing until it is flush with surface.
4. Install upper gear housing.

REAR BEVEL GEAR (25 HP)

Removal/Installation

1. Remove upper gear housing.
2. Slide rear bevel gear and thrust washer off propeller shaft as shown in **Figure 34**.
3. Installation is the reverse of these steps.

BEVEL PINION (25 HP)

Removal/Installation

1. Remove lower unit.
2. Remove upper gear housing.

3. Remove rear bevel gear.

4. Remove propeller shaft assembly from lower gear housing.

5. Remove bevel pinion as shown in **Figure 35**.

6. Installation is the reverse of these steps.

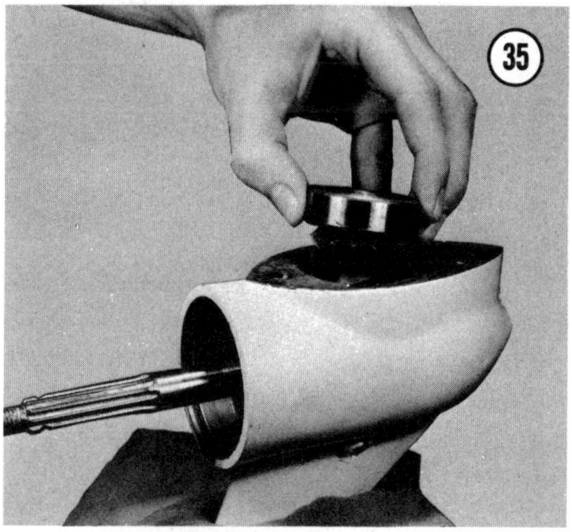

FRONT BEVEL GEAR (25 HP)

Removal/Installation

1. Remove lower unit.

2. Remove upper gear housing.

3. Pull propeller shaft assembly with rear bevel gear from lower gear housing.

4. Remove bevel pinion.

5. Slide front bevel gear out of bore in lower gear housing.

6. Installation is the reverse of these steps.

CLUTCH (25 HP)

Removal

1. Remove lower unit.

2. Remove upper gear housing.

3. Pull propeller shaft assembly out of lower gear housing.

4. Slide rear bevel gear and thrust washer off propeller shaft.

5. Pull shift pin out of bore in propeller shaft.

6. Slide clutch against spring and install ⅛ in. diameter drift punch through clutch slot in propeller shaft. This prevents damage to clutch slots when removing spring pin from clutch. See **Figure 36**.

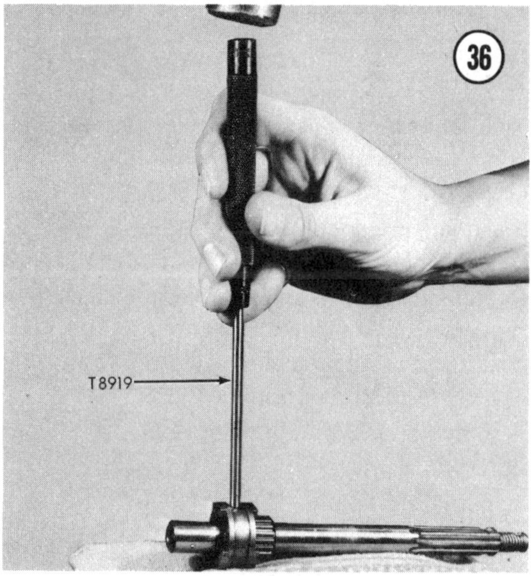

7. Place propeller shaft with clutch on vise (partially opened). Cover jaws with a shop rag to prevent scratching machined surfaces.

8. Using pin remover (Special Tool T8919 or equivalent), drive spring pin out of clutch as shown in Figure 36.

9. Remove punches and slide clutch from propeller shaft.

10. Leave clutch spring in propeller shaft bore.

Installation

1. Drive spring pin partially in clutch.

2. Install clutch on propeller shaft. Align spring pin with slot in propeller shaft.

3

3. Clamp propeller shaft in vise as shown in **Figure 37**.

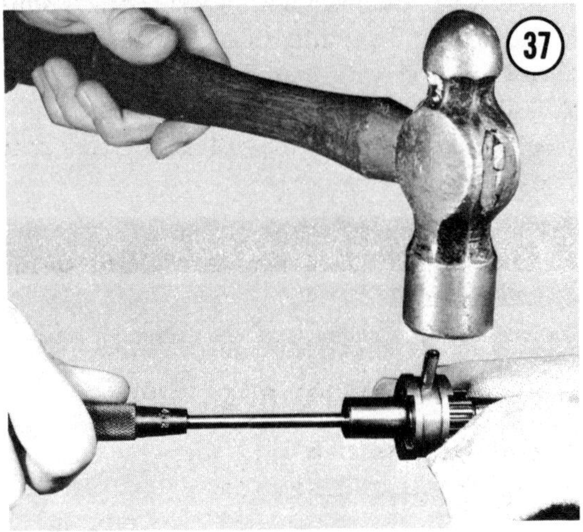

4. Compress clutch spring, shown in Figure 37. Align clutch so that spring pin does not contact either end of clutch slot in propeller shaft.

5. Drive spring pin in clutch until it contacts shank of pin remover as shown in Figure 37.

6. Remove propeller shaft assembly from pin remover. Reinstall pin remover to exert pressure against spring pin; this holds it away from edge of clutch slot in propeller shaft.

7. Drive spring pin in until flush with sides of clutch.

8. Install shift pin.

9. Complete assembly by reversing Steps 1-4 of *Removal* procedure above.

PROPELLER SHAFT (25 HP)

Removal/Installation

1. Remove lower unit.
2. Remove upper gear housing.
3. Pull propeller shaft assembly with rear bevel gear from lower gear housing.
4. Slide rear bevel gear and thrust washer from propeller shaft.
5. Remove shift pin from propeller shaft.
6. Remove clutch.
7. Installation is the reverse of these steps.

SHIFT CAM (25 HP)

Removal/Installation

1. Remove lower unit.
2. Remove upper gear housing.
3. Pull propeller shaft assembly out of lower gear housing.
4. Slide shift cam out of slot in lower gear housing as shown in **Figure 38**.

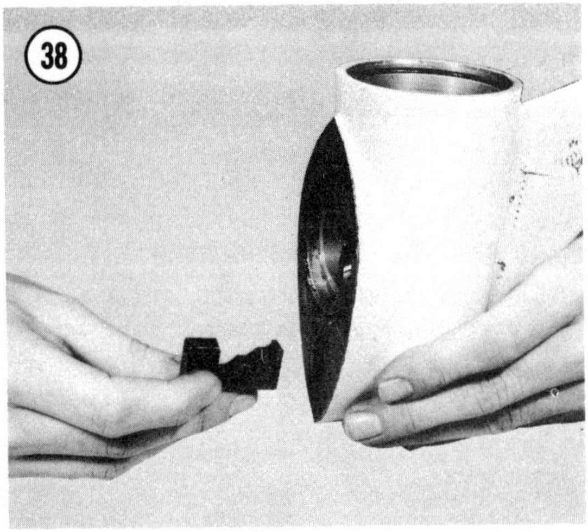

5. Installation is the reverse of these steps. Slide shift cam into slot in lower gear housing with threaded hole in shift cam up and flat side of cam toward nose of lower gear housing. See Figure 38.

LOWER GEAR HOUSING (25 HP)

Removal

1. Remove lower unit.
2. Remove upper gear housing.
3. Pull propeller shaft assembly from lower gear housing.
4. Remove bevel pinion.
5. Remove front bevel gear.
6. Remove shift cam.

Installation

1. Install shift cam.
2. Install front bevel gear.
3. Install bevel pinion.

4. Install propeller shaft assembly with rear bevel gear, thrust washer, and shift pin in lower gear housing.

5. Install shift cam detent spring in cavity in front of bevel pinion.

6. Install upper gear housing.

7. Install lower unit.

GEAR HOUSING (30 HP)

Lower Unit Removal

1. Drain lower unit by removing both FILL and VENT plug screws.

2. Remove 4 hex head screws and lockwashers securing upper gear housing to motor leg (motor leg extension on long leg motors).

3. Remove cotter pin securing shift rod pin to coupler of intermediate shift rod. Remove shift rod pin to free lower shift rod from coupler and pull lower unit from motor leg.

Installation

1. Apply anti-seize compound to crankshaft splines of drive shaft.

2. Turn lower shift rod clockwise until threads bottom in shift arm coupling. Turn shift rod counterclockwise until hole in shift rod faces port and starboard sides.

3. Install lower unit on motor leg. Insert lower shift rod in intermediate shift rod coupling. Align water line in water pump seal and engage drive shaft splines with crankshaft splines.

4. Install shift rod pin and cotter pin to secure lower shift rod to intermediate shift rod.

5. Have dealer pressure test gear housing.

6. Secure lower unit to motor leg with 4 lockwashers and screws. Coat threads with anti-seize compound.

LOWER SHIFT ROD (30 HP)

Removal/Installation

1. Remove lower unit.

2. Turn lower shift rod counterclockwise until shift rod threads out of shift arm coupling. Pull shift rod from lower unit slowly to avoid damaging seal.

3. Apply grease to threads of lower shift rod.

4. Install lower shift rod through shift rod seal. Slowly push rod down until it just contacts shift arm coupling. Turn shift rod clockwise to engage thread of rod with coupling. Turn rod until threads bottom in coupling. Turn rod counterclockwise until hole at top end of rod faces port and starboard sides.

5. Install lower unit.

6. Check shift adjustment as outlined under *Power Head*.

WATER PUMP (30 HP)

Removal/Disassembly

1. Remove lower unit.

2. Depress tabs on water line seal then pull seal from pump body.

3. Remove 4 screws securing water pump body assembly to upper gear housing and lift pump body assembly from lower unit.

4. Remove the water pump impeller from the pump body.

5. Drive the drive shaft seal from the pump body from inside the pump body.

6. Remove impeller drive pin from drive shaft.

7. Remove the water pump back plate from lower unit.

Assembly/Installation

1. Place water pump body on wood block to support it when installing seal. Press drive shaft seal (garter spring facing out) in pump body bore using seal installer (Special Tool T2907) as shown in **Figure 39**.

2. Install water pump impeller in pump body by turning impeller counterclockwise.

3. Install pump back plate on gear housing with slot toward the front on the port side.

> NOTE: *Holes in back plate will not line up exactly if plate is installed upside down.*

4. Install impeller drive pin in drive shaft.

5. Slide pump assembly down drive shaft. Align impeller slot with drive shaft drive pin.

3

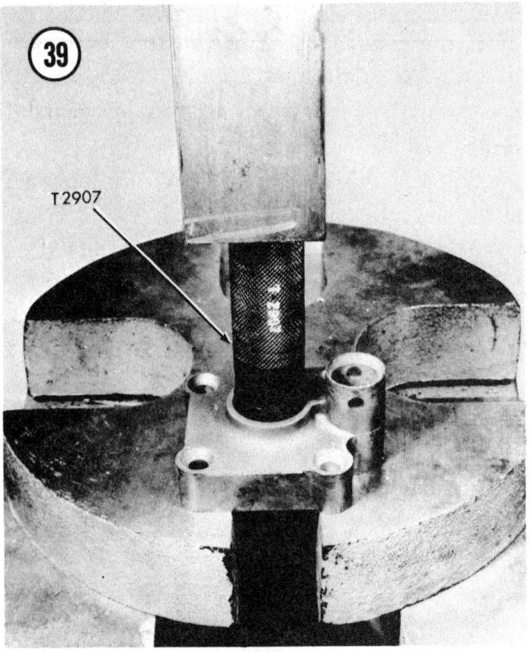

6. Apply anti-seize compound to threads of the 4 flat head screws and secure pump to upper gear housing.

7. Install water line seal in pump body bore. Make sure seal tabs seat in pump body holes.

8. Install lower unit.

PROPELLER SHAFT BEARING (30 HP)

Cage Removal

1. Remove propeller. Drain gear housing by removing FILL and VENT plugs.
2. Remove the 2 cap screws holding bearing cage on lower gear housing.
3. Install puller (Special Tool T8948) as shown in **Figure 40** and remove bearing cage assembly.
4. Remove bearing cage seal.

Cage Installation

1. Apply grease to bearing cage and install in bearing cage.
2. Apply grease between lips of propeller shaft seal. Install bearing cage assembly. Align groove of inner race of propeller shaft bearing with ball in propeller shaft.

> NOTE: *Upper hole in bearing cage has triangular flange.*

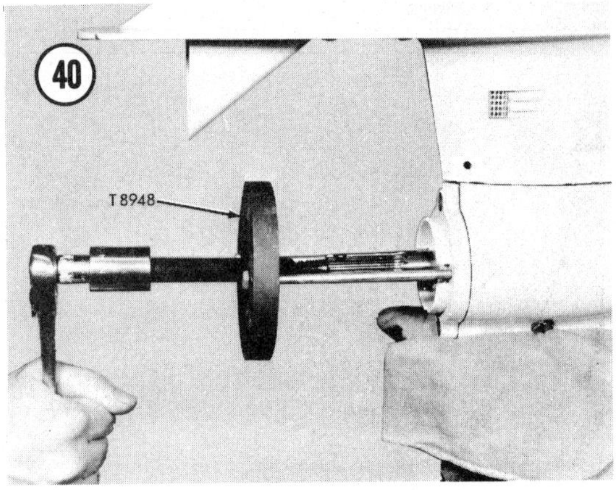

3. Push bearing cage in bore of lower gear housing. Do not force with hammer or gear housing screws.
4. Apply anti-seize compound to cap screw threads. Secure bearing cage to lower gear housing.
5. Apply anti-seize compound to propeller shaft splines. Install propeller, drive pin, seal, propeller nut, and cotter pin.
6. Have dealer pressure test gear housing. Fill gear housing with Chrysler Outboard Gear Lube.

Bearing Removal

1. Remove bearing cage.
2. Remove bearing as shown in **Figure 41**.

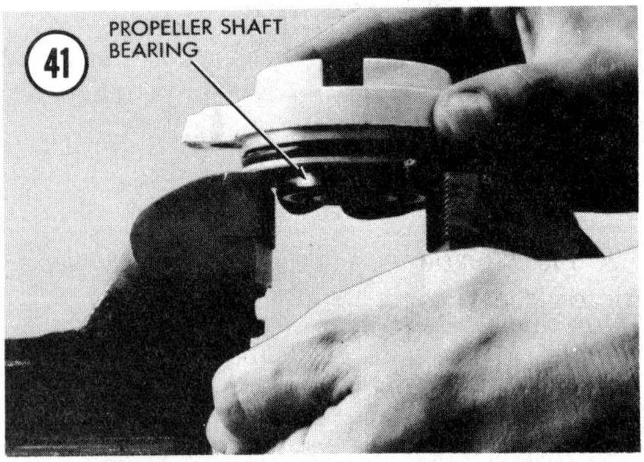

3. Pry seal from bearing cage as shown in **Figure 42**.

Bearing Installation

1. Apply grease between lips of seal. Position seal in bearing cage with garter spring toward

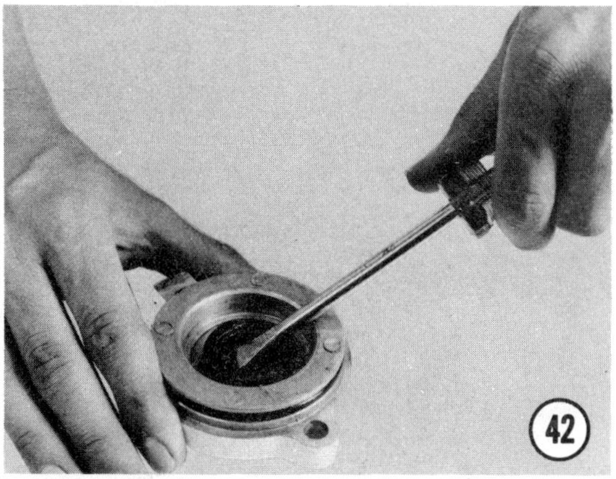

water side of bearing cage. Press seal into cage with seal installer (Special Tool T3431) as shown in **Figure 43**.

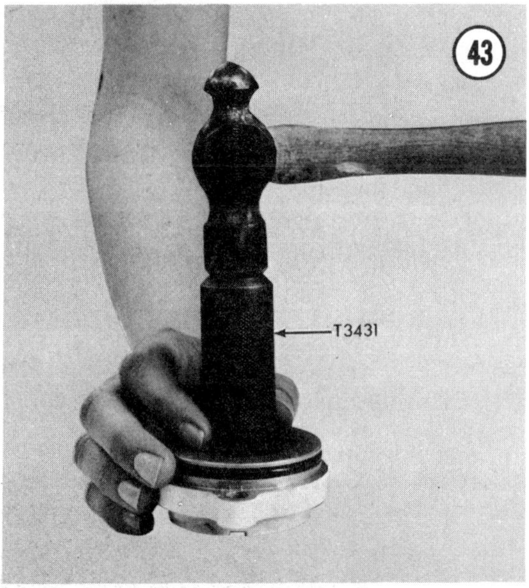

2. Place bearing in bearing cage and gently tap into place with a block of wood or plastic mallet.

CAUTION

Tap only on outer race of bearing.

3. Install propeller shaft bearing cage.

UPPER GEAR HOUSING BEARING (30 HP)

Removal

1. Remove water pump body and plate.
2. Pull drive shaft from lower unit.
3. Remove propeller shaft bearing cage.
4. Remove nut located behind rear bevel gear in lower gear housing.
5. Remove nut on stud in front of gearshift rod seal.
6. Separate the upper gear housing from the lower gear housing.
7. Remove drive shaft seal by inserting drive shaft bearing remover (Special Tool T8964) in bearing from underside. Press out bearing just enough to remove drive shaft seal. See **Figure 44**.

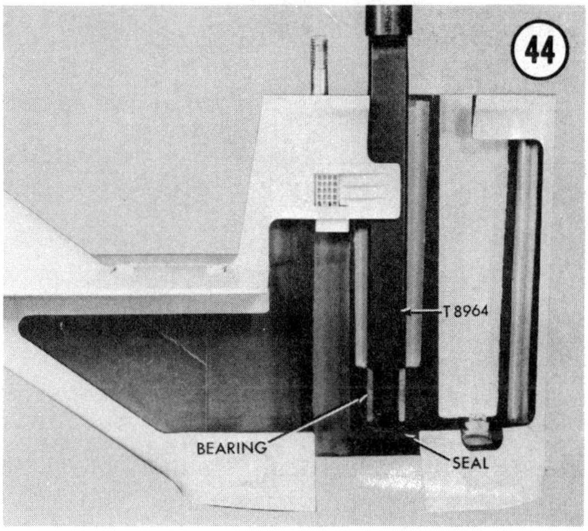

8. Press out the drive shaft bearing as described in Step 7.
9. Use hook and slide hammer to remove shift rod seal. See **Figure 45**.

Installation

1. Apply Loctite "H" sparingly to outside diameter of shift rod seal.
2. Place seal on installer (Special Tool T8957) with raised bead against shoulder of tool. Press seal in upper gear housing until flush with surface. See **Figure 46**.
3. Place bearing installer (Special Tool T8963) in drive shaft bearing and press in from top of upper gear housing until tool bottoms. See **Figure 47**.
4. Apply grease between lips of drive shaft seal. Place seal on installer (Special Tool T8972) with rubber coated side against shoulder of tool.

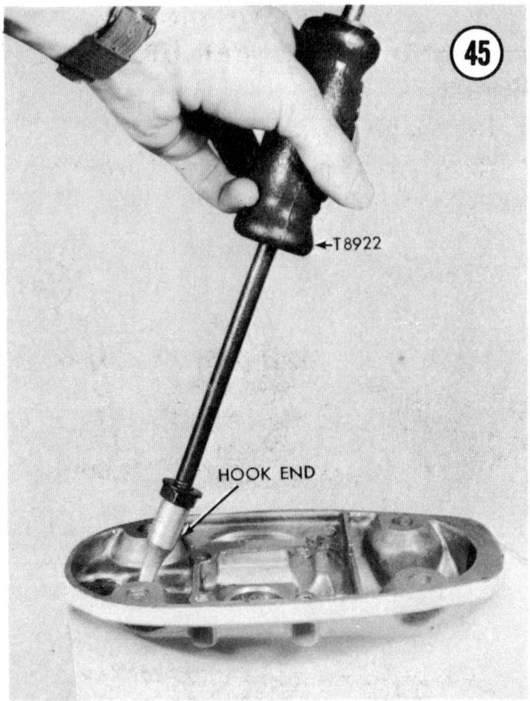

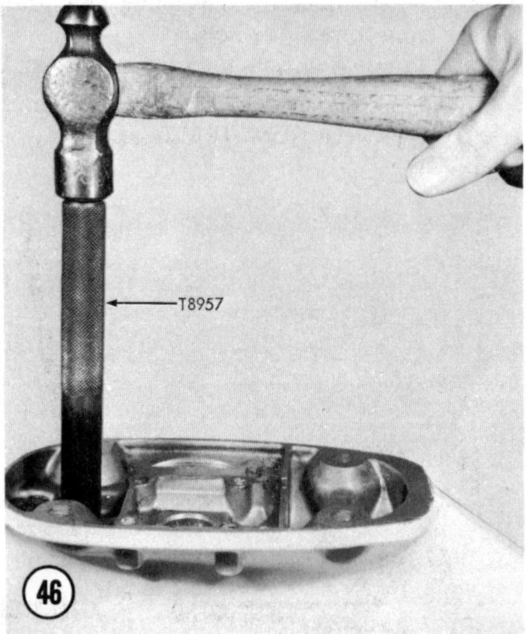

5. Drive seal into upper gear housing until it bottoms. See **Figure 48**.

6. Clean all mating surfaces of gear housing. Check condition of seal in lower gear housing; replace if necessary.

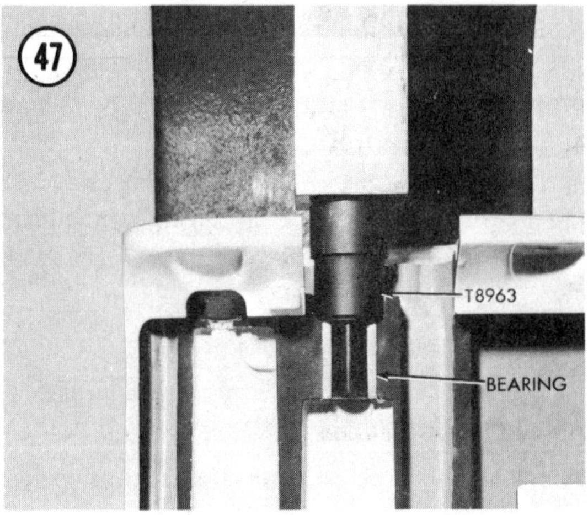

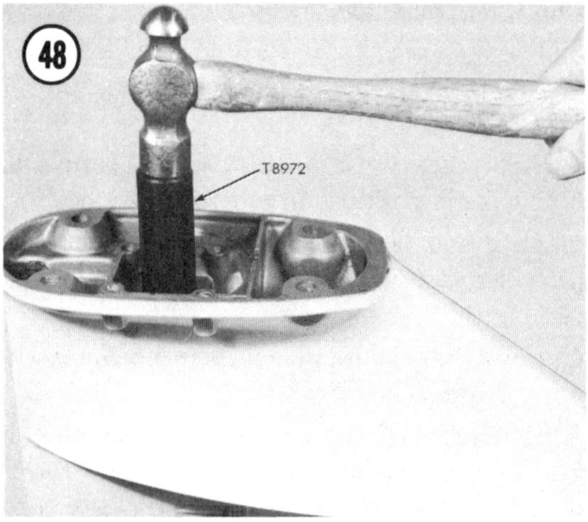

7. Secure lower gear housing to upper gear housing with 2 nuts and lockwashers.

> NOTE: *First torque each nut to 100 in.-lb. Increase torque in increments of 30-50 in.-lb. until 270 in.-lb. is reached.*

8. Install bearing cage.
9. Install lower unit.

PROPELLER SHAFT (30 HP)

Removal/Disassembly

1. Separate upper gear housing from lower.
2. Pull lower shift rod up as far as possible and then pull propeller shaft out of lower gear housing.

3. Remove ball from propeller shaft using magnet. Slide rear bevel gear and thrust washer off propeller shaft.
4. Remove yoke from shift pin.
5. Drive out spring pin securing clutch and shift pin to propeller shaft using spring pin punch (Special Tool T8919). Remove shift pin and clutch from propeller shaft.

Assembly/Installation

1. Install clutch on propeller shaft. Align spring pin holes with slot in propeller shaft.
2. Install shift pin in propeller shaft. Align hole with spring pin holes in clutch.
3. Drive spring pin through clutch, propeller shaft, and shift pin using spring pin punch (Special Tool T8919).
4. Apply heavy grease to shift pin groove to hold yoke in position. Install yoke in groove.
5. Slide rear bevel gear and thrust washer on propeller shaft with thrust washer between gear and clutch.
6. Insert ball in propeller shaft notch; use a little grease to hold it.
7. Carefully install propeller shaft assembly in gear housing. Make sure that lower shift rod is up as far as possible and that yoke pins are horizontal. Push propeller shaft assembly in until yoke pins align in slots of shift arm assembly as shown in **Figure 49**.
8. Install upper gear housing.

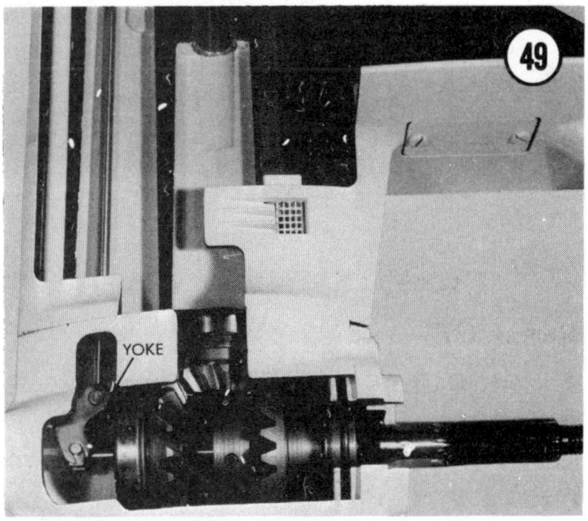

BEVEL PINION AND FRONT GEAR (30 HP)

Removal

1. Remove propeller shaft.
2. Remove bevel pinion and bevel pinion bearing cup as shown in **Figure 50**.

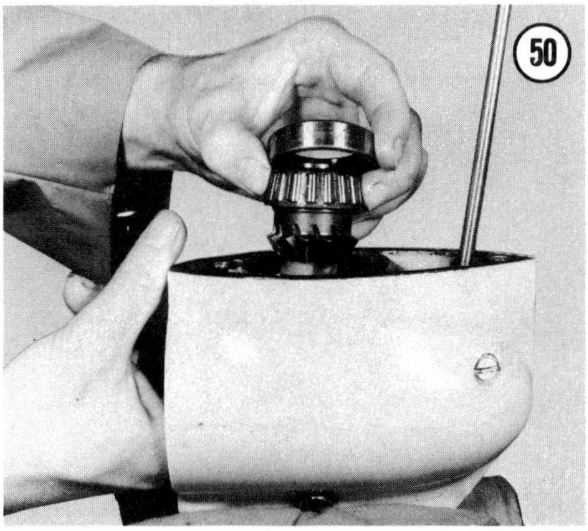

3. Remove front bevel gear assembly and thrust washer from lower gear housing.
4. Remove front bevel gear bearing cup using cup remover (Special Tool T8921) with bearing guide set (Special Tool T8918) as shown in **Figure 51**.

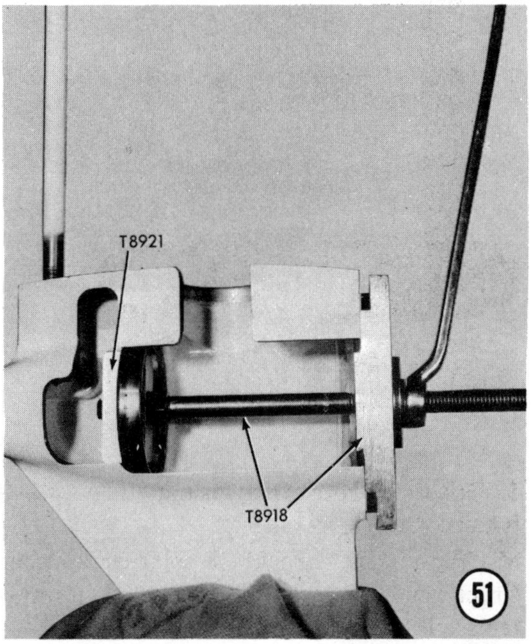

3

Installation

1. Press bearing cup in lower gear housing using cup installer (Special Tool T8904), driver hand (Special Tool T8907), and guide plate from bearing guide set (Special Tool T8918). See **Figure 52.**

52

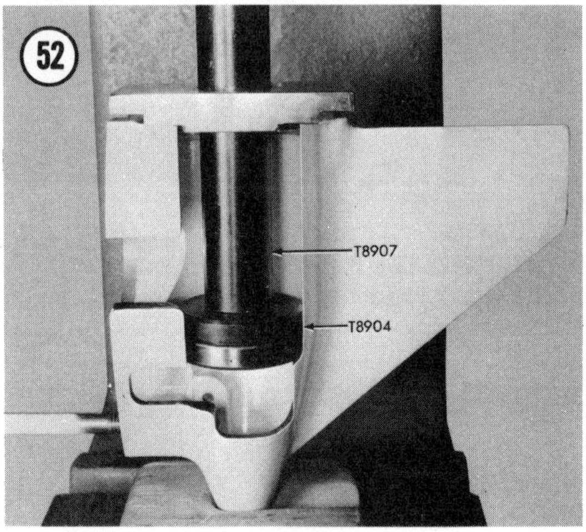

2. Install thrust washer and front bevel gear assembly with thrust washer on toothed side of front bevel gear.
3. Install bevel pinion and bearing cup.
4. Install propeller shaft assembly.

SHIFT ARM (30 HP)

Removal

1. Remove propeller shaft assembly.
2. Unscrew shift rod from shift arm.
3. Remove pivot screw securing shift arm to lower gear housing.
4. Remove shift arm from lower gear housing.

Installation

1. Install shift arm in lower gear housing with forked ends down.
2. Align pivot hole in shift arm with hole in lower gear housing and install pivot screw with nyltite washer.
3. Screw lower shift rod into shift arm until threads bottom.
4. Install propeller shaft assembly.

MANUAL STARTER

Removal

1. Remove 3 screws and lockwashers securing starter to power head.
2. Tilt starter to starboard side so interlock lever clears flywheel. Remove starter from power head.

Installation

1. With handle side forward, tilt starter to starboard so interlock lever hooks under flywheel.
2. Install 3 screws with lockwashers, but do not tighten.
3. Center starter by pulling starter handle so pawls engage the collar. Tighten the starter mounting screws.

Rope Replacement

1. Remove starter.
2. Remove 3 screws and retainer securing pawl plate to starter housing.
3. Remove 3 shims, pawl plate, and pawl plate spring.
4. Remove starter handle from end of rope. On hand start models, pry retainer from starter handle and remove rope from retainer. See **Figure 53.**

53

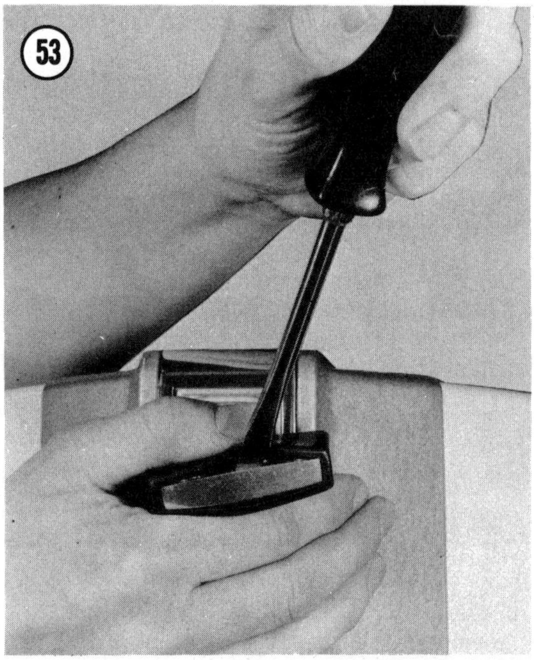

5. Using hand to slow pulley, press interlock lever and allow rewind spring to draw in starter rope.

6. Rotate pulley back and forth to make sure that there is no spring tension against pulley. Press interlock lever and lift pulley from starter housing.

7. Seize knot with needle nose pliers and pull rope from pulley.

8. Push new rope through hole between pulley flanges. Tie knot in end nearest pulley hub. Melt end of rope with match to fuse strands.

9. Wrap rope counterclockwise on pulley (interlock lugs facing viewer). Route rope through slot on pulley with about 9 in. protruding from slot.

10. With inner cavity of starter housing facing you and rope outlet boss at 12 o'clock, place the pulley in the housing with the rope groove at about 9 o'clock.

11. Place pawl plate spring over housing arbor with ends pointed up and toward gap between pawl guides.

12. Place pawl plate on arbor with pawl lever side toward pulley and slots over ends of pawl plate spring. See **Figure 54**.

54

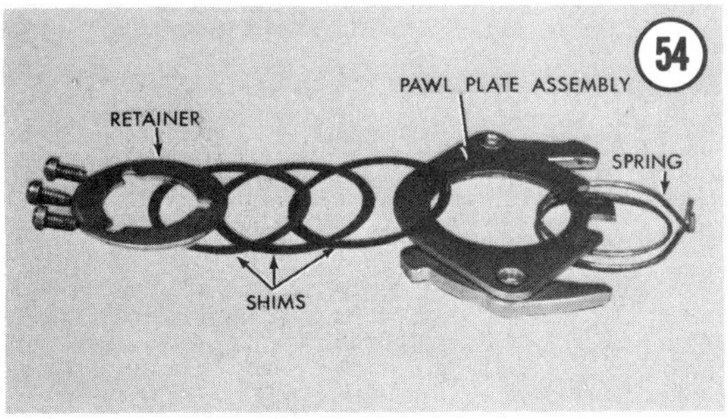

13. Place 3 shims on pawl plate and secure with retainer and 3 screws.

14. Rotate pulley 1¾ turns counterclockwise and guide rope through rope outlet boss.

15. On electric start models, tie knot in end of rope to retain handle. Melt rope end with match. On manual start models, route rope through handle and rope retainer as shown in **Figure 55**. Press retainer into handle.

16. Install starter.

55

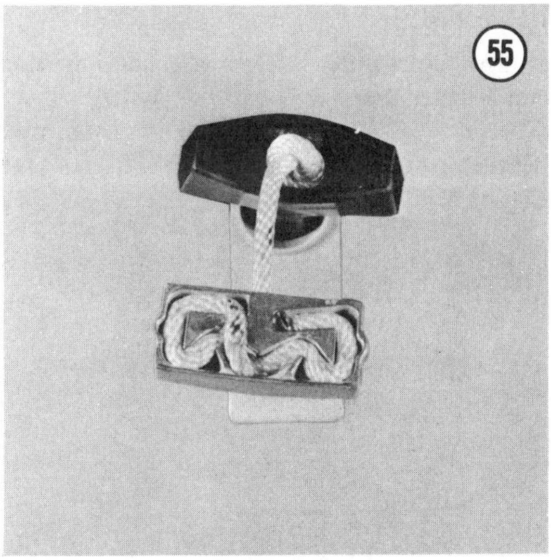

REWIND SPRING

Removal/Installation

1. Remove the pulley as described under *Rope Replacement*.

2. Remove spring from housing.

3a. If installing new spring, leave retainer on spring and go to Step 4.

3b. If installing old spring, grease spring. Clamp a pin punch in vise and hook center end of spring over it. Wind spring into a coil small enough to fit in starter housing.

4. Place spring in starter housing with outer end over spring retaining boss. Spring should run counterclockwise from retaining boss.

5. Reassemble starter pulley and rope.

STARTER SOLENOID

Removal

1. Disconnect battery leads from battery.

2. Remove nuts, leads, and lockwashers from terminal posts of starter relay.

3. Remove 2 screws securing starter relay. See **Figure 56**.

Installation

1. Secure starter to relay to starter bracket.

2. Install lockwasher, black striped yellow lead, and nut on port post of relay.

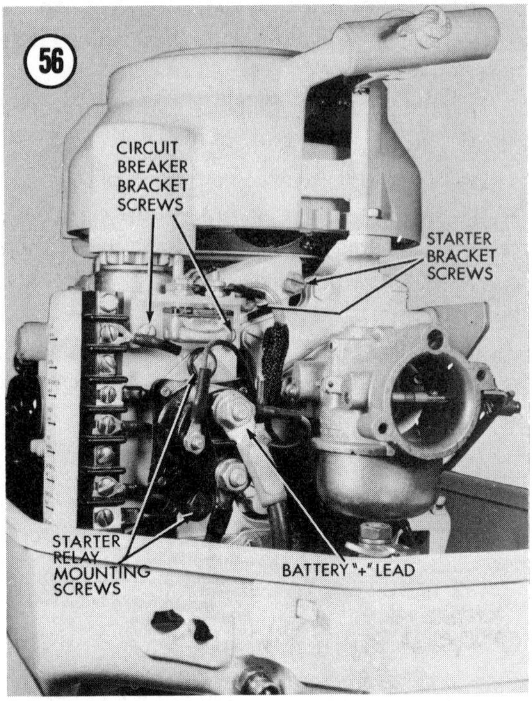

3. Install lockwasher, black lead, and nut on starboard post of relay.

4. Install lockwasher, red lead (black tip), and nut on lower post of relay.

5. Install white-striped red lead, lockwasher, positive battery lead (red tip), and nut on upper post of relay.

6. Connect battery leads to battery terminals.

CHOKE SOLENOID

Removal

1. Disconnect battery leads from battery.

2. Remove carburetor as described earlier.

3. Remove puddle drain hose from fitting on underside of crankcase cover.

4. Remove nut and green lead from post on side of choke solenoid.

5. Remove 2 screws securing solenoid bracket to crankcase cover. See **Figure 57**.

Installation

1. Install choke solenoid (terminal post at one o'clock), solenoid bracket, and 2 screws on crankcase cover. Turn screws alternately to ensure that bracket is pulled down evenly.

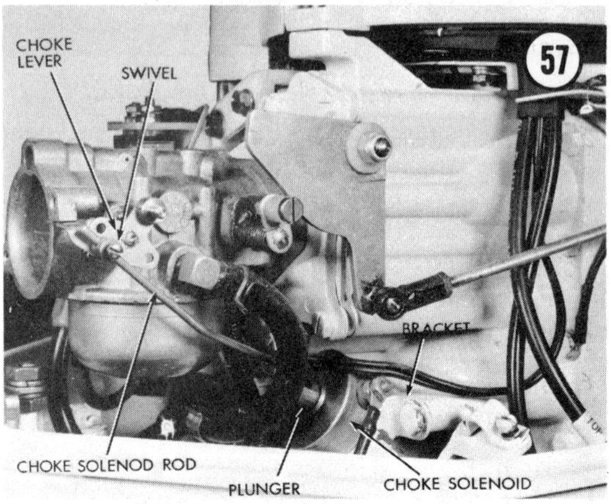

NOTE: *Make certain that the solenoid terminal is not grounded on the solenoid bracket.*

2. Install lockwasher, green lead, and nut on solenoid post. Secure lead to body of solenoid using nylon cable tie.

3. Install puddle drain hose on fitting on underside of crankcase cover.

4. Install carburetor and adjust solenoid as outlined under *Carburetor*.

5. Connect battery leads to battery terminals.

IGNITION SWITCH

Removal/Installation

1. Disconnect battery leads from battery.

2. Remove ignition switch from control box or dashboard of boat.

3. Disconnect lead wires from ignition switch.

4. Installation is the reverse of these steps. See **Figure 58**.

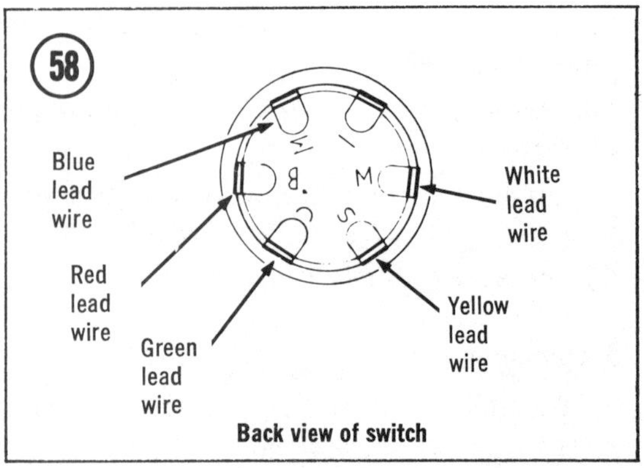

ELECTRIC STARTER

Removal

1. Disconnect battery leads from battery.
2. Remove nut and positive battery lead (red tip) from upper post of starter relay.
3. Remove 2 leads connected to interlock switch on exhaust port cover.
4. Remove lead connected to choke solenoid.
5. Remove ground lead from support plate.
6. Remove screw securing starter clamp to crankcase cover.
7. Remove 2 screws securing lower starter bracket to crankcase cover. See **Figure 59**.

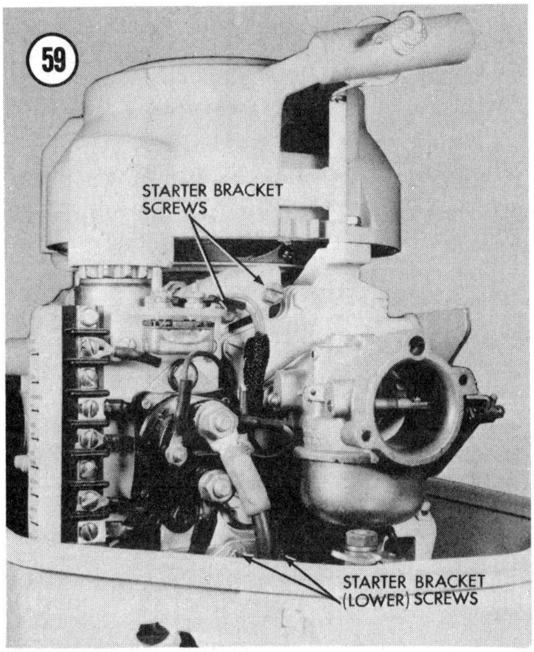

8. Remove 2 screws securing starter bracket to crankcase cover.
9. Remove starter bracket assembly from power head.
10. Remove red lead from lower terminal post of starter relay.
11. Remove 2 nuts and lockwashers from thru-bolts which secure starter to bracket.
12. Remove clamp from starter.

Installation

1. Slide clamp over starter with the most rounded corner of clamp up.
2. Insert starter thru-bolts through holes in starter bracket. Secure with lockwashers and nuts. See Figure 59.
3. Install lockwasher, red lead from starter, and nut on lower terminal post of starter.
4. Secure starter bracket to crankcase cover.
5. Secure lower starter bracket to crankcase cover. Clip for fuel line belongs under port screw and negative lead from battery belongs under starboard screw.
6. Use self-tapping screw and lockwasher to secure starter clamp to boss on power head. See **Figure 60**.

7. Install lockwasher, black double lead, and screw on support plate.
8. Install lockwasher, green lead, and nut on terminal post of choke solenoid.
9. Install lockwasher, yellow lead, and screw to underside of aft terminal of interlock switch.
10. Install lockwasher, black-striped yellow lead, and screw to underside of forward terminal of interlock switch.
11. Install white-striped red lead, lockwasher, positive battery lead (red tip), and nut on upper post of starter relay.
12. Connect battery leads to battery terminals.

POWER HEAD

Removal (Manual Start)

1. Remove retaining ring securing choke rod to choke lever on carburetor. Unhook choke rod from choke lever.

2. Remove magneto control shaft link as outlined under *Motor Leg*.

3. Use hose clamp pliers to slide hose clamp from fuel filter fitting. Remove hose.

CAUTION

Do not use hose camp pliers to pull hose off fitting; pliers can puncture the hose.

4. Loosen set screw in collar which holds gearshift control shaft. Pull shaft off upper gearshift rod.

5. Remove gearshift lever.

6. On 25 hp models, remove motor leg covers and screws securing motor leg to power head.

7. On 30 hp models, remove motor leg covers. Remove the screws securing the motor leg to the power head.

8. Remove power head.

9. Remove crankshaft spline seal from inside of crankshaft by prying downward with small screwdriver. See **Figure 61**.

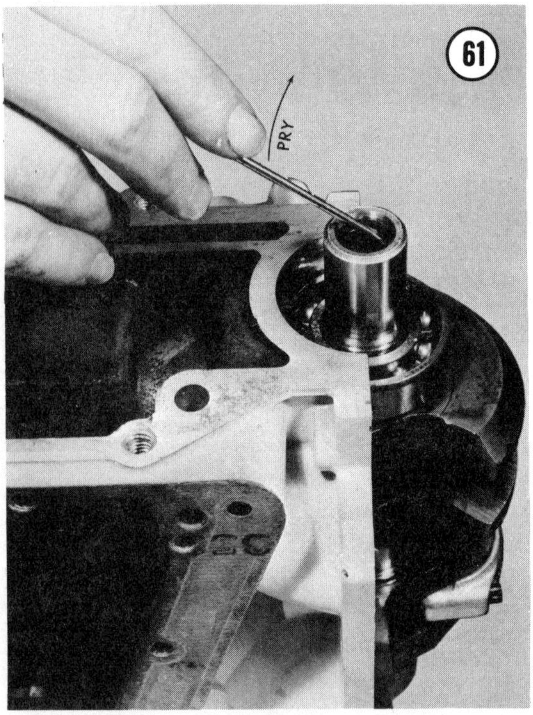

Installation (Manual Start)

1. Install crankshaft spline seal in bottom of crankshaft.

2. Clean gasket surface of power head and spacer plate. Install new cylinder exhaust gasket on spacer plate.

3. On 25 hp models, engage crankshaft splines with drive shaft splines by rotating flywheel or propeller. Ease power head onto spacer plate. Secure power head to motor leg and install motor leg covers.

4. On 30 hp models, position power head on spacer plate.

5. Install gearshift lever.

6. With spacer on end of gearshift control shaft, place end of shaft in nylon bearing in crankcase and hole in shaft arm over upper shift rod. Slide collar against rubber grommet and tighten the set screw.

7. Connect hose from bushing to fuel filter. Secure hose with clamp using hose clamp pliers.

8. Install magneto control shaft link.

9. Secure choke rod to choke lever with retaining ring.

Removal (Electric Start)

1. Disconnect battery leads from battery.

2. Disconnect red (+) lead from upper terminal post of starter relay.

3. Disconnect black (—) lead from crankcase.

4. Disconnect the double black lead from the support plate.

5. Use hose clamp pliers to slide hose clamp from fuel filter fitting. Remove hose.

CAUTION

Do not use hose camp pliers to pull hose off fitting; pliers can puncture the hose.

6. Remove gearshift lever.

7. On 25 hp models, remove motor leg covers and the screws securing the motor leg to the power head.

8. On 30 hp models, remove motor leg covers. Remove motor leg to power head screws.

9. Remove power head.

10. Remove crankshaft spline seal from inside of crankshaft by prying downward with small screwdriver. See Figure 61.

Installation (Electric Start)

1. Install crankshaft spline seal in bottom of crankshaft.
2. Clean gasket surface of power head and spacer plate. Install new cylinder exhaust gasket on spacer plate.
3. On 25 hp models, engage crankshaft with drive shaft splines by rotating flywheel or propeller. Ease power head onto spacer plate. Secure power head to motor leg and install motor leg covers.
4. On 30 hp models, position power head on spacer plate.
5. Install gearshift lever.
6. Connect hose from support plate bushing to fuel filter. Secure hose with clamp using hose clamp pliers.
7. Install lockwasher, double black lead, and screw on support plate.
8. Install lockwasher, black (—) battery lead, and screw in starboard hole of lower starter bracket on front of crankcase cover.
9. Install lockwasher, white-striped red lead, red lead, and nut on the upper terminal of the starter relay.
10. Connect leads to battery terminals.

CRANKSHAFT BEARING

Removal/Installation

1. Remove the magneto stator as outlined under *Magneto*.
2. Remove 4 screws securing bearing cage to power head.
3. Lift bearing cage with stator ring off power head. Slip cage over end of crankshaft.
4. Align link with plug lead retaining slot. Unhook stator ring from magneto control link.
5. Remove gasket from power head.
6. Align magneto control link with plug lead slot in stator ring. Hook link on ring by tilting ring. See **Figure 62**.
7. Place new bearing cage gasket on power head.
8. Apply grease between lips of crankshaft seal and insert seal protector (Special Tool T8967) in seal.

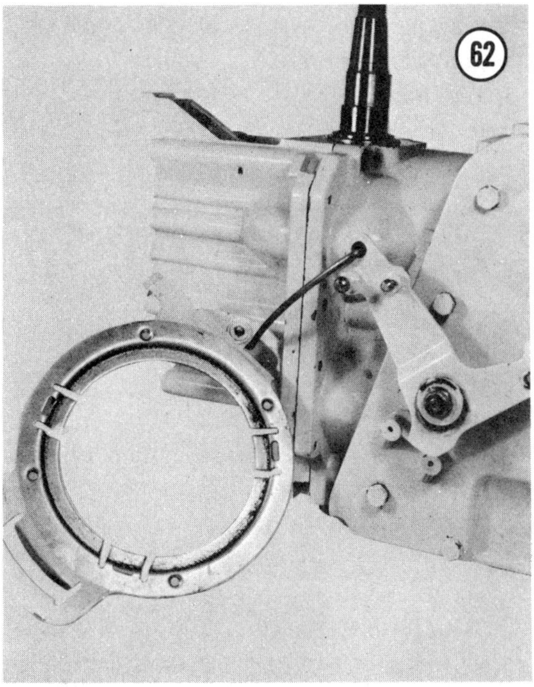
62

9. Apply sealant to threads of bearing cage screws. Secure cage to power head with 4 screws and torque to 70 in.-lb.
10. Install stator plate, outlined under *Magneto*.

Upper Crankshaft Seal Removal/Installation

1. Remove crankshaft bearing cage.
2. Use screwdriver to remove seal from bearing cage. See **Figure 63**.

63

3. Grease lip of seal. Place on seal protector (Special Tool T8967) with garter spring toward small end.

3

4. Slide protector onto crankshaft as far as it will go. See **Figure 64**.

64

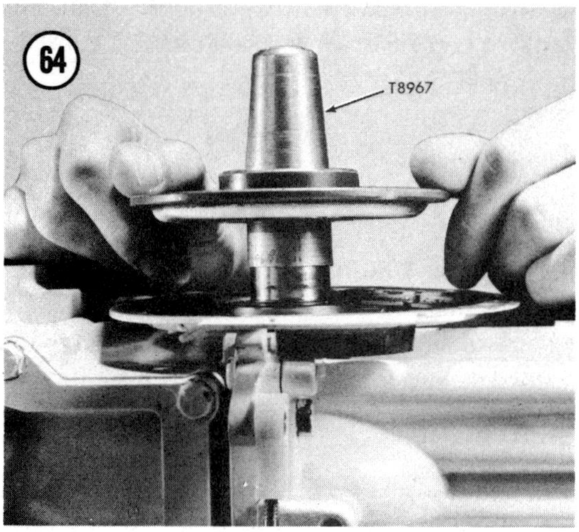

5. Use seal installer (Special Tool T8971) to drive seal into bearing cage. See **Figure 65**. Top of seal should be 0.070 ± 0.005 in. from bottom of bearing cage chamfer.

65

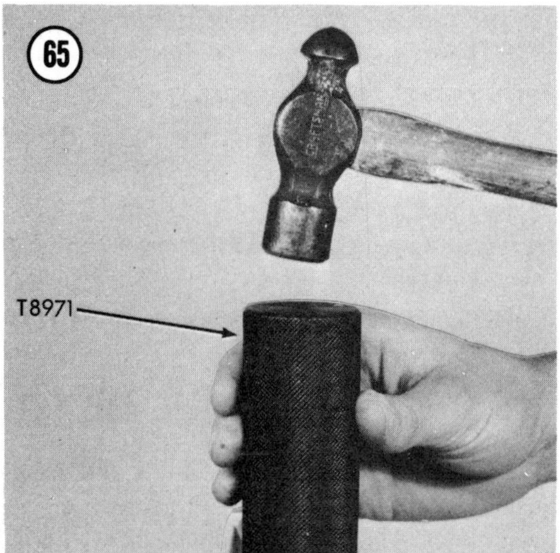

Cylinder Head Removal/Installation

1. Remove spark plugs from cylinder head.

2. Remove 10 bolts securing cylinder head to power head.

3. Remove cylinder head and gasket by prying at point shown in **Figure 66**.

66

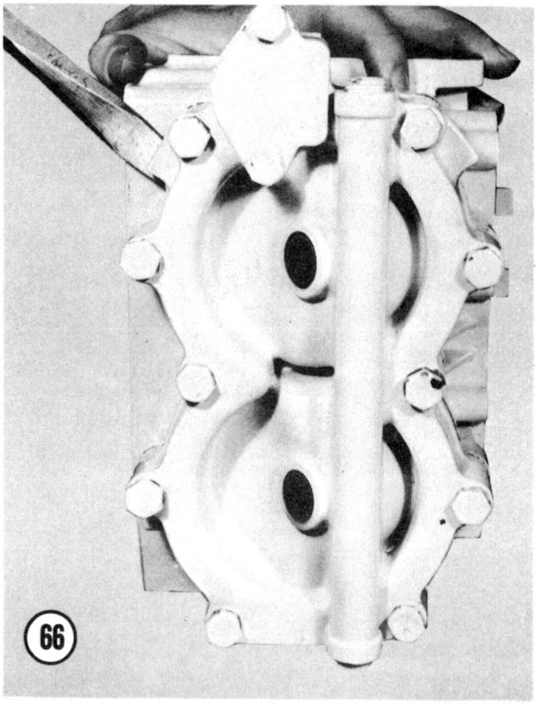

4. Remove 2 screws securing thermostat cover to head.

5. Install thermostat cover and gasket on head.

6. Align holes in cylinder head gasket with holes in head.

7. Install cylinder head and gasket on power head. Match intake side of cylinder head with intake side of cylinder. Refer to **Figure 67**.

67

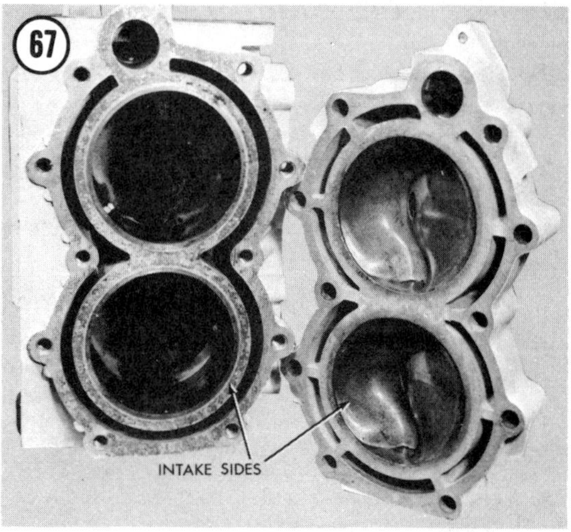

8. Apply anti-seize compound to first ¾ in. of cylinder head bolts. Torque head bolts to 270 in.-lb. following torque sequence as shown in **Figure 68**.

> NOTE: *Torque head bolts in steps. First torque bolts to 75 in.-lb. Continue in 30-50 in.-lb. increments to specified torque. This minimizes danger of warping cylinder head.*

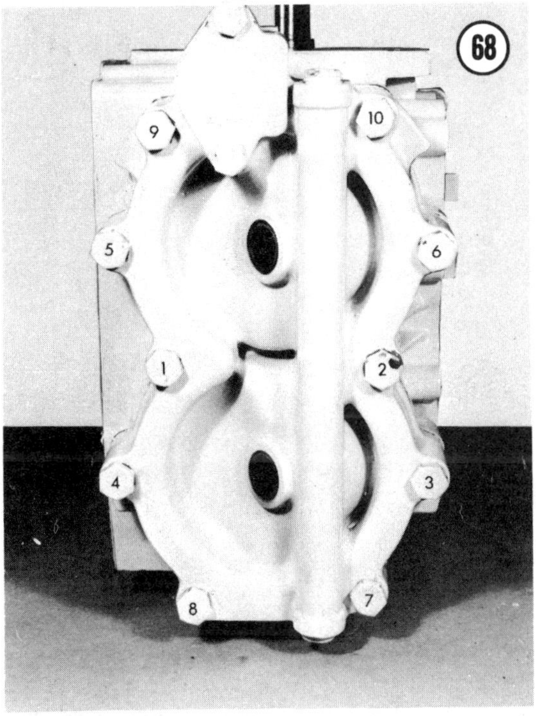

9. Run engine for at least 15 minutes and allow to cool off. Retorque cylinder bolts.

Exhaust Port Cover Removal/Installation

1. On electric start models, remove the interlock switch.
2. Unsnap throttle cam rod from magneto control lever.
3. Remove the 10 screws securing the cover to power head.
4. Remove cover, plate, and 2 gaskets.
5. Unscrew locknut securing magneto control lever to exhaust port cover.
6. Unscrew idle stop screw from boss on exhaust port cover.
7. Clean gasket surfaces on power head, cover, and plate.
8. Install one gasket between power head and exhaust port plate. Install other gasket between port plate and cover.
9. Secure cover to power head with 10 screws. Tighten center screws and work outward in a spiral pattern (torque to 70 in.-lb.).
10. Position nylon magneto control lever bearing on cover stud so that raised "step" is away from power head.
11. Position magneto control lever so that balljoints face away from power head. Install nylon bearing with slot in center, then secure control lever and bearings with stop nut.
12. Screw idle stop screw in boss from the top.
13. Install throttle cam rod.
14. Adjust throttle cam rod as outlined under *Tune-up*.
15. On electric start models, adjust idle stop screw as outlined under *Tune-up*.
16. On electric start models, install interlock switch.

Transfer Port Cover Removal/Installation

1. Remove shift lever.
2. Remove 10 screws securing transfer port cover to power head. Remove transfer port cover and gasket.
3. Remove the fuel pump as outlined under *Fuel System*.
4. Clean the gasket surfaces on cylinder and port cover.
5. Install new gasket on port cover and secure port cover to power head with 10 screws. The long screw belongs in the upper aft corner of the port cover. See **Figure 69**. Screws should be tightened in a spiral pattern starting with center screws (torque to 70 in.-lb.).
6. Install fuel pump.
7. Install shift lever.

Reed Assembly Removal/Installation

1. Unsnap throttle cam rod from throttle cam.
2. Remove the carburetor as outlined under *Carburetor*.

3

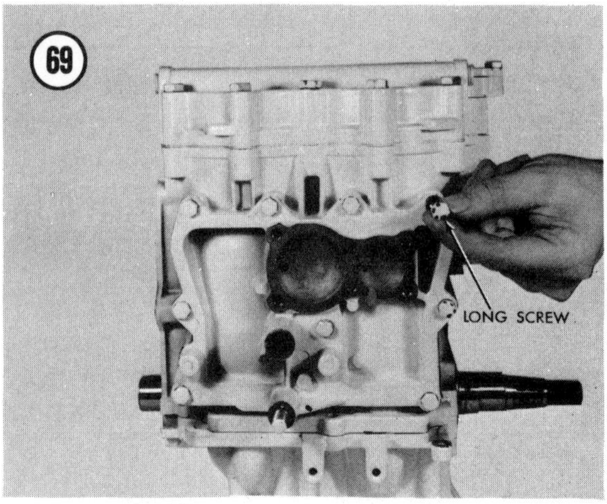

3. Remove 8 screws securing adapter flange to power head. Remove the adapter flange and reed assembly.
4. Separate adapter flange from reed assembly.
5. Remove screws securing reed plates to deflector plate. Remove reed plates and gasket.
6. Clean gasket surfaces of power head, reed plate, and adapter flange.
7. Install gasket with divided center between power head and deflector plate.
8. Secure reed plates over divided gasket on deflector plate.
9. Install gasket with undivided center between adapter flange and reed plate.
10. Secure adapter flange, reed assembly, and gaskets to power head.
11. Install the carburetor as outlined under *Carburetor*.
12. Secure throttle cam and bearings to adapter flange stud with locknut. Ball-joint side of cam should face away from power head. A nylon bearing should be on each side of cam and "steps" on bearings should be in hole in cam.

Reed Removal/Installation

1. Remove reed assembly as described above.
2. Remove screws securing stops and reeds to plates.
3. Secure reeds and stops to plate with screws and lockwashers. Reeds should be centered over openings.
4. Reed stops should be set at 0.28 ± 0.010 in. (measured from the tip of the reed stop to the deflector plate).
5. Reeds should neither stand open more than 0.010 in. nor exceed 0.005 in. twist.
6. Install reed plates.

Short Block Removal/Installation

1. Remove crankshaft bearing cage.
2. Remove power head.
3. On electric start models, remove starter bracket assembly and choke solenoid.
4. Remove reed assembly.
5. Remove cylinder head.
6. Remove exhaust port cover.
7. Remove transfer port cover.
8. Remove shift interlock lever.
9. Installation is the reverse of these steps.

Crankshaft Removal/Installation

1. Remove crankshaft bearing cage.
2. On electric start models, remove the starter bracket assembly.
3. Remove power head.
4. Remove reed assembly.
5. Remove transfer port cover.
6. Remove screws securing crankcase cover to cylinder (2 are inside, where reed plates were).
7. Drive out locating pins using pin punch (Special Tool T8919) as shown in **Figure 70**. Drive on flat end of pin.
8. Pry crankcase cover from cylinder using screwdriver at pry point. See **Figure 71**.
9. Remove exposed rollers and bearing race half from center main bearing.
10. Lift crankshaft and remove remaining rollers and bearing race half from bore.
11. Slide upper main bearing from crankshaft.
12. Slide lower main bearing seal collar from crankshaft.
13. Remove crankcase seal ring from middle of crankshaft.
14. Slide upper main bearing on crankshaft. Bearing should protrude ⅛ in. above top of cylinder bore.

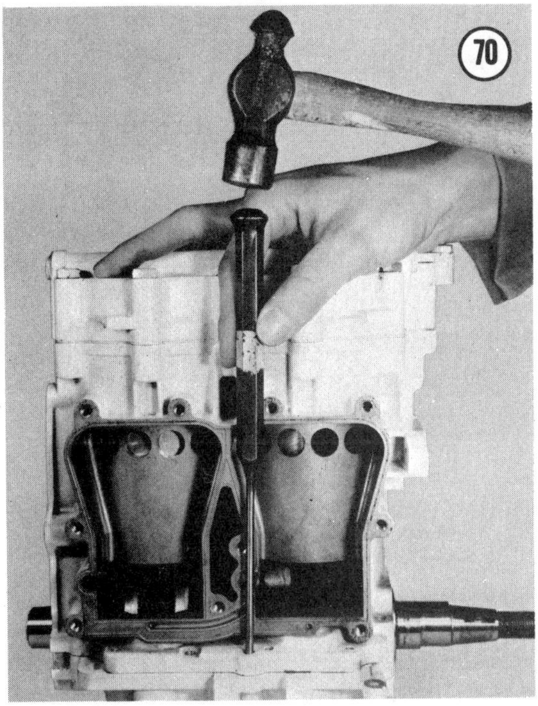

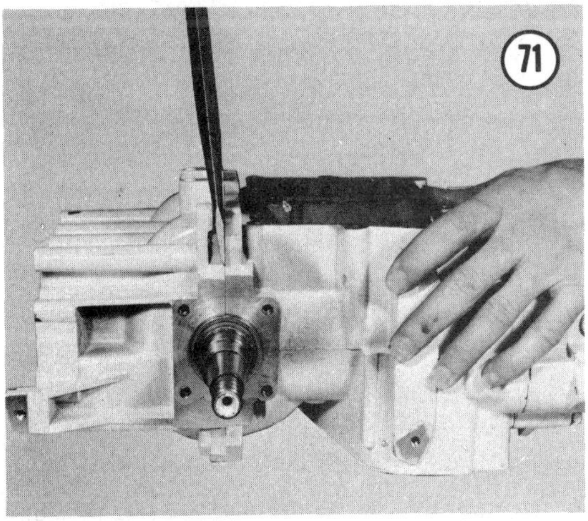

15. Install crankcase seal ring on crankshaft.

16. Place cylinder half of center main bearing race on peg in bearing bore. Coat race with grease and position 14 rollers on race.

17. Install crankshaft, grease journal, and position remaining 16 rollers on crankshaft.

18. Position other half of center main bearing race so that it dovetails with cylinder half of race.

19. Inspect parting line seal. If necessary, install new crankcase parting line seal in grooves in crankcase cover. Seal should be flush with sides of bearing bores.

20. Apply sealant to the 6 places shown in **Figure 72**.

21. Position crankcase cover on cylinder and drive in locating pins (drive on flat end).

22. Install crankcase screws (including 2 beneath reed plates). Torque bolts in a spiral from center. See cylinder head sequence shown in Figure 68. Ground lead belongs under head of second ¼ in. bolt from bottom on starboard side.

23. Insert seal protector (Special Tool T8976) in end of crankshaft (see **Figure 73**).

24. Apply grease between lips of seal. Push collar onto crankshaft, O-ring side first. Remove seal protector.

25. Make sure that O-ring is seated in groove in collar. Drive collar into power head with

3

collar installer (Special Tool T8977). See **Figure 74**. Collar should be flush to 0.010 in. above surface of power head.

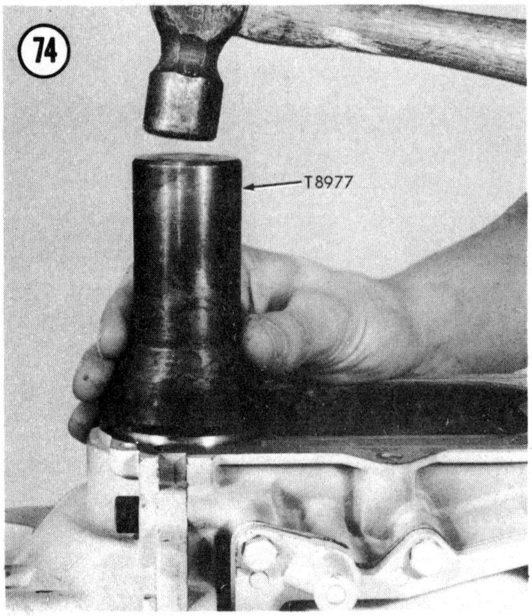

26. Install transfer port cover.

27. Install carburetor adapter flange and reed plate assembly.

28. Install power head.

29. On electric start models, install the starter bracket.

30. Install crankshaft bearing cage.

Connecting Rod Removal/Installation

1. Remove crankshaft as described earlier.

2. Mark rod caps and containers so that rollers, roller cages, and caps can be reassembled in their original positions on the crankshaft.

3. Remove rod caps from connecting rods using Special Tool T8929 as shown in **Figure 75**.

> NOTE: *To prevent needles from falling into cylinder while removing rod cap, place finger and thumb on each end of connecting rod flange at parting line of connecting rod and cap.*

> CAUTION
> *Do not handle needles with magnet. Magnetized needles wear quickly because they do not move freely in the bearing.*

4. Remove 9 rollers and half of roller cage from each connecting rod. Keep bearing cages, as well as rollers, separate.

5. Push pistons away from crankshaft. Remove the remaining rollers and roller cages from the connecting rods.

6. Lift crankshaft from cylinder.

7. Position crankshaft in cylinder.

8. Coat needle bearing portion of connecting rod with grease. Install half of roller cage and 9 rollers.

> CAUTION
> *Install crankpin roller cage halves with chamfered corner together and facing up. Do not mix roller cage halves.*

9. Slide connecting rods up to crankshaft. Coat crankpin with grease and install other roller cage and 7 rollers.

10. Position bearing caps on connecting rods, aligning match marks as shown in **Figure 76**. Apply Loctite Sealant Grade "D" to threads of connecting rods, not to screws.

11. Torque cap screws to a maximum of 10 in.-lb. and test alignment by running pencil up and down ground areas as shown in **Figure 77**. Joint between cap and rod must be almost imperceptible. If not, loosen screws and realign cap. If joints will not pass test, replace the connecting rods.

12. Torque connecting rod cap screws to 170 in.-lb. (rod screws must be torqued in steps—approximately 50 in.-lb increments).

76

77

13. Follow Steps 7 through 12 for remaining connecting rod.

Piston, Pin, and Ring Removal/Installation

1. Remove crankshaft.

2. Mark connecting rod and piston to identify which cylinder (top or bottom) these parts are being removed from. This is done to ensure that these parts will be assembled in their proper position if they are not being replaced.

3. Push connecting rod and piston assemblies out from cylinder.

4. Remove piston rings from each piston using piston ring expander (Special Tool T8926 or equivalent) as shown in **Figure 78**.

5. Remove piston pin retaining rings with retaining ring pliers.

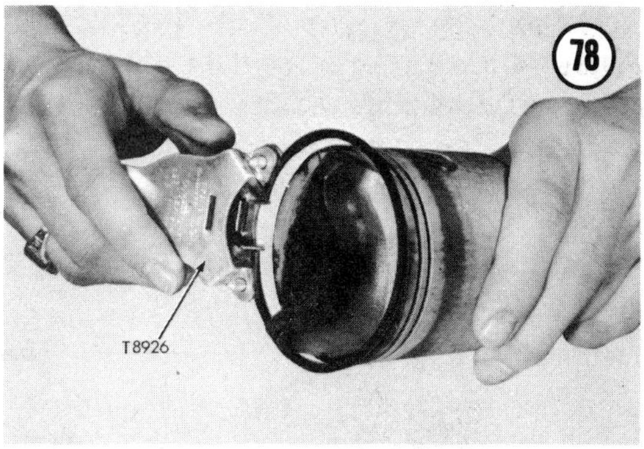

78

6. Remove piston pin by driving pin out. Use pillow block and drive pin (Special Tool T2900). See **Figure 79**.

7. Remove connecting rod from piston.

> NOTE: *Be sure to group top cylinder piston, connecting rod, piston pin, etc., and keep them separate from bottom cylinder parts to avoid confusion when it is time to assemble them.*

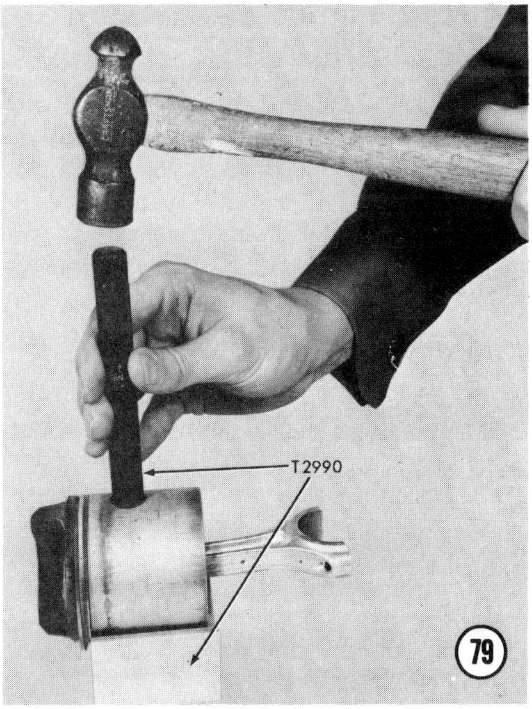

79

8. Before reassembly, heat pistons to approximately 200°F.

9. Drive piston pin in piston to secure connecting rod. (Place match marks on connecting rods on intake side of piston.)

10. Install retaining rings with retaining ring pliers.

11. Install piston rings with ring expander (Special Tool T8926 or equivalent).

> NOTE: *There is a bevel on one side of inner diameter of piston ring. See* **Figure 80**. *This side must be "up" or toward top of piston.*

12. Apply oil (SAE No. 30) to piston rings on piston. Install piston in ring compressor. Position ring gaps at spring pin, being careful not to catch end of ring with inside end of compressor band. Tighten ring compressor until rings are compressed sufficiently to enter cylinder.

> NOTE: *There are indentations at one end of ring compressor. These indentations are positioned on top of cylinder to prevent compressor from entering the cylinder.*

80

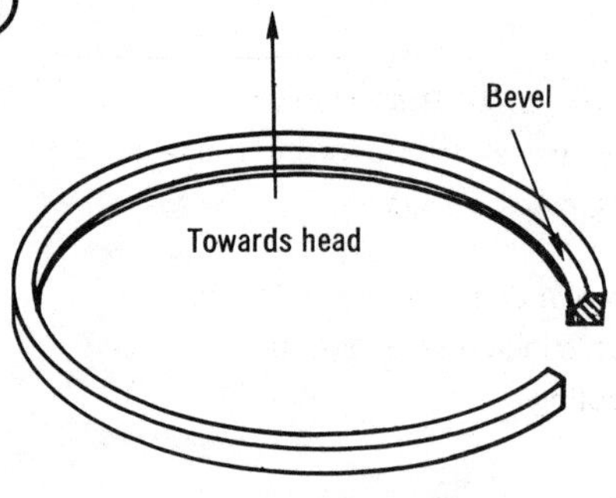

13. Position piston so that intake baffle on piston faces intake ports or transfer port cover. Push piston in cylinder. Refer to Figure 67.

14. Install connecting rod roller bearings.

15. Install crankshaft.

Table 1 ENGINE SPECIFICATIONS (25 AND 30 HP)

	25 HP	30 HP
Horsepower, BIA rated @	5,000 rpm	5,000 rpm
Recommended operating range	4,500-5,500 rpm	4,500-5,500 rpm
Engine — 2-cycle	Twin cylinder — alternate firing	Twin cylinder — alternate firing
Bore and stroke	2-3/16 in. x 2.300 in.	2-3/16 in. x 2.414 in.
Cubic inch displacement	28.57 cu. in.	29.99 cu. in.
Cooling	Water cooled — displacement type water pump	Water cooled — displacement type water pump
Propeller — standard	Aluminum alloy — 8½ in. diameter, 10 in. pitch, right-hand rotation, spline drive, 3 blade	Aluminum alloy — 10⅜ in. diameter, 13½ in. pitch, right-hand rotation, spline drive, 3 blade
Spark plug type	Champion L4J	Champion L4J
Spark plug gap	0.030 in.	0.030 in.
Breaker point gap	0.020 in.	0.020 in.
Compression (psi)	95-105	125-135
*Oil ratio per gallon of gas — break in	⅓ pint	⅓ pint
Oil ratio per gallon of gas — after break in	1/6 pint	1/6 pint
Transom height	15 in. or 20 in.	15 in. or 20 in.

***IMPORTANT** — When pistons, piston rings, piston pins, connecting rods, connecting rod bearings, crankshaft or crankshaft bearings are replaced, the break in oil ratio and procedure for new engines must be used.

Table 2 TORQUE SPECIFICATIONS (25 AND 30 HP)

Special Items		Standard Hardware	
Description	Torque	Screw Size	Torque
*Cylinder head	225 in.-lb.	10-24	30 in.-lb.
Flywheel	45 ft.-lb.	10-32	25 in.-lb.
Main bearing bolts	160 in.-lb.	12-24	45 in.-lb.
Connecting rod screws	165-175 in.-lb.	1/4-20	70 in.-lb.
Gear housing plugs	90-115 in.-lb.	5/16-18	160 in.-lb.
Spark plugs	120-180 in.-lb.	3/8-16	270 in.-lb.

*Torque from center out. Re-torque after run-in when engine has cooled.

CHAPTER FOUR

OUTBOARD MOTORS (35 TO 55 HP)

This chapter covers the tune-up, repair, and disassembly of all 35, 45, 50, and 55 hp outboard motors.

TUNE-UP

Spark Plugs

1. Remove spark plugs with deep socket, extension, and ratchet handle.
2. Inspect plugs for condition. Clean or replace plugs if necessary.
3. Check electrode gap on plugs with wire type feeler gauge. Reset to 0.030 in. Before setting the spark plug gap, file center electrode flat then make adjustment by bending the ground (side) electrode.
4. Install plugs and torque to 120-180 in.-lb.

Breaker Point Adjustment (All Models Except Magnapower)

1. Remove flywheel.
2. Inspect the breaker point contact surfaces. If they are burned or pitted, replace them. Do not file breaker points. Replace with new parts.

Breaker Point Adjustment (Magnapower Models)

1. Disconnect battery.

WARNING

The Magnapower ignition system operates at very high voltage. Always disconnect battery to avoid dangerous shock.

2. Remove the flywheel, spark plugs, and knock-off nut.
3. Inspect the breaker point contact surfaces. If the points are burned or pitted, replace them. Do not file breaker points. Replace with new parts.

NOTE: *Dirty points can be cleaned by using 320 grit emery paper to loosen film and then using a piece of clean hard surface cardboard to remove the residue.*

4. Set the throttle at WIDE OPEN position. This will establish a common location for setting the points.
5. Install flywheel knock-off nut on crankshaft. Using a box-end wrench, rotate crankshaft in the direction of engine rotation 2 full revolutions to establish a uniform grease film. If the crankshaft is moved too far, it must be rotated an additional revolution in the direction of engine rotation, and not backed up.

6. Rotate the crankshaft until the rubbing block of the point set being adjusted rests on the highest point of the breaker cam. At this point, the points are open to their widest.

7. On alternator models, continue to rotate the crankshaft 10° past the highest point on the cam.

8. On all models, mark the cam at the point just opposite the rubbing block. See **Figure 1**. This will be used as a reference point for adjusting the other set of points.

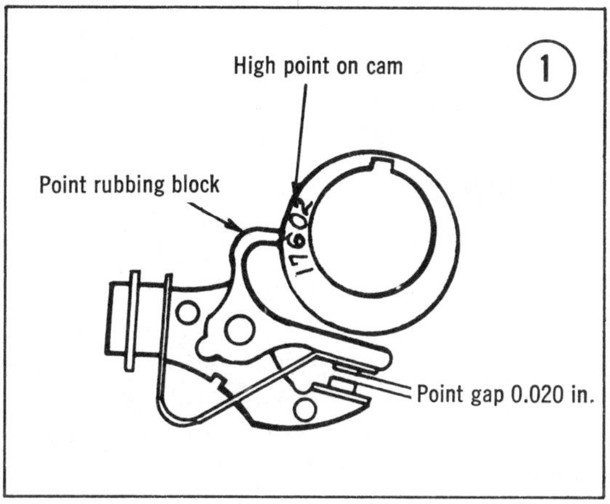

9. Measure point gap with a 0.020 in. metal feeler gauge. Adjust point gap until a slight drag is felt on the gauge when slipped between the points.

10. Rotate crankshaft one full turn. Align mark on cam with rubbing block on other set of points. Set point gap at 0.020 in. as described in Step 8.

11. Install flywheel.

Throttle Linkage Adjustment (All Models Except Magnapower)

The amount of throttle opening is synchronized with the degree of spark advance through the throttle cam and related linkage.

> NOTE: *This adjustment is necessary when the correct high speed neutral warm-up rpm cannot be reached. Correct high speed neutral warm-up is 1,800-2,500 rpm.*

1. Unsnap ball-joint connector from throttle tower shaft.

2. With throttle shutter in carburetor closed, adjust eccentric screw holding throttle roller to throttle shaft so that pick-up line on lower end of throttle cam is exactly centered on throttle roller.

3. Advance throttle tower shaft and throttle cam to full advance position (throttle shutter horizontal).

4. Adjust ball-joint connectors until spacing is identical to spacing between connector stud on throttle cam and throttle tower shaft.

5. Snap ball-joint connector in place on throttle tower shaft.

Throttle Linkage Adjustment (Magnapower Models)

1. Set tower shaft at idle position (throttle shutter of carburetor closed).

2. Disconnect throttle control rod from ball-joint on tower shaft. See **Figure 2**.

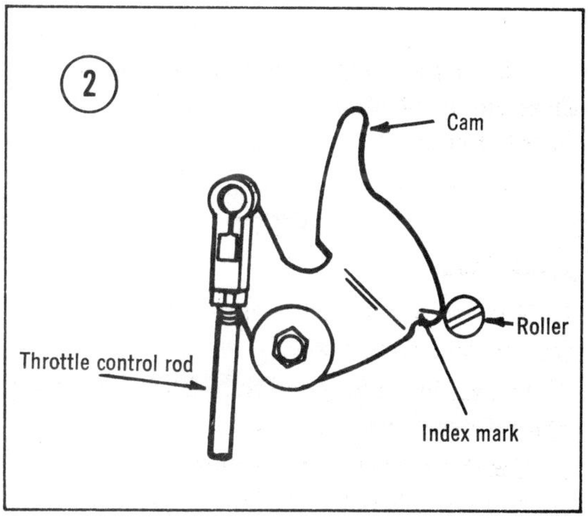

3. Hold throttle cam lightly against roller on throttle shaft of carburetor. Turn screw in roller until roller is centered on index mark of throttle cam.

Carburetor Adjustment

1. Turn the idle adjustment screw clockwise until it seats lightly. Do not overtighten, as needle and seat may be damaged. Back idle adjustment needle out one full turn.

2. Start engine and run until fully warmed up.

3. Move control lever to NEUTRAL position.

4. Turn the idle adjustment needle counterclockwise (open) until the engine loses power

and begins to "roll" or "gallop," due to an over-rich mixture. Slowly turn the needle clockwise (closed) until cylinders fire evenly and motor picks up speed. Continue turning clockwise until engine "pops" or "stalls" because of too lean a mixture. Set adjustment screw halfway between these 2 points.

5. Do not adjust leaner than necessary to obtain smooth idling. It is better to have the idle setting a little rich rather than too lean.

Wide Open Throttle (Magnapower Models)

1. Set tower shaft at full throttle position.

2. Adjust length of throttle control rod until throttle shutter of carburetor is in horizontal position. See Figure 2 for location of throttle control rod. Tighten locknut on throttle control rod.

Adjusting Idle Stop Screw (Magnapower Models)

1. Set remote control lever in NEUTRAL position.

2. Loosen locknut on throttle stop screw. See **Figure 3**.

3

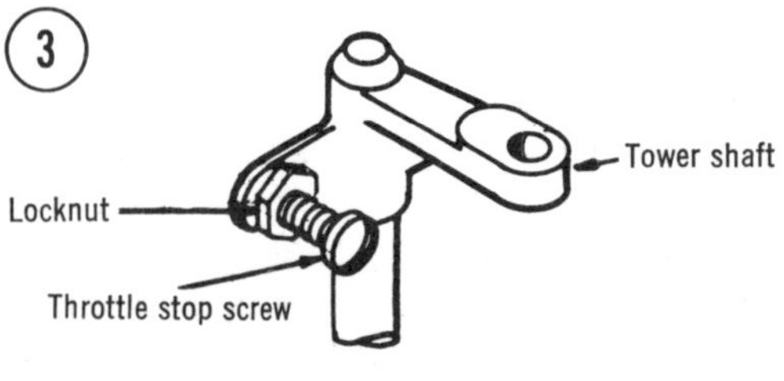

3. Turn throttle stop screw in or out until engine idles at 850-900 rpm in neutral.

4. Tighten locknut on throttle stop screw.

Timing (All Models Except Magnapower)

1. Select proper timing tool for timing engine. There are presently 2 timing tools available—one for 35 and 45 hp manual tiller engines (Special Tool T8938) and one for all other models from 35 through 55 hp (Special Tool T2937-1).

> NOTE: *Timing tool T8938 was designed specifically for 35 and 45 hp manual tiller engines beginning with the serial numbers shown in* **Table 1.**

2. Adjust the breaker points. Do not reinstall flywheel after adjusting points.

> NOTE: *Make sure that the breaker points are adjusted correctly. An error of 0.0015 inch in the setting will change engine timing as much as 1°.*

3. Check to make sure the throttle tower shaft is advanced to its maximum position (wide open stop arm on tower shaft against the crankcase cover).

4. Remove spark plug from top cylinder and install the barrel of the timing tool into the spark plug hole.

5. Install rod portion of timing tool (Special Tool T2937) into the barrel with the two 40 hp marks toward the outside.

6. Holding the rod tight against the piston, rotate the crankshaft in direction of engine rotation and locate top dead center (point at which piston is closest to cylinder head).

7. Screw the barrel of the timing tool in or out as required until the inside line of the two 40 hp marks on the rod lines up with the edge of the barrel. Refer to **Figure 4**.

Table 1 MANUAL TILLER ENGINE SERIAL NUMBERS

U. S. A.		Canada	
Model No.	Serial No.	Model No.	Serial No.
352HA	3001	352BA	3027
353HA	3001	353BA	3022
452HA	3001	452BA	3006
453HA	3001	453BA	3006

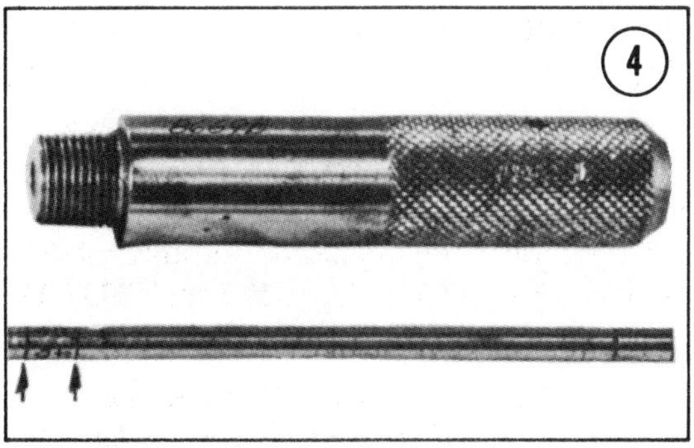

8. *Magneto Ignition Models* – Remove coil ground lead wires and attach a test light (Special Tool T2938) or continuity meter between lead wire and ground location on cylinder (**Figure 5**).

9. *Battery Ignition and Alternator/Generator Models*–Connect a test light (T2938) between the positive terminal of number 1 ignition coil and ground on cylinder head.

10. Turn crankshaft clockwise until the outer mark on the rod lines up with the edge of the barrel. The piston is now positioned exactly 32° before top dead center.

11. Turn crankshaft slowly until test light goes out.

12. Rock crankshaft back and forth. The test light should be adjusted to go on and off as the timing mark on the timing rod passes the edge of the timing tool barrel.

13. Loosen the locknut on the spark control link as shown in **Figure 6**. Adjust the spark con-

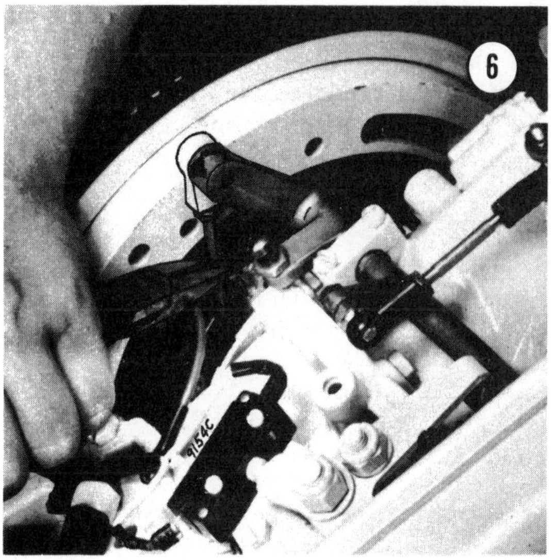

trol link in the direction required to obtain indication as in Steps 11 and 12 above.

14. Install flywheel.

Timing (Magnapower Models)

1. Remove flywheel.
2. Set throttle at wide open position.
3. Remove spark plugs from engine.
4. Install the barrel portion of the timing tool (TA2937-1) in spark plug hole of top cylinder.
5. Install rod portion of timing tool in barrel with the 2 marks on rod identified as "25 to 55 HP" facing toward outside of barrel as shown in **Figure 7**.

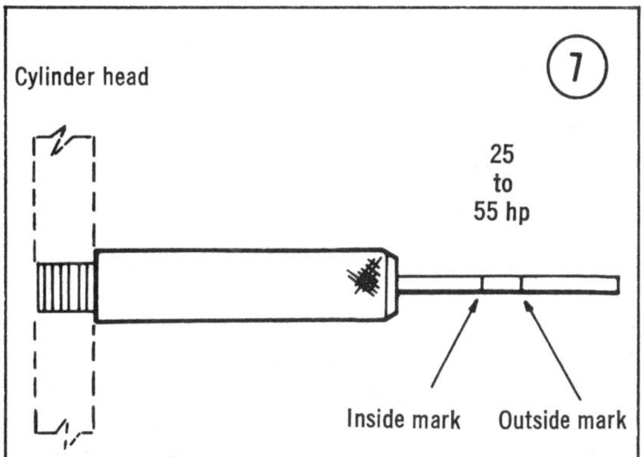

6. Holding the rod tight against top of piston, rotate crankshaft in direction of engine rotation and locate top dead center (point at which piston

4

is closest to cylinder head, also point at which rod extends maximum length from barrel of timing tool).

> NOTE: *Piston dome should be relatively free of "soft" carbon buildup prior to timing engine with timing rod to ensure constant rod position.*

7. Screw barrel in or out as required until inside mark on rod lines up with edge of barrel. Do not disturb position of barrel until Step 11 is completed.
8. Connect leads of test light (T2938-1) between terminal of number 1 cylinder breaker point (terminal to which White/Brown wire is connected) and ground. See **Figure 8**.

> NOTE: *The outer mark of timing tool will be aligned with edge of barrel when piston is at 32°* BTDC *and also at 32°* ATDC. *Always align mark with barrel when the rod is moving out of the barrel.*

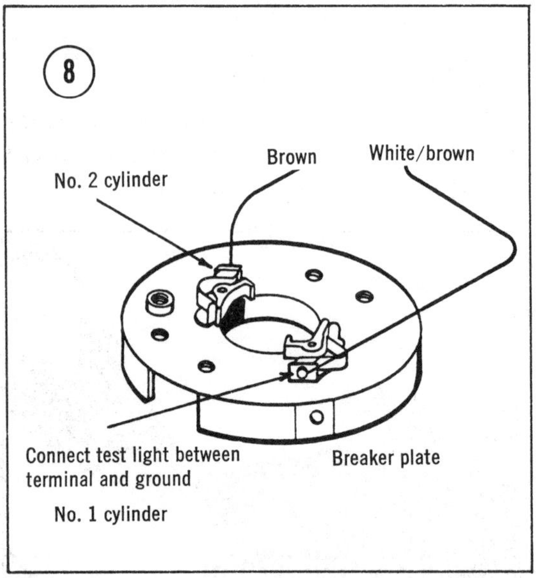

9. Rotate crankshaft in direction of engine rotation one full revolution until outer mark on rod is even with edge of timing tool barrel. This will locate piston at 32° BTDC.

> NOTE: *If crankshaft is turned too far, rotate crankshaft one full revolution until mark is aligned with edge of barrel. Do not back the crankshaft to align mark.*

10. Loosen locknut on spark control link. Turn spark control link, as necessary, until test light just goes out, indicating that points are fully open. Turn spark control link in opposite direction until test light just comes on and glows dimly, indicating that points are just beginning to close. Hold spark control link firmly and tighten locknut. Refer to **Figure 9**.

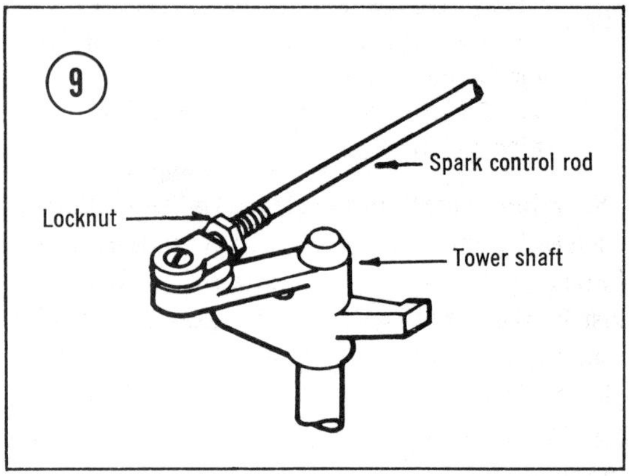

11. Rotate crankshaft one revolution and align outer mark on rod with edge of timing tool barrel. Test light should be just glowing dimly. Repeat Step 10 as necessary until light just glows dimly.
12. Proceed with timing number 2 cylinder by installing barrel of timing tool (TA2937-1) in spark plug hole of bottom cylinder.
13. Install rod portion of timing tool in barrel with the two marks on rod identified as "25 to 55 HP" facing toward outside of barrel as shown in Figure 7.
14. Holding the rod tight against top of piston, rotate crankshaft in direction of engine rotation and locate top dead center (point at which piston is closest to cylinder head, also point at which rod extends maximum length from barrel of timing tool).
15. Screw barrel in or out as required until inside mark on rod lines up with edge of barrel.
16. Connect leads of test light (T2938-1) between terminal of number 2 cylinder breaker point (terminal to which Brown wire is connected) and ground. See Figure 8.

> NOTE: *The outer mark of timing tool will be aligned with edge of barrel when piston is at 32°* BTDC *and also at*

32° ATDC. Always align mark with barrel when the rod is moving out of the barrel.

17. Rotate crankshaft in direction of engine rotation one full revolution until outer mark on rod is even with edge of timing tool. This will locate piston at 32° BTDC.

NOTE: *If crankshaft is turned too far, rotate crankshaft one full revolution until mark is aligned with edge of barrel. Do not back the crankshaft to align mark.*

18. When outer mark of rod is aligned with edge of barrel, test light should glow dimly. This indicates that points for number 2 cylinder are just beginning to open. Adjust gap of points for number 2 cylinder, as necessary, until test light glows dimly.
19. Remove test light and knock-off nut from the engine.
20. Install flywheel and flywheel nut. Torque nut to 80 foot-pounds.
21. Install spark plugs.

TROUBLESHOOTING

A 12-volt test light is a very simple and accurate device for the entire electrical circuit of battery ignition engines and the starter and choke circuits of magneto ignition-electric start engines. One lead of the test light must be connected to ground at all times, unless otherwise specified. If the other lead is linked to a hot circuit, the light will light up unless that circuit is grounded within itself.

Along with the 12-volt test light, it is recommended that a wiring diagram be used to assist in following the circuits being tested.

The following tests require that the battery be fully charged and the battery cables have a good connection to the battery. It is assumed that all engine wiring and remote electric harness wiring is connected and correct.

Circuit Breaker

Place the probe of the 12-volt test light on each terminal of the circuit breaker, as shown in **Figure 10**. A light should appear at each terminal. If a light appears at only one terminal, the circuit breaker is defective.

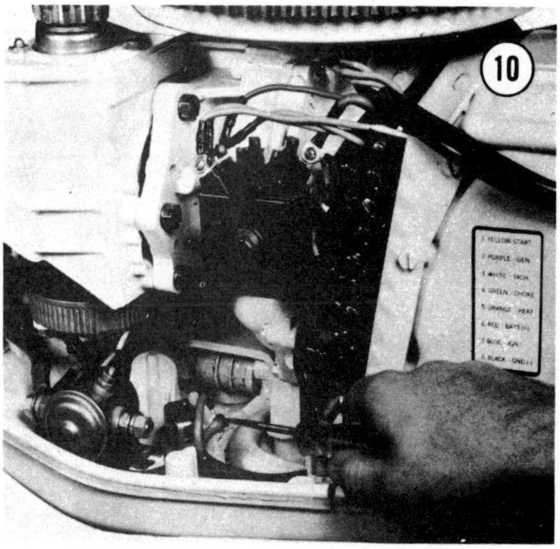

NOTE: *If the circuit breaker clicks continuously, it indicates a short circuit somewhere in the engine or remote electric harness wiring.*

Checking for Short Circuits

1. Disconnect either battery lead and insert the test light in series between the battery lead and the battery, as shown in **Figure 11**.

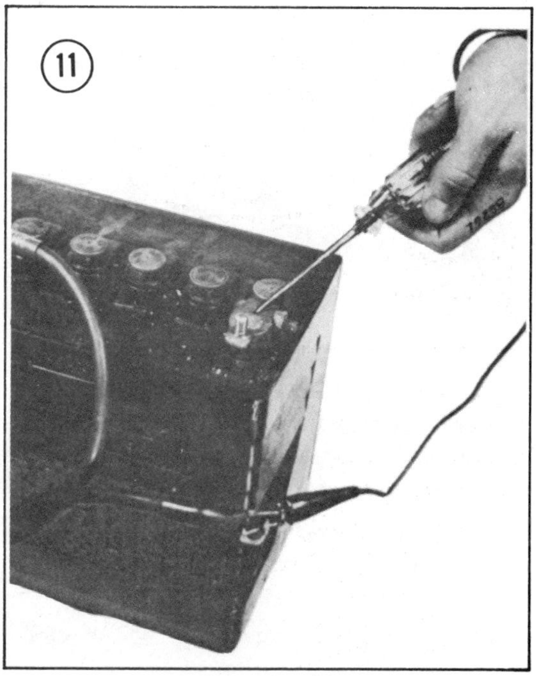

2. With the ignition switch off, there should be no light. A light at this point would indicate a flow of current, and thereby, a short.

3. On all two-cylinder generator models, if there is no light, there is no short in the electrical circuit up to the output side of the rectifier. This includes the battery or hot lead in the remote electric cable up to the ignition switch.

> NOTE: *If the battery cables are not attached to the correct terminals of the battery, a short circuit will occur, causing damage to the rectifier. If the ignition switch of a battery ignition engine is turned to the* ON *position, a short occurs and the light would come on.*

Choke Circuit

All tests must be made with the ignition switch in the CHOKE position—the key pushed into the barrel of the switch. If the 12-volt test light does not light during one step, proceed to the next step.

1. Check the green terminal of the engine terminal block, as shown in **Figure 12**. A light here indicates green lead wire or connection is faulty between terminal block and choke solenoid.

2. Check the terminal of the choke solenoid, as in **Figure 13**. A light at this point indicates:

   a. A faulty choke solenoid.

   b. Mechanical linkage faulty or out of adjustment.

3. Test the "C" (choke) terminal of the ignition switch as shown in **Figure 14**. A light at this point indicates a faulty green lead wire in the remote electric harness.

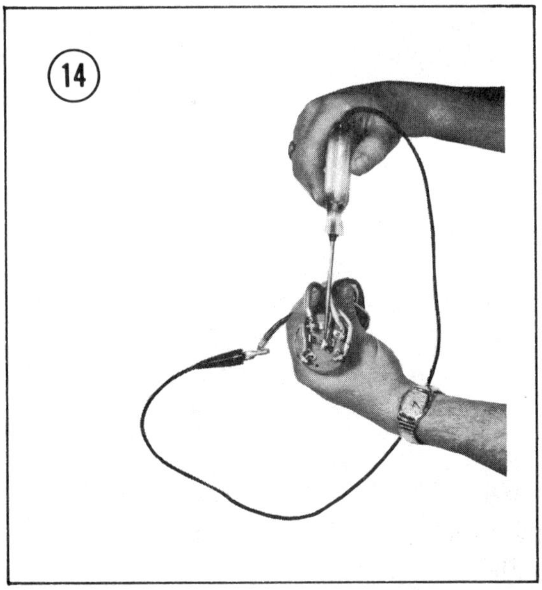

4. Check the "B" (battery) terminal of the ignition switch. A light here indicates a faulty ignition switch. No light at this point indicates an open circuit from the battery.

> NOTE: *If a dim light is noted in any of the preceding tests it can be assumed that the circuit has a poor connection or is shorted.*

Starter Circuit

All tests must be made with the ignition switch in the START position—the key turned all the way to the right. If the 12-volt test light does not light, proceed to the next step.

1. Check the terminal of the starter motor, as shown in **Figure 15**. A light at this point indicates a faulty starter motor.

> NOTE: *A dim light at this point could indicate either poor circuit conditions or a faulty starter.*

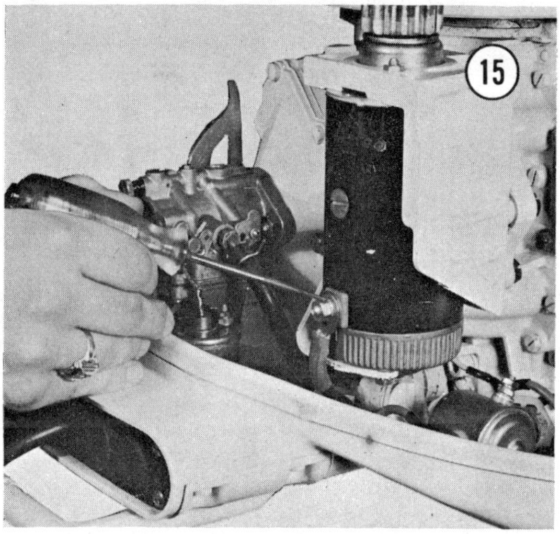

2. Check the small terminal of the starter relay, as shown in **Figure 16**. A light here indicates:

   a. A faulty starter relay.

   b. Starter relay not grounded.

   c. A faulty lead wire from relay to starter.

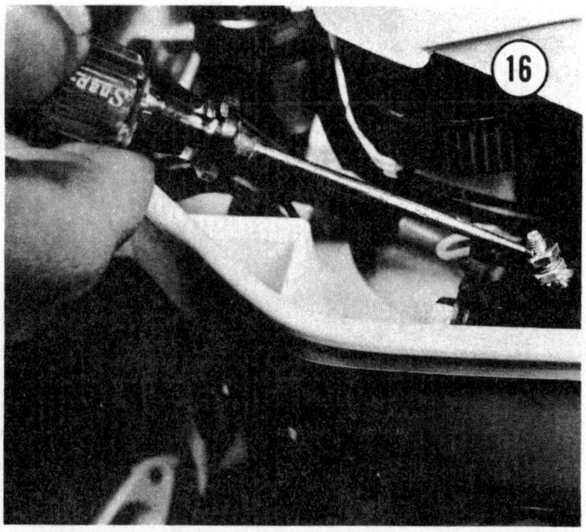

3. Check the output side of the neutral interlock switch, as shown in **Figure 17**. A light at this point indicates a faulty lead wire from interlock to starter relay.

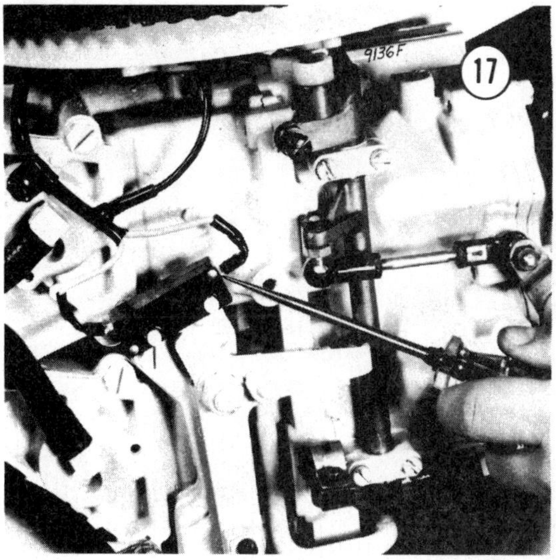

4. Check the input side of the neutral interlock switch. A light here indicates:

   a. Gear shift not in neutral.

   b. Interlock switch out of adjustment.

   c. A faulty neutral interlock switch.

5. Place the probe of the test light on the yellow terminal of the engine terminal block. A light here indicates a faulty lead wire between the terminal block and the neutral interlock switch.

6. Check the "S" (starter) terminal of the ignition switch, as shown in **Figure 18**. A light at this point indicates a faulty yellow lead wire in remote electric harness.

7. Test the "B" (battery) terminal of the ignition switch. A light here indicates a faulty ignition switch. No light at this point indicates an open circuit from the battery.

> NOTE: *If a dim light is noted in any of the preceding tests it can be assumed that the circuit has a poor connection or is shorted.*

Battery Ignition Circuit

Checking Ignition From Battery to Coil:

If the engine will not start, perform the following checks. The ignition switch must be in the

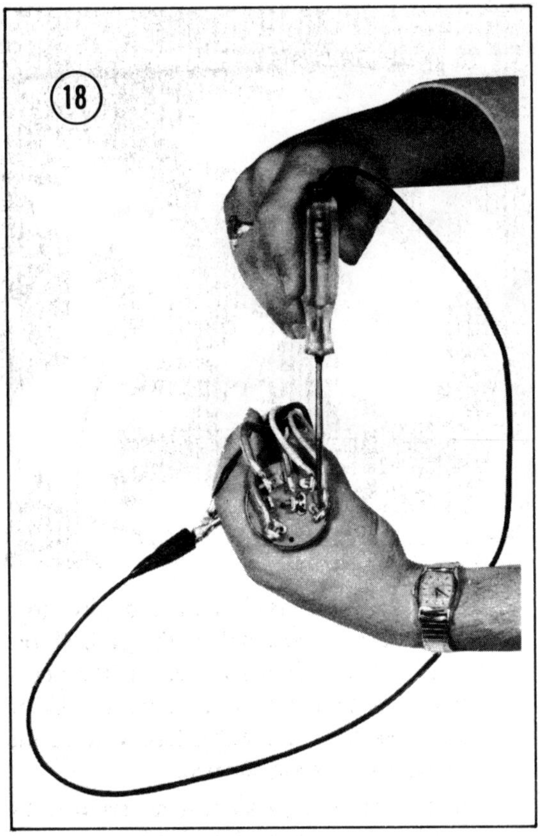

18

ON position and engine not running. (Avoid leaving switch in the ON position for prolonged periods.) If the 12-volt test light does not light during one step, proceed to next step.

1. Place the probe of the 12-volt test light on the input, positive (+) terminal of the coils as shown in **Figure 19**. A light at this point indicates the ignition circuit to be OK up to the coils. Refer to last procedure in this section for further checks of the ignition circuit from the coil to the breaker point.

2. If no light appears on the positive (+) terminal on 50 hp battery ignition models, place the probe of the test light on the blue connector of the terminal block. A light here indicates blue ignition lead wire faulty between terminal block and coils.

3. Place the probe of the 12-volt test light on the "I" (ignition) terminal of the ignition switch. A light here indicates blue ignition lead in remote electric harness faulty.

4. Place the probe of the test light on the "B" (battery) terminal of the ignition switch. A light

19

here indicates a faulty ignition switch. No light at this point indicates an open circuit from the battery.

5. If a dim light is noted in any of the previous tests, that circuit has a poor connection or is shorted.

Testing the Ignition Circuit With the Engine Running:

The following tests are especially helpful in locating a misfiring or dead cylinder. The checks should be made with the engine running in "Neutral", at 800 to 1,000 rpm.

1. With engine running, place the probe of the test light on the negative (—) terminal of the coil. The test light should flicker on and off as the breaker points open and close. The spark plugs will stop firing on the cylinder being checked, since the test light is shorting the primary circuit.

2. If test light remains on or off continuously, refer to procedure below for additional tests.

3. If the test light flickers as it should, but there is no loss in engine rpm, it can be assumed that the primary circuit of the ignition is OK, and the problem must be in the secondary circuit. The secondary circuit of the ignition consists of the secondary windings in the coil, the hi-tension lead wire, and the spark plug. It is not possible to test the secondary circuit with the 12-volt test light since the voltage in this circuit is approximately 20,000 volts.

4. To test the secondary circuit, proceed as follows:

a. Stop the engine and remove spark plugs.

b. Attach the hi-tension lead wires to the spark plugs.

c. With the ignition switch in the ON position and the spark plugs grounded to the cylinder head, crank the engine. A healthy, blue spark should be observed. If the spark plug does not fire, check the spark plug, the hi-tension lead wire, and its connection to the coil and spark plug.

d. A coil tester must be used to test the secondary windings of the coil.

Testing the Ignition Circuit from Coil and Condenser to Breaker Point:

All checks are to be made with the ignition switch ON and the engine not running.

1. Place the probe of the 12-volt test light on the positive (+) input terminal of the coil to be sure there is current to this point.

2. Place the probe of the test light on the negative (—) output terminal of the coil. If the breaker points are closed, the light will not come on. If the breaker points are open, the light will come on.

NOTE: *Be sure the spark plugs are removed so that the engine does not start accidentally.*

3. Rotate the engine clockwise 360°, as shown in **Figure 20**. The light should come on for 90° and stay off for 270°.

4. If test light remains on while rotating engine 360°, it indicates an open circuit caused by:

a. Breaker points insulated or not closing.

b. A faulty lead wire from coil to breaker points.

5. If the test light remains off while rotating the engine through 360°, a closed or shorted circuit is indicated. Proceed as follows:

a. Rotate the engine so that the breaker points of the faulty cylinder are in open position.

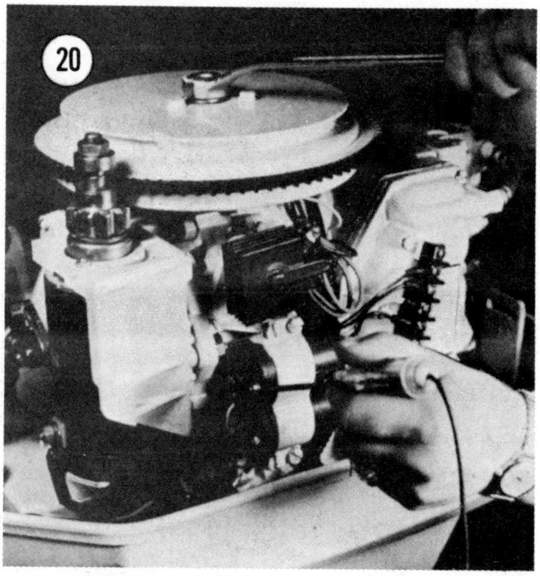

b. Remove the breaker point lead wire from negative (—) terminal of the coil. If the test light now shows current at the negative (—) terminal of the coil, it can be assumed that the breaker lead wire or the breaker points are shorted.

c. If the test light does not light, remove the condenser lead wire. If a light now appears, the condenser is shorted.

d. *No. 1 Cylinder Only*—Remove the tachometer lead wire (White) from the negative (—) terminal. If the light now lights, the tachometer or the tachometer circuit is shorted.

e. At this point, all wires are removed from the negative (—) terminal. If there is still no light, it can be assumed the coil is faulty.

Testing Alternator Output

The following tests are used to determine whether an alternator is actually charging a battery or not. All tests must be made with the engine running at 1,000 to 1,100 rpm.

1. Run the engine at the rpm indicated above and disconnect either battery cable from the battery. The engine should continue to run.

2. If the engine stops when the battery cable is disconnected, the alternator does not have full output, or has no output at all.

CAUTION

Do not run the engine for extended periods, or at higher rpm, with the battery cable disconnected. A current indicator may be used for more accurate checking of alternator output.

3. Run the engine at the rpm listed above. Place the probe of a 12-volt test light on the 3 input terminals of the rectifier, as shown in **Figure 21**. (Input terminals are the 3 in line with yellow dots.) A light should appear on each of the 3 terminals. No light at this point indicates a faulty stator.

Alternator Rectifier Check (All Models)

All checks are to be made with the engine not running and the ignition switch turned to the ON position. (Avoid leaving switch in the ON position for prolonged periods.)

1. Place the probe of the test light on the output terminal of the rectifier, as shown in **Figure 22**. (This is a single terminal with a heavy red wire attached.) The test light should indicate voltage at this point. If there is no light, the red output lead wire must be checked from the rectifier to the circuit breaker.

2. Place the probe of the test light on each of the 3 input terminals of the rectifier, as shown in Figure 21. (Input terminals are the 3 in line.)

3. A light at any of these 3 terminals indicates reverse current flow and a faulty rectifier.

Starter Motor

1. Starter motor engages but does not have sufficient power to turn engine over.

   a. Battery not fully charged. Check battery and make sure it is charged to full capacity. Make sure correct type battery is used.

   b. Starter motor windings damaged or burned. Take the starter to an authorized repair center.

   c. Power head components seized. Try turning engine over using a starter rope on flywheel emergency starter ring. If engine is tight and can't be turned over, it will be necessary to make major repairs. Refer to *Power Head* section of this chapter for details.

2. Starter motor turns but does not engage flywheel.

   a. Check starter motor "Bendix Drive" located on top of starter motor. If the "Bendix Drive" is found to be defective, it must be replaced as a complete unit.

   b. Lubricate "Bendix Drive".

3. Starter motor does not turn. The following test should be made using a test light.

   a. Connect one test light lead wire to the small terminal located on top of the starter relay. The starter relay is located near the front of the support plate on the "port" side just under the starter motor.

b. Connect the other test light lead wire to a ground location on the engine and turn the ignition key to the START position. If the test light comes on, the starter relay is defective and must be replaced. If the test light does not come on, check the battery connections, neutral interlock switch, ignition switch and all engine wiring between the START terminal on back of the ignition switch and top terminal of starter relay.

FUEL SYSTEM

Fuel Pump Removal/Installation

1. Remove fuel lines from inlet, outlet, and air pressure fittings on fuel pump.
2. Remove screws which retain fuel pump bracket assembly to cylinder and remove pump.
3. Installation is the reverse of these steps. Use new gaskets.

Inspection

1. Diaphragm must be free from holes or breaks of any kind and must completely cover the crankcase gasket surface.

Carburetor Removal/Installation

NOTE: *When disconnecting throttle link from carburetor, exercise caution, as the link must not be bent out of shape. If the link is bent, it must be replaced with a new one.*

1. Remove fuel line from carburetor.
2. Disconnect choke wire from choke shaft.
3. Remove nuts which hold the carburetor to the adapter flange.
4. Pull carburetor forward and off the studs.
5. Installation is the reverse of these steps. Use new gasket and adjust carburetor as outlined under *Tune-up*.

FLYWHEEL

Removal/Installation

1. Remove flywheel nut.
2. Install flywheel knock-off nut (T2910) to crankshaft. Turn knock-off nut down to within 2 turns of the flywheel. Lift up on edge of flywheel when striking nut. Strike knock-off nut with a medium (16 oz.) weight hammer. The blow should be centered as much as possible.

CAUTION

Do not use a heavy hammer or strike too hard, as possible damage to the crankshaft and bearings could result.

3. Remove knock-off bolt and lift flywheel from crankshaft.
4. Carefully inspect the flywheel for cracks and breaks.

WARNING

Cracked or chipped flywheels must be replaced. At high engine rpm a damaged flywheel may fly apart throwing shrapnel over a large area.

5. Whenever the flywheel is removed for any reason, the tapered bore must be cleaned and inspected for evidence of fretting or working. If there is evidence of fretting or working, or if the engine has had in excess of 25 hours of operation, the flywheel bore must be lapped as described below.
6. Install Woodruff key, flywheel, new lockwasher (if any removed), and nut. Tighten the nut to 80 ft.-lb.

NOTE: *Do not reuse old lockwasher. Always use new one.*

Lapping

1. Apply a light coat of valve grinding compound to the tapered portion of the crankshaft.
2. Assemble flywheel to crankshaft and rotate flywheel gently back and forth about ¼ turn. Do not spin flywheel completely around the crankshaft.
3. Move the flywheel 90° and repeat the above operations.
4. Remove flywheel, wipe compound off crankshaft and flywheel, and inspect. The tapered bore in the flywheel should have a minimum of 90% surface contact to the taper on the crankshaft.
5. If the above conditions are satisfactory, wipe all grinding compound from the flywheel and

crankshaft. Install flywheel key, flywheel, lockwasher (if used), and flywheel nut to crankshaft. Tighten flywheel nut to 80 ft.-lb.

NOTE: *Whenever a flywheel is removed the old lockwasher should be discarded and replaced with a new one.*

MAGNETO

Removal/Installation

Refer to **Figure 23** for following procedure.

1. Remove flywheel.
2. Remove screw retaining spark control bearing to throttle tower shaft.
3. Remove 4 screws which retain magneto to stator ring.
4. Remove spark plug lead wires and magneto ground wire from center-forward screw in upper transfer port cover.
5. Disengage wiring harness from terminal connector plate.
6. Lift magneto up and off the engine.

NOTE: *If power head repairs are to be made, remove magneto cam and key.*

7. Lubricate all moving parts, linkages, magneto pilot bore, stator plate, and cam wiper felts with Rykon 2EP.

NOTE: *Install magneto breaker cam and key, if removed. Install cam with arrow or part number "up."*

8. Installation is the reverse of these steps.

Coil Removal/Installation

The coils are held in place with coil wedge springs which pass between the coil and core.

1. To remove coil, disconnect primary and secondary lead wires and pry on end of coil wedge spring attached to coil core. It may be necessary to bend one of the coil core laminations to remove coil.
2. After removing spring and bending lamination, use 2 screwdrivers and pry coil from core.
3. Installation is the reverse of these steps.

NOTE: *When replacing coil, bend core lamination down to ensure against coil moving out and striking flywheel.*

Condenser Removal/Installation

1. Disconnect lead wire attached to breaker point and remove screw securing it to stator plate.
2. Installation is the reverse of this step.

CHARGING SYSTEM

Alternator Removal/Installation

1. Remove flywheel.
2. Disconnect the breaker point lead wire and breaker lead wire to the ignition coils from the dual male terminals mounted on the stator, as shown in **Figure 24**.

NOTE: *The yellow coil lead wire will have to be pulled through the holes in the floor of the stator. Make a note of the correct routing of this lead wire for reassembly later.*

24

3. Remove the 3 breaker plate shoes from stator as shown in **Figure 25**.

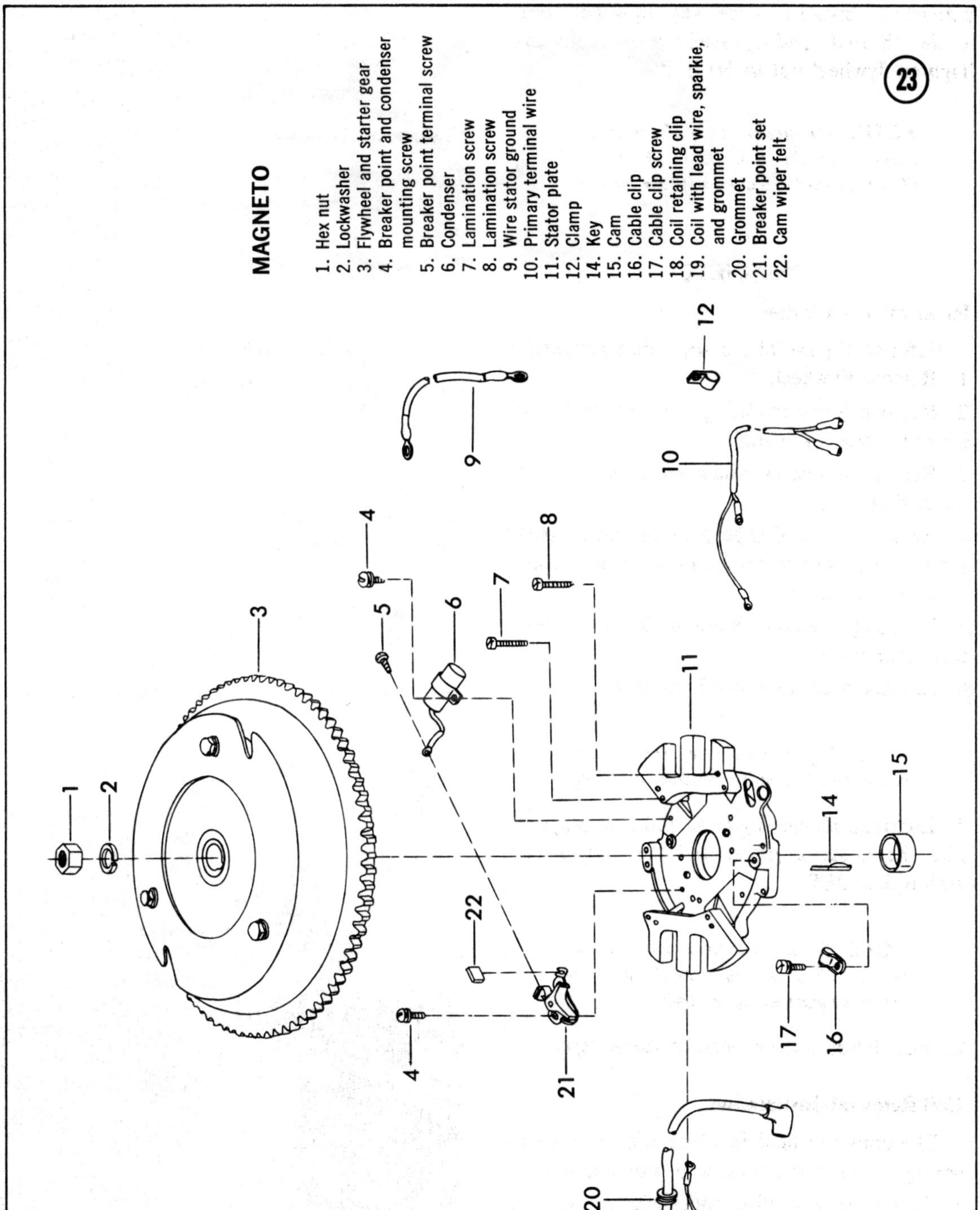

MAGNETO

1. Hex nut
2. Lockwasher
3. Flywheel and starter gear
4. Breaker point and condenser mounting screw
5. Breaker point terminal screw
6. Condenser
7. Lamination screw
8. Lamination screw
9. Wire stator ground
10. Primary terminal wire
11. Stator plate
12. Clamp
14. Key
15. Cam
16. Cable clip
17. Cable clip screw
18. Coil retaining clip
19. Coil with lead wire, sparkie, and grommet
20. Grommet
21. Breaker point set
22. Cam wiper felt

(23)

4. Remove the 3 gray stator lead wires attached to the rectifier and lift stator group up and off the engine.

5. Installation is the reverse of these steps.

Rectifier Removal/Installation

1. Remove black and purple lead wires from terminals on rectifier.

2. Remove the 2 screws attaching the rectifier mounting bracket to the cylinder as shown in **Figure 26**.

3. Installation is the reverse of these steps.

CAUTION

Always remove the rectifier from the engine as described above to prevent damaging the protective coating. Do not use a wrench on the coated mounting bolt head, as this will cause internal shorting of the rectifier plates.

ELECTRIC STARTER

Removal

1. Remove electrical connections from starter.

2. Remove bolts securing starter mounting bracket to engine and remove starter.

Installation

1. If starter was removed from bracket, reinstall in bracket using 2 long thru-bolts. Do not tighten at this time.

CAUTION

When removing thru-bolts from starter hold starter end assemblies together, and do not allow starter motor to become disassembled.

2. Install starter and bracket assembly to engine but do not tighten mounting screws at this time.

3. After all starter mounting bracket screws have been installed, torque screws holding the lower mounting bracket to crankcase cover. Torque to 70 in.-lb.

4. After screws have been torqued, torque 3 screws securing upper starter mounting bracket to large flange on the crankcase cover. Torque to 160 in.-lb.

5. Tighten thru bolts. Turn armature shaft by hand while tightening to prevent binding of the armature shaft.

NOTE: *Apply Loctite "D," to three 5/16-18 x 1 starter mounting screws when installing.*

6. After complete starter assembly and pinion gear are installed, the mesh clearance between pinion gear and ring gear on flywheel must be 0.015 to 0.040 in.

Starter Relay Removal/Installation

1. Remove all lead wires from terminals on starter relay.
2. Remove 2 screws retaining relay to support plate as shown in **Figure 27**.
3. Installation is the reverse of these steps.

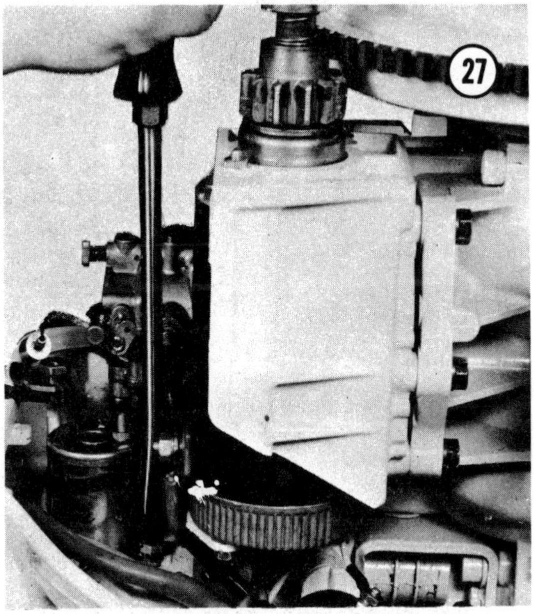

Choke Solenoid Removal/Installation

1. Remove green lead wire from terminal on top of choke solenoid.
2. Remove choke plunger wire from choke arm on carburetor.
3. Remove 2 screws retaining solenoid to support plate as shown in **Figure 28**.
4. Installation is the reverse of these steps.

MANUAL STARTER

Rewind Spring Replacement

1. Remove pinion pin retaining screws as shown in **Figure 29**.

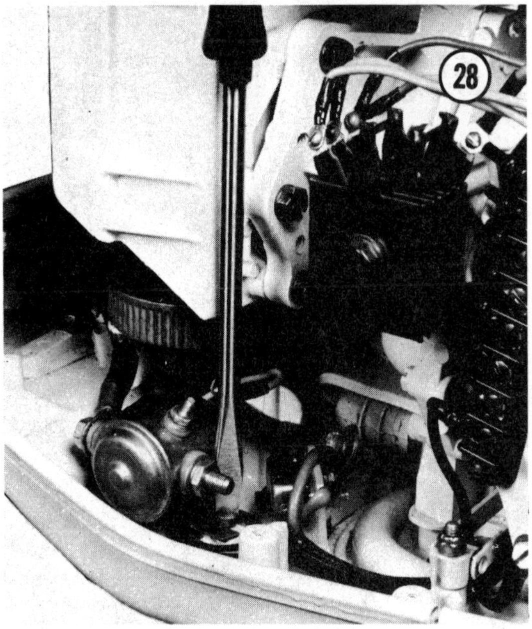

2. Insert Special Tool T3139 into the hole from which retaining screw was removed. Tighten tool securely. Push starter pinion pin out carefully. See **Figure 30**.
3. Lift starter rewind spring drive, rewind spring, guide post, and lower retainer out of starter spool bore.
4. Grease the starter spool bearings, rewind spring, spring guide post, spring drive, and retainer liberally with cam grease, or equivalent.

4

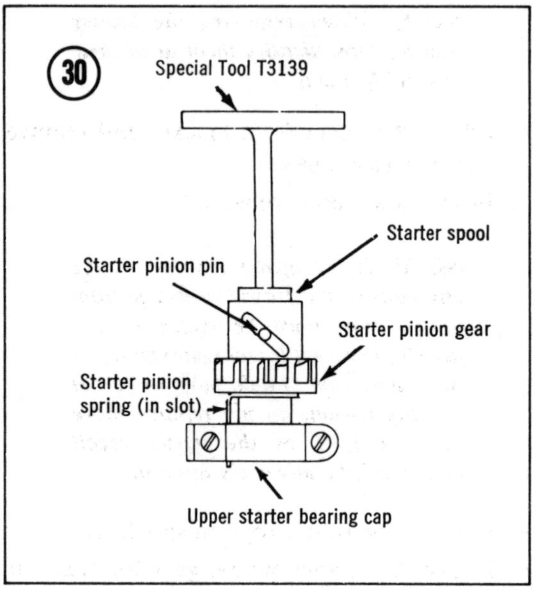

5. Insert the rewind spring retainer inside the rewind spring with the rectangular lug toward the flat end of the rewind spring. Turn the spring retainer until the rectangular lug extends beyond the flat end of the rewind spring. Engage the lower eye of the rewind spring with the pin on the rewind spring retainer. Refer to **Figure 31**.

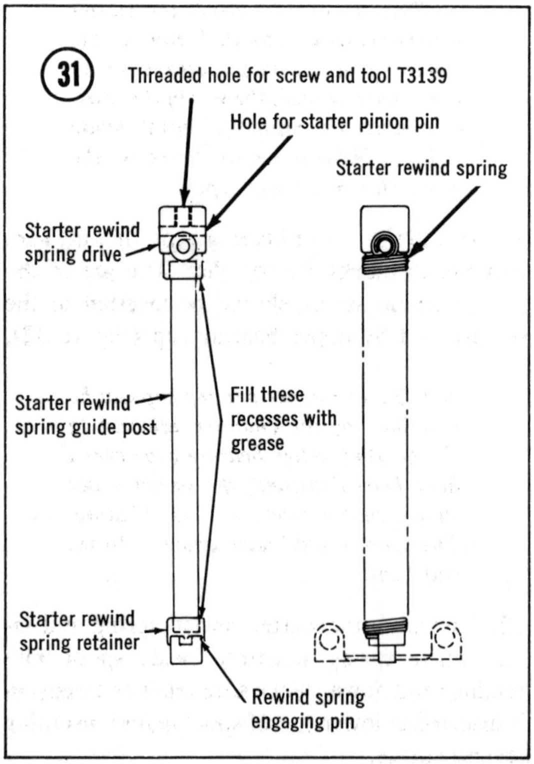

6. Insert rewind spring guide post inside of rewind spring. Engage upper eye of rewind spring with pin on rewind spring drive. Refer to Figure 31.

7. Insert the entire assembly inside of starter spool with the retainer end down. See **Figure 32**.

> NOTE: *If the starter retainer extension, located on the bottom of the starter assembly has been removed for any reason, it must be inserted into the bottom of the starter spool prior to installing starter spring-retainer assembly.*

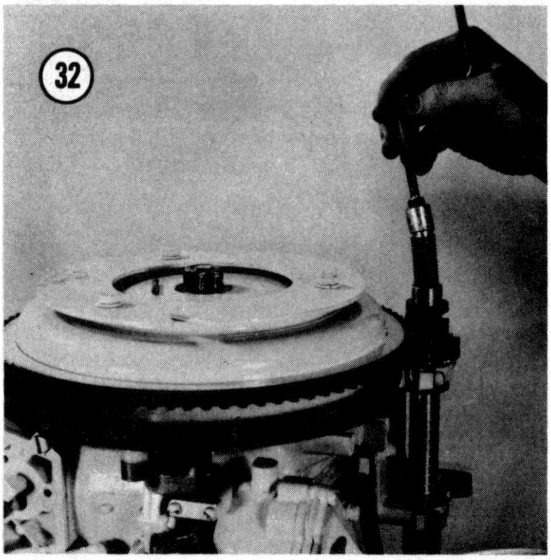

8. Install the starter retainer extension on the bottom of the spool. Insert the starter rope guide through the hole in the extension and install guide to lower inside screw which retains the lower starter bearing cap.

9. Make sure the starter rope is fully wound on spool. Hold spool firmly with rope fully wound.

10. Turn Special Tool T3139 and rewind spring assembly 8 turns counterclockwise to establish the proper initial tension on rewind spring. See **Figure 33**.

11. Align hole in starter rewind spring drive wtih hole in spool and insert starter pinion pin through diagonal slot in starter pinion gear so pinion pin engages all parts (Figures 29 and 30).

> NOTE: *Inspect the starter pinion pin for burrs. Remove burrs or replace with new pin.*

12. Remove Special Tool T3139 and install screw used to retain starter pinion pin.

Starter Rope Replacement

1. Remove plug button and handle. Allow rope to rewind on starter spool.
2. Remove screw which retains starter pinion pin. Insert Special Tool T3139 into the hole from which the screw was removed. Tighten tool securely.
3. Drive starter pinion pin out carefully. Starter rewind spring will unwind when this pin is removed.

> NOTE: *It is not necessary to remove starter from engine to replace starter rope. Simply allow the rewind spring to unwind, remove old starter rope and replace with new rope. Then, follow winding procedure for starter spring. If the starter is removed from the engine, follow all steps as follows.*

4. Lift starter spring drive, spring, and retainer out of starter spool as an assembly.
5. Remove the 4 screws which attach the starter bearing caps. Remove starter bearing caps and starter rope guide.

> NOTE: *When removing the starter bearing caps, identify them as to their original location.*

6. Lift starter spool from bracket and remove damaged starter rope.
7. Install new starter rope.

> NOTE: *If the starter rope is cut for any reason, the frayed or cut portion of the rope must be sealed with a match to prevent it from unraveling. If the starter rope should have to be cut for any reason, do not remove more than ½ inch, as the starter recoil action will be adversely affected.*

8. Rewind new starter rope on spool.
9. Inspect the starter pinion gear for wear. If worn excessively, replace. Starter pinion spring should have only a light tension on the gear. Lubricate the shaft portion of the starter spool before installing the starter pinion gear.
10. Lubricate the bearing surface of the starter spool, then assemble spool and rope to the carburetor adapter flange (or mounting bracket).

> NOTE: *Be sure to install the starter retainer extension to the bottom of the starter spool and then insert the starter rope guide through the sole in the starter retainer extension and install guide to lower inside screw which retains the lower starter bearing cap.*

11. Install the starter bearing caps, making sure that match marks are together. The leg of the starter pinion spring should be inserted in the slot formed by upper bearing cap (Figure 32).

> NOTE: *The upper bearing cap can be identified by the chamfer adjacent to the bearing. After bearing cap screws have been tightened, the starter spool should rotate freely without binding. The spool should have about 1/16 in. end float.*

12. Lubricate the starter rewind spring and insert entire spring assembly inside spool with retainer end down. Make sure retainer extension is inserted in lower end of spool before installing rewind spring.

4

13. Pull starter rope through engine control panel and attach starter handle and plain washer. Tie knot in end of starter rope and pull knot securely into cavity of handle. Install plug button to starter handle.

14. Perform Steps 8 through 12 under *Rewind Spring Replacement.*

> NOTE: *If full throttle operation cannot be obtained, the probable cause is the starter pinion gear restricting the throttle cam operation by riding up on the starter spool shaft. If this condition exists, perform the following steps.*

15. Remove starter pinion gear and spring from starter.

16. Remove the pinion spring from gear.

17. Compress pinion spring until ends contact each other. This will increase the tension on the starter pinion gear.

18. Lubricate groove in pinion gear with Rykon 2EP and reinstall spring.

19. Reinstall starter pinion and rewind starter.

20. Check starter and full throttle operation. If pinion is too tight, simply spread spring ends until spring has firm drag but does not cause a sluggish recoil action.

POWER HEAD

Removal

1. On manual starter models, remove the starter handle and tie a knot in starter rope to prevent it from rewinding on starter spool. This procedure will eliminate rewinding starter spring when reassembling power head.

2. Remove E-ring from stablizer link located on the port side of the cylinder block just to the rear of the crankcase parting line (1966 and earlier models).

3. Remove the magneto or alternator as outlined under *Magneto* or *Alternator Generator*.

4. Remove fuel line from carburetor inlet and puddle drain hoses from fittings on carburetor adapter flange.

5. Remove the carburetor, fuel pump, and reed plate.

6. Remove the thermostat water tube and the cylinder head.

7. Remove the 2 screws which attach the upper shock mount engine bracket to the upper shock mount (located directly above the kingpin nut).

8. Remove the hex nut from the shift arm bracket and gearshift rod on the starboard side of the power head as shown in **Figure 34**.

> NOTE: *If the cylinder is to be replaced, remove as many components as possible from the power head before removing power head from motor leg. this allows better leverage when removing heavily torqued screws.*

9. Remove the power head-motor leg attaching screws. One of these screws is located under the motor leg exhaust cover, as shown in **Figure 35**. On models equipped with motor leg covers, the covers must be removed to gain access to these screws.

10. Lift power head up and off, separating the power head from the spacer plate at the upper cylinder exhaust gasket.

Disassembly

Refer to **Figure 36** (p. 70) for this procedure.

1. Remove 4 crankshaft bearing cage attaching screws and remove bearing cage.

2. Remove main bearing bolts and dowel pins.

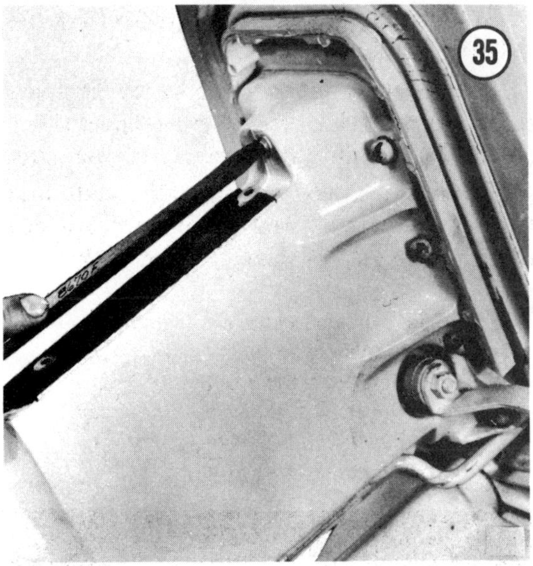

3. Remove throttle tower shaft from starboard side of power head.

4. Remove all crankcase cover-to-cylinder attaching screws.

5. Separate the crankcase cover from the cylinder by inserting a screwdriver into the slotted openings near the dowel pin holes. Pry the halves apart.

6. Loosen connecting rod cap screws and remove cap and screws from rod.

> NOTE: *Mark the caps so as to identify the matching connecting rod.*

7. Remove the crankpin rollers and cages. Keep the cages and rollers in sets and mark them to identify the matching connecting rod. To prevent loss of the connecting rod needles, lay the cylinder on its side and place a cloth below it. Rotate the crankshaft to the bottom of the stroke. This will permit the needles to drop free instead of dropping into the cylinder when the rod cap is removed.

8. Remove crankshaft.

9. Pull connecting rod and piston assemblies out of cylinder and mark with a "T" and "B" to identify at top or bottom cylinder.

10. If the piston is to be removed from the connecting rod, remove using Special Tool J-8718 as shown in **Figure 37**.

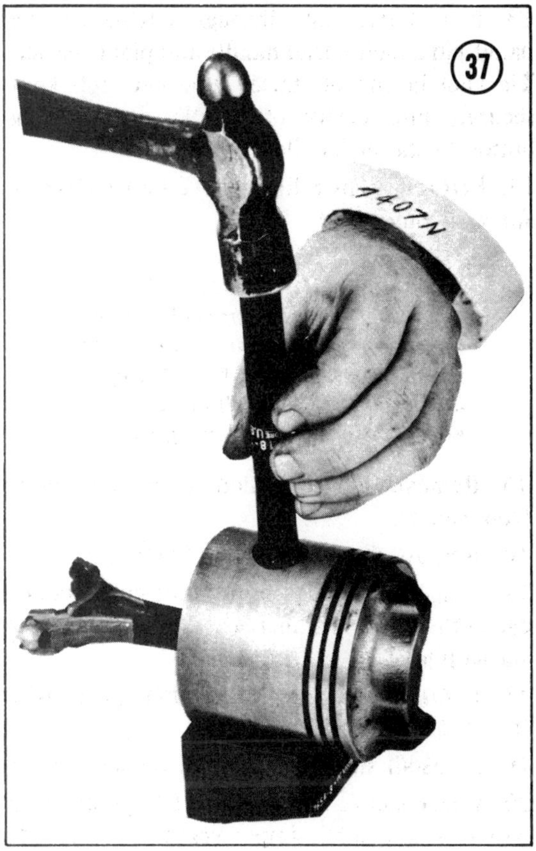

> NOTE: *On all models, serial number 3001 and later, perform Steps 12 through 15 for piston pin removal.*

11. Remove piston rings from piston using Special Tool J-8743.

12. Place piston on pillow block with piston pin aligned with hole in pillow block.

13. Place necked down end of drive pin in I.D. of piston pin.

14. Drive piston pin from piston.

15. Remove connecting rod and piston pin spacers from piston. Exercise caution so as not to lose needle bearings from connecting rod.

> NOTE: *There are 26 needles per bearing.*

Inspection

1. Inspect cylinder bore for rust, scoring, or pitting. Replace if scored, out-of-round, or tapered. Inspect all water passages for any obstructions.

36

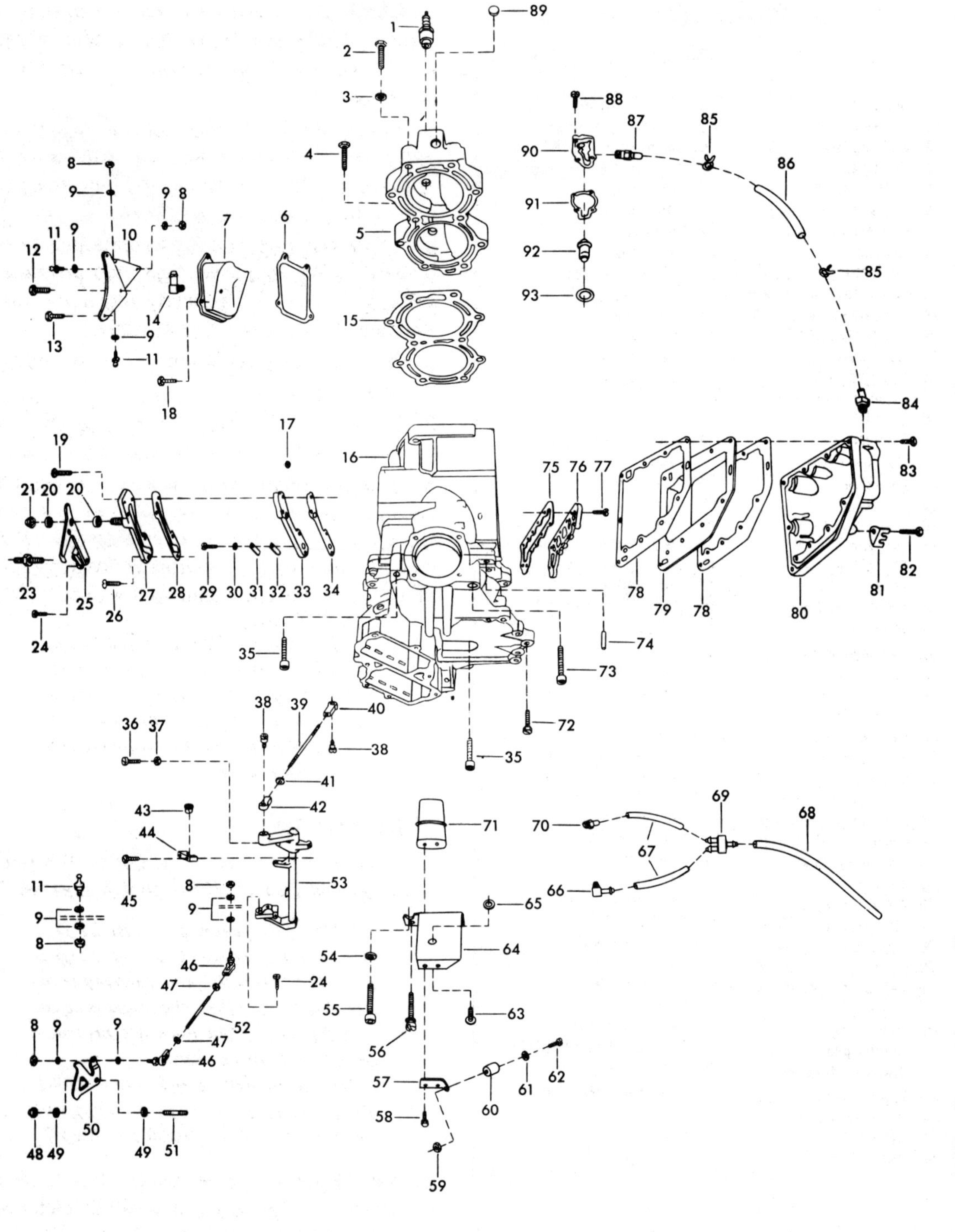

POWER HEAD

1. Spark plug
2. Cap screw
3. Plain washer
4. Cap screw
5. Cylinder head
6. Transfer port cover gasket
7. Transfer port cover
8. Hex nut
9. Internal tooth lockwasher
10. Connector stud bracket
11. Rod end connector stud
12. Fillister head screw
13. Hex screw
14. Fuel line elbow
15. Cylinder head gasket
16. Cylinder
17. Cylinder drain reed plate screen
18. Hex screw
19. Hex screw
20. Shift arm bearing
21. Stop nut
22. Elastic stop nut
23. Stud
24. Fillister head screw
25. Shift arm
26. Flat head screw
27. Cylinder drain cover
28. Cylinder drain cover gasket
29. Pan head screw
30. Plain washer
31. Cylinder drain reed stop
32. Cylinder drain reed
33. Cylinder drain reed plate
34. Cylinder drain reed plate gasket
35. Screw
36. Fillister head screw
37. Hex jam nut
38. Spark control swivel
39. Spark control link
40. Left spark control bearing
41. Hex nut
42. Right spark control bearing
43. Tower shaft bearing
44. Tower shaft bearing cap
45. Fillister head screw
46. Ball-joint
47. Hex nut
48. Elastic stop nut
49. Throttle cam bearing
50. Throttle cam
51. Throttle cam stud
52. Throttle link
53. Tower shaft
54. Lockwasher
55. Allen screw
56. Fillister head screw
57. Center bumper bracket
58. Hex screw
59. Stop nut
60. Bumper
61. Plain washer
62. Fillister head screw
63. Flat head screw
64. Upper engine bracket shock mount
65. Plain washer
66. Elbow
67. Short crankcase drain line
68. Long crankcase drain line
69. Check valve Y-fitting
70. Drain fitting
71. Upper shock mount
72. Allen screw
73. Allen screw
74. Dowel pin
75. Exhaust water jacket cover gasket
76. Exhaust water jacket cover
77. Fillister head screw
78. Exhaust port plate gasket
79. Exhaust port plate
80. Exhaust port cover
81. Lead wire clip
82. Hex screw
83. Allen screw
84. Thermostat fitting
85. Clamp
86. Thermostat water tube
87. Thermostat fitting
88. Fillister screw
89. Welch plug
90. Thermostat cover
91. Thermostat cover gasket
92. Thermostat
93. Thermostat grommet

2. Inspect crankshaft journals, keyway, and splines. Replace if scored, rusted, pitted, or discolored from excessive heat.

3. Check all bearings for rust, corrosion, or pitting. Replace as indicated. Under normal conditions, all bearings will last the life of the engine.

4. Inspect the connecting rod and cap, piston, and piston pin for wear. Replace piston if scored or pitted. Replace connecting rod if rusty, pitted, or discolored from excessive heat.

5. Check the main bearing locating pins in the cylinder. They should be tight, and protrude a sufficient amount to properly retain the main bearings. Remove any burrs visible.

6. Clean all old sealer from crankcase and cylinder mating surfaces.

7. Clean all carbon and water by-product deposits from exhaust chamber and water jackets.

8. Inspect piston rings for wear at gap and also for side clearance. Cylinder walls, after running, acquire a hard, tough glaze, causing new piston rings to require an abnormally long break-in period to attain top engine performance.

> NOTE: *The glaze on the cylinder walls can be removed through the use of a cylinder hone or de-glazer. Extreme care must be exercised, as only a very minute amount can be removed from the cylinder walls.*

Piston Assembly

1. Assemble the connecting rod to the piston using Special Tool J-8718 as shown in **Figure 38**.

> NOTE: *The piston pin must be centered in the connecting rod so that when the connecting rod is moved from one side to the other, the travel is equal and the piston pin does not protrude beyond the piston skirt.*
>
> *On all models, serial numer 3001 and later, perform Steps 2 through 6. On earlier models, proceed to Step 7.*

2. Slip alignment pin in piston. Install piston pin spacer on alignment pin. Small diameter end of spacer must face toward inside of piston.

3. Install needle bearings in connecting rod. If old bearings are being installed, coat interior of

4

piston pin bore in connecting rod with Rykon 2EP grease or equivalent and press the needles in place.

> NOTE: *There are 26 needles per bearing.*

4. Slip alignment pin through connecting rod. Install second piston pin spacer on alignment pin. Slip alignment pin into piston pin bore on other side of piston.

> NOTE: *Match marks on connecting rod must face toward crowned side of piston.*

5. Place piston assembly on pillow block. Place piston pin in bore of piston. Place necked down end of drive pin in I.D. of piston pin. Drive piston pin down until it is centered in piston.

6. Apply liberal coating of motor oil to needle bearings at piston pin. Piston pin must be free enough to slide easily up and down in clearance space between connecting rod and piston pin spacers.

7. Assemble piston rings to piston (as shown in **Figure 39**) using Special Tool J-8743. Align open ends of rings with anchor pin in piston and install to piston with the inside beveled edge to the top.

> NOTE: *The connecting rod must be installed to the piston so that when the complete piston assembly is installed to the power head, the sloping side of the piston dome will face the exhaust chest of the cylinder. Also, the match marks and oil hole in the connecting rod must be facing "up," toward the flywheel. When installing the connecting rod, inspect the bearing in the piston pin eye. If this bearing is damaged, the complete connecting rod must be replaced.*

8. Coat pistons, rings, and cylinder walls with a light coating or oil and install pistons in cylinder using the piston ring compressor as shown in **Figure 40**.

Crankshaft Assembly

The crankshaft used on 35 through 50 hp models uses an upper main thrust bearing. This bearing is pressed onto the crankshaft and is not available as a service replacement part due to the specialized equipment for its installation. However, if this bearing must be replaced, contact an authorized dealer.

Inspect the crankshaft journals, keyway, spline, bearings, and seal. Replace crankshaft, bearings, or seal if scored, rusted, pitted, discolored from excessive heat, torn, cracked, or distorted.

If the center main bearing has been removed or must be replaced, assemble to crankshaft as follows.

1. Coat each half of bearing race with a light coating of grease and lay on bench.
2. Arrange race halves so that snap ring groove lies to the bottom of the crankshaft.
3. Coat both bearing cage halves with a light coating of grease. Carefully observe the cages. One edge of each cage has a small cutout. Place cages in races so that cutouts lie together and point to the top of the crankshaft (flywheel end).
4. Install 16 bearing rollers in cage halves.
5. Install ½ of bearing to underside of crankshaft center main journal. Make sure that the snap ring groove lies to the bottom of crankshaft.
6. Place the remaining half of bearing on crankshaft. Make sure cage cutouts and snap ring grooves match.
7. Install snap ring in groove.

Connecting Rod Needle Bearings Installation

1. Place crankshaft in position on cylinder. Lift connecting rods toward the crankshaft until the crankshaft bearing surfaces of the connecting rods are about ⅛ in. below the crankshaft mating surfaces. Adjust piston and connecting rod, if necessary, to align the bearing surfaces. Remove crankshaft from cylinder.
2. Coat bearing surfaces of connecting rod with a light coating of grease.

> NOTE: *The needle bearings used on 35 through 55 hp models use caged needle bearings. Sixteen needle bearings are used in each connecting rod.*

3. Place one half of bearing cage on the bearing surface of lower connecting rod with the cutouts facing "up" toward flywheel. Install 8 needle bearings in recesses of bearing cage.

> NOTE: *The bearing cages are machined together for accuracy. For this reason, the cages must be installed in pairs.*

4. Repeat Step 3 for upper connecting rod.
5. Carefully set crankshaft in position on cylinder so as not to disturb the needles on the connecting rods. Rotate center main bearing race and lower main bearing until locating pins in cylinder fit into the holes in the bearings.
6. Apply a light coating of grease to the top half of the crankshaft journal.
7. Lay remaining bearing cage over exposed half of crankshaft journal making sure the cutouts of the 2 cage halves match. Place remaining 8 needles in recesses of cage.
8. Install connecting rod caps carefully so that loose needles are not disturbed. Caps must be installed to the connecting rod from which they were removed, with the marks on the rod and cap together and "up," toward the flywheel.
9. Install connecting rod screws. Tighten screws gradually and move cap back and forth gently until it is properly aligned with the connecting rod. Inspect joint—if joint is visible, improper alignment is indicated. Refer to **Figure 41** for proper joint alignment. Torque connecting rod screws.

Crankcase Closure

1. Using a clean rag soaked in cleaning solution or pure grain alcohol, wipe cylinder/crankcase parting line, crankshaft bearing cage mounting surface, and O-ring recess clean.
2. Apply Sealer 1000 to cylinder and crankcase parting line. Wipe all excess sealer from crankcase bearing cage mounting surface and O-ring recess. Keep sealers away from bearing surfaces. Apply sealer as follows.
   a. Apply Permatex No. 1 to all screws with holes through crankcase.

4

41

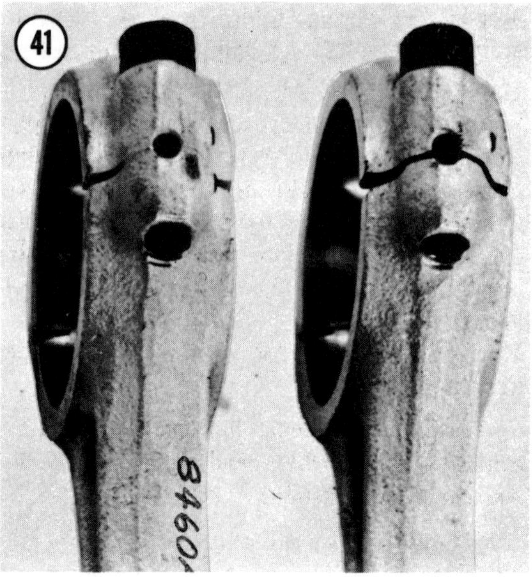

b. Apply Loctite "D" (T-2963) to upper and lower main bearing bores in cylinder and crankcase cover. Apply sparingly. Using new parting line seal (long rubber type seal), lay new seal in cylinder groove and cut off flush to bearing O.D.

c. Apply sealer from O.D. of upper main bearing bore to outside edge of ⅜ in. tapped hole, avoiding parting line seal by ⅛ in. on both sides. Apply from O.D. of central main bearing bore to within ⅛ in. of parting line seal, entire web, both sides. Apply ½ in. band along side lower main bearing bore, avoiding parting line seal by ⅛ in. on both sides.

d. Apply Permatex No. 1 to all cylinder head screws, motor leg-to-power head screws on exhaust side that break into exhaust cavity, all screws with holes through crankcase and two ⅜ in. screws at center main bearing.

> NOTE: *The welch plug in the top of the cylinder head is replaceable. When installing, make sure counterbore in head is free of burrs or foreign material. Coat outside edge of plug with Loctite "D" (T-2963) before inserting plug into counterbore with convex side "up." Drive plug against seat until flat and then stake in 3 places around diameter to prevent it from loosening.*

3. Install and torque all main bearing bolts holding crankcase cover to cylinder.

> CAUTION
>
> *Turn engine over using a vise block to ensure all parts are free and smoothly operating. If binding or unusual sounds occur, the power head must be disassembled and the fault corrected before proceeding.*

Crankshaft Bearing Cage and Seal

> NOTE: *The crankshaft bearing cage can be serviced without removing the power head. Remove flywheel, stator, magneto key and cam, and top 2 screws attaching crankcase cover to cylinder. The bearing cage is now completely accessible.*

1. Inspect the bearing and seals in and on the crankshaft bearing cage.
2. If the bearings are scored, pitted, or rusted, the complete bearing cage must be replaced. Specialized equipment is required to install the bearing.
3. There are 2 seals on the bearing cage. One seal is pressed into the top of the cage, and the other is an O-ring seal. If the seals are cracked, torn, or distorted, replace with new seals. If the pressed-in seal must be replaced, simply pry old seal out, being careful not to gouge the seal bore.
4. Apply Sealer 1000 to O.D. of seal prior to installing.
5. Grease sealing lip of seal liberally with cam grease before installing seal.
6. Assemble seal with garter spring down (toward cylinder) using seal punch T-3510 (35 through 50 hp). Press the seal into the seal bore so that the lower edge (sealing lip or garter spring) extends to within 0.150 in. from recess on bottom of bearing cage.

> NOTE: *35 through 55 hp models using A203144 or A213144 Bearing Cage—bearing is pressed onto the crankshaft.*

7. Apply Sealer 1000 to crankshaft bearing cage mounting surface on cylinder.
8. Install Special Tool T-3512 seal protector over end of crankshaft.

9. Apply Rykon 2EP Lubricant to recess on I.D. of magneto stator ring and hold ring to underside of crankshaft bearing cage.

10. Install bearing cage/stator ring assembly to cylinder using 4 flat head screws. Before installing bearing cage, make sure rubber O-ring seal is installed to lower side.

Installing Lower Crankshaft Seal

1. Apply cam grease to inside sealing lip of lower crankshaft seal.

2. Install seal to lower end of crankshaft with garter spring "down," toward motor leg.

3. Tighten the main bearing bolts, 2 screws directly below crankshaft bearing cage, and screws on lower end of cylinder. Tighten all remaining crankcase cover attaching screws. Torque main bearing bolts to 270 in.-lb.

Power Head Assembly/Installation

1. Lightly lubricate the spline in lower end of crankshaft and spline on drive shaft down to rubber O-ring seal with cam grease. Make sure the O-ring seal is in place on the drive shaft as shown in **Figure 42**.

42

2. Place new cylinder exhaust gasket on motor leg and install power head.

> NOTE: *Apply Permatex No. 1 to both sides of cylinder exhaust gasket, across the front of the gasket and on the rear 1½ inch.*

3. Clean all carbon buildup from dome cavities in cylinder head. Check flatness of cylinder head and mating surface with a straightedge.

4. Install cylinder head and new gasket. Make sure head gasket is positioned properly. Some head gaskets are marked to facilitate installation. Others must be laid up against the gasket surface of the cylinder to match the configurations. Incorrect installation will cut off power head cooling water supply.

5. Apply Loctite "H" (T-2962) sealer to cylinder head bolts.

6. Torque cylinder head bolts starting from the center of the cylinder head and working outward in either direction.

> NOTE: *The cylinder head bolts must be re-torqued after run-in. See procedure under* Tune-up. *When re-torquing bolts, hold torque for 15 seconds to allow torque to set.*

7. Install thermostat, grommet, thermostat gasket, and cover to cylinder head. Thermostat must be installed with "V" slot up. Install thermostat fitting to exhaust port cover if removed.

8. Install spark plugs.

9. Install the exhaust water jacket cover and gasket to the exhaust chamber on the port side of the cylinder.

10. Install exhaust port plate gasket, exhaust port plate, exhaust port cover gasket, and exhaust port cover on cylinder, in order as listed.

> NOTE: *Apply Sealer 1000 to both sides of exhaust port plate gasket (between cylinder and exhaust port plate) around the rear lower inlet hole, from top forward mounting hole, across top to thin section of gasket, and entire forward lower corner to just above first mounting hole.*

11. Using a new gasket(s), install transfer port cover(s) to starboard side of engine.

Installing Fuel Lines

Fuel Line–Pump to Carburetor: Route fuel line down from pump outlet in front of power head ground strap behind gearshift arm, under cylinder drain cover, up to carburetor inlet.

4

Completing Power Head Assembly

1. Assemble 2 split, flanged bearings to throttle tower shaft with shoulder up on top bearing and down on lower bearing. Lubricate I.D. of bearings when installing. See **Figure 43**.

2. Lubricate tower shaft bearing surfaces on crankcase cover and I.D. of tower shaft bearing caps.

3. Place tower shaft in position on crankcase cover and install bearing caps. Tighten bearing caps so that tower shaft will move free without excessive binding. See **Figure 44**.

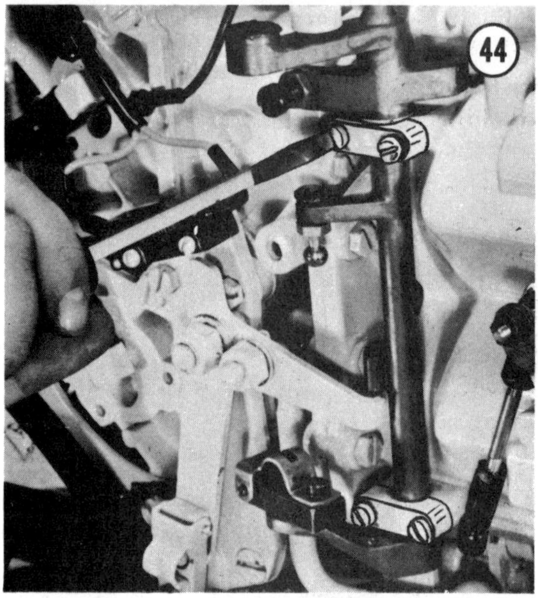

4. Install throttle link assembly from throttle cam to ball connector on tower shaft (**Figure 45**).

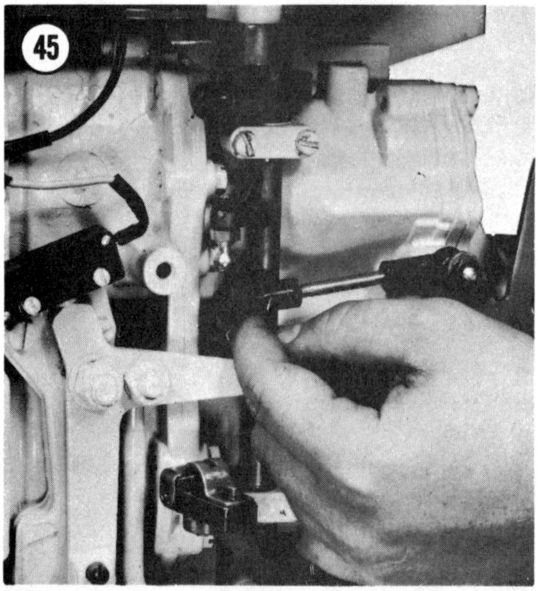

5. Assemble puddle drain lines to carburetor adapter flange.

6. Install screws which attach upper shock mount engine bracket to upper shock mount, using the lower set of mounting holes in the bumper bracket. These screws are located directly above the kingpin nut.

7. Install stabilizer link over stabilizer screw and assemble E-ring on screw to lock assembly in place. See **Figure 46** for stabilizer location.

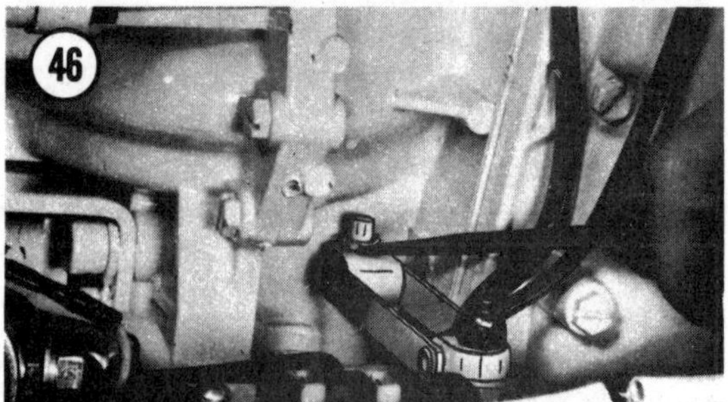

8. Assemble shift arm bearing over stud in cylinder drain cover.

9. Insert cotter pin through hole in gearshift rod. Assemble plain washer over shift rod and up against cotter pin.

10. Install shift arm over stud on cylinder drain cover and gearshift rod with "hooked" arm forward. See **Figure 47**.

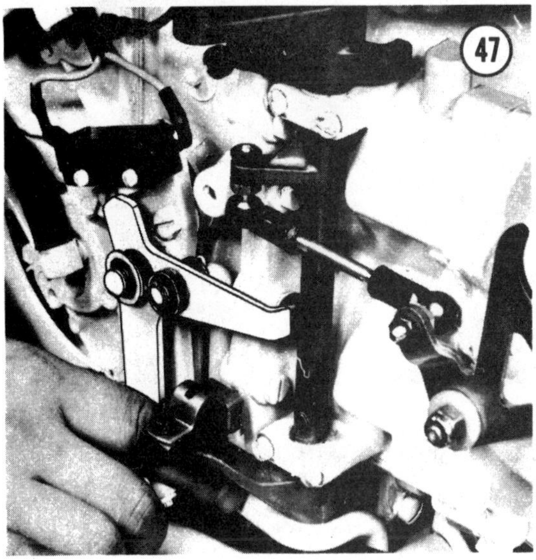

11. Assemble shift arm bearing over stud in cylinder drain cover and plain washer over end of gearshift rod.

12. Lubricate bearings and washers on shift rod and cylinder drain cover stud liberally.

13. Install long elastic stop nut to stud on cylinder drain cover and short elastic stop nut to gearshift rod. Tighten locknuts securely and then back off just enough to ensure free movement of shift arm mechanism.

14. Install neutral interlock switch to top 2 holes in cylinder drain cover with button down. See **Figure 48**. Do not tighten switch mounting screws too tight as the plastic case of the switch may crack. No adjustments of the switch are required as the switch is self-aligning. Adjust gearshift rod.

15. Assemble electrical system components as outlined in appropriate sections.

16. Install "White" spark control bearing and locknut to spark control link from magneto or alternator. Assemble spark cotnrol link/bearing assembly to top arm on throttle tower shaft using a shoulder screw. See **Figure 49**.

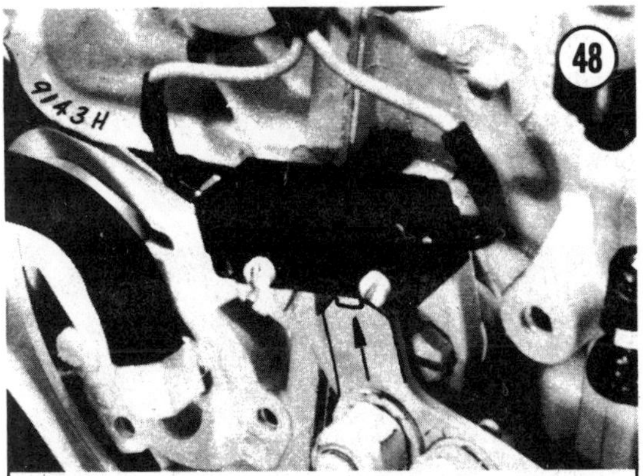

Install switch with button down and point of shift arm centered on switch button

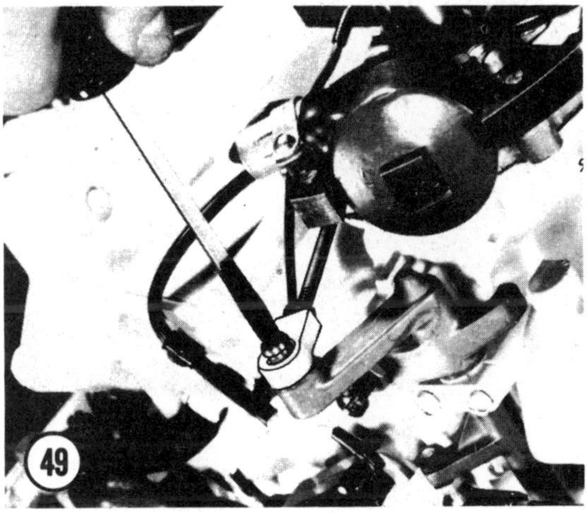

17. Adjust all linkages, point of throttle opening, and engine timing, outlined under *Tune-up*.

GEAR HOUSING

Lower Unit Removal

1. Disconnect coupler between intermediate shift rod and upper shift rod as shown in **Figure 50**. On models with acoustical leg cover, remove the covers to reach the coupler.

2. Remove screws that attach gear housing to the motor leg and remove gear housing.

Lower Unit Disassembly

Refer to **Figure 51** for this procedure.

1. Remove motor leg covers from motor leg.

2. Loosen the upper gear housing-to-motor leg screws, but do not remove.

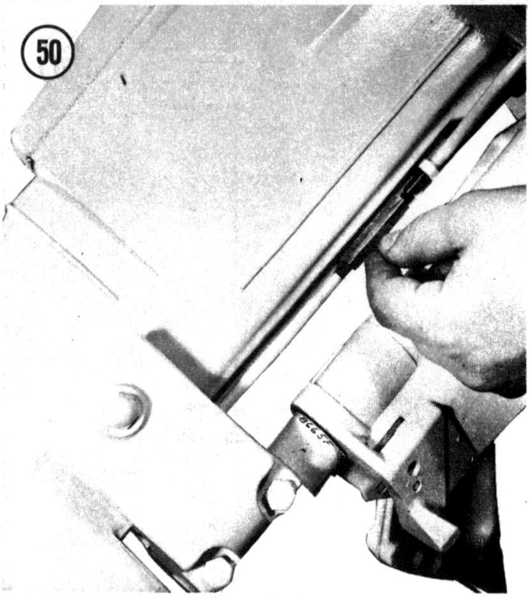
50

3. Disconnect upper gearshift rod from intermediate rod by loosening jam nut and removing the coupler.

4. Remove the upper gear housing-to-motor leg screws and remove lower unit from motor leg.

5. Remove water pump body screws and pull drive shaft with water pump assembly from lower unit.

6. Slide water pump body and impeller up to expose impeller drive pin. Remove impeller drive pin from drive shaft.

7. Slide water pump body and impeller from drive shaft.

8. Remove water pump back plate from upper gear housing.

9. Disconnect intermediate gearshift rod from lower rod by loosening upper coupling from lower coupling. Thread intermediate rod from lower coupling. Remove lower coupling from lower rod.

10. Drain lower unit grease by removing both FILL and VENT plug screws.

11. Remove nut from stud securing upper gear housing to lower gear housing. See **Figure 52**.

12. Remove propeller from lower unit.

13. Remove screws securing propeller shaft bearing cage to lower gear housing.

14. Remove propeller shaft bearing cage using puller (Special Tool T8948). See **Figure 53**.

1. Propeller pin
2. Propeller nut
3. Propeller nut seal
4. Cotter pin
5. Propeller
6. Allen screw
7. Propeller shaft seal
8. Propeller shaft bearing cage
9. Propeller shaft ball bearing
10. Propeller shaft bearing cage seal
11. Rear bevel gear
12. Bevel gear thrust washer
13. Propeller shaft
14. Gearshift pin
15. Clutch
16. Spring pin
17. Front bevel gear
18. Propeller shaft thrust bearing cup
19. Lower gear housing
20. Gear housing plug
21. Gear housing plug washer
22. Gearshift arm pin
23. Nyltite washer
24. Spring pin
25. Spring pin
26. Gearshift arm yoke
27. Gearshift arm
28. Shift arm coupling
29. Bevel pinion
30. Lower gearshift rod
31. Long stud
32. Lockwasher
33. Hex nut
34. Seal retainer
35. Shift rod lower seal
36. Shift rod seal spacer
37. Shift rod seal retainer
38. Short stud
39. Gear housing gasket
40. Fillister head screw
41. Inlet water plate
42. Inlet water tube
43. Upper gear housing
44. Drive shaft seal
45. Water pump back plate
46. Lower gearshift rod coupling
47. Hex nut
48. Water pump impeller
49. Water pump top plate
50. Water pump body
51. Intermediate gearshift rod
52. Lower inlet water line seal
53. Inlet water line extension
54. Flat head screw
55. Motor leg extension
56. Hex bolt
57. Seal
58. Plain washer
59. Drive shaft
60. Inlet water line
61. Water pump impeller drive pin

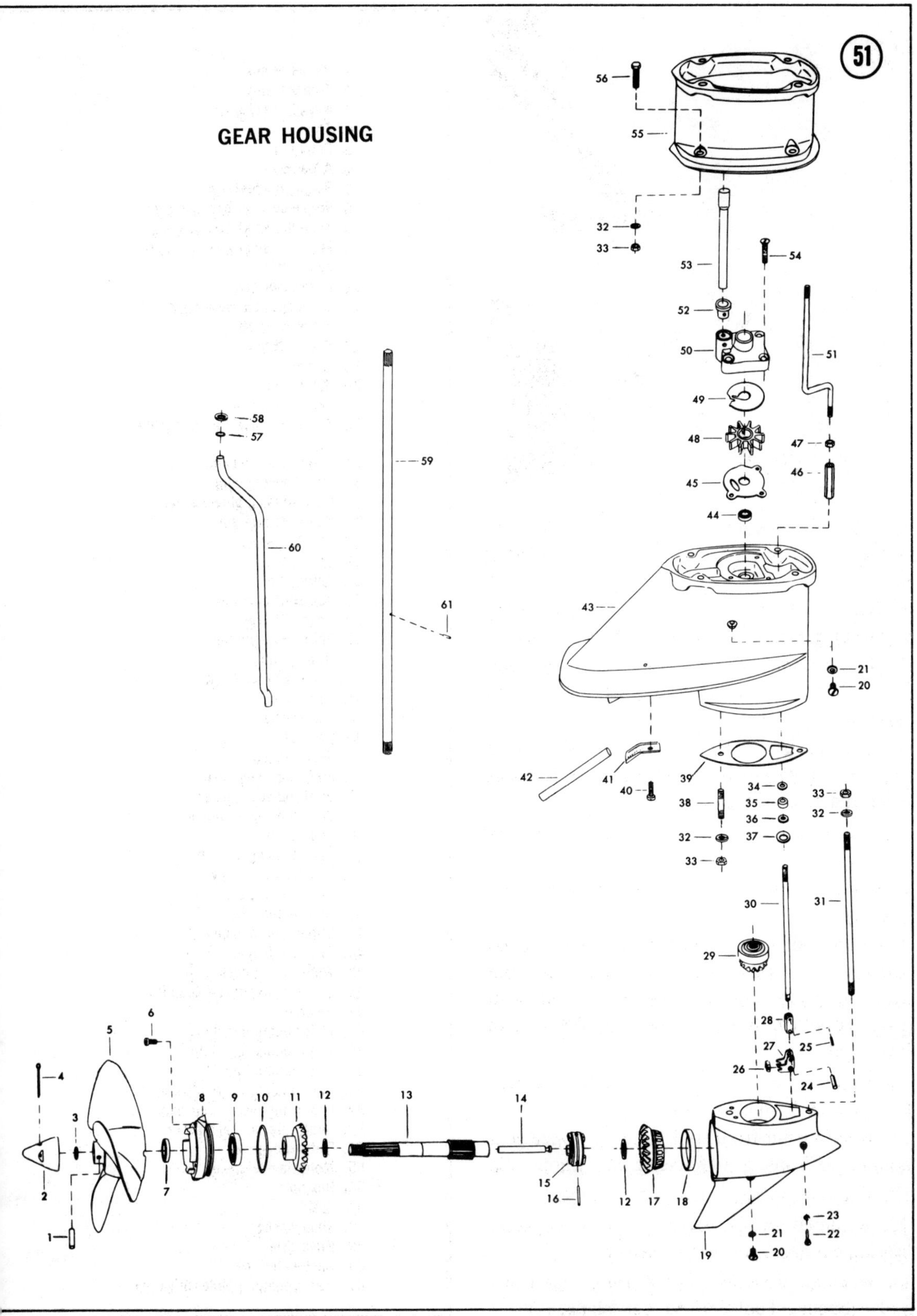
51
GEAR HOUSING
1
2
3
4
5
6
7
8
9
10
11
12
13
14
15
16
12
17
18
19
20
21
22
23
24
25
26
27
28
29
30
31
32
33
34
35
36
37
38
39
40
41
42
43
44
45
46
47
48
49
50
51
52
53
54
55
56
57
58
59
60
61

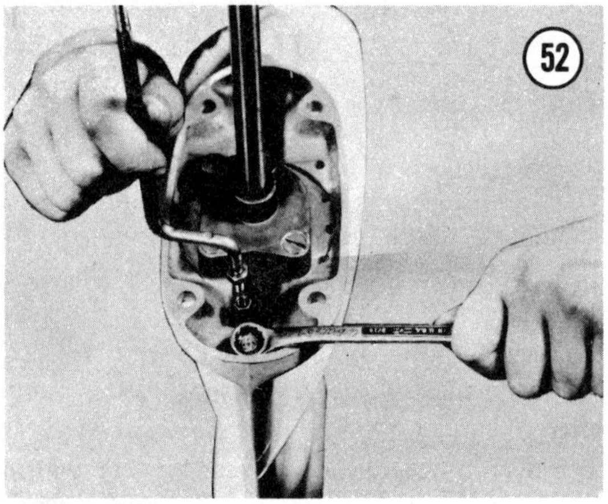
52

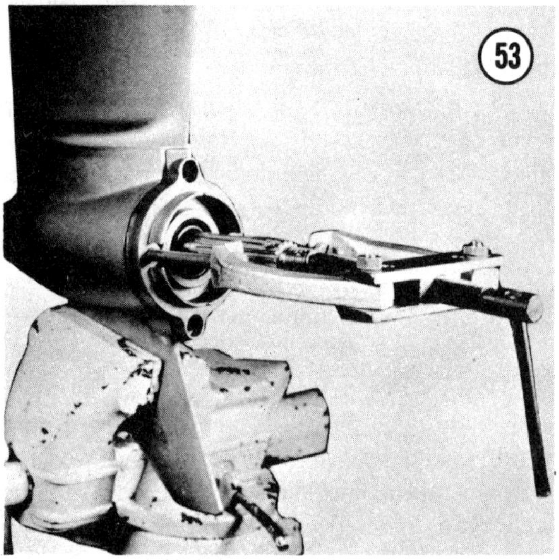
53

15. Slide propeller shaft ball bearing from propeller shaft. Remove steel ball in cavity of propeller shaft which prevents inner race of ball bearing from turning on propeller shaft.

16. Remove hex nut and spring lockwasher from stud securing lower gear housing to upper gear housing. See **Figure 54**.

17. Pull upper gear housing from lower gear housing.

18. Pull propeller shaft with rear bevel gear, clutch, shift pin, and yoke from lower gear housing. See **Figure 55**.

19. Slide rear bevel gear and thrust washer from propeller shaft.

20. To remove clutch and shift pin from propeller shaft, drive spring pin from clutch and slide clutch and shift pin from propeller shaft.

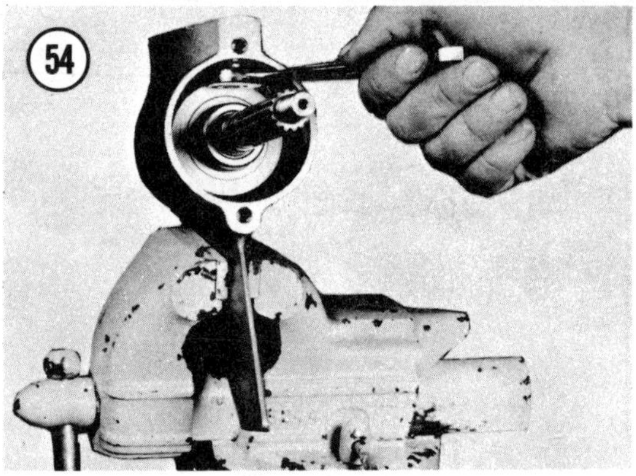
54

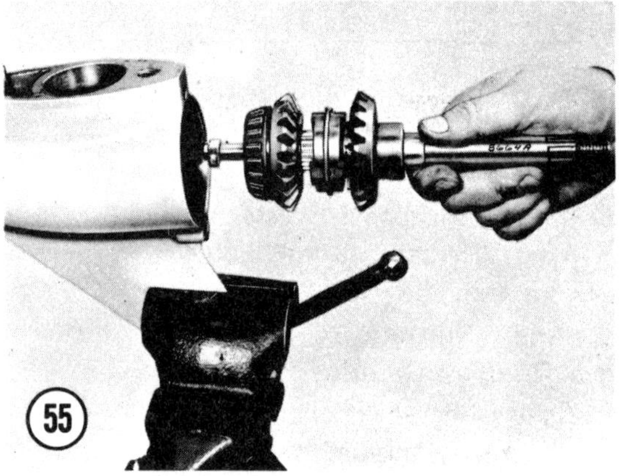
55

21. Lift bevel pinion from lower gear housing.

22. Remove forward bevel gear from lower gear housing.

23. Remove gearshift arm pin from lower gear housing.

24. Lift lower gearshift rod with shift arm from lower gear housing.

Lower Unit Assembly

1. Clean gasket surfaces of upper gear housing and lower gear housing.

2. Install clutch and shift pin on propeller shaft and secure with spring pin. See **Figure 56**.

3. Install thrust washer for front bevel gear on propeller shaft.

4. Install forward bevel gear on propeller shaft.

5. Install thrust washer for rear bevel gear on propeller shaft, then install rear bevel gear.

6. Apply heavy grease on shift pin yoke. Install shift pin yoke on shift pin with groove on yoke positioned down.

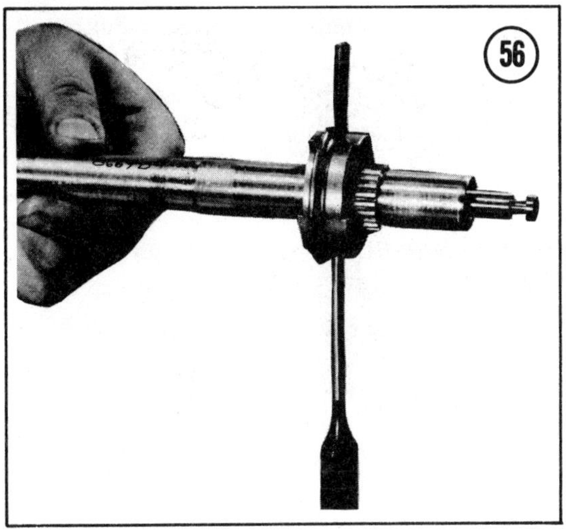

7. Install lower shift rod assembly with grooves on shift arm toward forward bevel gear to receive shift pin yoke.

8. Install propeller shaft assembly in lower gear housing with tabs on yoke aligned in grooves of shift arm.

9. Secure shift arm in position with shift arm pin and nyltite washer.

10. Install bevel pinion gear assembly in bore of lower gear housing.

11. Apply sealant on both sides of new gear housing gasket. Install gasket on lower gear housing.

12. Install upper gear housing on lower gear housing. Use caution when sliding lower gear-shift rod through shift rod seal on upper gear housing.

13. Install hex nut and spring lockwasher on stud immediately behind rear bevel gear and tighten securely.

14. Install hex nut and spring lockwasher on stud in front of water pump area on upper gear housing and tighten securely.

15. Apply a small quantity of grease to cavity on propeller shaft. Install propeller shaft ball in cavity.

16. Install propeller shaft ball bearing on propeller shaft so that groove in inner race slides over ball on shaft.

17. Install propeller shaft bearing cage on lower gear housing. Secure bearing cage to lower gear housing with screws.

18. Apply anti-seize compound to splines on propeller shaft and install propeller, propeller pin, seal, and propeller nut. Secure propeller nut to shaft with cotter pin.

19. Slide water pump body and impeller up drive shaft. Install impeller drive pin in drive shaft and slide impeller and water pump body down on drive pin with groove of impeller over drive pin.

20. Install water pump back plate on upper gear housing and install drive shaft with water pump in upper gear housing.

21. Secure water pump to gear housing with 4 flat head screws.

22. Check lower unit for leaks with Special Tool T8950. If no leaks are indicated, proceed with assembly.

23. Install short coupling with counter bore up tight against bend in new longer intermediate shift rod. Install longer coupling with counter bore down on intermediate shift rod against short coupling. Jam longer coupling tightly against short coupling.

24. Install intermediate rod with couplings on lower shift rod.

25. With lower unit in FORWARD gear position (lower shift rod pushed all the way down), turn intermediate rod with couplings in lower rod until bend in intermediate rod is 1/16 in. above water pump body. Position bend in rod above starboard side pump body screw.

26. Apply anti-seize compound or equivalent to splines on top of drive shaft.

27. Install lower unit on engine by inserting drive shaft up motor leg and in crankshaft splines and inserting shift rod through motor leg.

28. Align water line in water pump seal and secure lower unit to motor leg extension.

29. Before tightening lower unit to motor leg extension screws, connect intermediate rod to upper rod with coupler.

30. Torque lower unit to motor leg extension screws to 270 in.-lb.

31. Shift engine in NEUTRAL gear position. Initially adjust coupler between intermediate rod and upper rod until shift arm on power head is at center of travel over neutral throttle stop on tower shaft (engine in NEUTRAL gear position).

32. Determine center of travel by turning propeller and moving shift lever slowly until clutch dogs just contact gear dogs. This is not the fully engaged condition. Mark that position on intermediate shift rod where it enters near bottom of motor leg.

33. Move shift lever in opposite direction until same condition occurs. Mark this position on the intermediate shift rod near bottom of motor leg.

34. Measure distance between marks and mark half-way point. This is the center of shift linkage travel or exact NEUTRAL gear position.

35. Set intermediate shift rod at center mark. Adjust coupler until shift lever is exactly centered over neutral stop on tower shaft and center mark is at opening near bottom of motor leg.

36. Tighten jam nut against coupler to secure shift adjustment.

37. Install motor leg covers on motor leg.

38. Fill lower unit with Chrysler Outboard Gear Lubricant. If this lubricant is not available, use a non-corrosive, leaded EP90 Outboard Gear Lubricant. Do not use a corrosive, hypoid lubricant.

Lower Unit Installation

1. Install the upper drive shaft spline seal to the drive shaft.

2. Apply a coating of grease to end of water line so it will engage easily into water pump body boss. Apply a generous amount of grease to spline on drive shaft.

3. Assemble gear housing to motor leg guiding shift rod and drive shaft into place.

4. Ensure inlet water line is engaged properly to water pump body boss, then install screws and nuts retaining gear housing to motor leg. Torque to 256-275 in.-lb.

5. Assemble gearshift rod coupling between upper and lower shift rod. Be sure the right-hand thread in the coupler is to the top.

Water Pump Removal/Installation

1. Remove lower unit.

2. Remove screws that attach water pump body to gear housing.

3. Slide water pump body and impeller off drive shaft.

4. Remove impeller drive pin and water pump back plate.

5. Install water pump back plate to upper gear housing.

6. Install water pump drive pin and slide impeller down over drive shaft.

7. Place water pump top plate in pump body. Use a small amount of grease on back of top plate to retain it to pump body.

8. Slide pump body down over drive shaft. Rotate drive shaft and push pump body over impeller. Install pump body retaining screws.

9. Install lower unit.

Gearshift Linkage Adjustment

1. Shift gear housing into FORWARD gear by moving shift arm or handle into the FORWARD position.

2. Scribe a mark on gearshift rod where it emerges from motor leg. See (A), **Figure 57**.

57

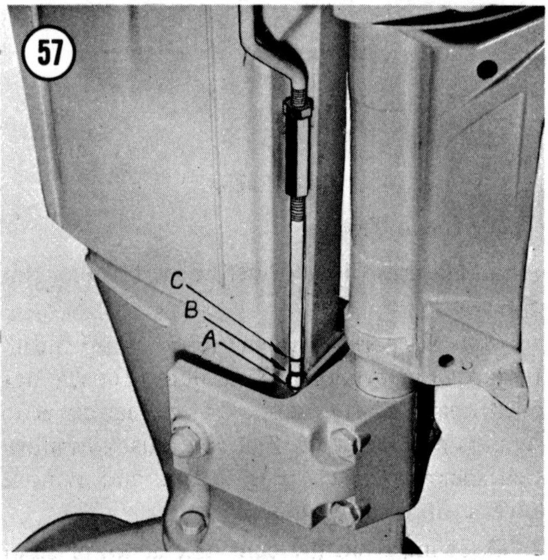

3. Shift engine into NEUTRAL. Again, scribe a mark on gearshift rod. See (B), Figure 57.

4 Shift engine into REVERSE and again scribe a mark on gearshift rod. See (C), Figure 57. This distance between the marks should be equal.

5. Adjust gearshift rod coupling clockwise or counterclockwise (whichever is necessary) to align marks an equal distance apart.

CHAPTER FIVE

OUTBOARD MOTORS (60 HP)

Ths chapter covers the tune-up, repair, and disassembly of all 60 hp outboard motors, including models with Magnapower II ignition systems. **Table 1** provides general specifications. **Table 2** provides tightening torques for fasteners. Both tables are at the end of the chapter.

TUNE-UP

Compression Testing

Engine must be cool before performing this procedure.

1. Remove spark plug cover from cylinder head. Remove top cylinder spark plug. Loosen hex head screw securing support plate rear cover to support plate retainer. Pull cover back to allow clearance for spark plug socket and remove lower cylinder spark plug.
2. Disconnect throttle cam link at tower shaft and move throttle cam to wide open throttle (WOT) position. Hold in this position by tightening elastic stop nut securing cam to stud.
3. Connect compression gauge following manufacturer's instructions.
4. Crank engine until compression gauge needle stabilizes. Compression of each cylinder should be 155 ± 5 psi.

NOTE: *Add 5 pounds to compression range of engine having 15 hours or more of running time.*

Torquing Cylinder Head

Loosen each bolt slightly, then torque bolt to 225 in.-lb. Follow torquing sequence as shown in **Figure 1**.

CAUTION
Do not over torque cylinder head bolts. The cylinder bores or head may be distorted. Do not under torque or the cylinder gasket may leak.

Spark Plugs

1. Remove spark plugs as outlined under *Compression Testing*.
2. Inspect plug condition. Clean or replace plugs if necessary.
3. Check electrode gap on plugs with wire type feeler gauge. Before setting gap, file the center electrode flat. Adjust to 0.030 in. by bending ground (side) electrode.
4. Install plugs and torque to 120-180 in.-lb.

Timing Engine

1. Remove spark plugs as described under *Compression Testing*.

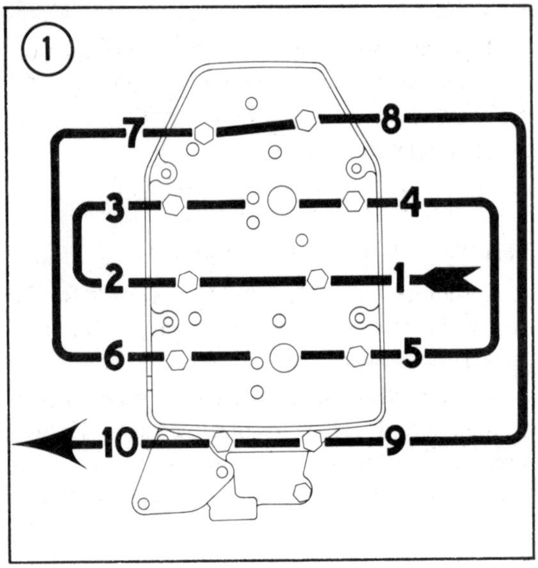

2. Install timing tool (Special Tool T2937-1) in top cylinder spark plug hole. Insert rod portion of timing tool in barrel with 2 marks identified as "25-55 hp" outside of barrel.

3. Holding rod tight against piston, slowly rotate flywheel in direction of engine rotation to locate top dead center (TDC) or point at which marks on rod extend furthest from barrel. Screw barrel of the timing tool in or out as required until inside line of the timing rod lines up with edge of barrel. See **Figure 2**.

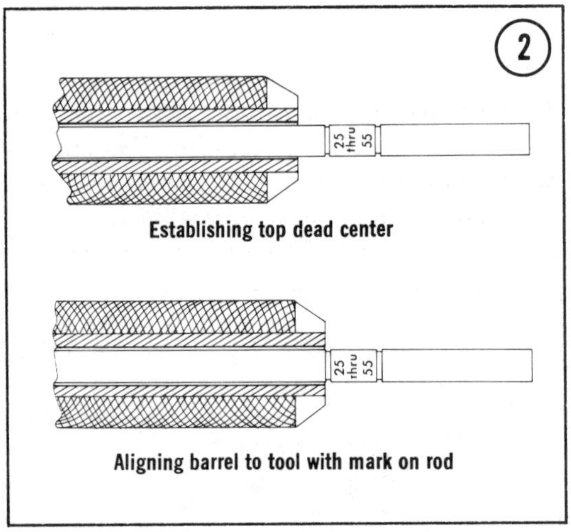

Establishing top dead center

Aligning barrel to tool with mark on rod

4. Apply slight pressure to end of rod with finger and turn flywheel clockwise in direction of engine rotation approximately ¾ around until outer line of rod lines up with edge of barrel. This line represents 32° before top dead center (BTDC). See **Figure 3**.

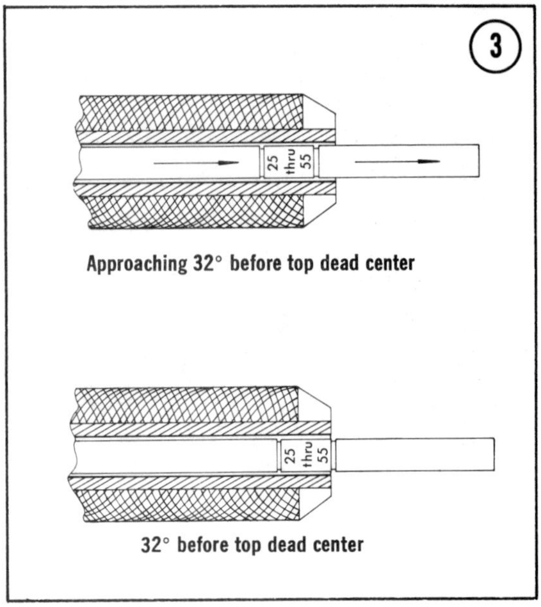

Approaching 32° before top dead center

32° before top dead center

5. Check decal on ring gear of flywheel for alignment with index mark on top of carburetor adapter flange. The 32° BTDC mark on decal must line up with index mark. If marks do not align, install new decal or otherwise make new mark.

6. With engine in test tank or on boat in water, connect timing light (Special Tool T8978 or equivalent to top spark plug. Start engine and run at full retard position. Timing must be relatively close (TDC mark on decal in relationship to index mark on carburetor adapter flange).

> NOTE: *If* TDC *mark on decal is not close or within 3° of index mark, recheck timing as outlined in Steps 2 through 5.*

7. Start engine and accelerate to WOT. Engine rpm's MUST be within operating range, (5,000 to 5,500 rpm). With timing light connected to top cylinder spark plug lead wires, observe alignment of timing marks (32° mark on decal to index mark on carburetor adapter flange). If marks are not aligned, retard throttle and shut engine off. Adjust link between tower shaft and timing ring under flywheel. One full turn on link represents approximately 2°. To advance timing,

turn link counterclockwise (as viewed from front of engine). To retard timing, turn link clockwise. See **Figure 4**.

CAUTION

Do not adjust link while engine is running.

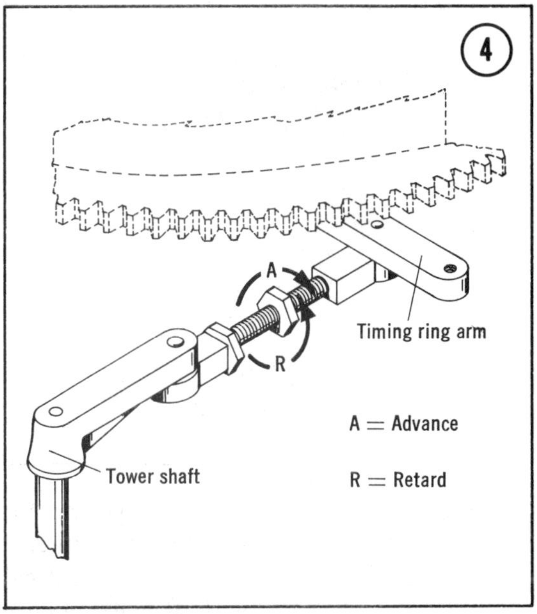

Synchronizing Throttle Shutters

1. Snap throttle link off tower shaft and pivot throttle cam away from throttle roller on the carburetor.
2. Remove retaining ring securing throttle tie bar to top carburetor throttle arm.
3. Loosen throttle tie bar screw as shown in **Figure 5**.

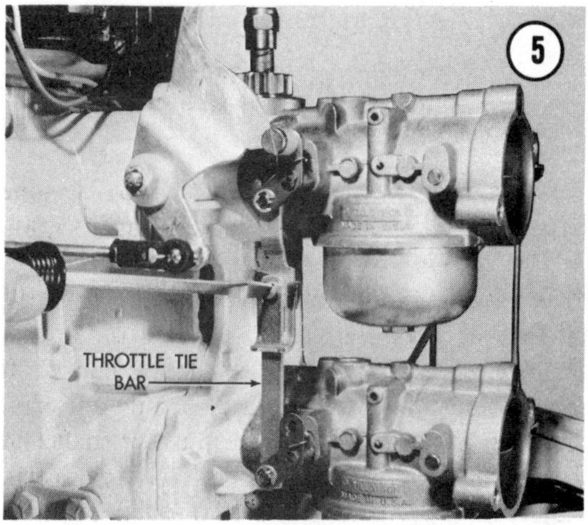

4. Make sure that throttle shutters are closed.
5. Tighten throttle tie bar screw (see Figure 5) and make sure tie bar end pivot goes in and out of carburetor throttle arm freely.
6. Install retaining ring.
7. Snap throttle link on tower shaft.

Throttle Pick-up Point Adjustment

1. Disconnect throttle link at tower shaft. Do not disconnect throttle link at throttle cam or throttle cam may be distorted.
2. Loosen stop nut on eccentric screw which secures nylon roller to throttle arm. Tighten stop nut just enough to take up clearance between eccentric screw, roller, throttle arm and stop nut.
3. Pivot throttle cam so that throttle pick-up mark on cam is in the approximate area where contact with roller will occur.
4. Rotate eccentric screw clockwise until roller is at maximum distance from pick-up point mark on throttle cam.
5. Rotate eccentric screw clockwise until roller just contacts pick-up mark on throttle cam. Rotate throttle cam so that pick-up mark on cam moves up and away from roller. Rotate throttle cam back to contact roller, if pick-up mark is not centered in relationship to throttle cam, readjust by turning eccentric screw.
6. Tighten nut on eccentric screw being certain not to rotate eccentric screw.
7. Insert paper lightly between cam and the roller from top side and then from bottom side noting gap between edge of paper and mark on throttle cam. If gaps are equal, mark on cam is at center of contact with roller. See **Figure 6**.

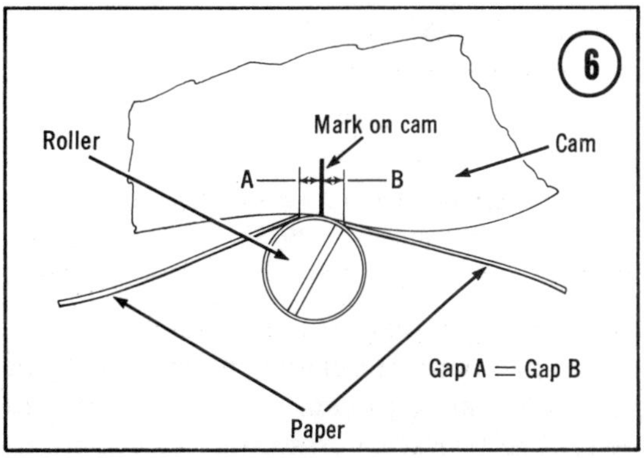

5

8. Connect throttle link on tower shaft and rotate until nylon throttle stop on tower shaft is against cylinder. Check to see if throttle shutter is horizontal in carburetor. If not, loosen jam nut, and turn end of link to lengthen or shorten link until above condition is met. Tighten jam nut on link.

Carburetor Adjustment

1. Turn idle adjustment screw clockwise until it seats in the carburetor.

CAUTION
Do not force idle adjustment screw or the tip will be damaged.

2. Open idle adjustment screw 1 turn counterclockwise.
3. Shift engine to NEUTRAL and start motor. Allow the engine to warm up to operating temperature.
4. Shift engine to FORWARD. Throttle engine back to lowest reliable throttle setting.
5. Turn idle adjustment screw on carburetor clockwise ⅛ turn at a time, pausing at least 10 seconds between each adjustment until the engine begins to "pop" from the lean fuel/air setting. Note position of screwdriver slot on idle adjustment screw.
6. Turn idle adjustment screw counterclockwise to original position. Turn idle adjustment screw counterclockwise ⅛ turn at a time pausing at least 10 seconds between each adjustment until the engine begins to "roll or gallop" from the rich fuel/air setting. Note the idle adjustment screw setting.
7. Turn idle adjustment screw to midpoint between the settings noted in Steps 5 and 6.
8. Adjust idle stop screw on tower shaft as necessary until engine idles between 750-800 rpm in FORWARD.

Synchronizing Choke Shutters

1. Loosen screws on both choke swivels to free choke link.
2. Position top end of link approximately 1/16 to ⅛ inch beyond top of top carburetor choke swivel. Tighten screw to secure link in swivel.
3. Close top and bottom carburetor choke shutters fully. Tighten bottom carburetor choke swivel screw to secure link to swivel.
4. Loosen 2 screws securing choke solenoid just enough so that solenoid can move easily.
5. Slip a piece of paper approximately ½ inch wide in both carburetor air horns.

NOTE: *The paper insures proper clearance between choke shutter and carburetor air horn to prevent shutters from sticking in the closed position.*

6. With pieces of paper in air horns of carburetors, close choke shutters fully against the pieces of paper by pushing only on choke solenoid plunger as shown in **Figure 7**.

7

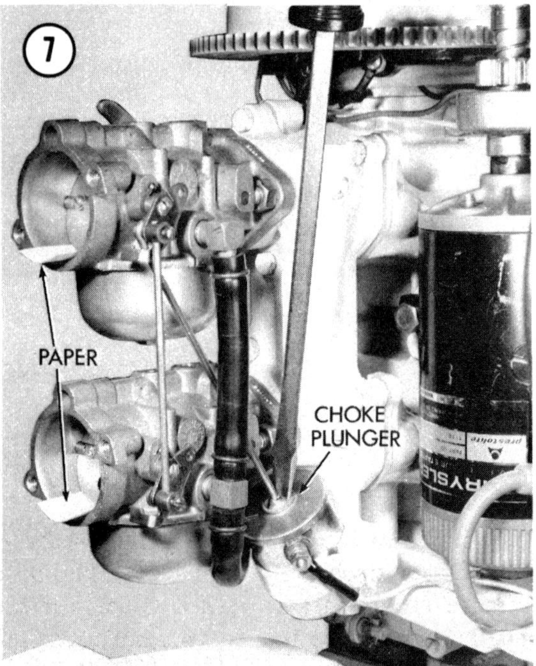

7. While holding choke shutters closed by the choke plunger, slide choke solenoid against plunger. Tighten screws to secure choke solenoid in position.
8. Release choke solenoid plunger and push plunger back in solenoid. Pull paper out of carburetor air horns; paper must slide out of carburetor easily or with a slight drag. If not, adjust solenoid position as outlined in Step 7.

9. Release choke solenoid plunger and check to see that choke shutters are horizontal. If they are not, bend groove pin (shutter stop) in air horn of carburetor.

Checking Lower Unit Grease

1. With engine vertical (running position), remove FILL plug from lower gear housing. See **Figure 8**. Allow a small amount of grease to flow from the hole.

> NOTE: *Do not check gear housing grease immediately after running engine. Allow engine to stand in the running position for at least 2 hours before checking gear grease. If water is present in lower unit, this time will allow water to settle to the bottom of lower unit.*

8

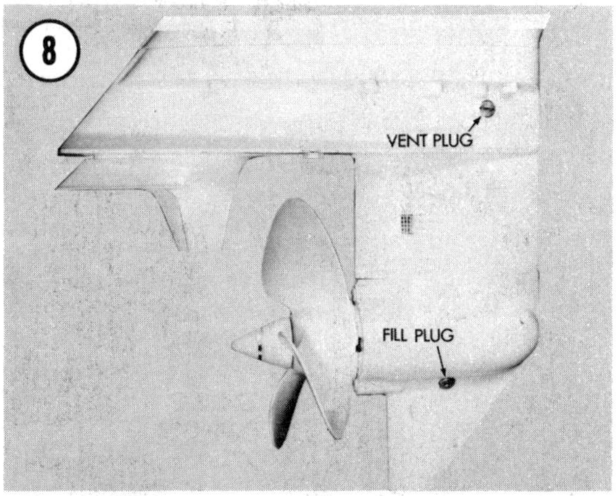

2. If no water is present, screw FILL plug back in 2 turns. Remove VENT plug and washer, then remove FILL plug and washer. Quickly insert nozzle of gear lube tube in FILL hole and add gear lube until it appears at VENT hole. Reinstall VENT plug and nyltite washer. Remove nozzle of gear lube tube and install FILL plug and nyltite washer.
3. If water is present, take motor to your dealer. Have him pressure test lower unit to determine where water leakage occurs.

TROUBLESHOOTING MAGNAPOWER II IGNITION SYSTEM

The Magnapower II ignition system is a breakerless, capacitor discharge magneto ignition system. Magnapower II has no moving components to wear or require periodic adjustment. The ignition system consists of a flywheel, C-D module, two trigger modules, a capacitor module, timing ring and 2 ignition coils. There is no distributor, timing belt, breaker cam or breaker points in this system. No battery voltage is applied to the ignition system. Ignition voltage is generated by the spinning magnet imbedded in the flywheel passing the coil windings of the C-D module. See **Figure 9** for Magnapower components.

Use following procedure to find the trouble when engine will not start or misses on one cylinder.

> NOTE: *This procedure requires the use of an ignition triggered timing light. If one is not available have tests performed by an authorized service center. See* **Figure 10** *for Magnapower schematic diagram.*

1. Connect timing light to top spark plug.
2. Crank engine (450 rpm minimum) or start engine and run at idle. Depress button on timing light. If the timing light flashes, the top cylinder is firing.
3. Repeat Steps 1 and 2 for the bottom cylinder to determine if it is firing. Do not turn ignition key off after determining which cylinder is not firing. Choke to stop.

> NOTE: *Always leave ignition switch in the* ON *position while troubleshooting. This is necessary to retain the charge stored in the capacitor.*

CAUTION

After completing Step 1, remove spark plug lead wires from spark plugs to prevent engine from starting while troubleshooting.

4. Using a screwdriver, check capacitor charge at the T-1 and T-4 terminals on the C-D module. See **Figure 11**.

WARNING

Use only a plastic handled or wood handled screwdriver to prevent electrical shock.

5

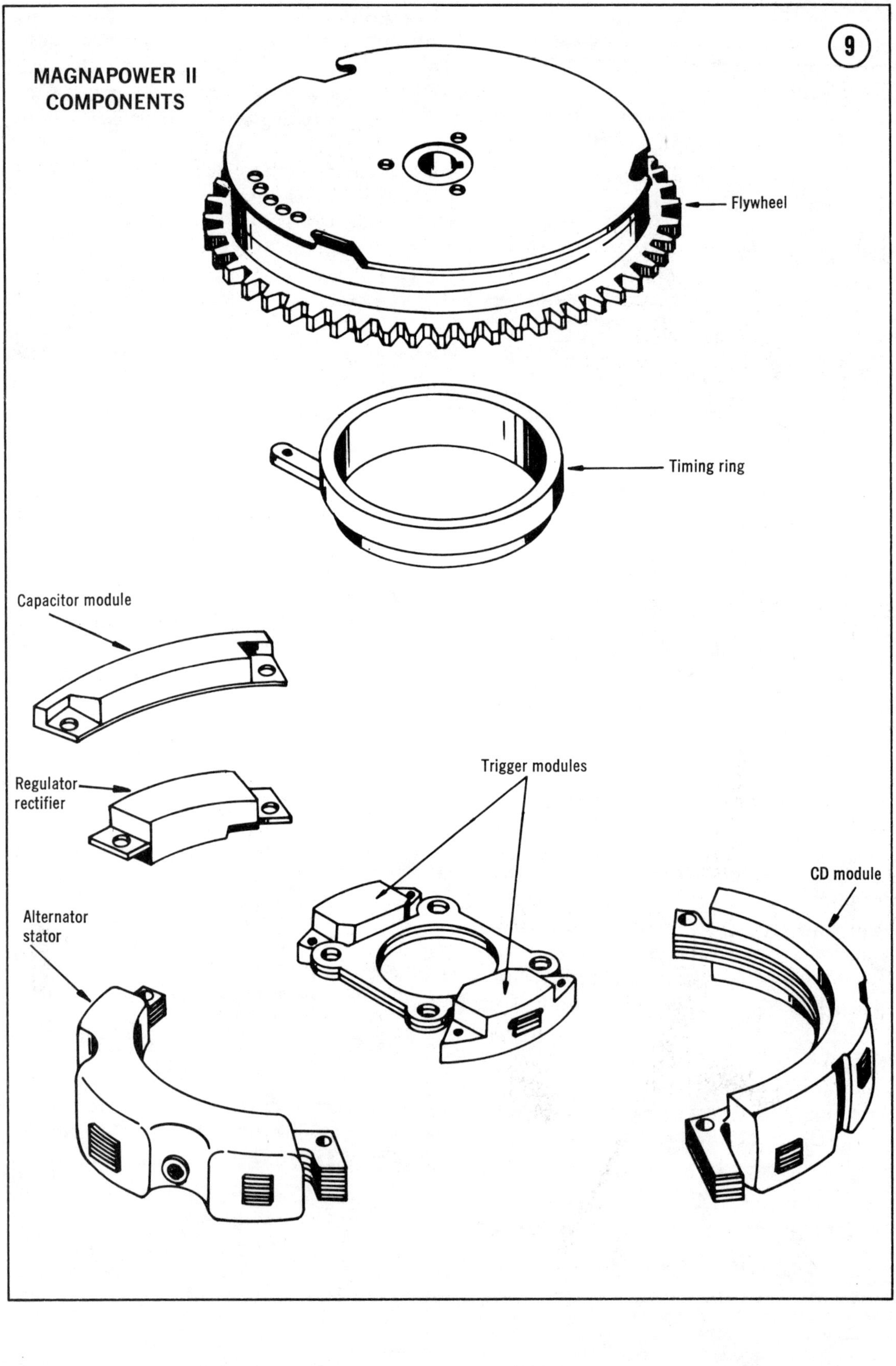
9
MAGNAPOWER II
COMPONENTS
Flywheel
Timing ring
Capacitor module
Regulator
rectifier
Trigger modules
CD module
Alternator
stator

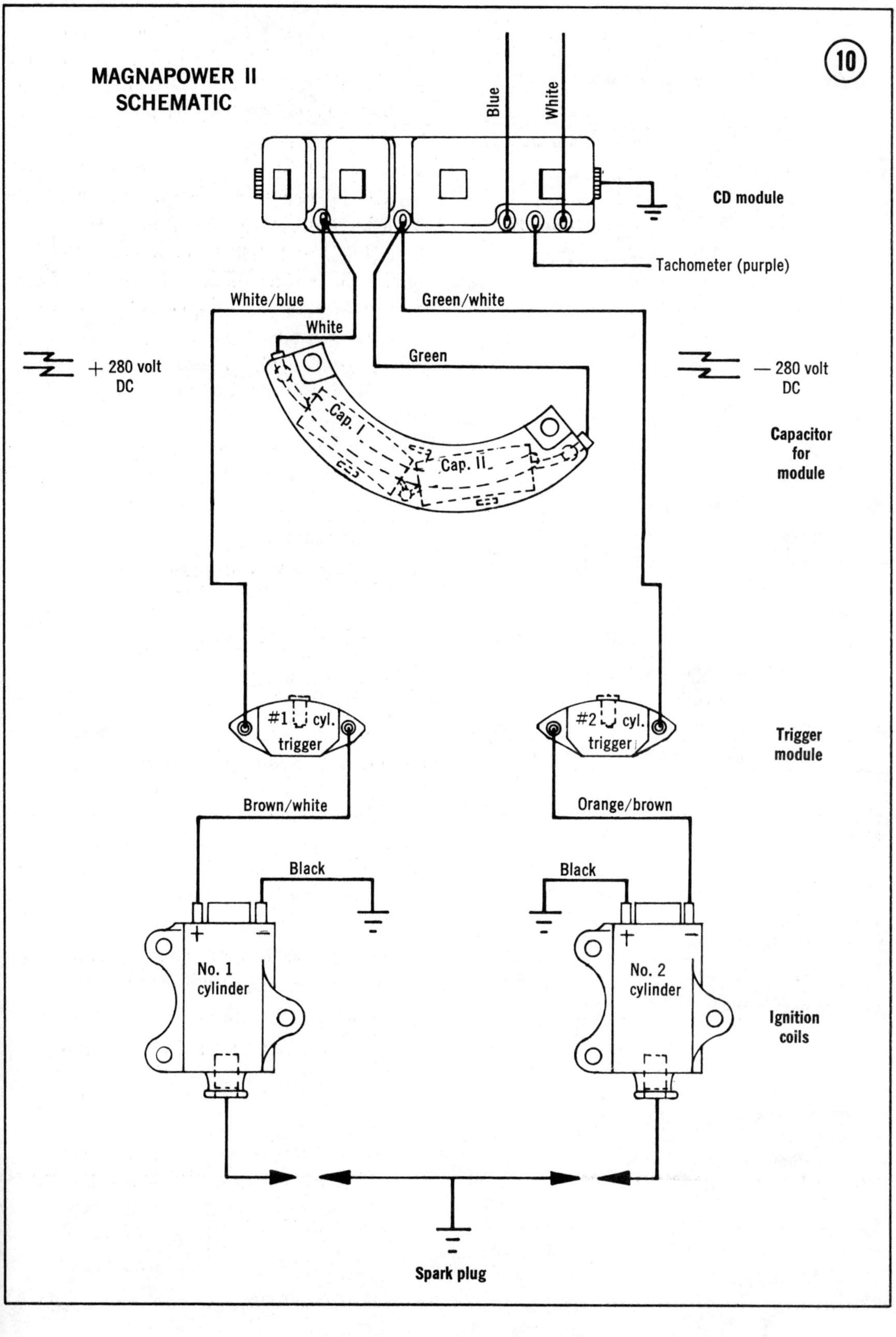
10
MAGNAPOWER II
SCHEMATIC
Blue
White
CD module
Tachometer (purple)
White/blue
Green/white
White
Green
+ 280 volt
DC
— 280 volt
DC
Cap. I
Cap. II
Capacitor
for
module
#1 cyl.
trigger
#2 cyl.
trigger
Trigger
module
Brown/white
Orange/brown
Black
Black
No. 1
cylinder
No. 2
cylinder
Ignition
coils
Spark plug

5

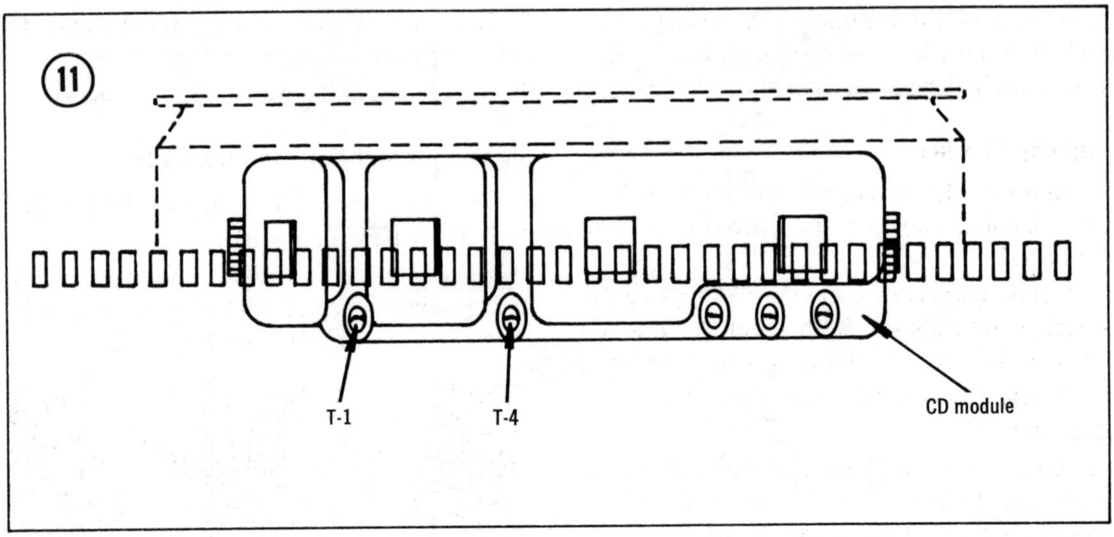

Ground screwdriver to flywheel first. Move screwdriver in to make contact with T-1 terminal. There should be a good arc from terminal to screwdriver. Repeat on T-4 terminal.

If little or no arc is present at one of the terminals, check the triggers as follows:

1. Remove flywheel as described elsewhere.
2. Disconnect leads from trigger modules.
3. Remove 4 bolts securing trigger assembly to bearing cage and rotate trigger assembly 180°. The top cylinder trigger now becomes the bottom trigger and vice versa.
4. Install flywheel and crank engine (450 rpm minimum) or start engine. Choke engine to stop. (Leave ignition switch in ON position.)
5. Recheck T-1 and T-4 terminals for spark. If opposite terminal now fails, the trigger is defective. Replace it.
6. If same terminal indicates little or no spark, C-D module or capacitor has failed.

> NOTE: *Special test equipment is required to test C-D module and capacitor and trigger modules. Replace suspected unit or have it further tested by an authorized service center.*

If a good arc is present at both terminals, the C-D module and capacitor module are good. If engine still misses, interchange the ignition coils. If the opposite cylinder misses, replace the defective coil.

FLYWHEEL

Removal

1. Remove flywheel nut.
2. Install flywheel puller (Special Tool T8948) on flywheel.
3. Turn forcing screw as tight as possible against crankshaft while holding bar to prevent puller plate from turning.
4. Using large screwdriver or wedge to apply an upward force on flywheel, strike top of forcing screw with hammer. Flywheel will loosen from taper on crankshaft.

> CAUTION
> *Do not strike forcing screw with excessive force as this may damage crankshaft and crankshaft bearings.*

5. Remove flywheel puller and flywheel from crankshaft.
6. Pry flywheel key out of slot in crankshaft.
7. Carefully inspect the flywheel for possible cracks or breaks.

> WARNING
> *Cracked or chipped flywheel must be replaced. At high rpm a damaged flywheel may fly apart throwing shrapnel over a large area.*

8. Inspect tapered bore of flywheel and taper on crankshaft for fretting or working. If there

is evidence of this condition or if the engine has had 25 or more hours of operation, the flywheel bore must be lapped. See procedure below.

Lapping Flywheel

1. Apply a light coating of a 240 grit water base valve lapping compound to tapered portion of crankshaft.
2. Install flywheel on crankshaft and rotate flywheel gently back and forth about ¼ turn—do not spin flywheel completely around crankshaft.
3. Rotate flywheel 90° and repeat the above operation.
4. Remove flywheel, wipe compound off crankshaft and flywheel. Taper in bore of flywheel should have a minimum of 80% surface contact with taper on crankshaft.

> NOTE: *To check percentage of contact, use soft lead pencil and draw 3 vertical lines on crankshaft taper 120° apart. Mount flywheel on crankshaft and rotate flywheel 360° or one full turn exerting light downward pressure. Remove flywheel and check percentage of pencil lines that have been rubbed off. If 80% or more of the pencil lines have been removed and no rocking is evident, then clean the tapers and reinstall the flywheel. Repeat the procedure if less than 80% of the lines have been removed. If lapping cannot correct taper contact to crankshaft, replace the flywheel. If new flywheel does not lap in, then replace the crankshaft.*

5. Thoroughly clean compound from flywheel, crankshaft and key way.

Installation

1. Install flywheel key in slot of crankshaft.
2. Install flywheel on crankshaft and torque flywheel nut to 90 ft.-lb.

STARTER SYSTEM

Starter Motor Removal/Installation

1. Disconnect battery leads from battery.
2. Remove nut and lead from stud on lower side of starter.
3. Remove 3 screws securing starter motor to crankcase cover and remove starter motor.
4. Installation is the reverse of these steps.

Starter Solenoid Removal/Installation

1. Disconnect battery leads from battery.
2. Remove port support plate.
3. Remove positive battery lead wire (black with red end) and small red lead wire from lower terminal of starter relay. See **Figure 12**.

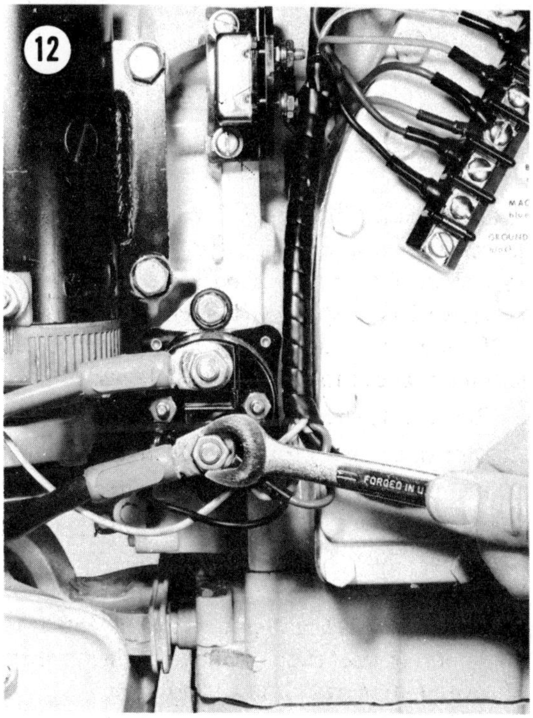

4. Remove yellow lead wire from rear terminal of starter relay.
5. Remove red lead wire (relay to starter motor lead) from top terminal of starter relay.
6. Remove black lead from forward terminal of starter relay.
7. Remove screws securing starter relay to the crankcase cover and remove starter relay.
8. Installation is the reverse of these steps.

IGNITION SYSTEM

Ignition Switch Removal/Installation

1. Remove ignition switch from control box or dashboard of boat.

2. Disconnect lead wires from ignition switch.

3. Installation is the reverse of these steps. See **Figure 13** for proper connection of ignition switch wires.

13

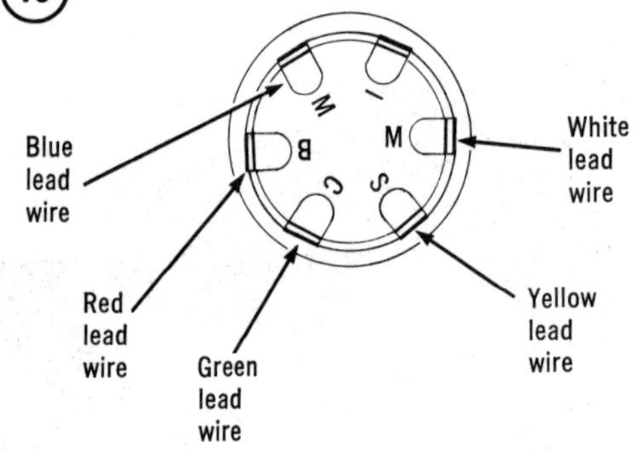

Back view of switch

Ignition Coil Removal/Installation

1. Disconnect the primary lead wire from the top of coil.

2. Remove screws securing coil to cylinder head cover and remove coil as shown in **Figure 14**.

14

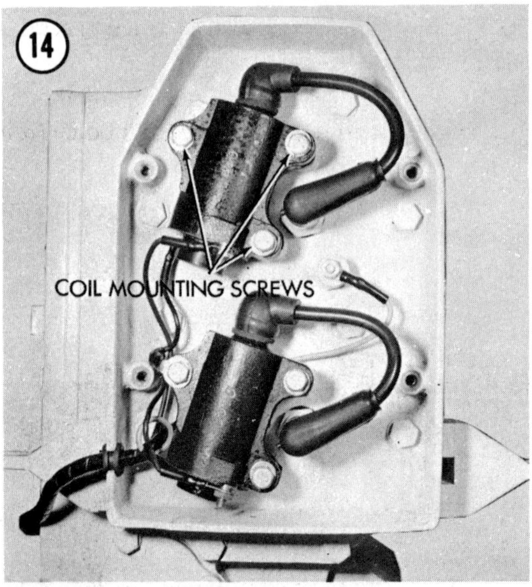

3. Remove nuts, lockwashers and lead wires from bottom of coil. See **Figure 15**.

> NOTE: *When removing bottom coil, remove rear support plate cover.*

4. Installation is the reverse of these steps.

15

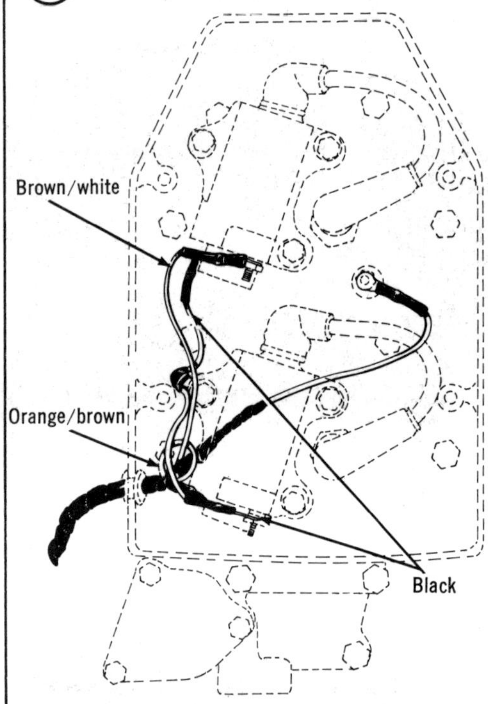

C-D Module Removal/Installation

1. Remove flywheel.

2. Remove timing ring retainer.

3. Remove 5 screws, lead wires and lockwashers from C-D module.

4. Remove 2 studs securing C-D module to bearing cage and remove C-D module from engine. See **Figure 16**.

5. Place C-D module on bearing cage. Install studs and tighten securely.

> NOTE: *When tightening mounting studs, push in on module to seat module properly against bearing cage.*

6. Install screws, lead wires and lockwashers to C-D module. See **Figure 17** for proper connection of lead wires.

7. Install 4 bowed washers, timing ring retainer and 4 stop nuts. Tighten stop nuts down evenly using a 0.003 feeler gauge between retainer and timing ring at retainer legs. There should be drag on feeler gauge. See **Figure 18**.

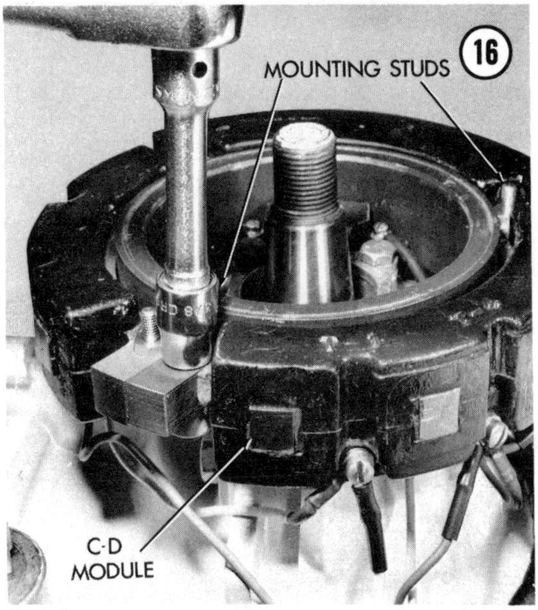

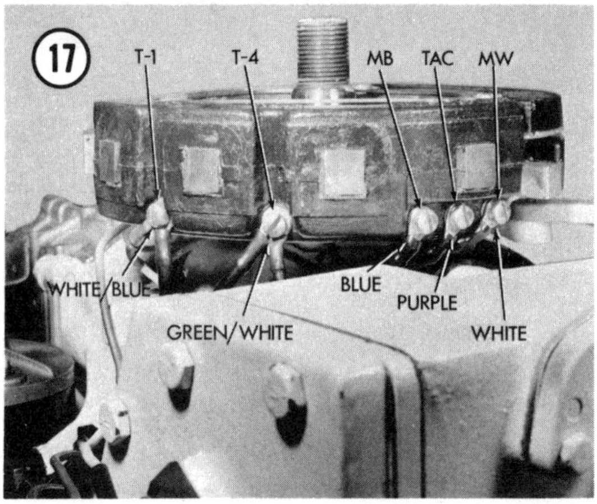

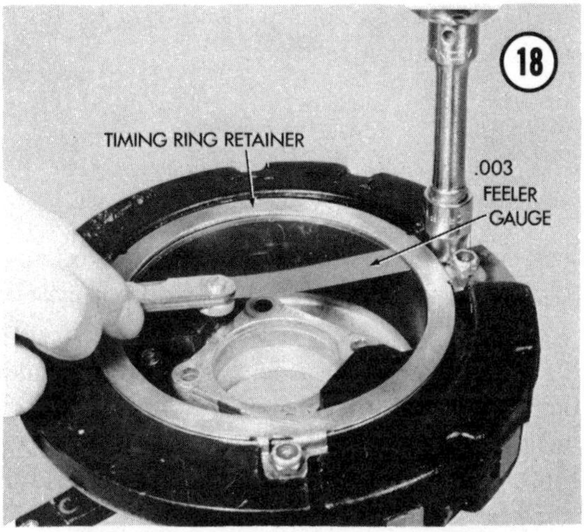

8. Check friction of timing ring by rotating it with a spring scale attached to outside hole of pivot arm. Reading should be 4 to 6 lbs. Readjust stop nuts to get proper friction if required. See **Figure 19**.

9. Install flywheel.

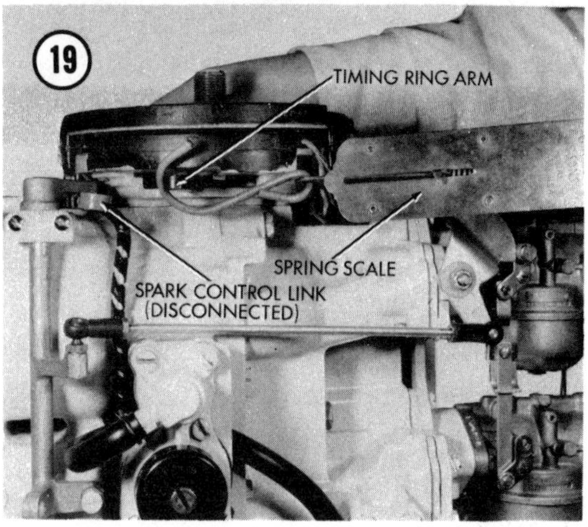

Capacitor Module Removal/Installation

1. Remove flywheel.
2. Remove timing ring retainer.
3. Remove screws and lockwashers securing capacitor leads to C-D module.
4. Remove studs securing capacitor module to bearing cage and remove capacitor module from bearing cage. See **Figure 20**.

5

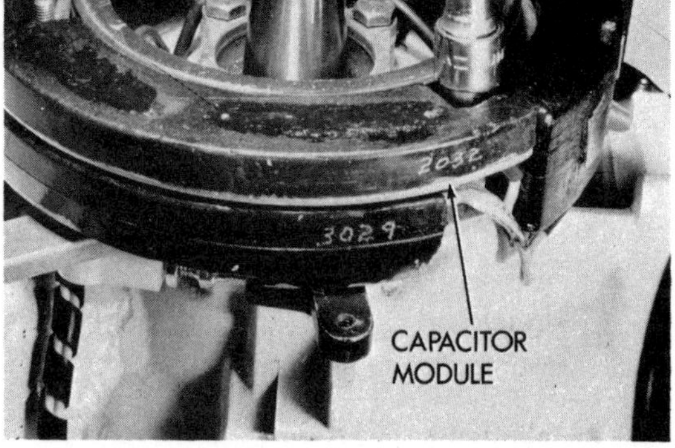

5. Installation is the reverse of these steps. See **Figure 21** for proper connection of capacitor leads to C-D module.

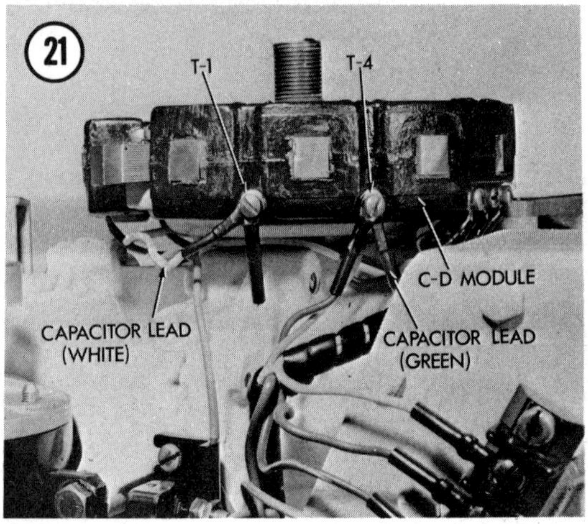

Timing Ring Removal/Installation

1. Remove flywheel.
2. Remove screws securing spark control link to timing ring as shown in **Figure 22**.

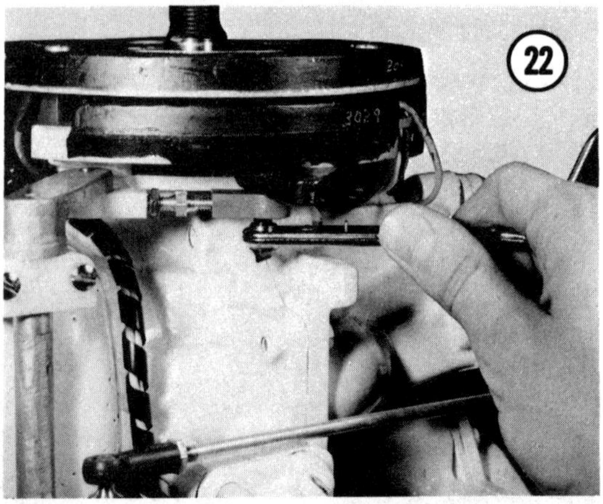

3. Remove timing ring retainer.
4. Remove regulator-rectifier as described later and remove timing ring from bearing cage.
5. Installation is the reverse of these steps. Before installing, apply grease to bearing cage. Lay timing ring in bearing cage with timing ring arm to starboard side.

Trigger Module Removal/Installation

1. Remove flywheel.
2. Remove timing ring.
3. Remove screws, lockwashers and lead wires from trigger modules.
4. Remove screws securing trigger assembly to bearing cage. Pry up on trigger assembly with screwdriver and remove same from bearing cage as shown in **Figure 23**.

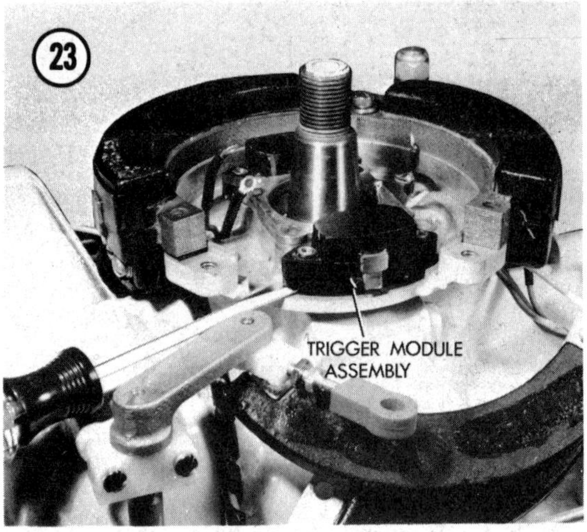

5. Remove trigger module from mounting plate by bending metal clip down and sliding module from plate as shown in **Figure 24**.

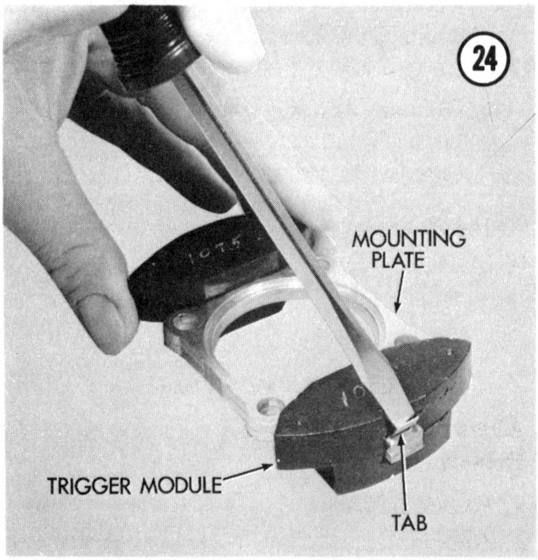

6. Install trigger module on mounting plate, terminals up and secure by bending metal clip down. Refer to Figure 24.
7. Place trigger assembly on bearing cage and secure with screws.

8. Install screws, lockwashers and lead wires on trigger modules as follows (see **Figure 25**):

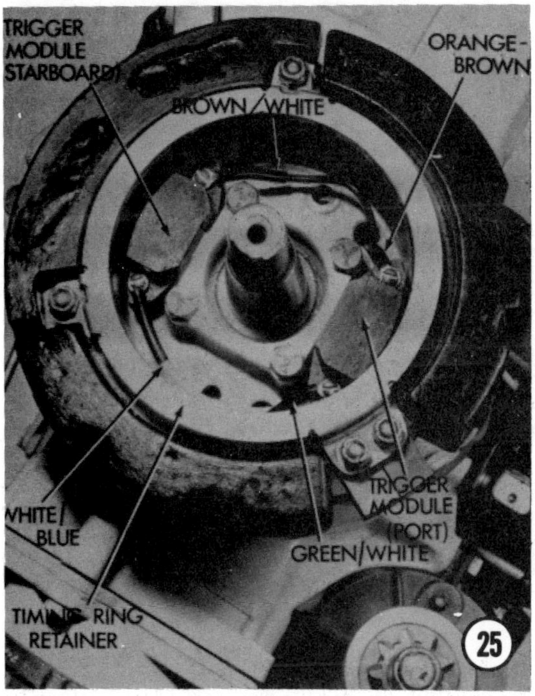

a. Top Cylinder Trigger (Starboard Side)
White/Blue Lead—Forward Terminal
Brown/White Lead—Rear Terminal
b. Bottom Cylinder Trigger (Port Side)
Green/White Lead—Forward Terminal
Orange/Brown Lead—Rear Terminal

9. Install timing ring.

10. Install flywheel.

CHARGING SYSTEM

Alternator Stator Module Removal/Installation

1. Remove flywheel.

2. Remove screws and lockwashers securing lead wires to alternator stator module.

3. Remove timing ring retainer.

4. Remove studs securing the alternator stator module to bearing cage. See **Figure 26**.

5. Installation is the reverse of these steps. See **Figure 27** for proper connection of leads.

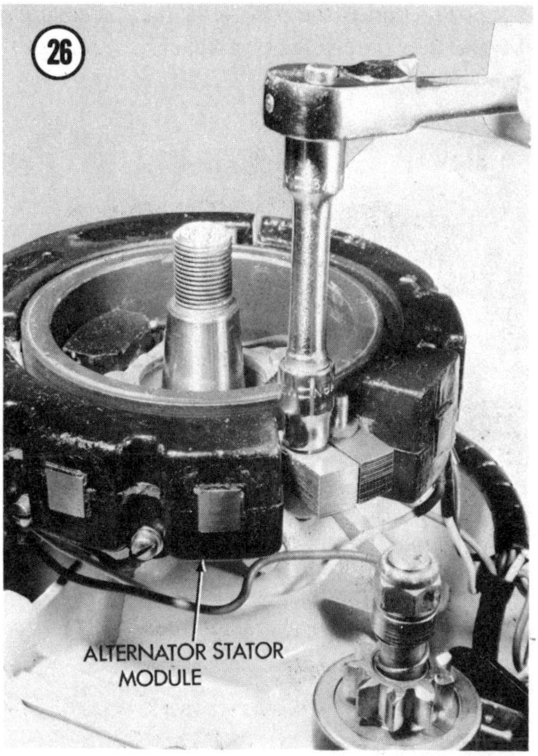

Regulator-Rectifier Module Removal/Installation

1. Remove flywheel.

2. Remove capacitor module.

3. Remove screws and lockwashers securing regulator-rectifier leads to alternator module and remove one screw securing regulator-rectifier lead to terminal block.

5

4. Remove screws and lockwashers securing regulator-rectifier to bearing cage as shown in **Figure 28** and remove it.

5. Installation is the reverse of these steps. See **Figure 29** for proper connection of regulator-rectifier leads.

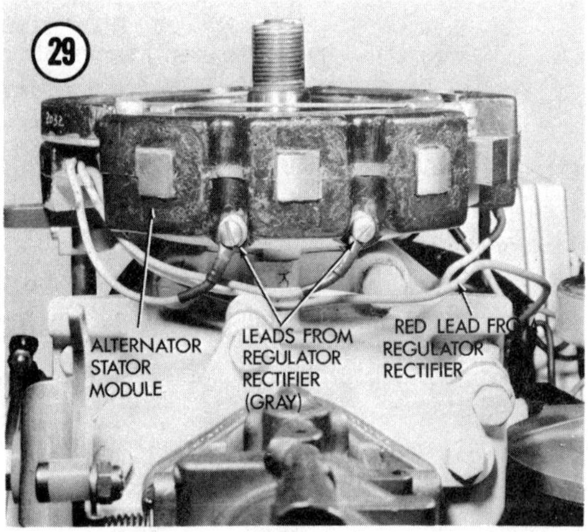

FUEL SYSTEM

Top Carburetor Removal

1. Remove carburetor intake with cover as shown in **Figure 30**. Also remove carburetor intake gaskets.

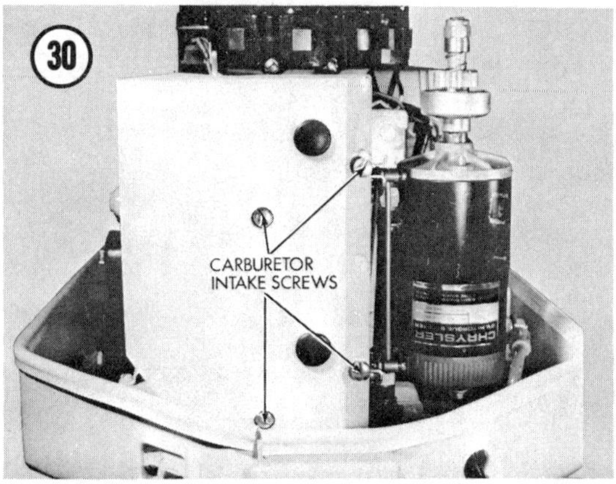

2. Remove retaining ring securing throttle tie bar to carburetor throttle arm. Remove screw securing end to tie bar. See **Figure 31**.

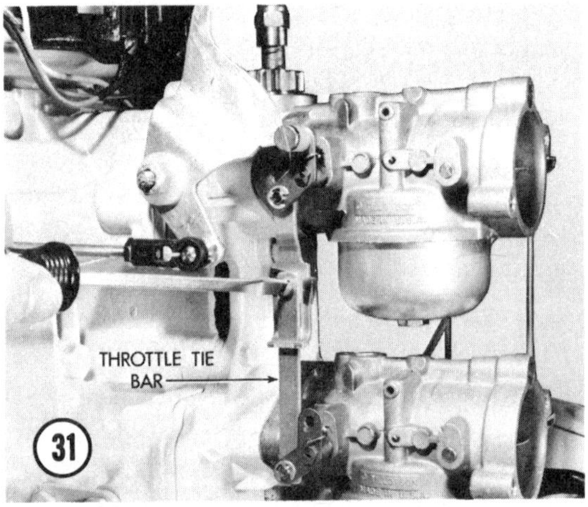

3. Loosen each choke swivel screw and allow choke link to slide down.

4. Remove cotter pin securing choke swivel to choke lever arm of carburetor. Remove plain washer, O-ring, choke rod, and choke swivel from choke lever arm.

5. Using hose clamp pliers slide hose clamp down and pull fuel hose from inlet fitting on carburetor.

CAUTION

Do not use hose clamp pliers to pull hose from fitting; pliers may puncture the hose.

6. Remove nuts securing carburetor to carburetor adapter flange and remove carburetor.

7. Remove fuel inlet fitting from carburetor.

8. Remove throttle roller shaft and roller from throttle shaft arm of carburetor by removing stop nut from roller shaft.

Top Carburetor Installation

1. Install throttle roller shaft and roller in top hole of throttle shaft arm. Secure roller shaft to stop nut, but do not tighten. Refer to *Tune-Up* for adjustment of throttle pick up after completion of assembly.
2. Apply sealant to threads of fuel inlet fitting. Install fitting on carburetor and position barb at 6 o'clock position.
3. Install new carburetor gasket on studs of carburetor adapter.
4. Install carburetor and secure with nuts.
5. Install choke swivel through choke shutter arm and rod end of choke solenoid plunger assembly. Install plain washer and secure swivel with cotter pin.
6. Slide choke rod up through choke swivel and secure with screw. Tighten screw on choke swivel on lower carburetor. Synchronize choke shutters as outlined under *Tune-Up*.
7. Connect fuel line to inlet fitting and secure with hose clamp using hose clamp pliers.
8. Install tie bar end on throttle tie bar. Secure with fillister head screw but do not tighten. Position tie bar end pivot through bottom hole on throttle shaft arm and secure with retaining ring. See Figure 31. Synchronize carburetor shutters as outlined under *Tune-Up*.
9. Install carburetor intake with cover being sure that gaskets are in place and secure with 4 screws. See Figure 30.

Bottom Carburetor Removal

1. Remove carburetor intake with cover as outlined under *Top Carburetor Removal* procedure.
2. Remove retaining ring securing throttle shaft tie bar to throttle shaft arm. Remove tie bar from throttle shaft arm.
3. Loosen screw securing choke rod to swivel on choke shaft arm. Remove rod from swivel.
4. Slide hose clamps from each barb on inlet fuel fitting using hose clamp pliers and disconnect hoses from fuel fitting.

CAUTION

Do not use hose clamp pliers to pull hose from fitting; pliers may puncture the hose.

5. Remove nuts securing carburetor to carburetor flange and remove carburetor.
6. Remove cotter pin securing choke swivel to choke arm of carburetor. Remove plain washer, and 2 seals. Remove swivel from choke arm.
7. Remove inlet fuel fitting from carburetor.

Bottom Carburetor Installation

1. Apply sealant to threads of fuel inlet fitting. Install fitting on carburetor and position fitting with barbs pointing at 12 o'clock and 6 o'clock.
2. Install O-ring on choke swivel. Install choke swivel with O-ring on choke shaft arm. Install O-ring, plain washer, and secure choke swivel with cotter pin.
3. Install new carburetor gasket on studs of carburetor adapter.
4. Install carburetor on carburetor adapter and secure with 2 nuts.
5. Install choke rod in choke swivel and secure by tightening screw on swivel against rod. Synchronize the choke shutters as outlined under *Tune-Up*.
6. Install throttle shaft tie bar in lower hole of throttle shaft arm of carburetor and secure with retaining ring. Synchronize throttle shutters as outlined under *Tune-Up*.
7. Connect fuel lines to inlet fuel fitting and secure with clamps.
8. Install carburetor intake with cover being sure that gaskets are in place and secure with 4 screws. See Figure 30.

Carburetor Disassembly

1. Remove carburetor from engine.
2. Remove 2 screws holding throttle shutter in shaft, as shown in **Figure 32**.
3. Move throttle lever until throttle shutter is wide open. (Shutter horizontal). Use needle nose pliers to remove shutter. Do not force shutter out. Note that edge of shutter is beveled. See **Figure 33**.

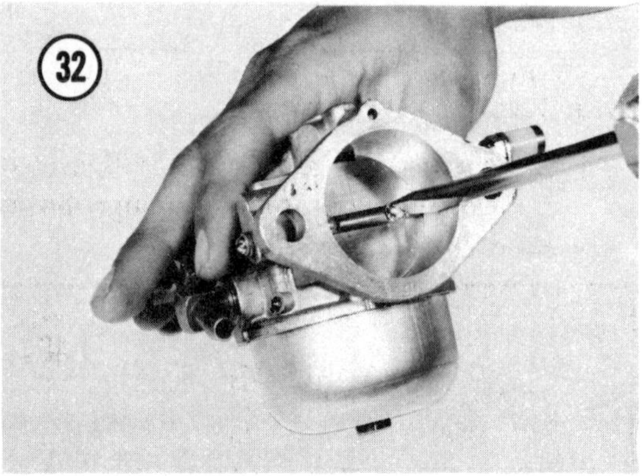

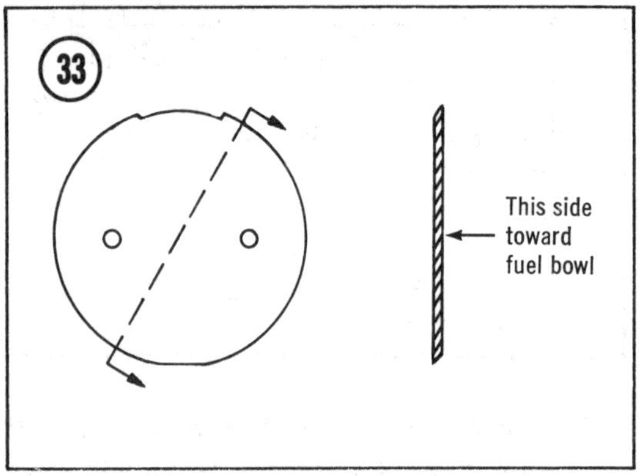

4. Unhook throttle return spring from pin on carburetor body.

5. Remove screw with lockwasher and washer from port end of throttle shaft.

6. Pull throttle shaft from carburetor body.

7. Remove nut securing throttle roller shaft (eccentric screw) and roller to throttle arm.

8. Remove spring from throttle shaft.

9. Remove 2 screws securing choke shutter to choke shaft. Use needle nose pliers to gently pull choke shutter from choke shaft.

10. Pull choke shaft out just enough to free choke lever from stop on carburetor body, relieving tension of choke shaft return spring.

11. Unhook choke shaft return spring from choke lever and pull choke lever with shaft from carburetor.

12. Straighten cotter pin and remove it from choke rod swivel on choke lever.

13. Remove choke swivel, washer and seals from choke lever.

14. Remove idle adjustment screw.

15. Examine screw for deep grooves on tapered portion of point. If deep grooves are present, replace screw.

16. Remove screw securing fuel bowl to carburetor as shown in **Figure 34**.

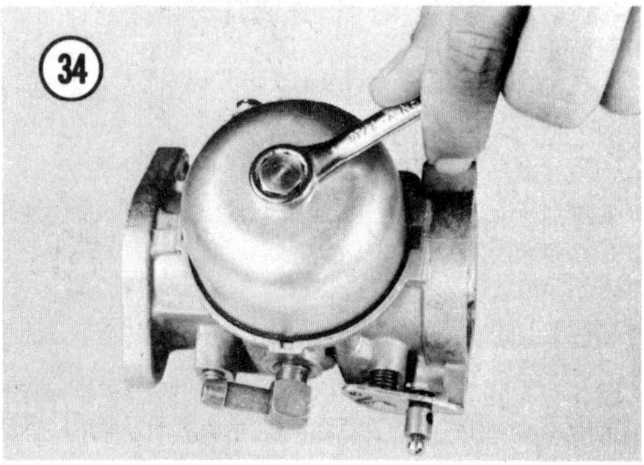

17. Remove fuel bowl. See **Figure 35**.

18. Remove main nozzle as shown in **Figure 36**.

19. Remove main fuel jet as shown in **Figure 37**.

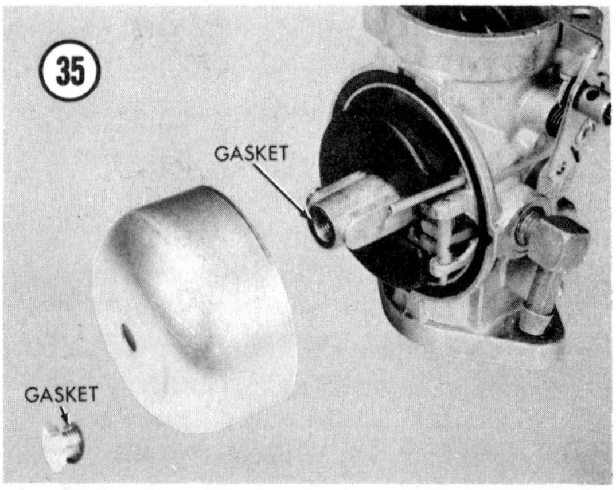

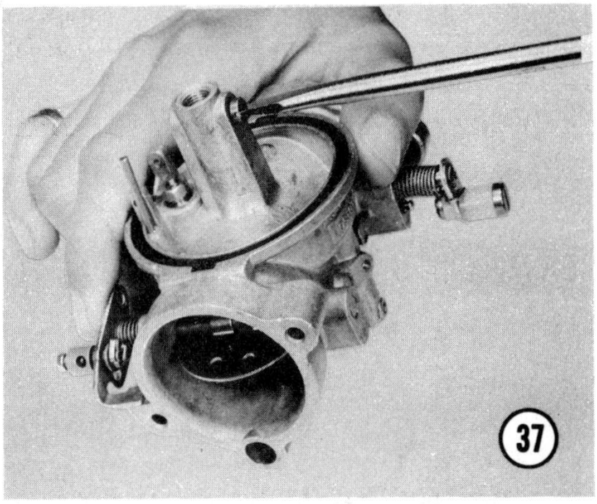

20. Use pin punch to drive out the float lever pin from the protruding (unknurled) end. See **Figure 38.**

21. Remove inlet needle as shown in **Figure 39.**

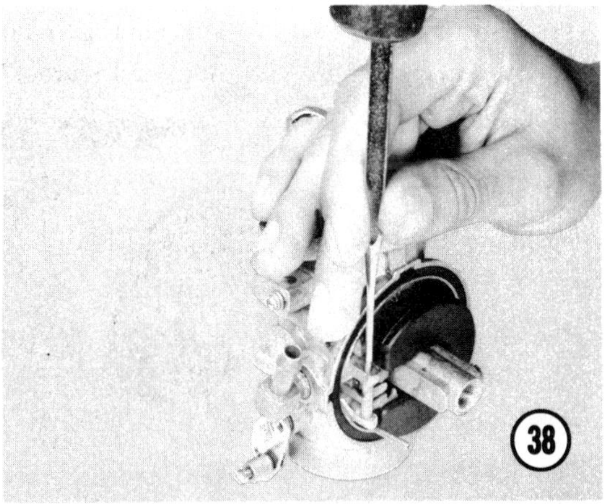

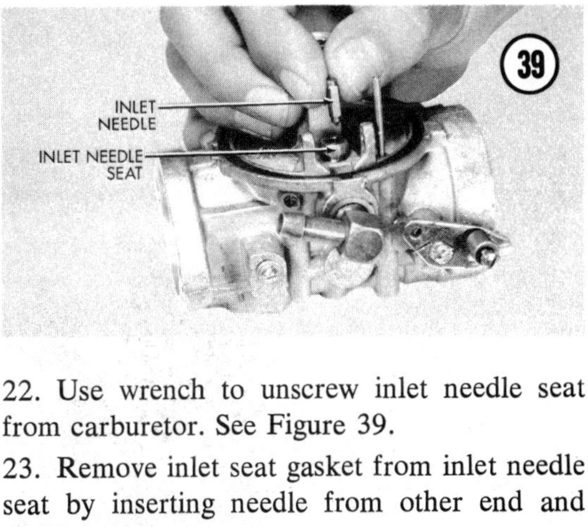

22. Use wrench to unscrew inlet needle seat from carburetor. See Figure 39.

23. Remove inlet seat gasket from inlet needle seat by inserting needle from other end and pushing gasket out.

Assembly

Assembly is the reverse of disassembly. Keep the following points in mind.

a. Measure float height, shown in **Figure 40**. If measurement is not within range shown, bend tab as shown in Figure 20.

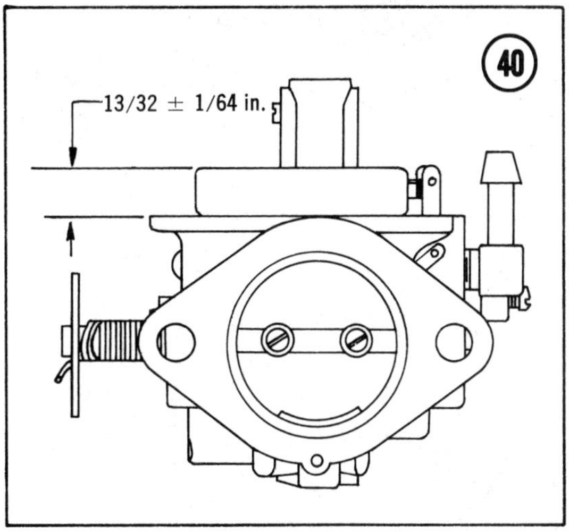

b. Knurled end of float lever pin must be flush with pivot hole in carburetor body. See **Figure 41**.

c. Place float in carburetor with tab near pivot toward carburetor body.

d. Insert inlet needle, pointed end first.

e. Insert inlet seat gasket, flat end first, in large end of inlet needle seat.

f. Install new fuel bowl gasket and 2 fuel bowl retaining screw gaskets (Figure 35).

g. Apply light coat of Sealer 1000 or equivalent to threaded portion of float lever pin and shutter screws.

h. Place an O-ring seal on choke rod swivel.

i. Secure choke shutter to choke shaft by installing 2 screws with lockwashers in recessed side of choke shaft.

j. Insert choke shutter in slot in choke shaft with beveled edge down.

k. Turn choke lever counterclockwise and push it in so lever is stopped by stop on carburetor body.

l. Hook small loop of choke shaft return spring around peg on carburetor body. Hook other end around carburetor body.

m. Insert choke shaft in carburetor body from port side.

n. Slide choke shaft return spring on choke shaft so small loop will be toward the carburetor body.

o. Insert throttle shaft in carburetor from starboard side.

p. Install carburetor.

q. Adjust the carburetor as outlined under *Tune-up*.

Sediment Bowl and Filter (Screen) Removal/Installation

1. Loosen knurled screw on sediment bowl and remove bowl.

2. Remove gasket and screen. See **Figure 42**.

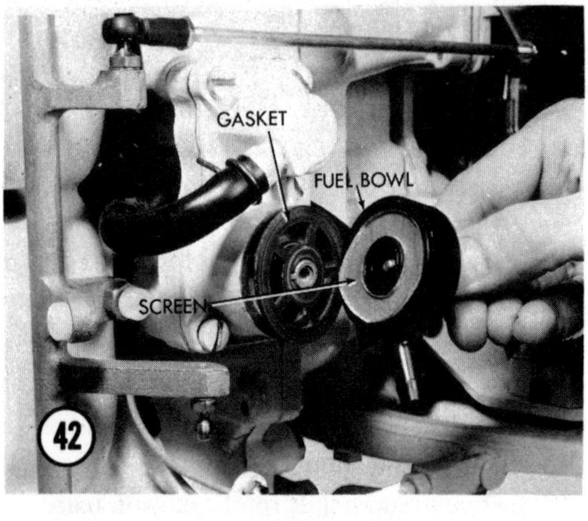

3. Use hose clamp pliers to slide hose clamp about one inch down hose from sediment bowl. Pull hose off sediment bowl.

CAUTION

Do not use hose clamp pliers to pull hose off fitting; pliers can puncture the hose.

4. Installation is the reverse of these steps.

Fuel Pump Diaphragm Removal/Installation

1. Remove sediment bowl.

2. Use hose clamp pliers to slide hose clamp on fuel pump outlet fitting about one inch down hose. Pull hose off fitting.

CAUTION

Do not use hose clamp pliers to pull hose off fitting; pliers can puncture the hose.

3. Remove screws securing fuel pump assembly to power head. Remove fuel pump assembly. See **Figure 43**.

4. Remove screws securing fuel pump body to fuel pump cover. Separate cover from fuel pump body and remove the fuel pump gasket and diaphragm.

5. Remove O-ring seals from back of fuel pump cover. See **Figure 44**.

6. Installation is the reverse of these steps. See **Figure 45**.

Fuel Pump Body Removal/Installation

1. Remove fuel pump body.

2. Remove screws securing central valve to fuel pump body. Remove fuel pump valve and gasket as shown in **Figure 46**.

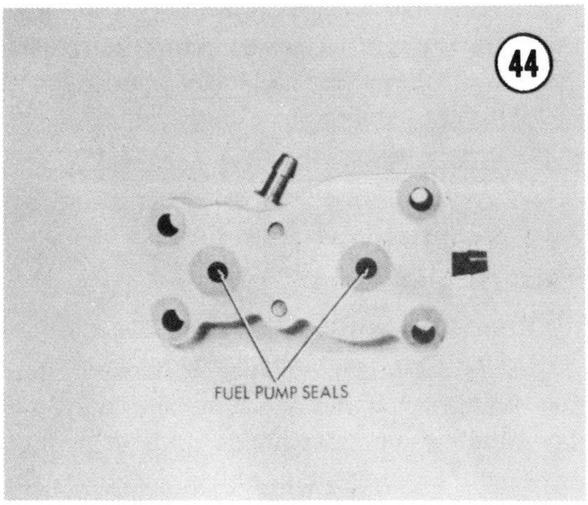

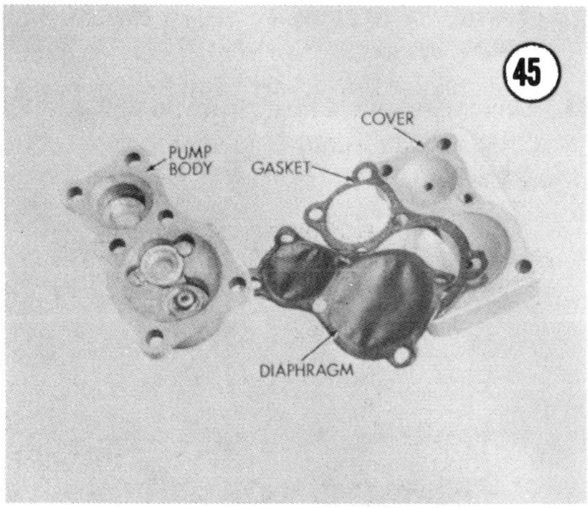

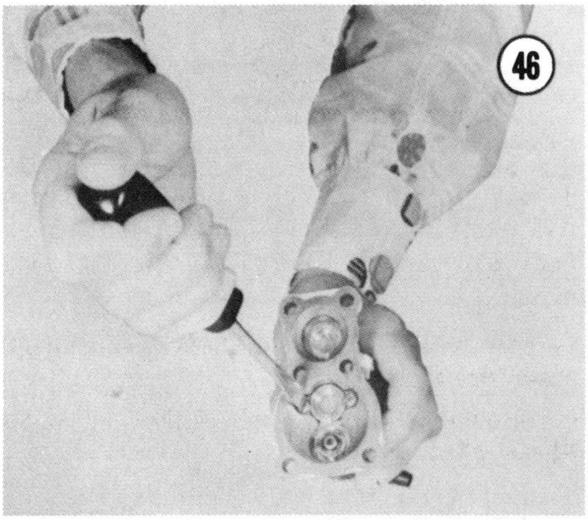

3. Unscrew fuel line fitting from body of fuel pump.

4. Apply sealant to threads of fuel line fitting. Install fitting in fuel pump body.

5. Place fuel pump valve gasket on valve seat in fuel pump body. Place valve on valve seat so that brass ring on valve is toward power head.

6. Use 2 screws to secure the valve to the fuel pump body.

7. Install fuel pump body.

Prime Bulb Removal/Installation

1. Dip prime bulb portion of fuel line in hot water (180-200°F) for a few minutes until hose becomes soft and pliable.

2. Pull hose and ferrule from adapter on each end of prime bulb.

3. Installation is the reverse of these steps.

GEAR HOUSING

Lower Unit Removal/Installation

1. Remove the bolts securing lower unit to motor leg.

2. Pull lower unit down enough to expose cotter pin and clevis pin securing lower shift rod to upper shift rod.

3. Remove cotter pin from clevis pin. Then remove clevis pin securing lower shift rod to upper shift rod.

4. Remove lower unit from motor leg.

5. Apply anti-seize compound to drive shaft splines.

6. Install lower unit on engine by inserting drive shaft up motor leg and engaging drive shaft splines with crankshaft splines.

7. Insert lower shift rod in coupler of upper shift rod. Secure lower shift rod to coupler of upper shift rod with clevis pin and cotter pin.

8. Check water line for alignment in water pump seal.

9. Apply anti-seize compound to threads of gear housing screws. Install screws to secure lower unit to motor leg.

Lower Shift Rod Removal/Installation

1. Remove lower unit.

2. Unscrew lower shift rod from shift arm.

3. Apply grease to threads of lower shift rod.

4. Insert lower shift rod through shift rod seal until it makes contact with shift arm. Turn shift

rod clockwise until thread bottoms. Turn rod counterclockwise until hole at top of rod faces port and starboard.

5. Install lower unit.

Water Pump Removal/Installation

1. Remove lower unit.
2. Remove water line seal from body by depressing tabs on seal, then pulling seal from pump body.
3. Remove screws securing water pump body assembly to upper gear housing and lift pump body assembly from lower unit.
4. Remove the water pump impeller from the pump body.
5. Drive the drive shaft seal out from inside pump body.
6. Remove water pump back plate and gasket from lower unit.
7. Support inside top surface of water pump body on wood block to prevent body from collapsing when installing drive shaft seal. Press drive shaft seal (garter spring on major sealing lip positioned out) in pump body with seal installer (Special Tool T3012) as shown in **Figure 47**.

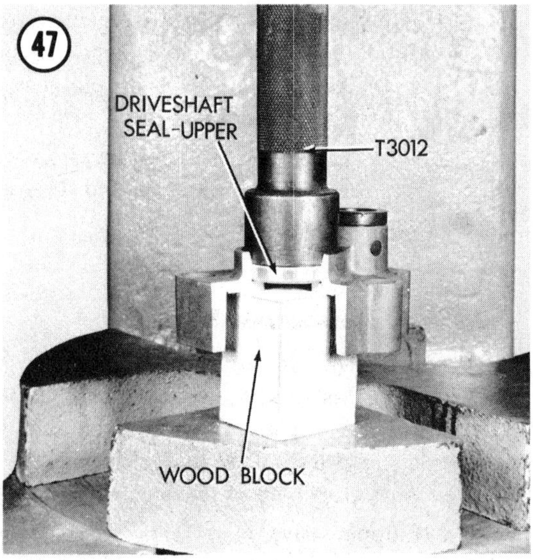

8. Install water pump impeller by turning impeller in pump body in a counterclockwise direction.
9. Clean gasket surface on upper gear housing. Install new pump gasket on upper gear housing. Install pump back plate so that holes in plate and gasket line up exactly with holes in upper gear housing.

NOTE: *Holes in back plate will not line up exactly if plate is installed upside down. It is important to install plate correctly or water pump will not supply sufficient cooling water.*

10. Install pump assembly down drive shaft on back plate aligning slot of impeller with dry key on drive shaft.
11. Install water pump centering tool (Special Tool T8979) down drive shaft to center pump body in relationship to drive shaft (**Figure 48**).

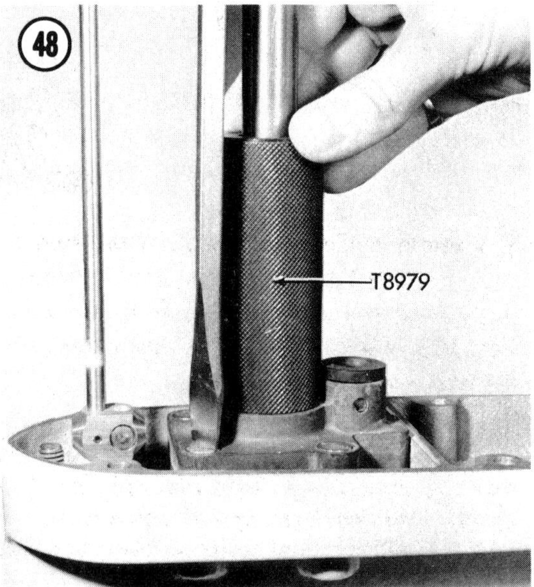

12. Apply anti-seize compound to threads of flat head screws which secure pump body to upper gear housing. While applying downward force on centering tool, install and tighten 4 flat head screws on pump body. Torque screws to 70 in.-lb. Remove centering tool.
13. Install water line seal in seal bore of pump body making sure that tabs on seal are seated in holes in seal bore of pump body.
14. Install lower unit.

Upper Gear Housing Removal

1. Remove lower unit.
2. Remove propeller and drain gear housing by removing FILL and VENT plugs.
3. Remove screws securing propeller shaft bearing cage to lower gear housing.
4. Install puller (Special Tool T8948 or equivalent) as shown in **Figure 49** and remove bearing cage assembly.

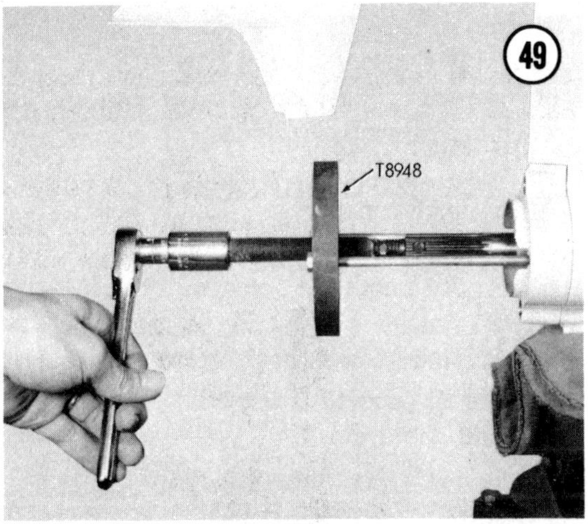

5. Remove nut and lockwasher from stud located behind rear gear in lower gear housing.
6. Remove nut and lockwasher from stud in front of gearshift rod. Separate upper gear housing from lower gear housing.
7. Remove water pump.
8. Remove shift rod seal by threading a 5/16 in. diameter lag screw in shift rod seal. Insert ¼ in. diameter rod from opposite side and press both seal and lag screw out of seal bore as shown in **Figure 50**.

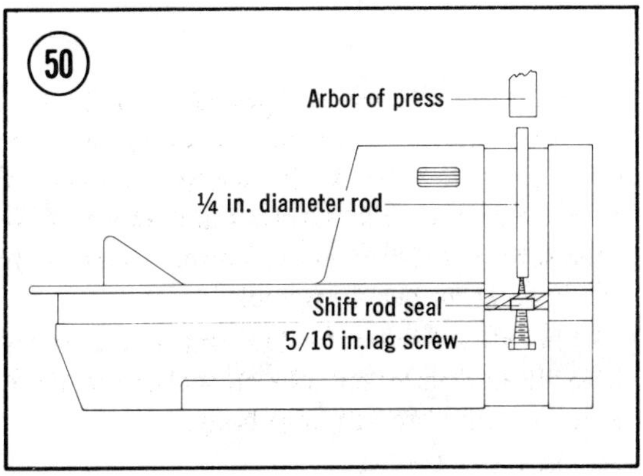

9. Remove screw and plain washer securing bevel pinion to drive shaft. Remove bevel pinion with bearing and cup.
10. Press drive shaft out of upper gear housing as shown in **Figure 51**. This operation will also remove drive shaft seal. Remove seal from drive shaft.

11. Remove upper drive shaft bearing cup from upper gear housing by tapping lightly from lower gear housing side with spring pin punch (Special Tool T8919) and hammer.
12. Remove exhaust snout from gear housing by removing socket head cap screw and retainer securing same to upper gear housing.

Upper Gear Housing Installation

1. Apply Loctite "H" on outside diameter of shift rod seal. Install seal on seal installer (Special Tool T8957) with raised bead on seal in cavity machined in tool. Press seal in until tool bottoms on top of bore as shown in **Figure 52**.
2. Install upper drive shaft bearing cup (large diameter end up) in upper gear housing by tapping lightly around circumference of bearing cup with punch and hammer until cup bottoms completely in bore.

5

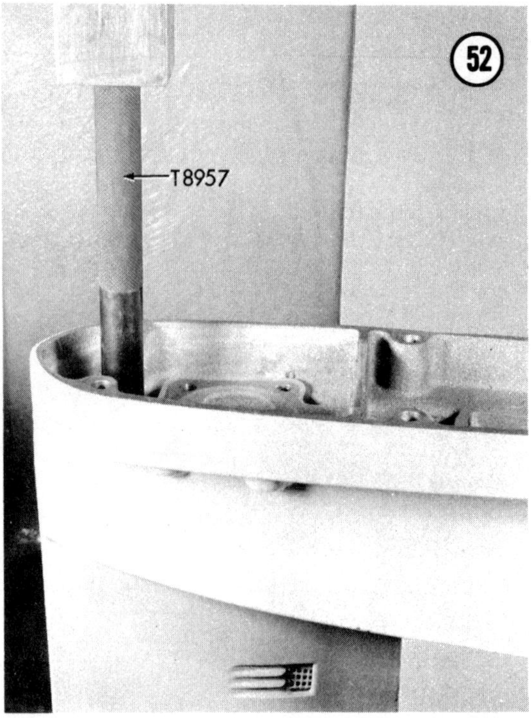

3. Install drive shaft with bearing cone in upper gear housing.

4. Clean bevel pinion bearing cup bore in upper gear housing. Install bearing cup and bevel pinion.

5. Apply grease between sealing lips of drive shaft seal. Slide seal down drive shaft. Using seal installer (Special Tool T8985) as a slide hammer, drive seal in bore until top of seal is flush with top of bore. See **Figure 53**.

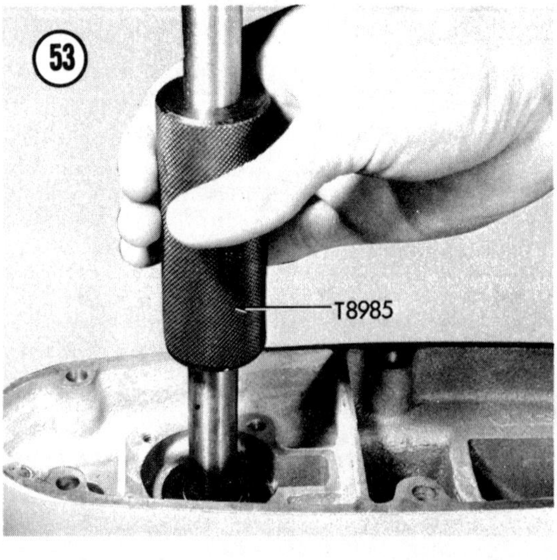

6. Clean mating surfaces of both upper and lower gear housings. Inspect gear housing seal for cracks or cuts. Replace if necessary.

7. Install upper gear housing on lower gear housing. Secure upper gear housing to lower gear housing with 2 nuts and lockwashers.

> NOTE: *Torque each nut to 100 inch-pounds. Increase torque in increments of 30-50 inch-pounds to 270 inch-pounds.*

8. Apply grease to bearing cage seal and to lips of propeller shaft seal. Install bearing cage assembly on propeller shaft.

9. Apply anti-seize compound to threads of 2 Allen head cap screws. Secure bearing cage assembly to lower gear housing with screws.

10. Apply Loctite to threads of exhaust snout screws. Install exhaust snout on upper gear housing and secure with 2 screws.

11. Install propeller, drive pin, seal, propeller nut, and cotter pin.

12. Install water pump.

13. Install lower unit.

Bevel Pinion Removal/Installation

1. Remove lower unit.

2. Remove upper gear housing.

3. Remove screw and washer securing bevel pinion to drive shaft and remove bevel pinion and bearing cup.

4. Clean threads on drive shaft end and prime with Locquic. Apply Loctite "D" to threads of bevel pinion retaining screw.

5. Install bearing cup and bevel pinion on drive shaft aligning cup in bore of upper gear housing.

6. Install bevel pinion retaining screw and washer. Do not tighten screw at this time.

7. After installing screw in drive shaft, clamp drive shaft in vise (with protective jaws) with drive shaft horizontal.

8. Swing upper gear housing on drive shaft. Note how freely gear housing swings. Tighten retaining screw while swinging gear housing as shown in **Figure 54** until gear housing just starts to bind.

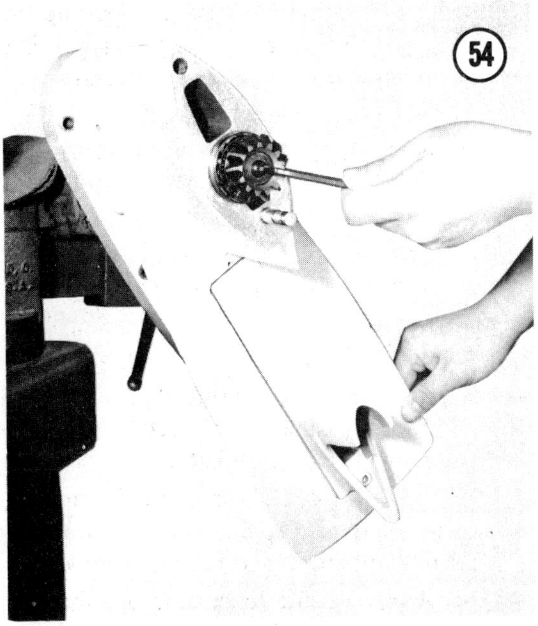

NOTE: *If not previously removed, remove drive shaft seal before performing Step 8 so that gear housing swings freely on drive shaft.*

9. Seat bearing (drive shaft and bevel pinion) by tapping retaining screw on end of drive shaft 2 times as shown in **Figure 55**.

CAUTION
Do not hit face of gear with hammer. This may damage bevel pinion.

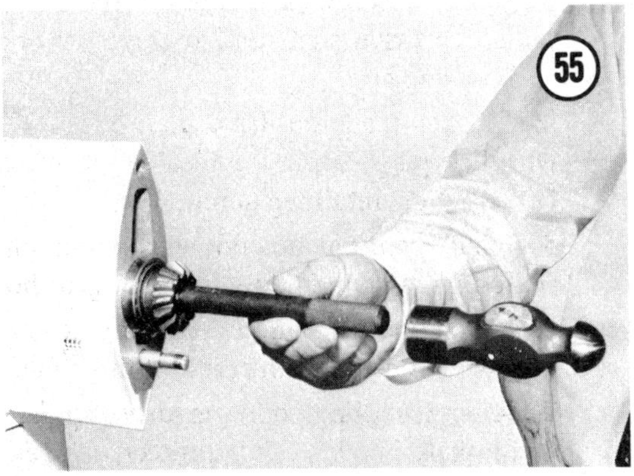

10. Swing upper gear housing again and check to see that gear housing swings freely. If it still binds slightly, loosen screws just enough so that gear housing swings freely.
11. Install upper gear housing.

Lower Gear Housing Removal/Installation

1. Remove lower unit.
2. Remove upper gear housing assembly and remove lower gear housing complete.
3. Remove bevel pinion and bearing cup from upper gear housing.
4. Installation is the reverse of these steps.

POWER HEAD

Exhaust Port Cover Removal/Installation

1. Remove port support plate.
2. Remove 2 screws securing terminal block to exhaust port cover. Pull terminal block forward away from exhaust port cover.
3. Remove screws securing exhaust port cover to power head. Remove exhaust port cover, plate, and gaskets.
4. Clean all gasket surfaces.
5. Apply anti-seize compound to threads of exhaust port cover screws.
6. Install exhaust port cover, plate, and gaskets as shown in **Figure 56**.

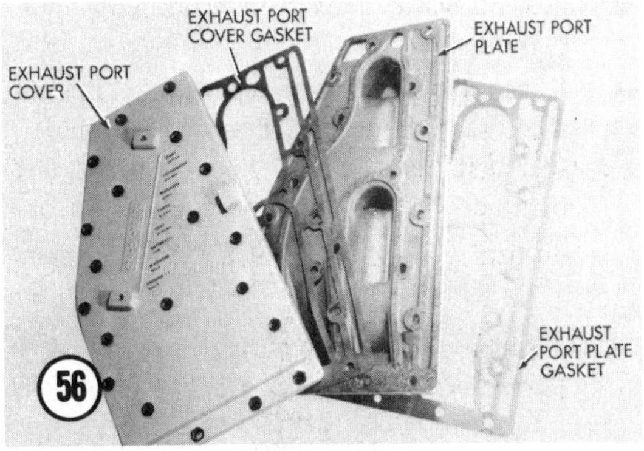

7. Install exhaust port cover screws and torque from the center out to 70 $\pm$ 5 in.-lb.
8. Secure terminal block to exhaust port cover.
9. Install port support plate.

Bypass Valve Cover Removal/Installation

1. Remove screws securing bypass valve cover to power head and remove bypass valve cover and gasket.

2. Installation is the reverse of this step. Install new gasket.

Thermostat Removal/Installation

1. Remove port support plate.
2. Remove screws securing thermostat cover to cylinder head. See **Figure 57**.

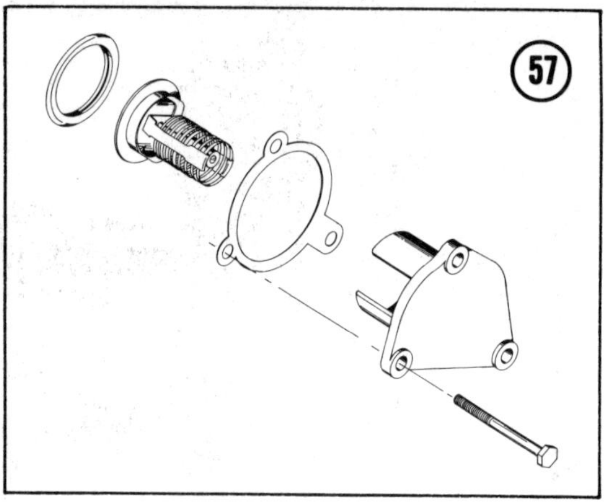

3. Remove thermostat cover gasket.
4. Remove thermostat and grommet from cylinder head.
5. Installation is the reverse of these steps.

Cylinder Head Removal

1. Remove spark plug cover.
2. Remove port and starboard support plates.
3. Remove coils as described earlier.
4. Remove spark plugs from cylinder head.
5. Remove thermostat.
6. Remove 11 bolts securing cylinder head to power head. Pry cylinder head from power head as shown in **Figure 58**.
7. Remove 3 screws and thermoswitch securing cylinder head cover to cylinder head. Remove cylinder head cover and gasket.
8. Remove rear stabilizer from cylinder head.

Cylinder Head Installation

1. Install rear stabilizer on cylinder head.
2. Clean all gasket surfaces.
3. Install gasket and cover on cylinder head and secure with 3 screws and thermoswitch. See **Figure 59**.

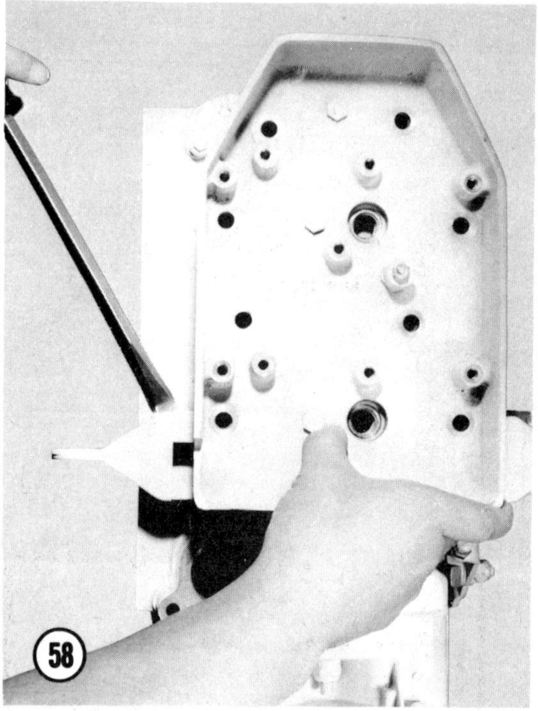

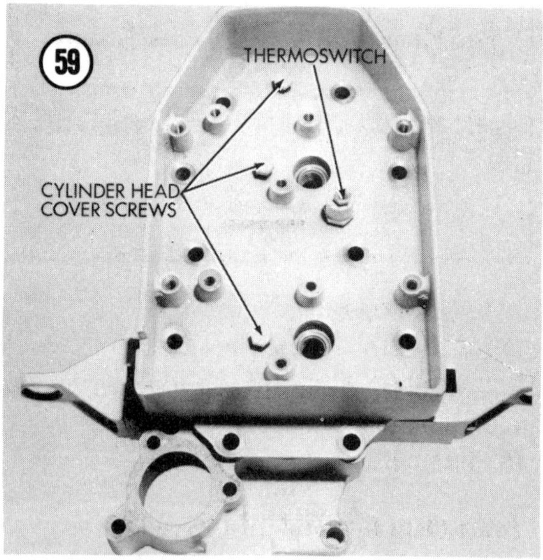

4. Apply anti-seize compound to threads of cylinder head bolts.
5. Install cylinder head gasket, cylinder head, bolt washers, and cylinder head bolts as shown in **Figure 60**. Torque head bolts initially to 70 in.-lb. as shown in **Figure 61**. Increase torque in 30-50 in.-lb. increments until bolts are torqued to 225 in.-lb.

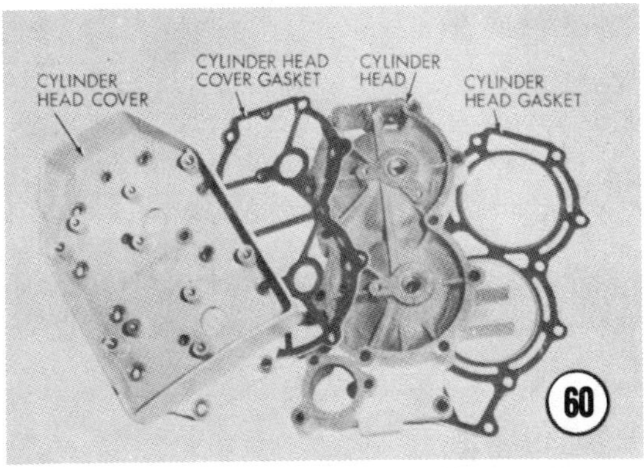

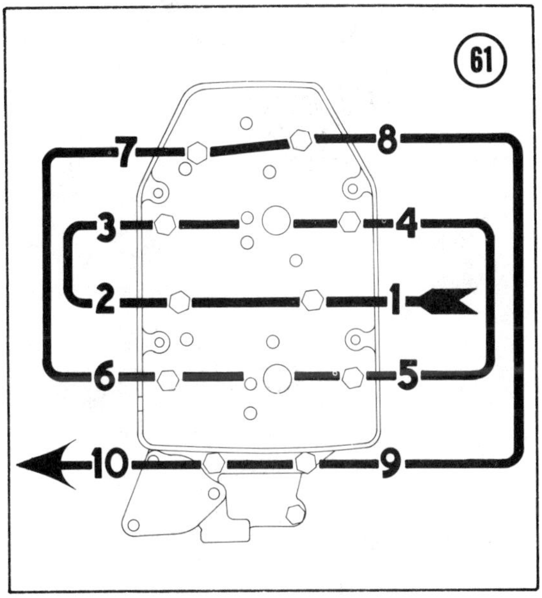

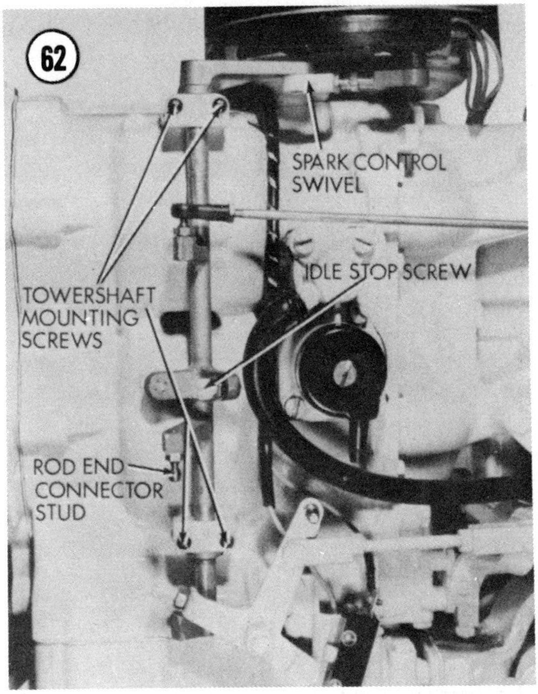

6. Install thermostat.

7. Install spark plugs and torque 120-180 in.-lb.

8. Install coils as described earlier.

9. Install spark plug cover.

10. Install port and starboard support plates.

Tower Shaft Removal/Installation

1. Remove starboard support plate.

2. Remove spark control swivel securing spark control bearing to top of tower shaft.

3. Unsnap throttle link from tower shaft.

4. Remove screws securing upper and lower tower shaft bearings to power head. Remove tower shaft. See **Figure 62**.

5. Unscrew idle stop screw and nut from tower shaft.

6. Drive plastic rivet out from back of tower shaft with pin punch.

7. Remove rod end connector stud and lockwasher from tower shaft.

8. Remove ball-joint and lockwasher from tower shaft.

9. Install ball-joint on tower shaft with lockwasher between tower shaft and ball-joint. See Figure 62.

10. Install lockwasher and rod end connector stud on tower shaft.

11. Push plastic rivet into hole in tower shaft. Secure plastic rivet by pushing in rod that protrudes from rivet.

12. Install the idle stop screw and nut on the tower shaft.

13. Apply Loctite "D" to first 4 threads of tower shaft bearing screws. Use 4 screws to secure upper and lower tower shaft bearings to power head. See Figure 62.

14. Snap the throttle link on ball-joint of the tower shaft.

15. Use spark control swivel to secure spark control bearing to top of tower shaft.

16. Install starboard support plate.

17. Tune up engine as outlined under *Tune-up*.

Shift Arm Removal/Installation

1. Remove starboard support plate.

2. Remove cotter pin, plain washer, bearing, and gearshift pin securing gearshift coupler to shift arm as shown in **Figure 63**.

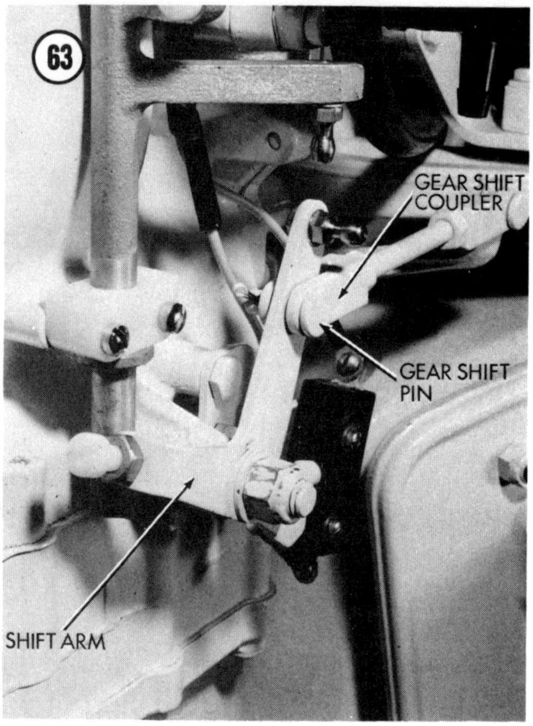

3. Remove stop nut and bearings securing shift arm to power head and remove shift arm.

4. Remove nut and lockwashers securing rod end connector stud to shift arm.

5. Remove neutral throttle stop screw and nut from shift arm.

6. Install nut and neutral throttle stop screw on shift arm.

7. Install rod end connector stud and 2 lock-washers in top hole on shift arm and secure with nut.

8. Install shift arm on its stud with one shift arm bearing on each side of arm. Secure with elastic stop nut just snug enough to prevent binding.

9. Align gearshift coupler with hole in shift arm. Install bearing and gearshift pin and secure with cotter pin. See Figure 63.

10. Install starboard support plate.

Reed Plate Removal

1. Remove the carburetors as outlined under *Carburetor*.

2. Unsnap throttle link from throttle cam.

3. Remove screws securing carburetor adapter and reed plate to crankcase. Remove assembly from engine. See **Figure 64**.

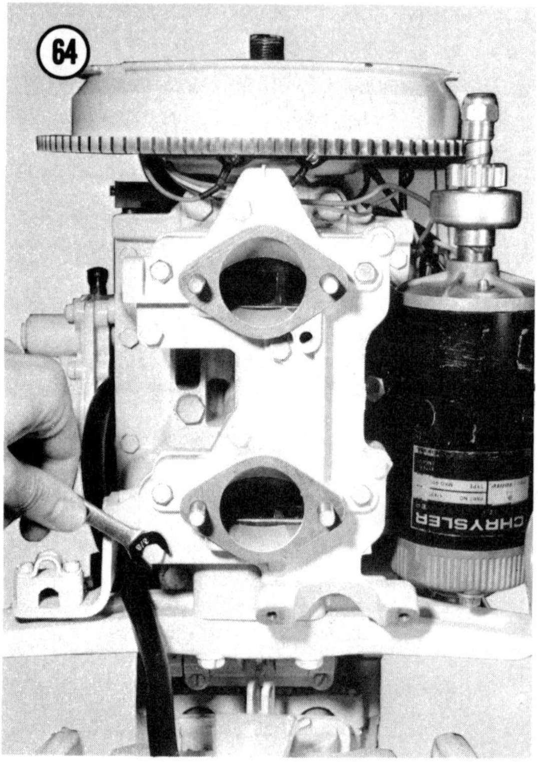

4. Remove screws securing reed plate to carburetor adapter as shown in **Figure 65**. Separate assembly and remove gaskets.

Reed Plate Installation

1. Install reed plate assemblies on adapter with 2 gaskets. Install carburetor adapter on reed plate adapter with gasket. See **Figure 66**. Refer to Figure 65 for location of screws.

2. Install carburetor adapter assembly on crankcase. Secure screws and torque from the center out.

3. Snap throttle link on connector stud on throttle cam.

4. Install the carburetors as outlined under *Carburetors*.

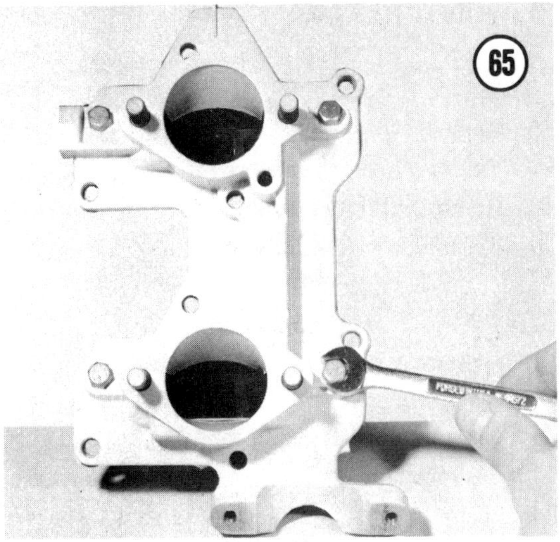

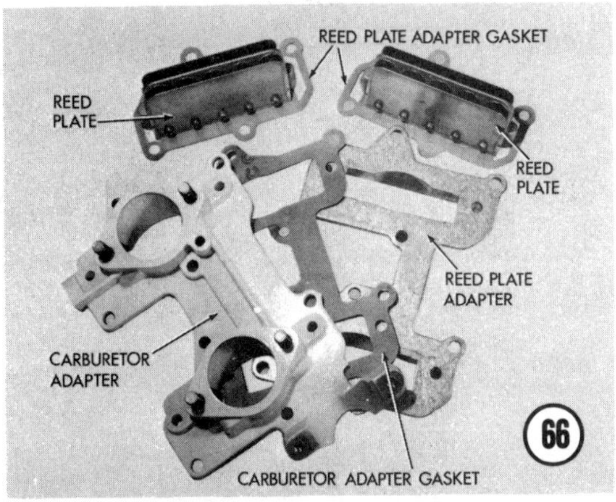

Reed Removal/Installation

1. Remove carburetor adapter assembly.
2. Remove 5 screws and lockwashers securing reed stop and reeds to each side of plate.
3. Install reed, reed stop, and 5 screws and lockwashers on each side of reed plates. Reed plate assembly must meet specifications shown in **Figure 67**.
4. Bend reeds and stops until they are within specifications. There must not be sharp angles or kinks in reeds or stops.
5. Install carburetor adapter assembly.

Upper Crankshaft Bearing Removal/Installation

1. Remove flywheel as described earlier.
2. Remove C-D module.

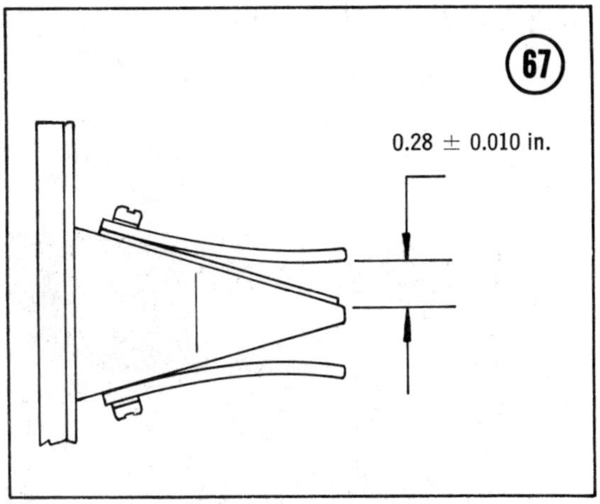

3. Remove alternator stator module.
4. Remove capacitor module.
5. Remove regulator-rectifier module.
6. Remove timing ring.
7. Remove trigger module assembly.
8. Remove 2 screws securing crankshaft bearing cage to cylinder. Remove bearing cage and gasket.
9. Installation is the reverse of these steps. Apply grease between lips of seal.

POWER HEAD

Removal

1. Remove port and starboard support plates.
2. Remove inlet fuel line from sediment bowl.
3. Remove cotter pin, plain washer, and gearshift pin securing upper gearshift rod to gearshift pivot.
4. Remove 8 stop nuts securing power head to motor leg as shown in **Figure 68** and one stop nut securing power head to spacer plate. Lift power head from spacer plate.
5. Remove cylinder exhaust gasket.

Installation

1. Clean gasket surfaces of cylinder and spacer plate.
2. Install new gasket on spacer plate. Apply anti-seize compound to splines on drive shaft. Install power head and secure to spacer plate and motor leg with stop nuts.

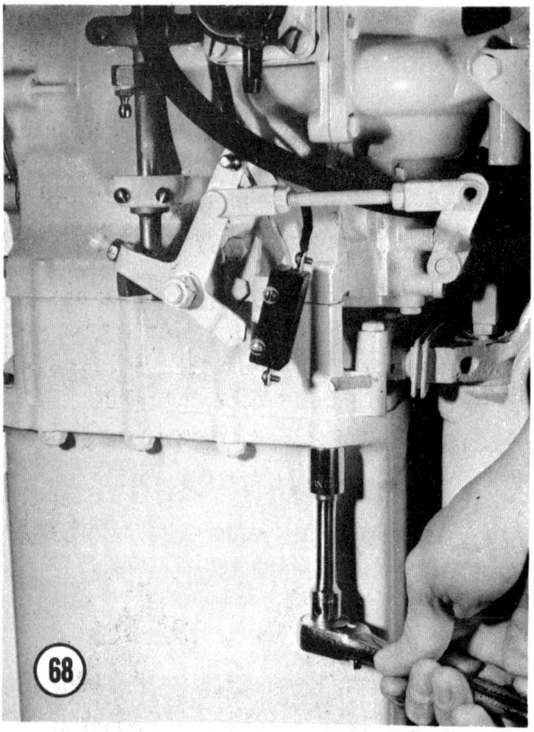

3. Install gearshift pin through coupler on upper gearshift rod and gearshift pivot. Secure with plain washer and cotter pin. See **Figure 69**.

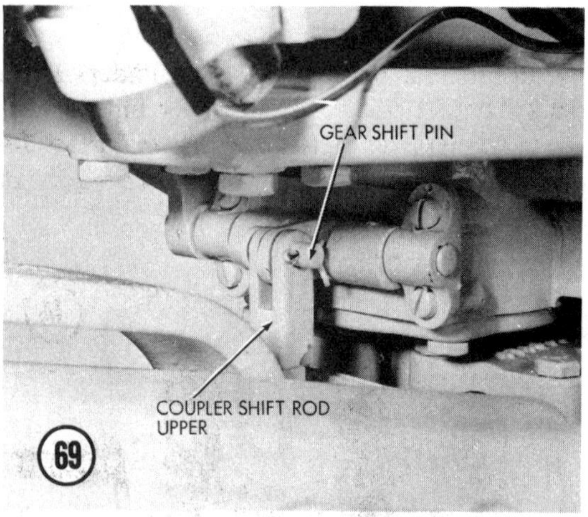

4. Connect the fuel line to fitting on the fuel sediment bowl.
5. Install port and starboard support plates.

Short Block Removal/Installation

1. Remove port and startboard support plates.
2. Remove crankshaft bearing cage.
3. Remove carburetor adapter.
4. Remove starter motor.
5. Remove circuit breaker.
6. Remove starter relay.
7. Remove exhaust port cover.
8. Remove cylinder head.
9. Remove tower shaft.
10. Remove gearshift arm.
11. Remove interlock switch bracket.
12. Remove the fuel pump as outlined under *Fuel System*.
13. Remove remote cable bracket.
14. Remove front stabilizer.
15. Remove gearshift lever assembly.
16. Remove power head.

Lower Crankshaft Bearing Removal

1. Remove short block.
2. Remove 6 main bearing bolts and 8 crankcase parting line screws.
3. Drive out 2 dowel pins positioning crankcase cover on cylinders as shown in **Figure 70**.

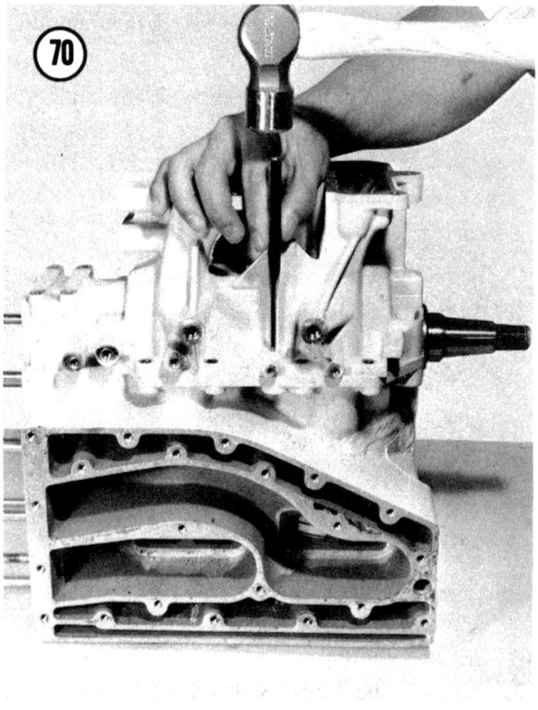

4. Remove screws securing lower crankshaft bearing to cylinder and crankcase as shown in **Figure 71**.

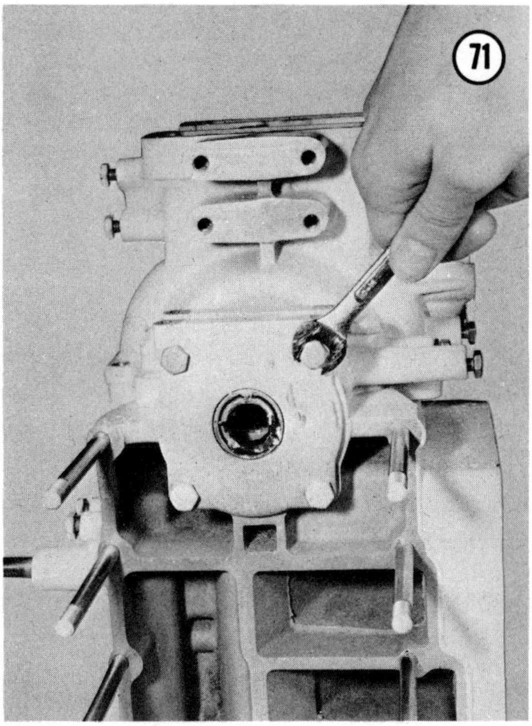

5. Pry crankcase cover from cylinder with a large screwdriver at each pry point as shown in **Figure 72**. Lift crankcase cover from cylinder.

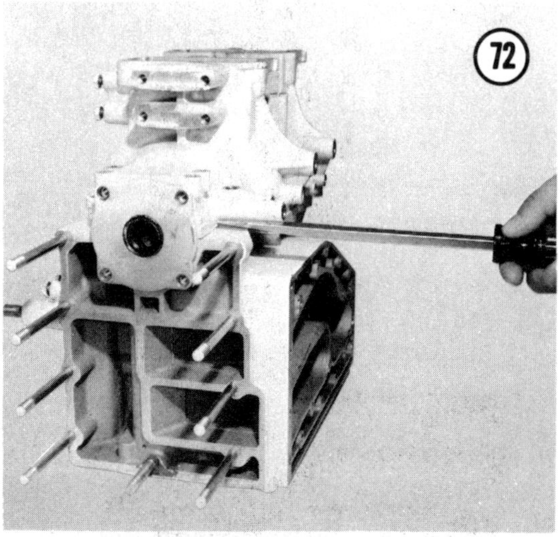

6. Remove crankcase partling line seal from groove in cylinder.

7. Remove the lower crankshaft bearing cage with seals.

8. Remove O-ring seal from outer diameter of bearing cage.

Lower Crankshaft Bearing Installation

1. Install O-ring seal in channel at upper end of bearing cage.

2. Apply grease between lips of seals and install bearing cage on crankshaft.

3. Clean crankcase parting line surface and install new crankcase parting line seal in grooves of cylinder.

4. Scrape old Loctite off outer diameter of lower main bearing. Clean bearing surface with Locquic. Apply a bead of Loctite retaining compound around outer surface of bearing.

5. Apply sealant to areas shown in **Figure 73**.

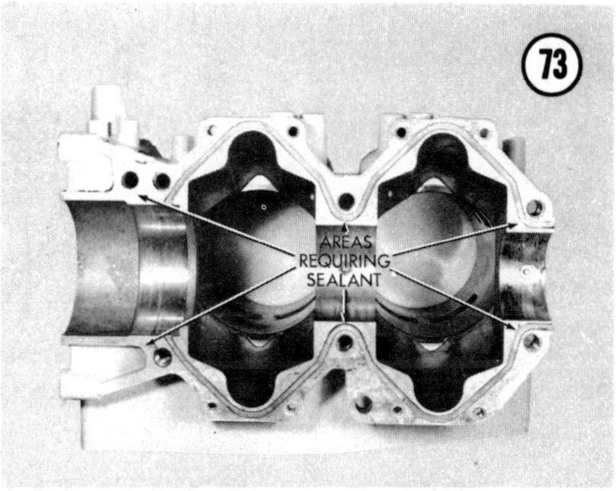

6. Install crankcase cover on cylinder. Drive in 2 locating pins to locate cover on cylinder. Install crankcase bolts as shown in **Figure 74**. Torque bolts to 270 in.-lb. from the center of crankcase and outward.

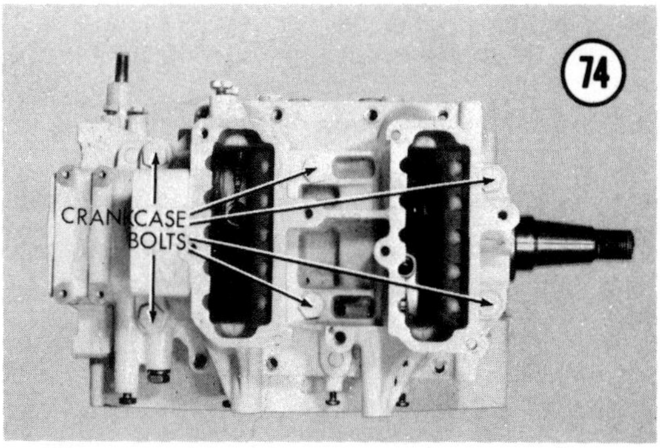

7. Apply anti-seize compound to threads of lower crankshaft bearing screws. Install screws and tighten securely.

8. Install short block.

5

Crankshaft Removal

1. Remove short block.
2. Remove lower crankshaft bearing.
3. Remove connecting rod cap screws using 12-point socket as shown in **Figure 75**. Mark each rod cap showing position in cylinder as rod caps are removed.

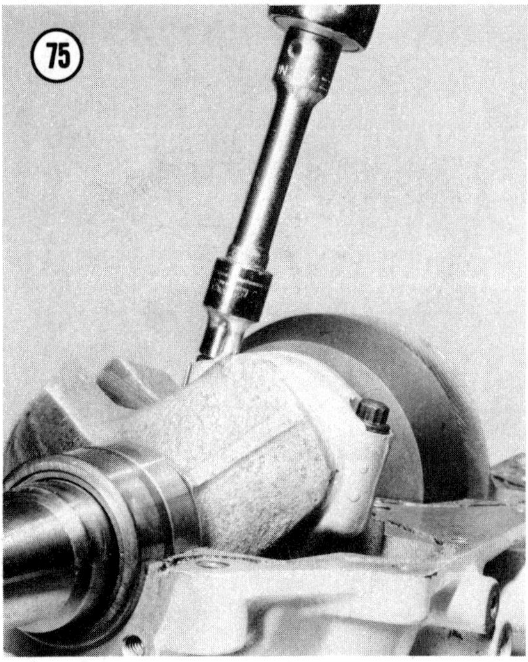

4. Remove crankpin needle bearings and cages from crankshaft throws.

> NOTE: *Be sure to group rollers and cages with respective rod cap. Do not mix needles and/or cages of one rod cap with another.*

5. Lift crankshaft with main bearings from cylinder.
6. Remove snap ring from groove in main bearings as shown in **Figure 76**. Remove center main bearing race and caged rollers. Remove crankcase seal from groove in crankshaft next to main bearing.
7. Slide upper main bearing off top end of crankshaft.

Crankshaft Installation

1. Install upper main bearing on upper end of crankshaft.

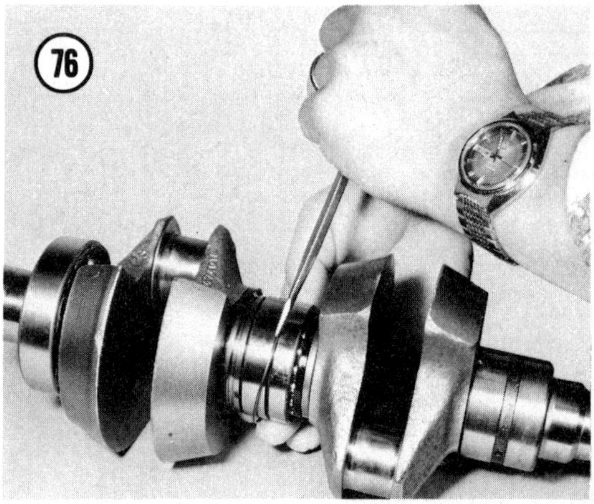

2. Install center main bearing on crankshaft with holes in bearing race down toward bottom of crankshaft. Secure race on crankshaft with snap ring. Do not have gap of snap ring over fracture in main bearing race.
3. Apply grease to crankcase seal groove in crankshaft to retain seal in groove. Install crankcase seal in groove in crankshaft.
4. Scrape old Loctite off outer diameter of lower main bearing. Clean bearing surface with Locquic. Apply a bead of Loctite retaining compound around outer surface of bearing.
5. Install crankshaft assembly on cylinder. Align hole in upper main bearing with locating pin in cylinder bearing bore. Align hole in center main bearing with locating pin in cylinder bearing bore.
6. Install crankpin needle bearing cage half in connecting rod. Apply a light coating of grease on cage half. Install 7 needles in cage half. Pull rod with cage half and needles up and against crankpin throw. Install crankpin needle bearing cage half on crankpin throw. Apply a light coating of grease on cage half. Install the remaining 9 needles.
7. Install rod cap over crankpin needle bearings and cage. Match mark on rod shank with mark on rod cap as shown in **Figure 77**. If connecting rod has a sanded surface across fracture joint on screw bosses, torque rod cap screw to 10 in.-lb. maximum. Check for rod cap offset by lightly running a sharp lead pencil across sanded area. If offset is present, pencil will stop at fracture joint. Loosen rod cap screws. Reset rod cap on

connecting rod and torque rod cap screws to 10 in.-lb. Check again for offset. If offset is still present, replace connecting rod.

8. Torque cap screws to 275 ± 5 in.-lb. using torque wrench and 12-point socket.

9. Follow Steps 6 through 8 for remaining connecting rod.

10. Install lower crankshaft bearing.

11. Install short block.

Connecting Rod/Piston Removal/Installation

1. Remove crankshaft assembly.

2. Push piston assembly out of cylinder bore.

3. Install piston assembly in cylinder using ring compressor as shown in **Figure 78**. Position piston in cylinder with intake baffle on piston on intake side of cylinder.

4. Perform crankshaft assembly.

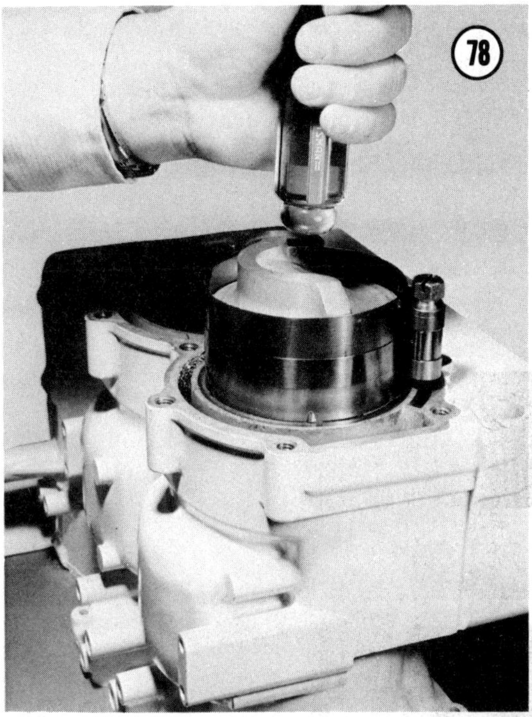

5

Table 1 ENGINE SPECIFICATIONS (60 HP)

Horsepower, BIA rated @	5,250 rpm
Recommended operating range	5,000-5,500 rpm
Engine—two cycle	Two cylinder
Bore and stroke	3⅜ x 2.8 in.
Cubic inch displacement	49.90 cu. in.
Cooling	Water cooled displacement type water pump
Propeller—standard	Aluminum alloy, 11 in. dia. x 13 in. pitch, right-hand rotation
Electric system	12 volt—negative ground
Alternator—output maximum	10 amps at 5,000 rpm, alternator cut in speed 1,000 rpm
Compression—average psi	150-160 psi
*Oil ratio per gallon of gas (break-in)	1/3 pint
Oil ratio per gallon of gas (after break-in)	1/6 pint

***Important**—When pistons, piston rings, piston pins, connecting rods, connecting rod bearings, crankshaft and crankshaft bearings are replaced, the break-in oil ratio and procedure for new engines must be used.

Table 2 TORQUE SPECIFICATIONS (60 HP)

Special Items		Standard Hardware	
Description	**Torque**	**Screw Size**	**Torque**
*Cylinder head	225 in.-lb.	10-24	30 in.-lb.
Flywheel	90 ft.-lb.	10-32	25 in.-lb.
Main bearing bolts	270 in.-lb.	12-24	45 in.-lb.
Connecting rod screws	270-280 in. lb.		
Gear housing plugs	90-115 in.-lb.	1/4-20	70 in.-lb.
Stern bracket pivot bolt	120 in.-lb.	5/16-18	160 in.-lb.
Spark plugs	120-180 in.-lb.		
King pin nut	50 ft.-lb.	3/8-16	270 in.-lb.

*Torque from center out. Re-torque after run-in when engine has cooled.

CHAPTER SIX

OUTBOARD MOTORS (70 TO 135 HP)

This chapter covers the repair and disassembly of 70, 75, 85, 90, 105, 120, 130, and 135 hp outboard motors. **Table 1** provides general specifications. **Table 2** provides tightening torque for fasteners. Both tables appear at the end of the chapter.

TUNE-UP

Checking Compression

Engine must be cool before performing this procedure.

1. Remove spark plugs from cylinder head.
2. Set throttle control at wide open throttle.
3. Connect compression gauge following the manufacturer's instructions.
4. Check compression of each cylinder. Each cylinder should be within specifications as listed in Table 1.

NOTE: *Add 5 pounds to compression range of engine tested with 15 hours or more running time.*

Torquing Cylinder Head

Loosen each bolt slightly, then tighten or torque bolt to the following specifications. Follow the sequence in **Figure 1**.

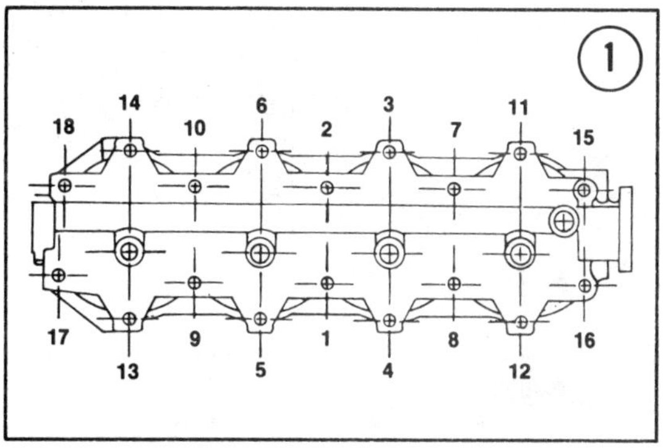

a. For engines with 3/8 in. head bolt, torque bolt to 270 ± 5 in.-lb.
b. For engines with 5/16 in. bolt, torque bolt to 225 ± 5 in.-lb.
c. For 120 hp and 130 hp, torque bolt to 225 ± 5 in.-lb.
d. For 135 hp with 3/8-16 studs, torque the nuts to 270 ± 5 in.-lb.
e. For 135 hp and 150 hp with 5/16-18 studs, torque nuts to 225 ± 5 in.-lb.

CAUTION
Do not over torque cylinder head bolts; cylinder bores or cylinder head may distort. Do not under torque or cylinder gasket may leak.

Spark Plugs

1. Remove spark plugs with 13/16 in. box-end wrench or socket.
2. Inspect plugs for condition. Clean or replace plugs if necessary.
3. Reinstall plugs and torque to 120-180 in.-lb.

Breaker Points

1. Disconnect battery leads from battery.
2. Remove distributor cap by loosening screws on cap retaining clips as shown in **Figure 2**.

3. Remove screws securing distributor to power head as shown in **Figure 3**. Slip off distributor belt and remove distributor.
4. Inspect breaker point contact surfaces visually. If they are burnt or pitted, they should be replaced. Do not file breaker points. Replace with new parts.
5. Set breaker points with feeler gauge to these specifications:
    a. 0.014 in. for 3-cylinder engines
    b. 0.010 in. for 4-cylinder engines

When setting breaker point gap, be certain follower arm of breaker point is on high point of one of the lobes on rotor shaft.

6. After setting breaker point gap, clean the breaker point contacts to remove any oily film

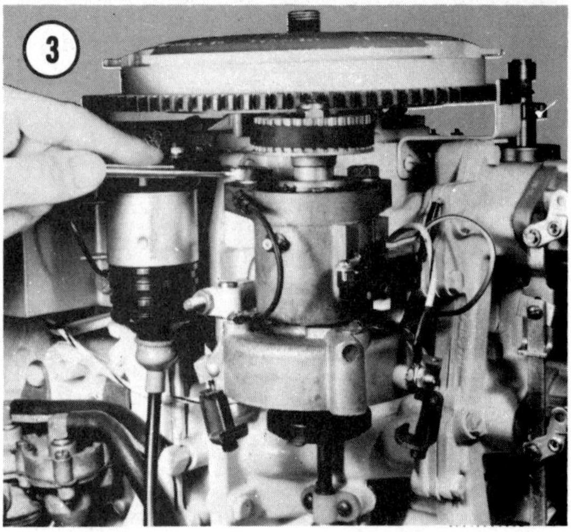

which may have been left by the feeler gauge. Insert a clean piece of hard surface cardboard between the contact surfaces and hold the points closed on the carboard. Rotate the cardboard using the points as a pivot. The cardboard should be used in several spots until no oily spots can be seen.

7. Install distributor cap on distributor housing by aligning locating pin in distributor housing with hole in distributor cap. Secure distributor cap to housing as shown in Figure 2.
8. Install distributor housing on power head as shown in Figure 3. Do not tighten screws at this time.
9. Time engine as described below.

Timing Engine

1. Disconnect battery leads from battery.
2. Remove all spark plugs from cylinder head.
3. Install barrel of timing tool (Special Tool T2937-1) in top cylinder spark plug hole. Screw barrel completely in spark plug hole.
4. Insert rod portion (Special Tool T2937A) of timing tool in barrel with marks identified as 70 HP AND UP toward the outside.
5. Holding the rod tight against the piston, rotate crankshaft in direction of engine rotation and locate top dead center (point at which piston is closest to cylinder head or point at which marks on rod extend furthest away from barrel). See **Figure 4**. Screw barrel of the timing tool in or out as required until inside line of the timing

4

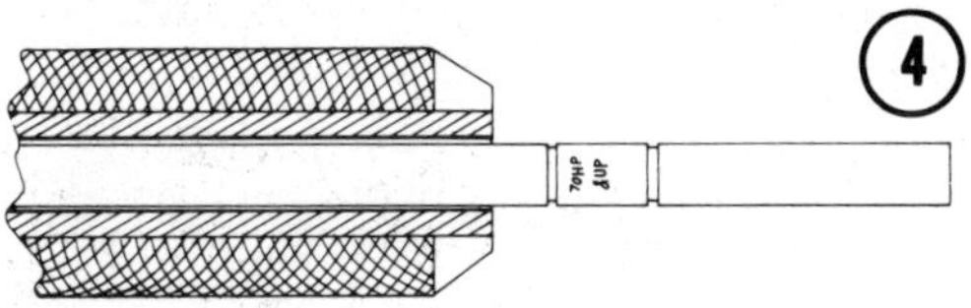

Establishing top dead center

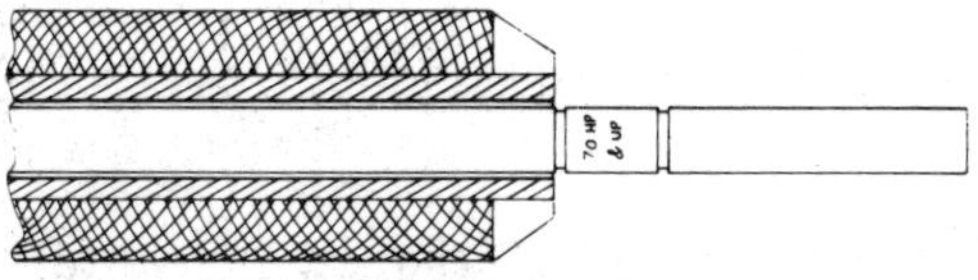

Aligning barrel of tool with mark on rod

rod lines up with edge of barrel as shown in Figure 4.

6. Apply slight pressure to end of rod with finger and turn crankshaft clockwise in direction of engine rotation until outer line of rod lines up with edge of barrel as shown in **Figure 5**. The piston is now positioned at 36° before top dead center.

5

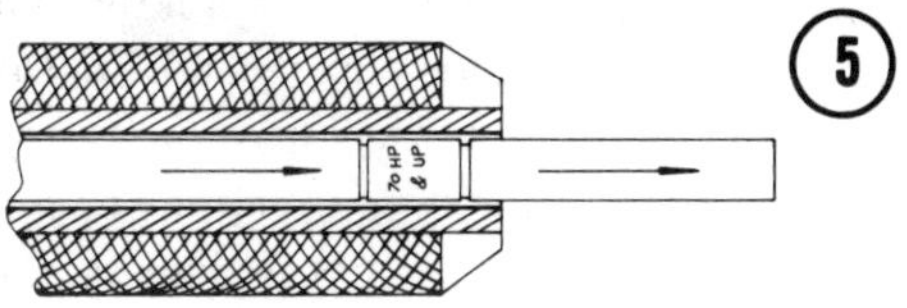

Approaching 36° before top dead center

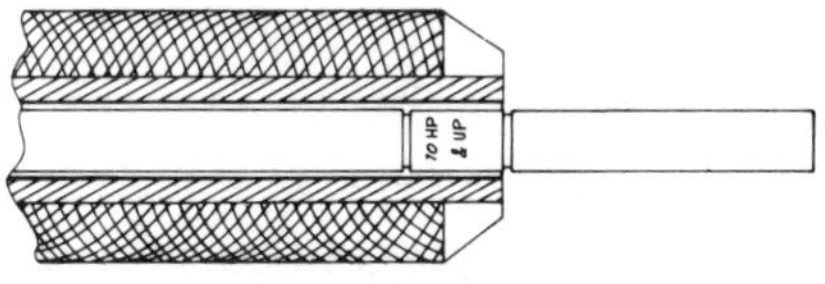

36° before top dead center

NOTE: *Rod will go completely in barrel of timing tool. Continue to hold finger over hole in barrel until rod comes back out. If finger is removed, rod will shoot out of barrel on compression stroke of piston. As rod comes out of barrel, periodically check to find location of outer line in relationship to end of barrel; if outer line goes beyond edge of barrel engine must be rotated clockwise again.*

7. The 36° mark on flywheel and the index line (I) on the timing pointer must align with each other; if not, shift timing point by loosening the 2 screws securing pointer to power head and align these 2 points.

8. Turn flywheel to align 0° mark on flywheel with pointer index line (I). Turn distributor pulley to match the index mark on distributor pulley with outside diameter of flywheel. See **Figure 6**. When the mark on the distributor pulley aligns with the outside diameter of flywheel, install distributor belt over pulley and adjust distributor to obtain a slight belt deflection (¼ in. with one pound force exerted). Tighten screws securing distributor bracket to power head as shown in Figure 3.

6

One method of adjusting distributor belt tension is to use a 0.008 in. thickness feeler gauge. Position tip of feeler gauge against middle of belt length and push against belt until feeler gauge bends with no further movement of belt. Belt should deflect from 3/16 in. to ¼ in. for proper tension. Belt should not deflect more than ¼ in. or it will be too loose and variation of timing may occur. Belt should not deflect less than 3/16 in. or it may cause tower shaft linkage to bind or excessively wear on tower shaft bearings. See **Figure 7**.

9. Remove throttle link from tower shaft. Set tower shaft at wide open throttle (nylon stop of middle tower shaft arm against crankcase cover).

10. Turn flywheel clockwise (same as engine rotation) to line up 36° mark on flywheel with

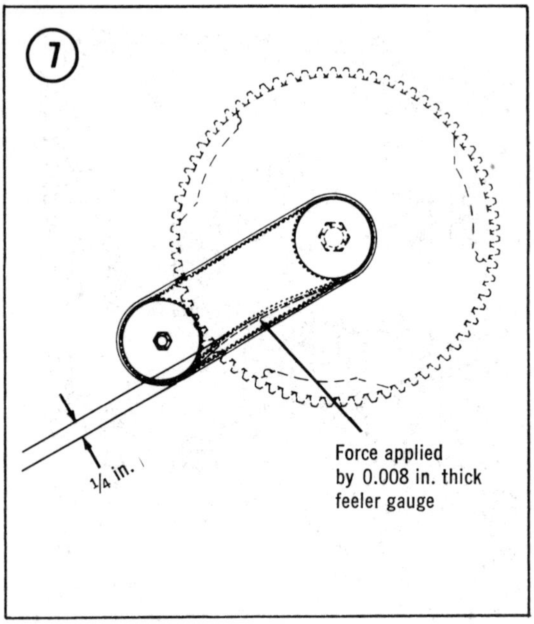

the appropriate mark on timing pointer as follows:

a. —4 mark (32° before top dead center) for all 3-cylinder engines and 105 hp. See **Figure 8**.

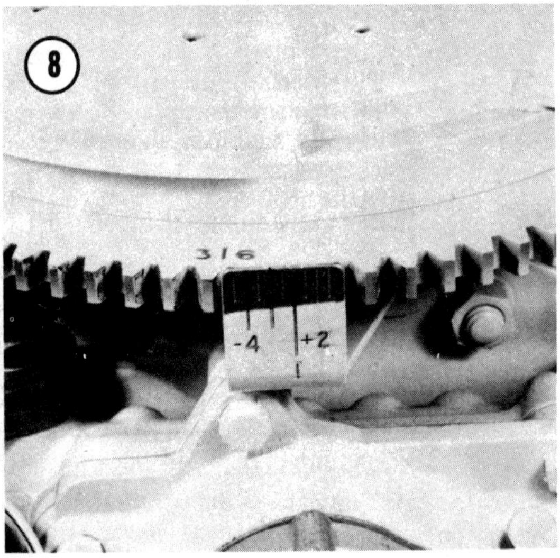

b. —2 mark (second mark to left of index mark (I) or 34° BTDC) for 120 and 130 hp. See Figure 8.

c. —6 mark (sixth mark to left of index mark (I) or 30° BTDC) for 135 and 150 hp. See Figure 8.

11. Connect leads of test light (Special Tool T2938-1 or equivalent) to distributor primary lead wire post and to ground (ground post on coil) as shown in **Figure 9**.

12. Loosen locknut on distributor control rod. If test light is on, turn distributor control rod counterclockwise until light just goes off or dims. If test light is off, turn distributor control rod clockwise until light just comes on. Check for proper adjustment by pushing lightly on distributor belt. Light should go on and off with each push.

> NOTE: *Distance between the nylon swivels should be between 3/8 and 1/2 inch when timing is properly adjusted. If it is more or less than specification, check the following:*

a. Flywheel turned to align 36° mark on flywheel and pointer from wrong direction (counterclockwise instead of clockwise).

b. Breaker point gap not within specifications.

c. Distributor belt not properly installed on distributor pulley (belt installed on distributor pulley when flywheel was not at top dead center). See Steps 4 through 9.

13. While holding the distributor control rod, tighten locknut to secure rod in position.

Neutral Interlock Switch Adjustment

1. Shift engine to NEUTRAL.
2. Advance tower shaft to neutral stop arm as shown in **Figure 10**.

3. Connect leads of test light (Special Tool T2938-1 or equivalent) to neutral interlock switch as shown in **Figure 11**.
4. Loosen screws securing switch cam to distributor housing.
5. Shift cam upward until test light just comes on.
6. Tighten screws on cam to secure position.

Neutral Interlock Switch Cam (Shift Arm) Adjustment

1. Shift engine to NEUTRAL.
2. Advance tower shaft to neutral stop as shown in Figure 10.
3. Connect the leads of test light (Special Tool T29384) to neutral interlock switch as shown in **Figure 12**.
4. Loosen screws securing switch cam to shift arm.

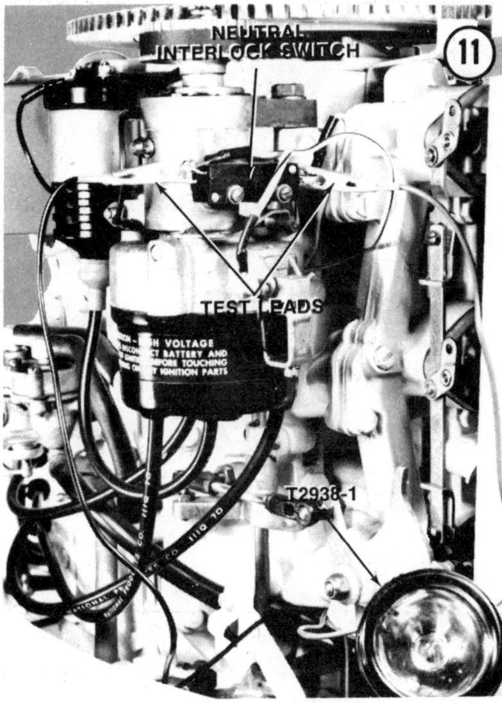

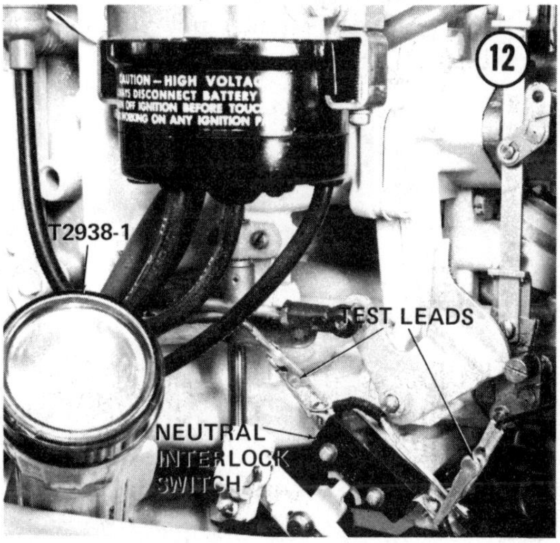

5. Slide cam upward until test light just comes on.
6. Tighten screws on cam to secure position.

Synchronizing Throttle Shutters (3-Cylinder Engines)

1. Snap throttle link off tower shaft and pivot throttle cam away from throttle roller on carburetor.

6

2. Loosen the throttle tie bar screws as shown in **Figure 13**.
3. Make sure that throttle shutters are closed.
4. Tighten throttle tie bar screws. See Figure 13.
5. Snap throttle link on tower shaft.
6. Set engine at wide open throttle and check throttle shutters to see if they are horizontal. Adjust link between throttle cam and tower shaft if necessary.

13

Synchronizing Throttle Shutters (4-Cylinder Engines)

1. Snap throttle link off tower shaft and pivot throttle cam away from throttle roller on carburetor.
2. Remove retaining ring securing throttle tie bar to top carburetor throttle arm.
3. Loosen throttle tie bar screws as shown in **Figure 14**.
4. Make sure that throttle shutters are closed.
5. Tighten throttle tie bar screws (see Figure 14) and check to see that throttle tie bar end pivot goes in and out of throttle arm of carburetor freely.

14

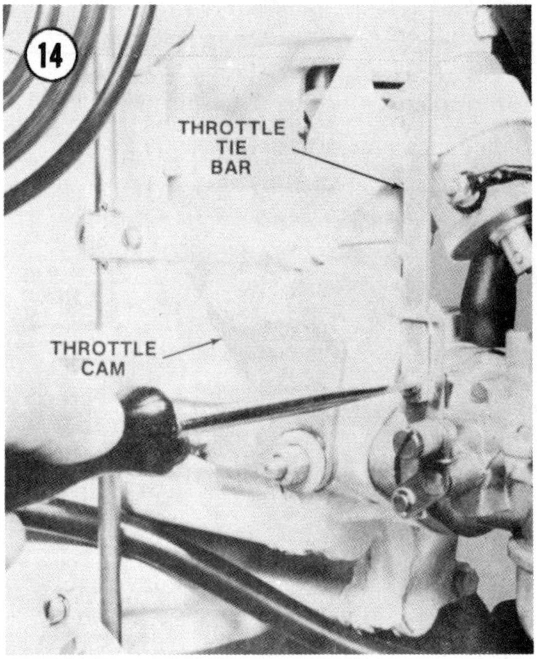

6. Install retaining ring to secure throttle tie bar to top carburetor throttle arm.
7. Snap throttle link on tower shaft.

Throttle Pickup Adjustment

1. Disconnect throttle link at tower shaft.
2. Adjust throttle roller shaft by loosening stop nut. Turn shaft until throttle roller just contacts the throttle cam at index line as shown in **Figure 15**.
3. Tighten stop nut.
4. Install throttle link on tower shaft.
5. Move tower shaft to wide open throttle stop.
6. Loosen jam nuts on throttle link between tower shaft and throttle cam.
7. Adjust throttle link until throttle shutters are horizontal.
8. Tighten jam nuts on throttle link to secure throttle link position.

Carburetor Adjustment

1. Turn idle adjustment screw clockwise until it seats in the carburetor.

CAUTION

Do not force idle adjustment screw or the tip will be damaged.

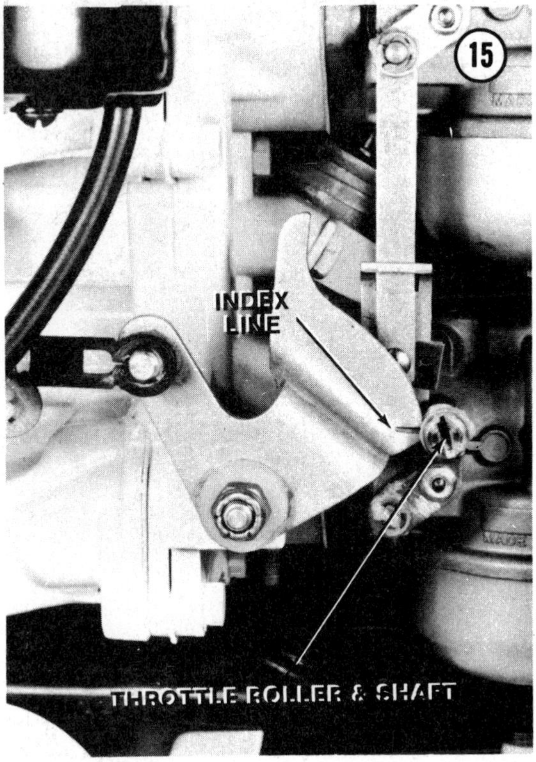

2. Open the idle adjustment screw one turn counterclockwise.

3. Shift engine to NEUTRAL and start motor. Allow the engine to warm up to operating temperature.

4. Shift engine to FORWARD. Throttle engine back to lowest reliable throttle setting.

5. Turn idle adjustment screw on carburetor clockwise ⅛ turn pausing at least 10 seconds between each adjustment until the engine begins to "pop" from the lean fuel/air setting. Note the position of screwdriver slot on the idle adjustment screw.

6. Turn idle adjustment screw counterclockwise to original position. Turn idle adjustment screw counterclockwise ⅛ turn at a time pausing at least 10 seconds between each adjustment until the engine begins to "roll or gallop" from the rich fuel/air setting. Note idle adjustment screw setting.

7. Turn idle adjustment screw to midpoint between the settings noted in Steps 5 and 6.

8. After top and middle carburetors have been adjusted, turn engine off. Turn each idle adjustment needle clockwise until it seats in carburetor noting number of turns on each carburetor. Average the 2 carburetors and set all 3 carburetors at this average. For example: Top carburetor is set at ⅞ turn and middle carburetor at ⅝ turn. Set all 3 carburetors at ¾ turn.

9. Adjust idle stop screw on tower shaft as necessary until engine idles between 700-900 rpm's in NEUTRAL gear.

Synchronizing Choke Shutters (4-Cylinder Engines)

1. Loosen screws on both choke swivels freeing choke link.

2. Position top end of link approximately 1/16 to ⅛ in. beyond top of top carburetor choke swivel. Tighten screw to secure link in swivel.

3. Close top and bottom carburetor choke shutters fully. Tighten bottom carburetor choke swivel screw to secure link to swivel.

4. Loosen 2 screws securing choke solenoid just enough so that solenoid can move easily.

5. Slip a piece of paper approximately ½ in. wide in both carburetor air horns.

> NOTE: *The paper insures proper clearance between choke shutter and carburetor air horn to prevent shutters from sticking in the closed position.*

6. With pieces of paper in air horns of carburetors, close choke shutters fully against the pieces of paper by pushing only on choke solenoid plunger as shown in **Figure 16**.

7. While holding choke shutters closed by the choke plunger, slide choke solenoid against plunger. Tighten screws to secure choke solenoid in position.

8. Release choke solenoid plunger and push plunger back in solenoid. Pull paper out of carburetor air horns; paper must slide out of carburetor easily or with a slight drag. If not, adjust solenoid position as outlined in Step 7.

9. Release choke solenoid plunger and check to see that choke shutters are horizontal. If they are not, bend groove pin (shutter stop) in air horn of carburetor.

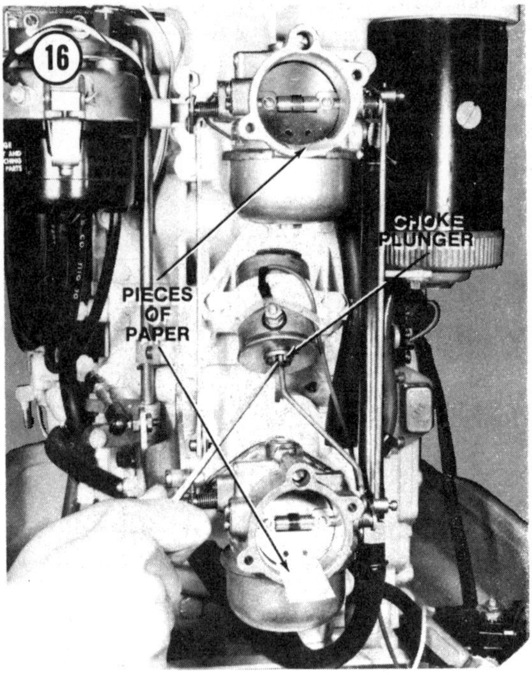

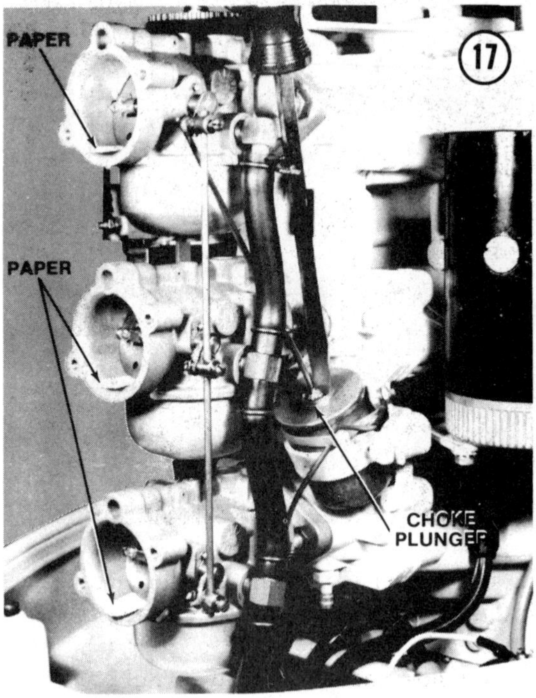

Synchronizing Choke Shutters (3-Cylinder Engine)

1. Remove carburetor intake cover.

2. Loosen screws on choke swivels freeing choke link.

3. Position top end of link approximately 1/16 to ⅛ in. beyond top of top carburetor choke swivel. Tighten screw to secure link in swivel.

4. Close top and middle carburetor choke shutters fully. Tighten middle carburetor choke swivel screw to secure link to swivel. Use same procedure for bottom carburetor choke shutter.

5. Loosen screws securing choke solenoid just enough so that solenoid can move easily.

6. Slip a piece of paper approximately ½ in. wide in both carburetor air horns.

> NOTE: *The paper insures proper clearance between choke shutter and carburetor air horn to prevent shutters from sticking in the closed position.*

7. With pieces of paper in air horns of carburetors, close choke shutters fully against the pieces of paper by pushing only on choke solenoid plunger as shown in **Figure 17**.

8. While holding choke shutters closed by the choke plunger, slide choke solenoid against plunger. Tighten screws to secure choke solenoid in position.

9. Release choke solenoid plunger and push plunger back in solenoid. Pull paper out of carburetor air horns; paper must slide out of carburetor easily or with a slight drag. If not, adjust solenoid position as outlined in Step 7.

10. Release choke solenoid plunger and check to see that choke shutters are horizontal. If they are not, bend groove pin (shutter stop) in air horn of carburetor.

Checking Lower Unit Grease

1. With engine vertical (running position), remove plug from grease FILL hole of lower gear housing. See **Figure 18**. Allow a small amount of grease to flow from FILL hole.

> NOTE: *Do not check gear housing grease immediately after running the engine. Allow engine to stand in the running position for at least 2 hours before checking gear grease. If water is present in lower unit, this time will allow water to settle down to the bottom of lower unit.*

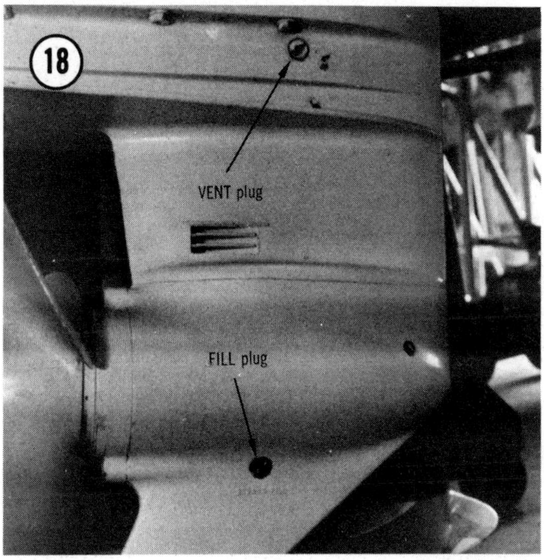

2. If no water is present, turn FILL plug back in 2 turns. Remove VENT plug, then remove FILL plug. Quickly insert nozzle of gear lube tube in FILL hole and add gear lube until it appears at VENT hole. Reinstall VENT plug and nyltite washer. Remove nozzle of gear lube tube and install FILL plug and nyltite washer.

3. If water is present, take motor to your dealer. Have him pressure test lower unit to determine where water leakage occurs.

ELECTRICAL TROUBLESHOOTING

A 12-volt test light is a very simple and accurate device for testing the entire electrical circuit of battery ignition engines and the starter and choke circuits of magneto ignition electric start engines. One lead of the test light must be connected to ground at all times, unless otherwise specified. If the other lead is linked to a hot circuit, the light will light up unless the circuit is grounded within itself.

The following tests require that the battery be fully charged and the battery cables have a good connection to the battery. It is assumed that all engine wiring and remote electric harness wiring is connected and correct.

Circuit Breaker

Place the probe of the 12-volt test light on each terminal of the circuit breaker, as shown in **Figure 19**. A light should appear at each terminal. If a light appears at only one terminal, the circuit breaker is defective. If the circuit breaker clicks continuously, it indicates a short circuit somewhere in the engine or remote electric harness wiring.

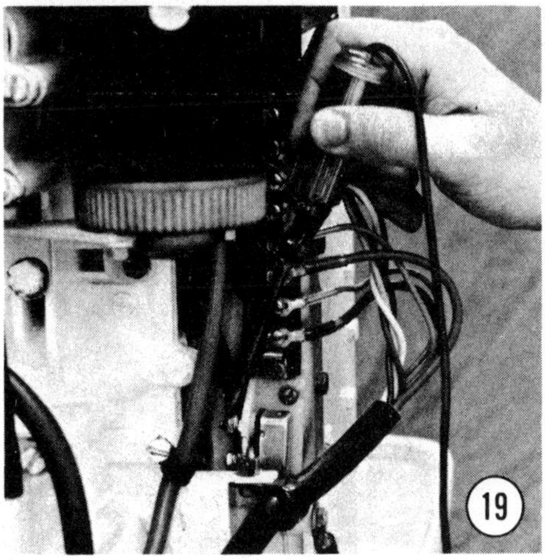

Checking for Short Circuits

Disconnect either battery lead and insert the test light in series between the battery lead and battery as shown in **Figure 20**. With the ignition OFF, there should be no light. A light indicates a short.

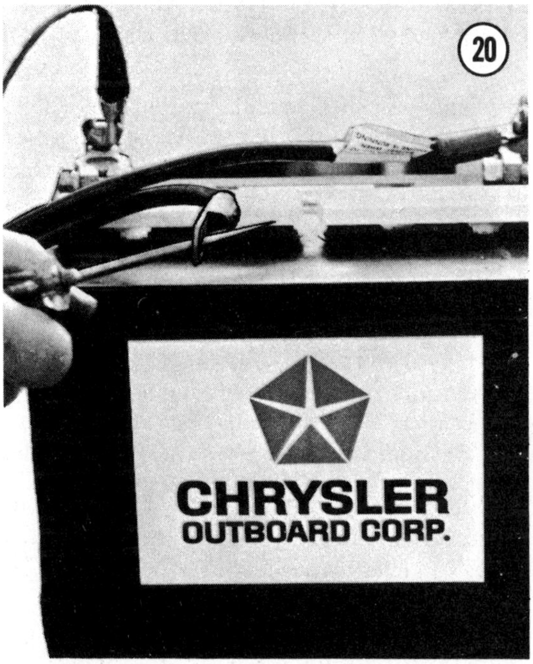

6

Choke Circuit

Make all tests with choke ON.

1. Check the choke solenoid terminal as shown in **Figure 21**. A light at this point indicates a defective choke solenoid, faulty or maladjusted mechanical linkage.

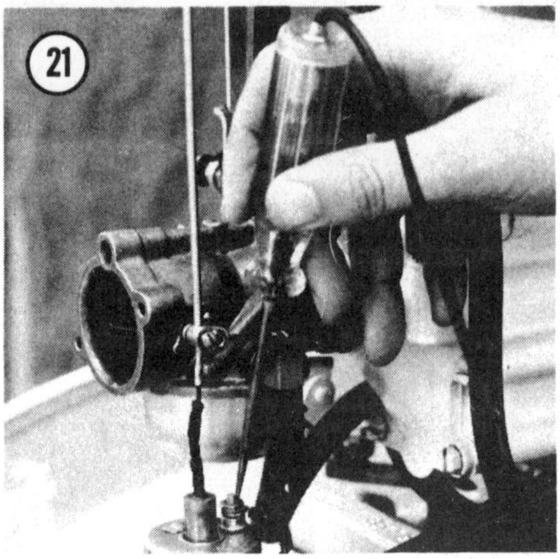

2. Check the green terminal on the terminal block as shown in **Figure 22**. A light indicates defective green lead wire or faulty connection between terminal plate and choke solenoid.

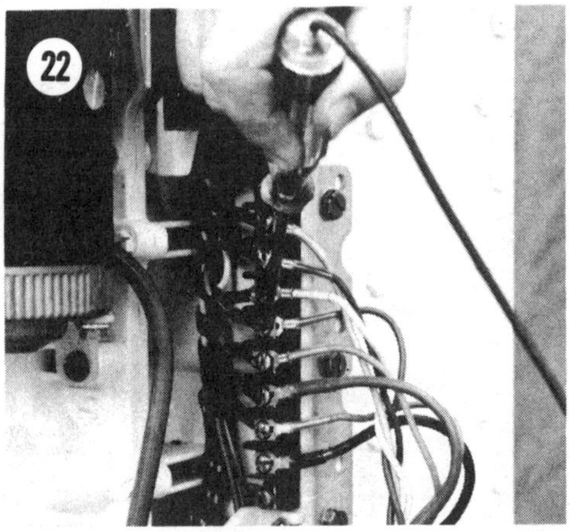

3. Test the "C" choke terminal of the ignition switch as shown in **Figure 23**. A light at this point indicates a faulty green lead wire in the remote electric harness.

4. Check the "B" battery terminal of the ignition switch. A light indicates a faulty ignition switch. No light indicates an open circuit from the battery.

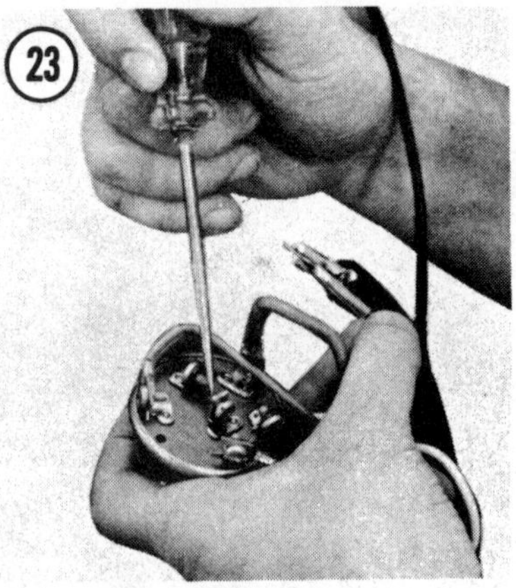

5. If a dim light is noted in any of the preceding tests, the circuit has a poor connection or is shorted.

Starter Circuit

All tests must be made with the ignition switch in the START position—the ignition key turned all the way to the right. If the 12-volt test light does not light during any step, go on to the next step.

1. Check the terminal of the starter motor as shown in **Figure 24**. A light indicates a faulty starter motor.

> NOTE: *A dim light at this point could indicate either poor circuit conditions or a faulty starter.*

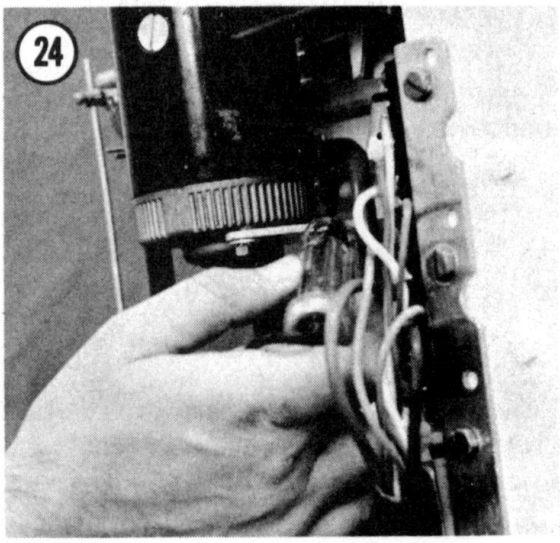

2. Check the small terminal of starter relay as shown in **Figure 25**. A light indicates a faulty starter relay, starter relay not grounded, or a faulty lead wire from relay to starter.

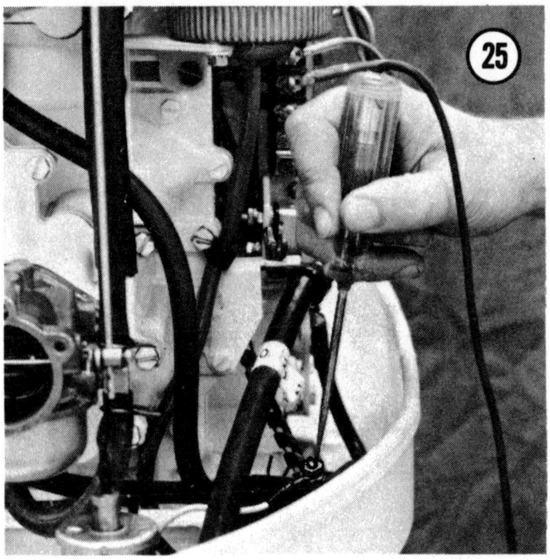

3. Test neutral interlock switch as shown in **Figure 26** (output side). A light indicates a faulty lead wire from interlock switch to starter relay.

4. Check input side of the neutral interlock switch. A light indicates gearshift not in NEUTRAL, interlock switch out of adjustment, or a faulty neutral interlock switch.

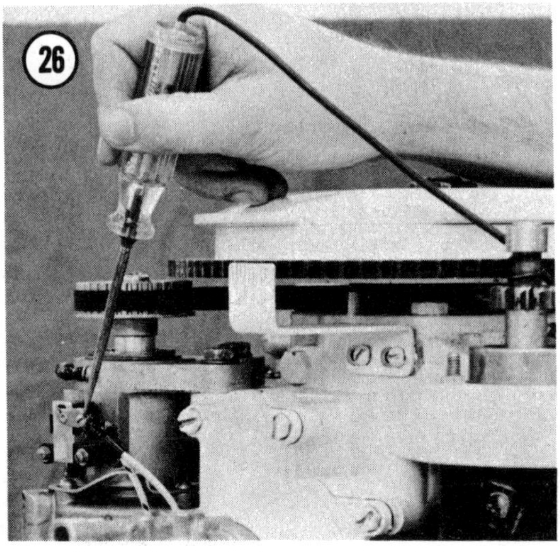

5. Place the probe of test light on yellow terminal of the engine terminal block as shown in **Figure 27**. A light indicates a faulty lead wire between the terminal block and the neutral interlock switch.

6. Check the "S" (starter) terminal of the ignition switch as shown in **Figure 28**. A light indicates a faulty yellow lead wire in remote electric harness.

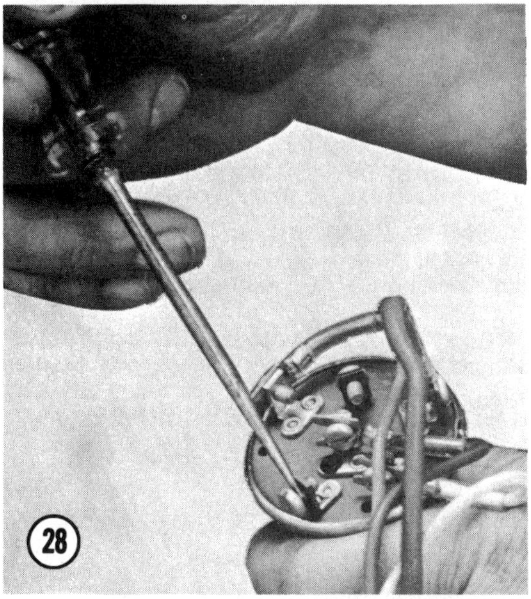

7. Test the "B" (battery) terminal of the ignition switch. A light indicates a faulty ignition switch. No light indicates an open circuit from battery.

8. If a dim light is noted in any of the preceding tests, the circuit has a poor connection or is shorted.

Magnapower C-D Unit

1. Turn ignition switch to ON and listen for high pitched singing noise from C-D unit. Tone should be smooth and steady.

NOTE: *Check that 12 volts DC is being supplied to BLUE WASHER terminal on C-D unit with test light. If no voltage is present, with ignition switch on* ON *position, the fault is in the engine electrical system rather than the C-D unit.*

2. Turn ignition switch OFF. Set engine controls at wide open throttle. Rotate flywheel until 36° mark on flywheel aligns with —4 mark on timing pointer. Connect test light between terminal on distributor and ground as shown in **Figure 29**. Test light should go on and off when distributor belt is depressed and released.

NOTE: *If circuit light will not go on and off, check the breaker point gap and engine timing. Refer to* Tune-Up *for procedure.*

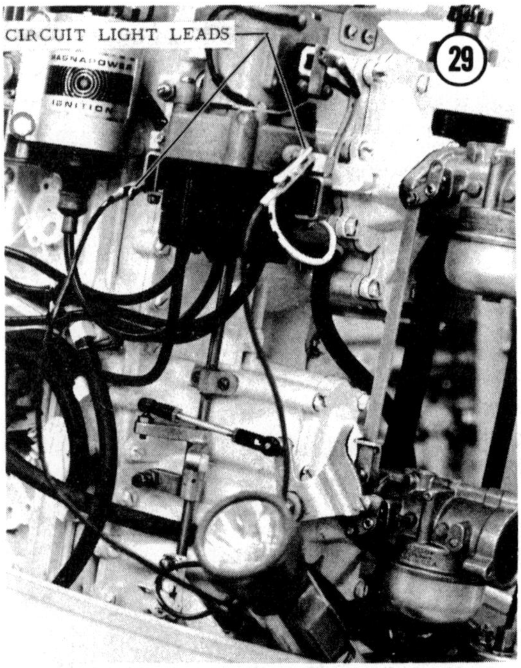

3. Turn ignition switch OFF. Remove test light leads from distributor. Remove top (No. 1) spark plug from cylinder.

WARNING
Use insulated tongs to hold spark plug.

4. Connect plug lead wire to No. 1 spark plug. Hold spark plug against unpainted portion of cylinder head next to spark plug hole. Turn ignition switch ON; depress and release distributor belt. Spark plug should fire momentarily when belt is depressed and released.

5. If no spark is observed in Step 2, replace the ignition coil.

6. If a continuous spark is observed in Step 2, replace C-D unit.

Magnapower Trip Regulator

Connect negative lead of test light to yellow washer terminal of trip regulator. Connect positive lead of test light to red washer terminal of trip regulator. The light should illuminate. If no light is observed, replace trip regulator.

FUEL SYSTEM (3-CYLINDER ENGINES)

Top Carburetor Removal

1. Remove carburetor intake with cover as shown in **Figure 30**. Also remove carburetor intake gaskets.

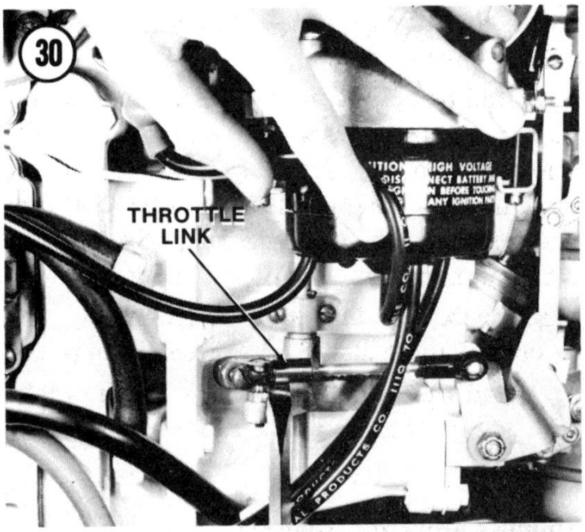

2. Remove retaining ring securing throttle tie bar to carburetor throttle arm. Remove tie bar end by removing screw securing end to tie bar.

3. Loosen each choke swivel screw and allow choke link to slide down.

4. Remove cotter pin securing choke swivel to choke lever arm of carburetor. Remove plain washer, choke rod, O-ring, and choke swivel from choke lever arm.

5. Using hose clamp pliers, slide hose clamp down and pull fuel hose from inlet fitting on carburetor.

6. Remove nuts securing carburetor to carburetor adapter flange.

7. Remove the carburetor inlet fitting from the carburetor.

Top Carburetor Installation

1. Apply sealant to threads of fuel inlet fitting. Install fitting on carburetor and position barb at 6 o'clock position.

2. Install carburetor on carburetor adapter flange and secure with nuts.

3. Install choke swivel through choke shutter arm with O-ring on choke swivel. Install another O-ring on choke swivel. Insert swivel into rod end of choke solenoid plunger assembly; install plain washer and secure swivel with cotter pin.

4. Slide choke rod up through choke swivel and secure with screw. Tighten other screws on choke swivel for both the middle and lower carburetors. Synchronize choke shutters as outlined under *Tune-up*.

5. Install tie bar end on throttle tie bar. Secure tie bar end to throttle tie bar with fillister head screw, but do not tighten. Position tie bar end pivot through bottom hole on throttle shaft arm and secure with retaining ring. Synchronize carburetor shutters as outlined under *Tune-up*.

6. Connect fuel line to inlet fuel fitting and secure with hose clamp using hose clamp pliers.

7. Install carburetor intake with cover. Make sure that gaskets are in place. See Figure 30.

Middle Carburetor Removal

1. Remove carburetor intake with cover.

2. Remove retaining ring securing throttle tie bar assembly on both top and middle carburetors. Swing tie bar assembly away to expose the nut securing carburetor to the carburetor adapter flange.

3. Loosen screw on choke swivel of each carburetor and remove choke rod.

4. Slide hose clamp from each barb on fuel inlet fitting and remove fuel hoses.

5. Remove nuts securing carburetor to carburetor adapter flange and remove carburetor.

6. Remove cotter pin securing choke swivel to choke lever arm of carburetor. Remove plain washer and O-ring and then remove choke swivel and other O-ring from choke lever arm.

7. Remove fuel inlet fitting from carburetor.

Middle Carburetor Installation

1. Apply sealant to threads of fuel inlet fitting. Install fitting on carburetor and position barbs at 12 o'clock and 6 o'clock position.

2. Install choke swivel with one O-ring on choke lever arm of carburetor. Install another O-ring, then washer and secure choke swivel to choke lever arm with cotter pin.

3. Install the carburetor onto the carburetor adapter flange.

4. Position throttle tie bar assembly aligning pivots with lower holes of throttle shaft arms of both top and middle carburetors. Secure pivots to throttle shaft arms with retaining rings. Synchronize carburetor shutters as outlined under *Tune-up*.

5. Connect fuel lines to inlet fuel fittings and secure with hose clamps.

6. Install choke rod through swivel of each carburetor and secure with fillister head screws. Synchronize choke shutters as outlined under *Tune-up*.

7. Install carburetor intake with cover. See Figure 30.

Bottom Carburetor Removal

1. Remove carburetor intake with cover.

2. Disconnect throttle link assembly from balljoint on tower shaft as shown in **Figure 31**.

3. Pivot throttle cam to expose fillister head screw securing throttle tie bar end to throttle tie bar. Remove screw. Remove retaining ring securing tie bar end pivot to throttle shaft arm, and remove tie bar end.

4. Loosen screw on choke swivel. Move swivel down to disconnect choke rod.

5. Slide hose clamps from barbs of inlet fuel fitting using hose clamp pliers and disconnect hoses from inlet fuel fitting.

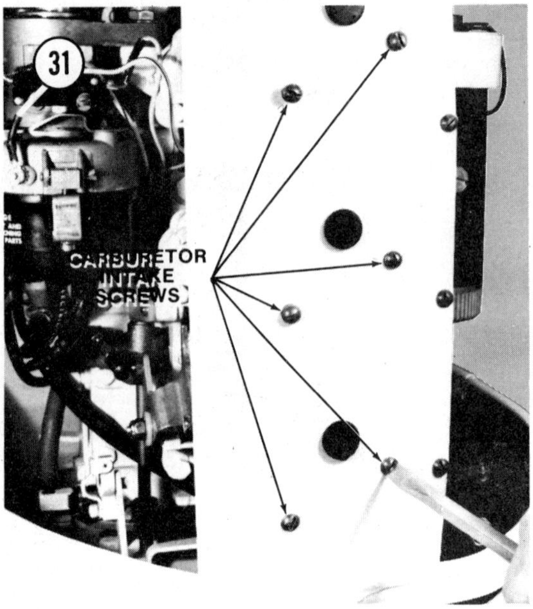

6. Remove nuts securing carburetor to carburetor adapter flange. Remove carburetor.

7. Remove cotter pin securing choke swivel to choke lever arm of carburetor. Remove plain washer, O-rings, and choke swivel from choke lever arm.

8. Remove shaft and roller from throttle shaft arm of carburetor by removing stop nut from roller shaft.

9. Remove carburetor inlet fuel fitting from carburetor.

Bottom Carburetor Installation

1. Apply sealant to threads of fuel inlet fitting. Install fitting on carburetor and position barbs at 12 o'clock and 6 o'clock position.

2. Install shaft and roller in top hole of throttle shaft arm. Secure roller shaft assembly to throttle shaft arm with hex stop nut, but do not tighten. Refer to *Tune-up* for adjustment of throttle pickup after completion of assembly.

3. Install choke swivel with one O-ring on choke swivel through choke shutter arm. Install another O-ring, plain washer, and secure assembly to choke lever arm with cotter pin.

4. Install carburetor on carburetor adapter flange.

5. Connect fuel lines to inlet fuel fittings. Secure fuel lines with hose clamps.

6. Connect choke rod to choke swivel and secure with screw. Synchronize choke shutters as outlined under *Tune-up*.

7. Install throttle tie bar end to throttle tie bar. Align pivot of tie bar end with bottom hole of throttle shaft arm of carburetor and secure pivot with retaining ring. Synchronize carburetor shutters as outlined under *Tune-up*.

8. Connect throttle link assembly to stud on tower shaft. See Figure 30.

9. Install carburetor intake with cover and gaskets. See Figure 31.

FUEL PUMPS

Two different fuel pumps are used. Refer to **Figures 32A and 32B** to determine which fuel pump you have.

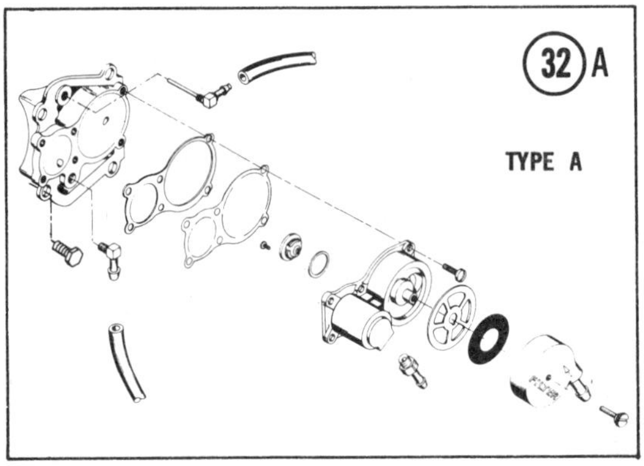

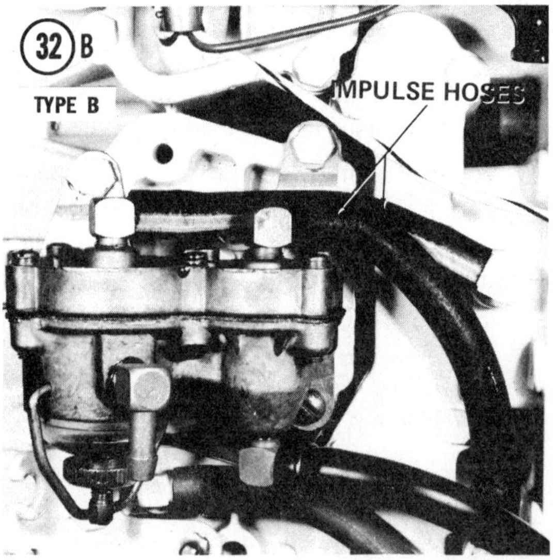

Type A Sediment Bowl and Filter (Screen) Removal/Installation

1. Loosen knurled screw on sediment bowl and remove bowl.
2. Remove gasket and screen.
3. Use hose clamp pliers to slide hose clamp about one inch down hose from sediment bowl. Pull hose off sediment bowl.

CAUTION

Do not use hose clamp pliers to pull hose off fitting; pliers can puncture the hose.

4. Install fuel intake hose on sediment bowl and secure with hose clamp.
5. Install screen in sediment bowl with turned over edge toward cylinder. See **Figure 33**.

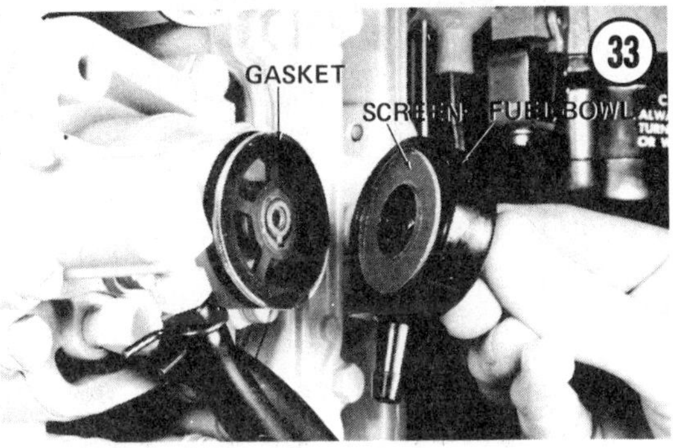

33

6. Place gasket on pump body so that slot in gasket is over key on pump body.
7. Position sediment bowl on pump body with hose fitting at 4 o'clock. Use knurled screw to secure sediment bowl to pump body.

Type A Fuel Pump Body and Diaphragm Removal/Installation

1. Remove sediment bowl.
2. Use hose clamp pliers to slide hose clamp about one inch down fuel pump outlet hose. Remove hose from fitting.

CAUTION

Do not use hose clamp pliers to pull hose off fitting; pliers can puncture the hose.

3. Remove screws securing fuel pump body to fuel pump cover. Remove fuel pump body, gasket, and diaphragm.
4. Installation is the reverse of these steps. Position fuel pump gasket and diaphragm on fuel pump body as shown in **Figure 34**. Install fuel pump body on fuel pump cover and secure with 6 screws.

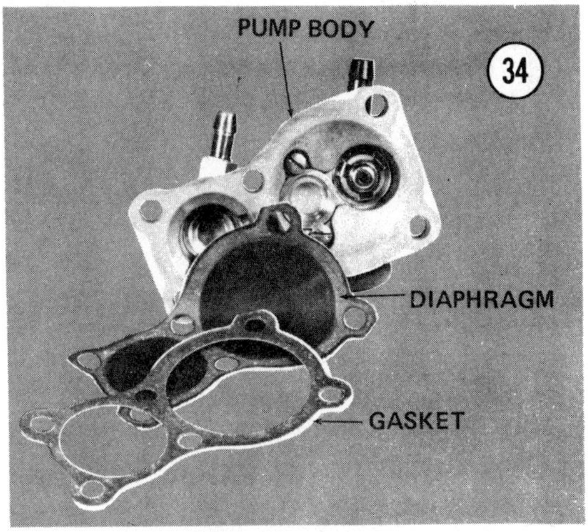

34

Type A Fuel Pump Valve Removal/Installation

1. Remove fuel pump body.
2. Remove screws securing central valve to fuel pump body as shown in **Figure 35**. Remove fuel pump valve and gasket from body.

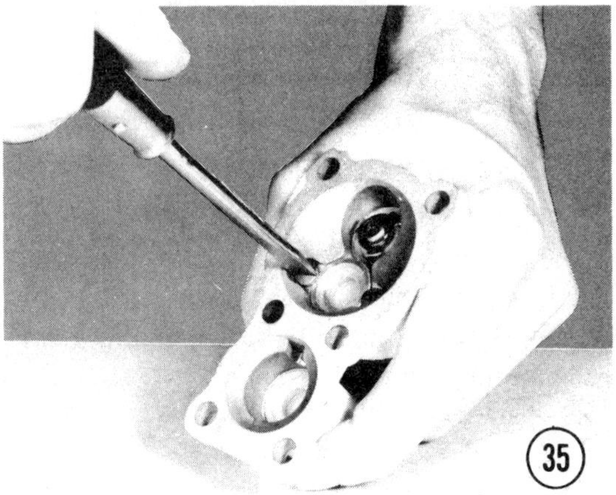
35

3. Remove outlet fuel line fitting from fuel pump body.
4. Apply sealant to threads of fuel line fitting. Install fitting in fuel pump body and tighten securely.
5. Place fuel pump valve gasket on valve seat in fuel pump body. Place valve on valve seat

so that brass ring faces power head. Install screws and tighten securely.

6. Install fuel pump body.

Type A Fuel Pump Cover Removal/Installation

1. Remove fuel pump body.
2. Remove impulse hose from lower fitting on fuel pump cover.

> NOTE: *On 4-cylinder engines remove recirculating hose from upper fitting on fuel pump cover.*

3. Remove screws securing fuel pump cover to power head and remove cover and gasket. See **Figure 36**.

4. Remove impulse hose fitting from fuel pump cover. On 4-cylinder models, remove recirculating hose fitting from fuel pump cover.
5. Installation is the reverse of these steps. Apply sealant to threads of impulse hose fitting. Install fitting in fuel pump cover and tighten securely. On 4-cylinder models, apply sealant to threads of recirculating hose fitting. Install fitting in fuel pump cover and tighten securely.

Type B Sediment Bowl and Filter (Screen) Removal/Installation

1. Remove screws securing fuel pump bracket to power head. Pull bracket with fuel pump away from power head.
2. Loosen knurl nut on bail and remove the fuel bowl.
3. Remove gasket and screen.
4. Installation is the reverse of these steps.

Type B Pump Cover and Diaphragm Removal/Installation

1. Remove inlet fuel line from inlet fitting. See **Figure 37**.

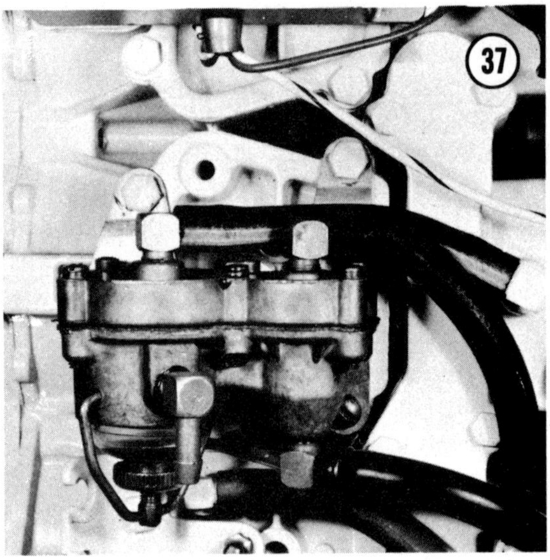

2. Remove screws securing fuel pump bracket to power head.
3. Remove impulse line from fitting on cover and remove pump assembly.
4. Remove fittings from pump cover.
5. Remove screws securing pump cover to body and remove cover.
6. Remove pump gasket and diaphragm.
7. Installation is the reverse of these steps. Apply Loctite "H" to threads of fittings and install on fuel pump cover. See Figure 37 for positioning of barbs.

Type B Fuel Pump Body Removal/Installation

1. Remove fuel pump cover.
2. Remove inlet fuel fitting from pump body.
3. Remove fitting from pump body.
4. Remove pump body from bracket.
5. Remove fuel bowl, screen, and gasket.
6. Remove bail and nut assembly from pump body by pulling bail ends out of counterbores.
7. Snap bail and nut assembly in place on fuel pump body.
8. Install screen, gasket, and fuel bowl.

9. Install fuel pump body assembly to bracket and secure with screws.

10. Apply Loctite "H" to threads of inlet fuel fitting and install fitting on body. See Figure 37.

11. Apply Loctite "H" to threads of fitting and install fitting on body. See Figure 37.

12. Complete fuel pump assembly.

Type B Fuel Pump Valves Removal/Installation

1. Follow disassembly procedures as outlined for Type A fuel pump valves.

2. Press out the 2 outside valves.

3. Remove screws securing middle valve to pump body. Remove middle valve.

4. Install a gasket in each counterbore for check valves.

5. Press outside valves in counterbores of pump body. See **Figure 38** for position of each valve.

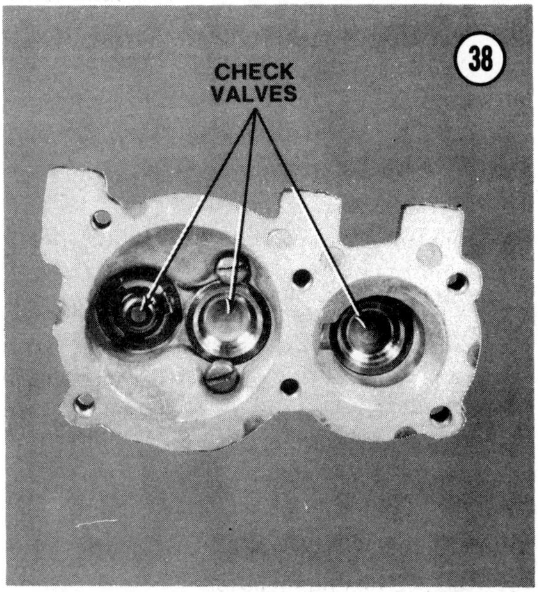

6. Install middle valve in middle counterbore of pump body and secure with screws. See Figure 38 for position of valve.

7. Complete assembly of fuel pump.

Prime Bulb Removal/Installation

1. Dip prime bulb portion of fuel line in hot water (180-200°F) for a few minutes until hose becomes soft and pliable.

2. Pull hose and ferrule from adapter on each end of prime bulb.

3. Installation is the reverse of these steps.

FUEL SYSTEM (4-CYLINDER ENGINE)

Top Carburetor Removal (WB Type)

1. Remove retaining ring securing throttle shaft tie bar to throttle shaft arm. Remove tie bar from throttle shaft arm.

2. Loosen screw securing choke rod to swivel on choke shaft arm. Remove rod from swivel.

3. Slide hose clamp from inlet fuel fitting on carburetor and disconnect hose from fuel fitting.

4. Remove nuts securing carburetor to carburetor adapter plate and remove carburetor.

5. Remove choke rod swivel from choke shaft arm.

6. Remove fuel inlet fitting from carburetor.

Top Carburetor Installation (WB Type)

1. Install choke swivel on arm of choke shaft using O-ring on each side of shaft arm. Install plain washer and secure swivel to shaft arm with cotter pin.

2. Apply sealant to threads of fuel inlet fitting. Install fitting on carburetor and position barb at 5 o'clock.

3. Install new carburetor gasket on stud of carburetor adapter.

4. Install carburetor on carburetor adapter.

5. Connect fuel line from bottom carburetor to inlet fitting on top carburetor. Secure hose with clamp.

6. Synchronize carburetor shutters as outlined under *Tune-up*.

7. Connect choke link in choke swivel and synchronize choke shutters as outlined under *Tune-up*.

Bottom Carburetor Removal (WB Type)

1. Remove retaining ring securing throttle shaft tie bar to throttle shaft arm. Remove tie bar from throttle shaft arm.

2. Slide hose clamps from each barb on inlet fitting. Remove fuel lines from each barb.

3. Loosen screw on choke swivel and remove choke link from swivel.

4. Remove nuts securing carburetor to carburetor adapter and remove carburetor from engine with choke solenoid plunger assembly.

5. Remove cotter pin securing choke swivel to choke arm of carburetor. Remove plain washer, seal, and another plain washer from swivel. Remove choke solenoid plunger assembly and choke swivel from choke arm of carburetor.

6. Remove throttle roller shaft and throttle roller from throttle arm of carburetor by removing stop nut from throttle roller shaft.

7. Remove inlet fitting from carburetor.

Bottom Carburetor Installation (WB Type)

1. Install O-ring on choke swivel. Install choke swivel with O-ring on choke shaft arm. Install choke solenoid plunger assembly, plain washer, O-ring, and another plain washer and secure choke swivel with cotter pin.

2. Apply sealant to threads of fuel inlet fitting. Install fitting on carburetor and position fitting with barbs pointing at 1 o'clock and 7 o'clock.

3. Install throttle roller on shaft. Install assembly on throttle shaft arm of carburetor. Secure throttle roller shaft to throttle shaft arm with stop nut, but do not tighten. Make final adjustment of throttle roller after mounting carburetor on carburetor adapter flange.

4. Install choke solenoid plunger in choke solenoid, then slip carburetor on the studs of the carburetor adapter flange. Secure carburetor to flange studs with nuts and tighten securely.

5. Install choke rod in choke swivel by pushing choke rod up and through choke swivel. Tighten swivel screw against rod. Synchronize choke shutters as outlined under *Tune-up*.

6. Install throttle shaft tie bar in lower hole of carburetor throttle shaft arm and secure with retaining ring.

7. Synchronize throttle shutters as outlined under *Tune-up*. Adjust throttle pickup as outlined in the same section.

8. Connect fuel lines to inlet fuel fitting and retain with clamps.

Top Carburetor Removal (TC Type)

1. Remove retaining ring securing throttle shaft tie bar to throttle shaft arm. Remove tie bar from throttle shaft arm.

2. Remove carburetor cover.

3. Loosen screw securing choke rod to swivel on choke shaft arm. Remove rod from swivel.

4. Slide hose clamp from inlet fuel fitting on carburetor and disconnect hose from fuel fitting.

5. Remove nuts securing carburetor to carburetor adapter plate and remove carburetor.

6. Remove choke rod swivel from choke shaft arm.

7. Remove fuel inlet fitting from carburetor.

Top Carburetor Installation (TC Type)

1. Install choke swivel on arm of choke shaft using O-ring on each side of shaft arm. Install plain washer and secure swivel to shaft arm with cotter pin.

2. Apply sealant to threads of fuel inlet fitting. Install fitting on carburetor and position barb at 5 o'clock.

3. Install carburetor on carburetor adapter with new gasket.

4. Connect fuel line from bottom carburetor to inlet fitting on top carburetor. Secure hose with clamp.

5. Install carburetor cover on carburetor.

6. Synchronize carburetor shutters as outlined under *Tune-up*.

Bottom Carburetor Removal (TC Type)

1. Remove retaining ring securing throttle shaft tie bar to throttle shaft arm. Remove tie bar from throttle shaft arm.

2. Remove screws securing carburetor cover to studs and remove cover.

3. Slide hose clamps from each barb on inlet fitting. Remove fuel lines from each barb.

4. Loosen screw on choke swivel and remove choke rod from swivel.

5. Remove carburetor from engine with choke solenoid plunger assembly.

6. Remove cotter pin securing choke swivel to choke arm of carburetor. Remove plain washer,

seal, and another plain washer from swivel. Remove choke solenoid plunger assembly and choke swivel from choke arm of carburetor.

7. Remove throttle roller shaft and roller from throttle arm of carburetor.

8. Remove inlet fitting from carburetor.

Bottom Carburetor Installation (TC Type)

1. Install O-ring on choke swivel. Install choke swivel with O-ring on choke shaft arm. Install choke solenoid plunger assembly, plain washer, O-ring, plain washer, and secure choke swivel with cotter pin.

2. Apply sealant to threads of fuel inlet fitting. Install fitting on carburetor and position fitting with barbs pointing at 1 o'clock and 7 o'clock.

3. Install throttle roller on shaft. Install assembly on throttle shaft arm of carburetor, but do not tighten nut. Make final adjustment of throttle roller after installing carburetor.

4. Install choke solenoid plunger in choke solenoid, then slip carburetor on the studs of the carburetor adapter flange. Secure carburetor to carburetor adapter flange studs with nuts and tighten securely.

5. Install choke rod in choke swivel by pushing choke rod up and through choke swivel. Tighten swivel screw against rod.

6. Install throttle shaft tie bar in lower hole of throttle shaft arm and secure with retaining ring.

7. Install carburetor cover on cover studs and secure with 3 screws.

8. Synchronize throttle shutters as outlined outlined under *Tune-up*. Adjust throttle pickup as outlined in the same section.

9. Connect fuel lines to inlet fuel fitting and retain with clamps.

FLYWHEEL

Removal

1. Remove nut securing flywheel to crankshaft.

2. Install puller (Special Tool T8948) on flywheel.

3. Turn forcing screw as tight as possible against crankshaft while holding bar to prevent puller plate from turning. See **Figure 39**.

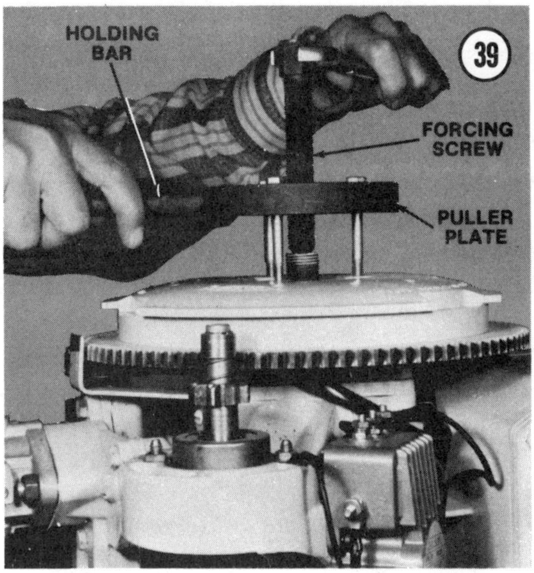

4. Using large screwdriver or wedge to apply an upward force on flywheel, strike top of forcing screw with hammer. Flywheel will loosen from taper on crankshaft.

CAUTION

Do not strike forcing screw too hard as this may damage crankshaft and crankshaft bearings.

5. Remove puller and flywheel from crankshaft.

6. Remove distributor belt.

7. Pry flywheel key out of slot in crankshaft.

8. Carefully inspect the flywheel for cracks or breaks.

WARNING

Cracked or chipped flywheel must be replaced. At high rpm a damaged flywheel may fly apart throwing shrapnel over a large area.

9. Inspect tapered bore of flywheel and taper on crankshaft for fretting or working. If there is evidence of this condition or if the engine has had 25 or more hours of operation, the flywheel bore must be lapped.

Lapping Flywheel

1. Apply a light coating of a water base valve lapping compound of 240 grit or finer to tapered portion of crankshaft.

2. Install flywheel on crankshaft and rotate flywheel gently back and forth about 1/4 turn—do not spin flywheel completely around crankshaft.

3. Rotate the flywheel 90° and repeat above operation.

4. Remove flywheel, wipe compound off crankshaft and flywheel. Taper in bore of flywheel should have a minimum of 80% surface contact with taper on crankshaft.

> NOTE: *To check percentage of contact, use a lead pencil (No. 2 or 2B grade lead) and draw 3 vertical lines on crankshaft taper 120° apart. Mount flywheel on crankshaft and rotate the flywheel 360° or 1 full turn exerting light downward pressure. Remove flywheel and check percentage of pencil lines that have been rubbed off. If 80% or more of the pencil lines have been removed and no rocking is evident, then clean the tapers and reinstall the flywheel. Repeat the above procedure if less than 80% of lines have been removed. If 3 lappings cannot correct taper contact to crankshaft, replace the flywheel. If new flywheel does not lap in, then replacement of crankshaft will be necessary.*

5. Thoroughly clean compound from flywheel, crankshaft, and key ways.

Installation

1. Install flywheel key in slot of crankshaft.

2. Install distributor belt as outlined under *Distributor*.

3. Install flywheel on crankshaft and torque flywheel to 90 ft.-lb.

IGNITION SYSTEM

Breaker Point Replacement

1. Remove battery leads from battery.

2. Remove distributor cap.

3. Remove bolts securing distributor belt to power head. Slip distributor belt off pulley. Pull distributor assembly away from power head.

4. Turn distributor over to expose breaker point set.

5. Remove screws securing breaker point set to distributor housing.

6. Lift points out of housing and remove screws securing lead wire to point set. Remove breaker point set.

7. Connect lead wire to new breaker point set and secure with screw.

8. Install breaker point set in distributor housing. Align pivot of breaker point set in pivot hole of distributor housing.

9. Secure breaker point set to distributor housing with 2 screws, but do not tighten securely (just enough to be able to adjust breaker point gap).

10. Adjust breaker point gap and complete assembly and tune-up procedures as outlined under *Tune-up*.

Distributor Belt Removal/Installation

1. Loosen bolts securing distributor to power head and slip distributor belt off pulley.

2. Remove flywheel as outlined under *Alternator* and remove distributor belt.

3. Installation is the reverse of these steps. Complete assembly and adjust belt tension as outlined under *Tune-up*.

Distributor Cap Replacement

1. Loosen screws on distributor retaining clips and remove distributor cap assembly from distributor.

2. Disconnect high tension lead wire from coil.

3. Remove spark plug lead wires from spark plugs and retaining clips.

4. Remove distributor cap assembly from engine.

5. Remove screws on distributor cover and pull cover with lead wires from cap.

6. Pull seal away from cover and pull lead wires from seal. Pull lead wires from cover.

7. Insert lead wires through cap cover and through seal. Align screw holes (cover to cap) and vent hole in cover with vent screen in seal. Allow at least one inch of lead wire to extend through cap seal as shown in **Figure 40**.

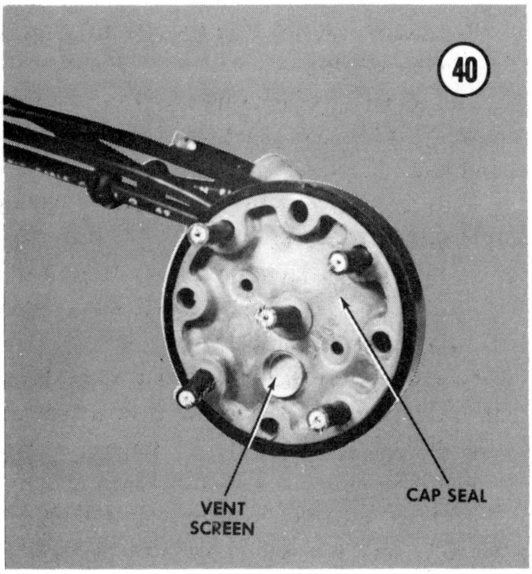

8. Insert lead wire ends in distributor cap against pointed contacts. Align screw holes (distributor cover to cap) and vent holes.

9. Draw distributor cover against cap using 2 screws and tighten until screws bottom.

10. Check lead wire continuity with a test light (Special Tool T2938-1 or equivalent) as shown in **Figure 41**. If test light does not light for any specific wire, remove distributor cover and repeat Steps 1 through 4.

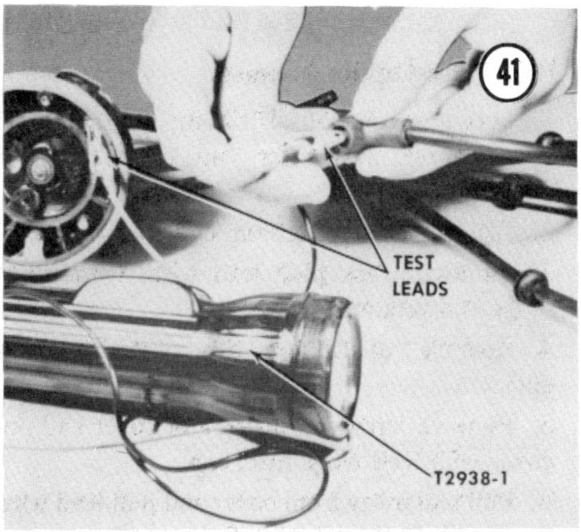

11. Install distributor cap on distributor. Align hole in cap wall with locating pin in distributor housing. Secure cap assembly to distributor with retaining clips.

12. Route center lead wire from cap assembly to coil and insert lead wire end firmly in coil. Push boot over end of coil.

13. Route spark plug lead wires to respective spark plugs. See **Figures 42 and 43** for identification of lead wires.

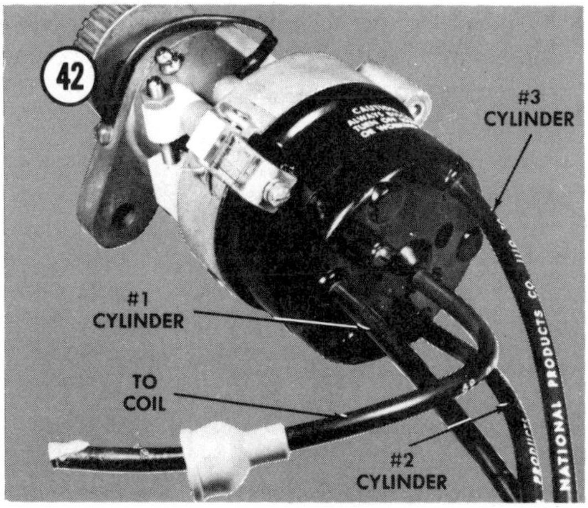

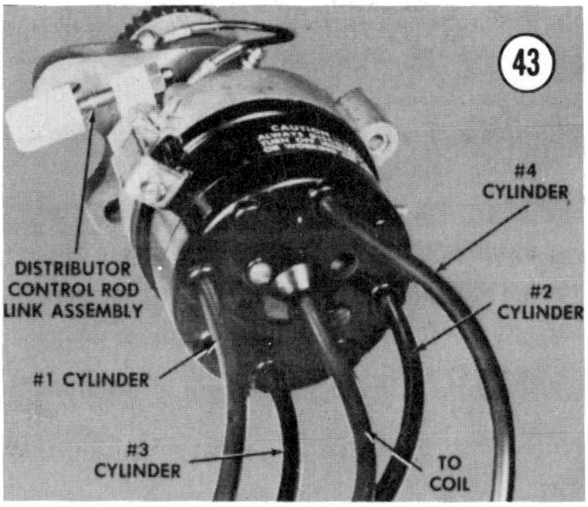

Distributor Pulley Removal/Installation

1. Remove screws securing interlock switch to distributor bracket and remove switch with wires from distributor.

2. Disconnect white/black stripe wire from terminal stud on distributor.

3. Remove distributor cap from distributor.

4. Remove bolts securing distributor bracket to power head and remove distributor.

5. Clamp distributor pulley lightly in a vise using soft jaws to prevent damage to pulley

teeth. Remove stop nut from end of distributor shaft and pull distributor from pulley.

6. Remove spacer and washers from distributor.

7. Remove distributor shaft and remove bronze spacer from underneath cam lobes on shaft.

8. Install Woodruff key in slot of distributor shaft and bronze spacer under cam lobes of shaft.

9. Install distributor shaft from breaker point side until bronze spacer on shaft bottoms against distributor housing.

10. Install small diameter washer on top of bearing in distributor (pulley end of shaft). Then install larger diameter washer on top of smaller diameter washer and install thick spacer.

11. Install distributor pulley on end of distributor shaft. Clamp distributor pulley in a vise using soft jaws to prevent damage to pulley teeth. Install stop nut on end of distributor shaft and tighten securely. Install distributor on power head and secure with bolts. Do not tighten these bolts yet.

12. Install distributor cap on distributor.

13. Connect white/black stripe wire to terminal stud on distributor and secure with nut and spring lockwasher.

14. Install the interlock switch to distributor bracket and secure with screws. Check interlock switch adjustment as outlined under *Tune-up*.

15. Install distributor belt.

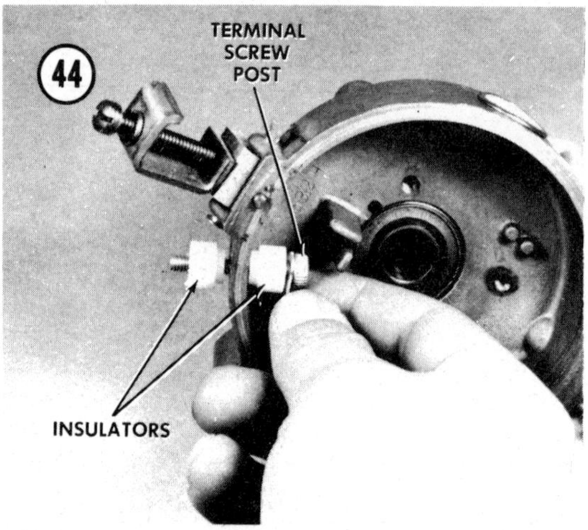

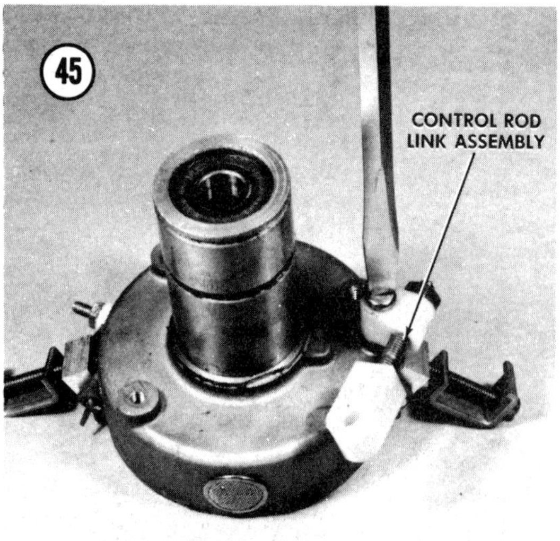

Distributor Housing Removal/Installation

1. Remove the distributor bracket, pulley, and shaft.

2. Remove breaker points.

3. Remove terminal screw post and insulators as shown in **Figure 44**.

4. Remove the distributor control rod link assembly. See **Figure 45**.

5. Remove interlock cam.

6. Disconnect ground wire from housing.

7. Installation is the reverse of these steps. Adjust interlock cam as outlined under *Tune-up*.

Delta C-D Unit Removal/Installation

1. Disconnect blue wire from blue washer terminal stud. See **Figure 46**.

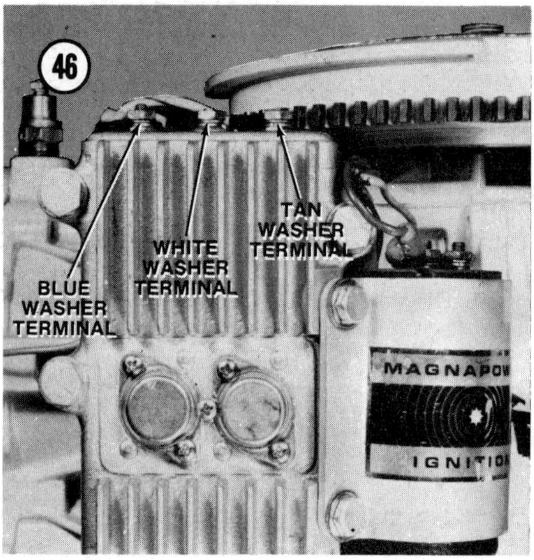

2. Disconnect white lead wire from white washer terminal stud.

3. Disconnect white/black lead wire from tan washer stud terminal.

4. Disconnect black lead wire from side terminal stud.

5. Disconnect white lead wire from (—) terminal on ignition coil.

6. Disconnect blue lead wire from (+) terminal on ignition coil.

7. Remove bolts securing C-D unit to power head and remove C-D unit with ignition coil.

8. Remove coil clamp and coil from C-D unit.

9. Installation is the reverse of these steps. Install assembly on power head. Torque bolts to 160 in.-lb.

Delta Ignition Coil Removal/Installation

1. Disconnect blue lead wire from (+) terminal stud on coil. See Figure 46.

2. Disconnect white lead wire from (—) terminal stud on coil.

3. Disconnect black lead wire from (G) terminal stud on coil.

4. Disconnect primary lead wire from bottom of coil.

5. Remove screws securing coil clamp to C-D unit and pull coil down from clamp.

6. Installation is the reverse of these steps.

CAUTION

Steel washer, fiber washer, and plastic washer must be correctly assembled or coil will not function properly.

Ignition Switch Removal/Installation

1. Remove the ignition switch from control box, dashboard, or boat.

2. Disconnect lead wires from ignition switch.

3. Installation is the reverse of these steps. See Figure 40.

Motorola C-D Unit (404301-1, 404301) Removal/Installation

1. Disconnect blue lead wire and white lead wire from terminal block.

2. Disconnect grey lead wire from (+) terminal stud on coil. See **Figure 47**.

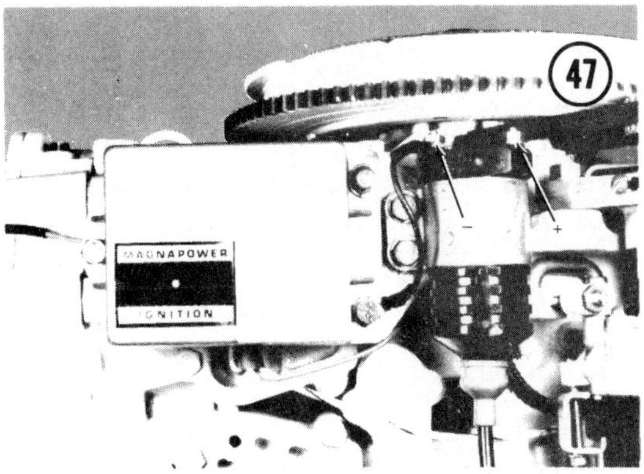

3. Disconnect white/black strip lead wire from distributor terminal stud.

4. Remove screws securing C-D unit to bracket and remove C-D unit.

5. Install C-D unit on bracket.

NOTE: *Connect black coil ground wire under bottom right side screw.*

6. Route blue lead wire and white lead wire behind C-D bracket and wrap around wiring harness to prevent wires from contacting flywheel.

7. Connect blue lead wire to second terminal screw from bottom of terminal block.

8. Connect white lead wire to third terminal screw from top of terminal block.

9. Connect grey lead wire to (+) terminal stud on coil.

10. Connect white/black strip lead wire to terminal stud on distributor.

Motorola C-D Unit (K404301-2) Removal/Installation

1. Remove hex nut and lockwasher securing white/black stripe wire to terminal on distributor bracket and remove wire.

2. Remove blue lead, red lead, and white lead (C-D unit to terminal block) from the terminal block.

3. Remove screws securing C-D unit to power head and remove C-D unit.

4. Install C-D unit on power head.

5. Route white wire/black stripe (from C-D unit) behind tower shaft and up to terminal on distributor and secure with hex nut.

6. Route remaining lead wires (blue, red, and white) up over power head, under flywheel, and down to terminal block. Connect leads to terminal block as specified on decal on exhaust port cover.

Motorola Ignition Coil Removal/Installation

1. Disconnect grey lead wire from (+) terminal stud on coil.

2. Disconnect black lead wire from (GND) terminal stud on coil.

3. Remove boot from coil and pull high tension lead wire from coil.

4. Remove screws securing coil clamp to C-D bracket. Remove coil, coil clamp, and spacer from power head.

5. Remove coil from coil clamp.

6. Install rubber band on top and bottom of coil. Install coil in coil clamp. Position spacer between ends of coil clamp and install assembly on power head. See Figure 47.

7. Secure coil clamp assembly to power head using 2 screws. Place steel plain washer then phenolic washer under head of each screw.

8. Connect high tension lead wire to coil.

9. Connect grey lead wire to (+) terminal stud on coil.

10. Connect black lead wire to (GND) terminal stud on coil.

Motorola Ignition Coil (K404301-2) Removal/Installation

1. Remove C-D unit.

2. Remove nuts and lead wires from terminals on ignition coil.

3. Remove screws and lockwashers securing coil and coil clamp to C-D unit. Remove coil and coil clamp.

4. Install ignition coil on C-D unit.

5. Connect grey lead from C-D unit to (+) terminal on ignition coil and black lead from C-D unit to terminal marked GND on ignition coil.

6. Install C-D unit.

CHARGING SYSTEM

Alternator Stator Removal/Installation

1. Remove flywheel.

2. Remove screws securing stator to crankshaft bearing cage.

3. Remove stator leads from rectifier.

4. Installation is the reverse of these steps. Install stator on bearing cage aligning holes in stator with holes in bearing cage.

Delta Rectifier (Silicone Bridge) Removal/Installation

1. Disconnect battery leads from battery.

2. Disconnect black lead wire from top left terminal post (—). See **Figure 48.**

48

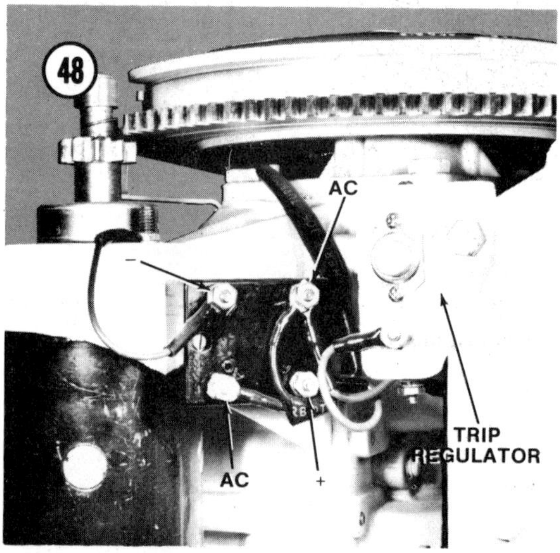

3. Disconnect black lead wire and purple lead wire from top right terminal post (AC).

4. Disconnect black lead wire from bottom left terminal post (AC). See Figure 48.

5. Disconnect red lead wire from bottom right terminal post (+). See Figure 48.

6. Remove screws securing rectifier to power head and remove rectifier.

7. Installation is the reverse of these steps.

Delta Rectifier (Selenium) Removal/Installation

1. Disconnect black lead wire and purple lead wire from inside terminal (marked with yellow paint). See **Figure 49.**

2. Remove red lead wire from middle terminal (marked with red paint).

3. Disconnect black lead wire from outside terminal (marked with yellow paint).

4. Remove screws securing rectifier bracket to power head.

5. Remove nut securing rectifier and trip regulator to rectifier bracket and remove rectifier.

CAUTION

When removing or installing rectifier, do not use wrench on outside hex head in middle of rectifier or rectifier could be damaged. Hold rectifier on large inside hex head.

6. Installation is the reverse of these steps.

Delta Trip Regulator Removal/Installation

When trip regulator is used with a silicone bridge type rectifier, proceed as follows.

1. Remove rectifier from cylinder exhaust cover. See **Figure 50**.

2. Disconnect red lead wire (from + terminal of rectifier) from yellow washer stud terminal.

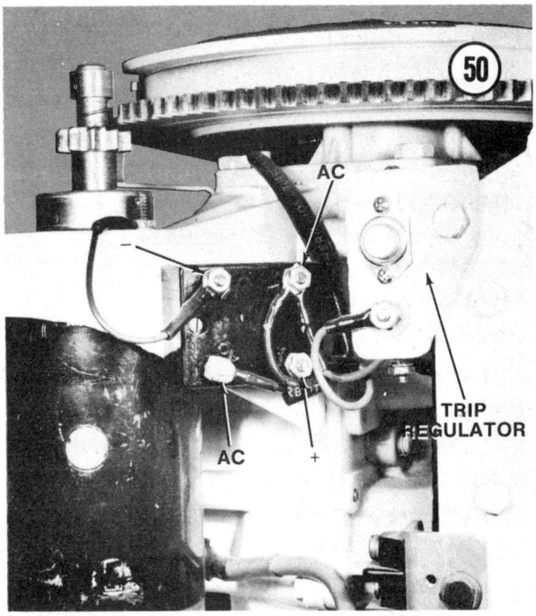

3. Disconnect red lead wire (from wiring harness) from red washer stud terminal.

When trip regulator is used with a selenium type rectifier, proceed as follows.

1. Remove rectifier.

2. Disconnect red lead wire (from + terminal of rectifier) from yellow washer stud terminal.

3. Disconnect red lead wire (from wiring harness) from red washer stud terminal.

4. Installation is the reverse of these steps.

Motorola Regulator/Rectifier Removal/Installation

1. Disconnect red lead wire from (+) terminal stud on regulator/rectifier. See **Figure 51**.

2. Disconnect 2 black lead wires and one purple lead wire from 2 AC terminal studs.

3. Disconnect black lead wire from side GND terminal stud.

4. Remove screws securing regulator/rectifier from power head and remove regulator/rectifier.

5. Install regulator/rectifier on power head.

6. Connect one black lead wire and one purple lead wire to top right side terminal stud (AC). See Figure 51.

7. Connect other black lead wire to middle terminal stud (AC).

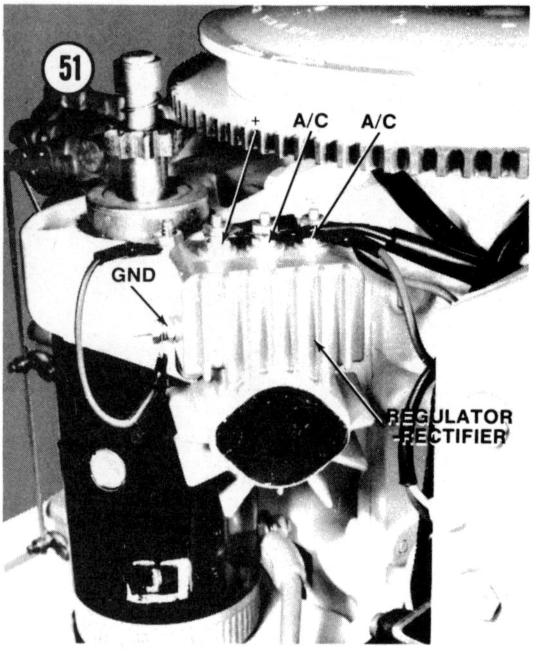

8. Connect red lead wire to left side terminal stud (+).

9. Connect black lead wire to side terminal stud (GND).

ELECTRIC STARTER

Removal

1. Disconnect battery leads from battery.
2. Remove bolts securing lower starter bracket to power head.
3. Remove locknuts on thru-bolts which secure lower starter bracket to starter.
4. Disconnect lead wire (starter relay to starter motor).
5. Thread thru-bolts out of flange on power head and remove starter motor assembly. Pull thru-bolts out of starter motor and remove lower starter bracket.

Installation

1. Install lower starter bracket on starter motor. Position starter motor so that terminal stud is toward one of the power head mounting legs on bracket. Install thru-bolts through lower starter bracket and starter motor.
2. Connect lead wire (starter relay to starter motor) to terminal stud of starter motor.
3. Install starter motor assembly on power head and thread thru-bolts of starter motor to flange on power head. Secure bolts with locknuts.

NOTE: *Some models have a ground wire which should be attached under one of these nuts.*

4. Install bolts to secure lower starter bracket to power head. Torque large bolt to 270 in.-lb. and smaller bolt to 70 in.-lb.
5. Connect battery leads to battery.

Starter Solenoid (Relay) Removal/Installation

1. Disconnect battery leads from battery.
2. Remove positive battery lead wire and red/white wire from forward side post of starter relay. See **Figure 52**.

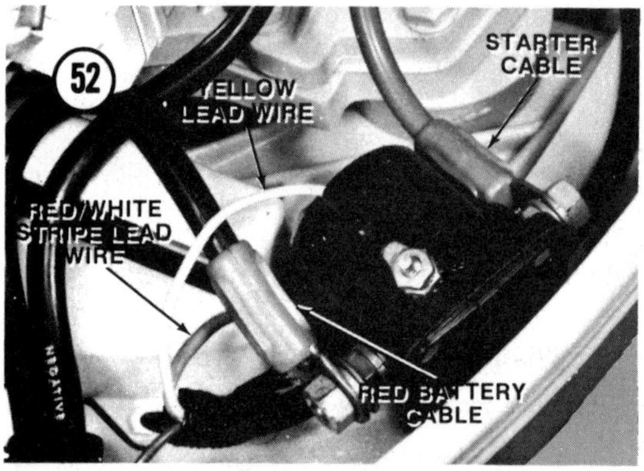

3. Remove yellow lead wire from top post on starter relay.
4. Remove red lead wire (relay to starter motor) from rear side post of starter relay.
5. Remove screws securing starter relay to support plate and remove starter relay.

NOTE: *1971 and later models have a ground wire under the head of the forward screw.*

6. Install starter relay on bosses provided in support plate.
7. On forward side post of relay, install red/white wire, then spring lockwasher, and then positive battery lead wire.

8. Install yellow lead wire to top post of relay.

9. Install red lead wire from starter motor to rear side post of relay.

GEAR HOUSING

Lower Unit Removal/Installation

1. Remove cotter pin securing shift rod pin to coupler of upper shift rod. Remove shift rod pin to free lower shift rod from coupler.

2. Remove screws and lockwashers securing upper gear housing to motor leg.

3. Remove rear screw and washer of exhaust snout and pull lower unit from motor leg.

4. Apply anti-seize compound to crankshaft splines of drive shaft.

5. Install lower unit to motor leg aligning lower shift rod through seal and gearshift rod coupling in motor leg, aligning water line in seal of water pump and engaging drive shaft splines in crankshaft of power head.

6. Apply anti-seize compound to threads of screws which secure upper gear housing to motor leg with spring lockwashers and screws.

7. Align lower shift rod through coupler of upper shift rod and secure with shift rod pin and cotter pin.

Water Pump Removal

1. Remove lower unit.

2. Remove water line seal from body by depressing tabs on seal then pulling seal from pump body.

3. Remove screws securing water pump body assembly to upper gear housing and lift pump body assembly from lower unit.

4. Remove the water pump impeller from the pump body.

5. Remove drive shaft seal from pump body by driving same out from inside pump body.

6. Remove water pump back plate and gasket from lower unit.

Water Pump Installation

1. Place water pump body on wood block which supports inside top surface of pump body to prevent top surface of pump body from collapsing when installing drive shaft seal. Press drive shaft seal (garter spring on major sealing lip positioned out) in seal bore of pump body using seal installer (Special Tool T3012) as shown in **Figure 53**.

2. Install water pump impeller by turning impeller in pump body in a counterclockwise direction.

3. Clean gasket surfaces on upper gear housing. Install pump back plate and new gasket on upper gear housing so that holes in plate and gasket line up exactly with holes in upper gear housing.

CAUTION

Holes in back plate will not line up exactly if plate is installed upside down. Install plate correctly or water pump will not supply engine with sufficient cooling water.

4. Install pump assembly down drive shaft on back plate aligning slot of impeller with drive key on drive shaft.

5. Install water pump centering tool (Special Tool T2992) down drive shaft to center pump body in relationship to drive shaft. (**Figure 54**).

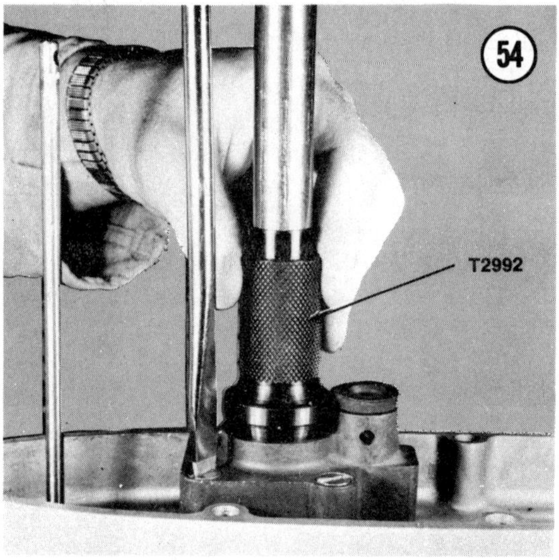

NOTE: *For water pump bodies without drive shaft seal, use end of centering tool opposite large tapered end.*

6. Apply anti-seize compound to threads of screws which secure pump body to upper gear housing. While applying downward force on centering tool, install and tighten screws on pump body. Torque screws to 70 in.-lb. Remove centering tool.
7. Install water line seal in seal bore of pump body making sure that tabs on seal are seated in holes in seal bore of pump body.
8. Install lower unit.

Lower Shift Rod Removal/Installation

1. Remove lower unit.
2. Turn lower shift rod counterclockwise until shift rod threads out of shift arm coupling. Pull shift rod from lower unit.
3. Apply grease to threads of lower shift rod.
4. Install lower shift rod through shift rod seal. Slowly push rod down until it just makes contact with shift arm coupling. Turn shift rod clockwise to engage thread of rod with coupling. Turn rod until threads bottom in coupling. Turn rod counterclockwise until hole at top end of rod is facing port and starboard sides.
5. Install lower unit.
6. Check shift adjustment as outlined under *Power Head.*

Upper Gear Housing Removal

1. Remove lower unit.
2. Remove stop nuts from studs securing upper gear housing to lower gear housing. Remove plain washers from front and rear studs. Remove spacer and O-ring seal from middle stud.
3. Lift upper gear housing from lower gear housing.
4. Remove shift rod seal by threading a 5/16 in. diameter lag screw in shift rod seal. Insert ¼ in. diameter rod from opposite side and press both seal and lag screw out of seal bore as shown in **Figure 55**.

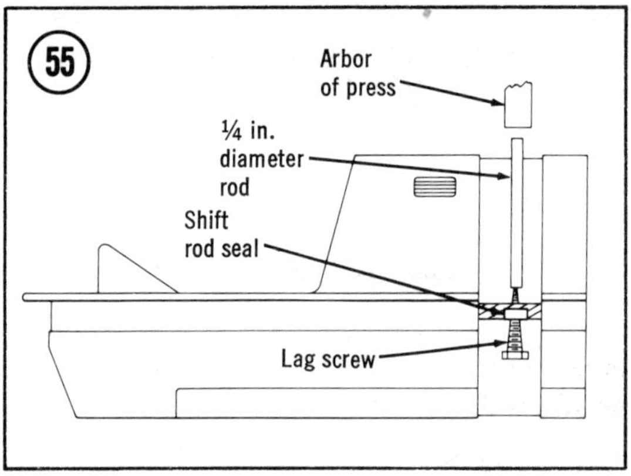

5. Remove bevel pinion nut and washer. Remove bevel pinion with bearing and cup.
6. Install knock-off nut (Special Tool T8911) over threaded portion of drive shaft and press drive shaft out of upper gear housing as shown in **Figure 56**. This operation will also remove drive shaft seal.
7. Remove upper drive shaft bearing cup from upper gear housing by tapping lightly from lower gear housing side using a spring pin punch (Special Tool T8919) and hammer.

NOTE: *Bearing cup is not a press fit in bore of upper gear housing.*

8. Remove exhaust snout from gear housing by removing flat head screw securing same and remove lockwasher.

Upper Gear Housing Installation

1. Apply Loctite "H" on outside diameter of shift rod seal. Install seal on seal installer (Special Tool T8957) with raised bead on seal in

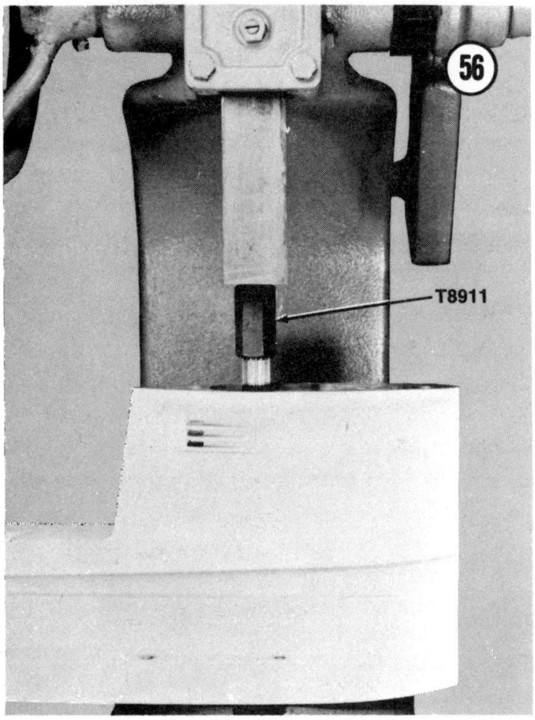

cavity machined in tool. Drive seal in seal bore until tool bottoms on top of seal bore as shown in **Figure 57**.

2. Install upper drive shaft bearing cup (with large diameter end of cup up) in upper gear housing by tapping lightly around circumference of bearing cup with punch and hammer until cup is bottomed completely in bore.

3. Install drive shaft with bearing cone in upper gear housing.

4. Clean bevel pinion bearing cup bore in upper gear housing. Install bearing cup and bevel pinion.

5. Apply grease between sealing lips of drive shaft seal. Slide seal down drive shaft with garter spring out or toward water pump, on top of seal bore in upper gear housing. Slide seal installer (Special Tool T8925) down drive shaft. Using seal installer as a slide hammer, press seal in bore until top of seal is flush with top of seal bore as shown in **Figure 58**.

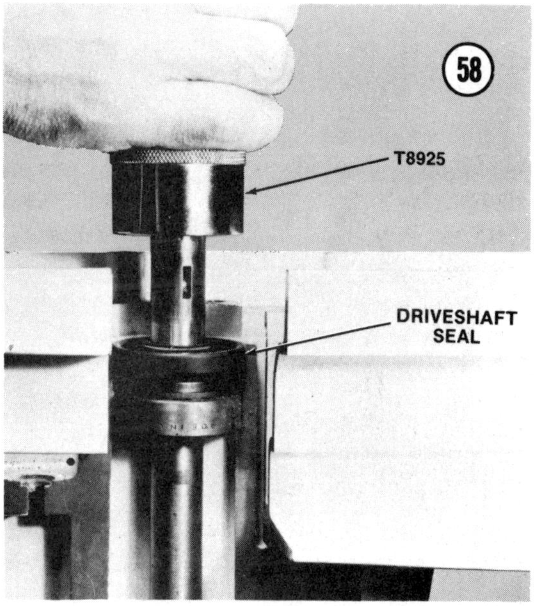

6. Clean mating surfaces of both upper and lower gear housings.

7. Apply sealant to lower gear housing in area where groove around pinion bearing cup meets seal groove. Just a little amount of sealant is required to hold seal in place until upper gear housing is installed. See **Figure 59**.

8. Install new gear housing seal in groove of lower gear housing.

9. Install upper gear housing on lower housing aligning studs and lower shift rod through upper gear housing and making sure O-ring seal stays in groove in lower gear housing.

6

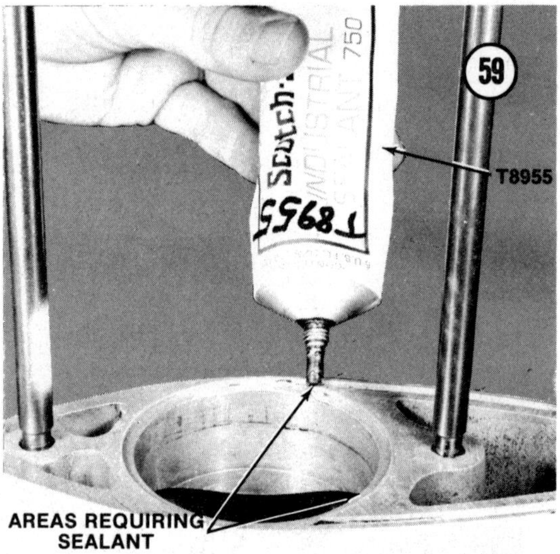

10. Secure upper gear housing to lower by installing washers and new stop nuts to front and rear studs. Install new O-ring, spacer, and new stop nut on middle stud. Torque stop nuts to 270 in.-lb.

> NOTE: *Torque each nut up to 100 in.-lb. first, then gradually increase torque in increments of 30-50 in.-lb. on each nut until the specified torque is reached.*

11. Install the exhaust snout and adjust as described later.

12. Install lower unit.

Bevel Pinion Removal/Installation

1. Remove lower unit.
2. Remove upper gear housing.
3. Remove retaining nut and washer securing bevel pinion to drive shaft and remove bevel pinion and bearing cup.
4. Clean threads on drive shaft end and prime with Locquic. Apply Loctite "D" to threads.
5. Install bearing cup and bevel pinion on drive shaft aligining cup in bore of upper gear housing.
6. Install bevel pinion retaining washer on drive shaft and then a new retaining nut. Do not tighten nut at this time.

CAUTION

Do not reuse old retaining nut. Once retaining nut is used, its locking ability is reduced; it may loosen, causing considerable damage to lower unit.

7. After installing nut loosely on drive shaft, clamp drive shaft in vise (with protective jaws) with drive shaft horizontal.
8. Swing upper gear housing on drive shaft. Note how freely gear housing swings.
9. Tighten retaining nut while swinging gear housing as shown in **Figure 60** until gear housing just starts to bind.

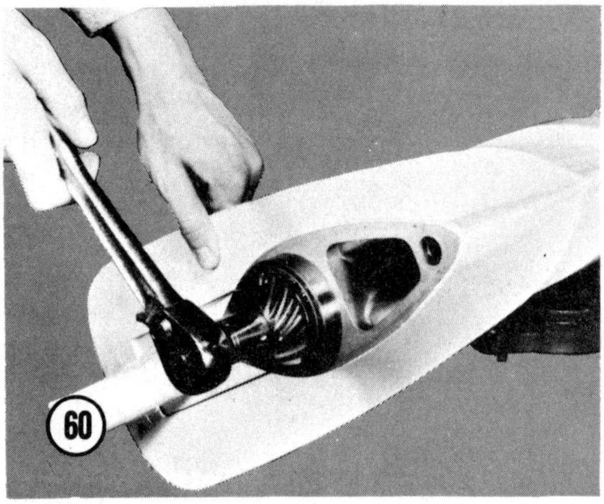

10. Seat bearings (drive shaft and bevel pinion) by tapping knock-off nut (Special Tool T8911) with hammer 2 times on end of drive shaft as shown in **Figure 61**.

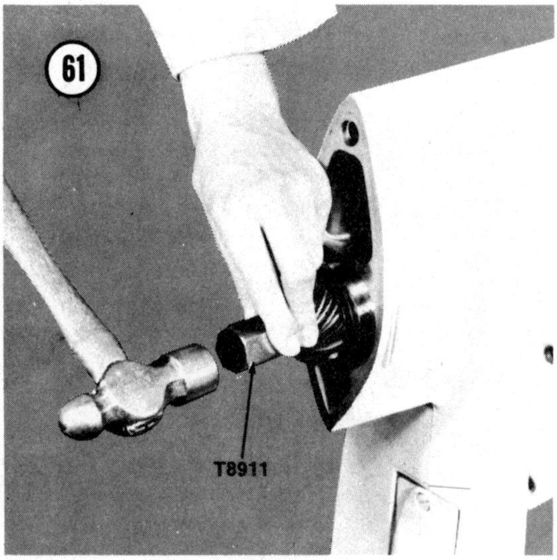

11. Swing upper gear housing again and check to see that gear housing swings freely. If it still

binds slightly, loosen nut just enough so that gear housing swings freely.

12. Install upper gear housing on lower gear housing and complete assembly of gear housing.

Drive Shaft Removal

1. Remove drive shaft with bearing.

2. Remove retaining ring positioning bearing on drive shaft using retaining ring pliers as shown in **Figure 62**.

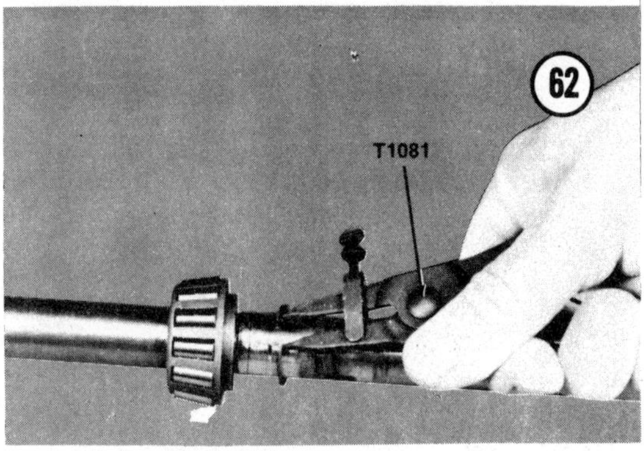

3. Press bearing off drive shaft using bearing remover (Special Tool T8905) and knock-off nut (Special Tool T8911) as shown in **Figure 63**.

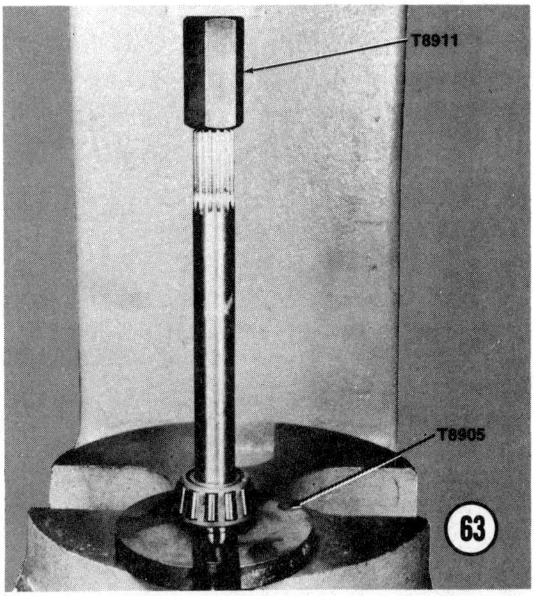

Drive Shaft Installation

1. Clean and degrease area of drive shaft where bearing is to be positioned. Spray this area with Locquic Primer and apply Loctite retaining compound.

2. Install retaining ring in groove of drive shaft using ring pliers.

3. Clamp drive shaft in vise (using protective jaws or rag) and drive bearing on drive shaft using bearing installer (Special Tool T8920) until bearing just bottoms against retaining ring as shown in **Figure 64**.

4. Complete assembly of gear housing.

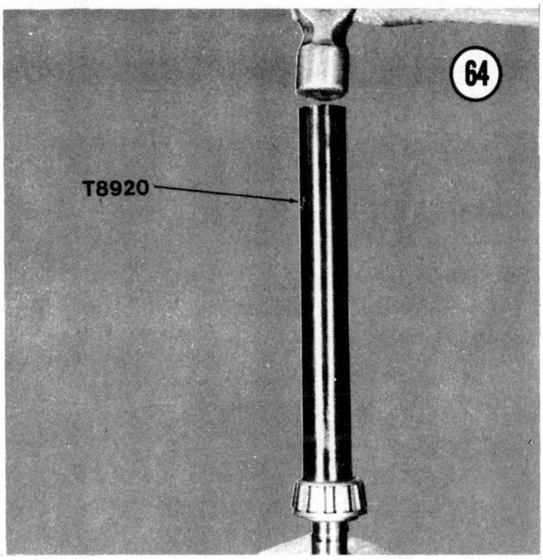

Bevel Pinion/Rear Bevel Gear Clearance

Proper bevel pinion/rear bevel gear clearance is important in order to minimize premature gear wear and/or bearing failure. Due to complexity of procedure and special tools required, have an authorized service center perform the procedure.

6

Propeller Shaft Bearing Removal/Installation

1. Remove propeller, propeller nut, cotter pin, seal, and drive pin.

2. Remove Allen cap screws securing bearing cage assembly to lower gear housing.

3. Install puller (Special Tool T8948) as shown in **Figure 65** and remove bearing cage assembly.

4. Remove bearing cage seal from groove in outer diameter of bearing cage.

5. Remove bearing cup from bearing cage using cup remover (Special Tool T8917) and slide

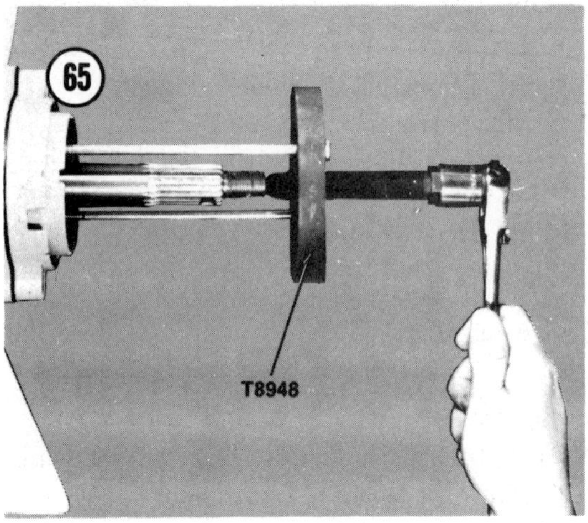

hammer (Special Tool T8922) as shown in **Figure 66** and remove shims.

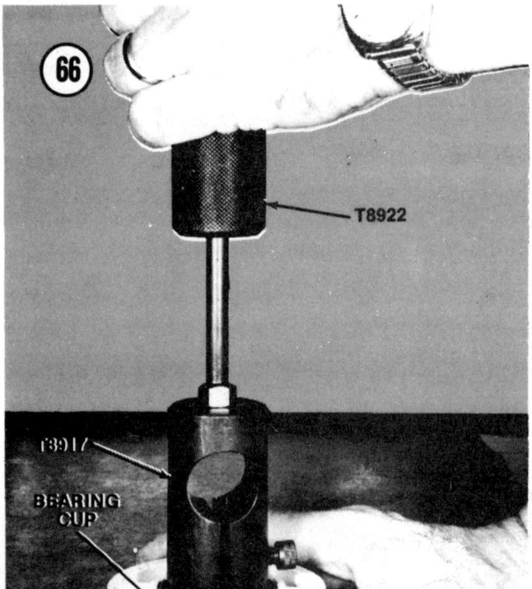

6. Remove propeller shaft seal by threading seal remover (Special Tool T8914) in seal as shown in **Figure 67**.

7. Press seal out as shown in **Figure 68**.

8. If propeller shaft bearing cage or bearing cup is replaced, bevel pinion/rear bevel gear clearance must be checked. Have it checked by an authorized service center.

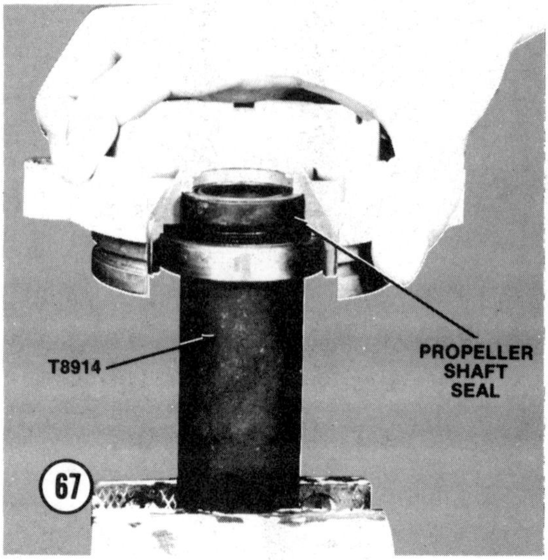

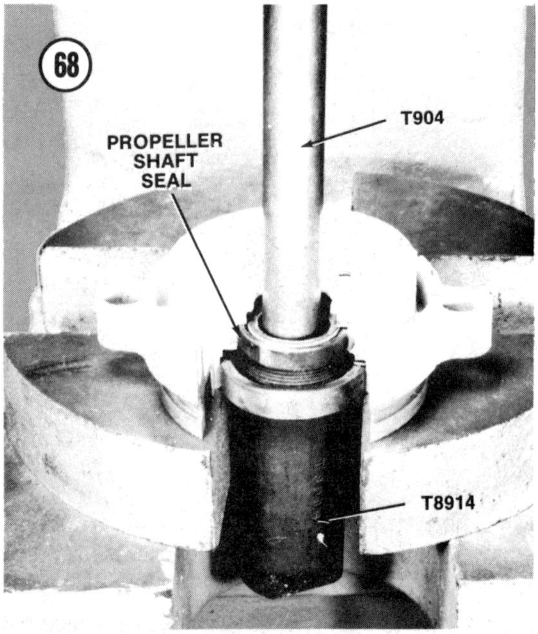

9. Install proper thickness of shims determined by service center. Install bearing cup in bearing cage using cup installer (Special Tool T8910) with driver handle (Special Tool T8907) as shown in **Figure 69**.

10. After installing bearing cup, install propeller shaft seal using seal installer (Special Tool T8908) and driver handle (Special Tool T8907) as shown in **Figure 70**.

11. Apply grease to bearing cage seal and install in groove of bearing cage.

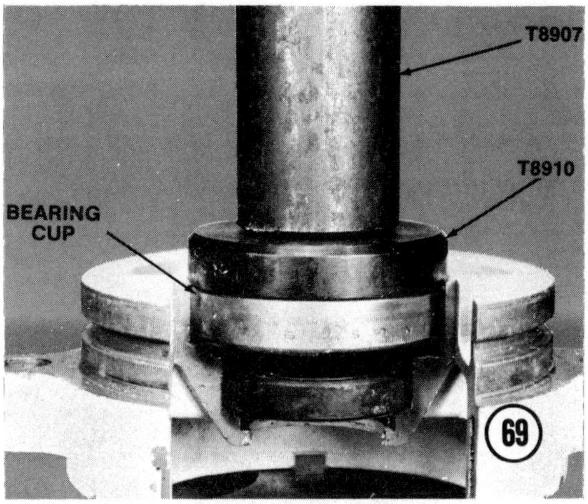

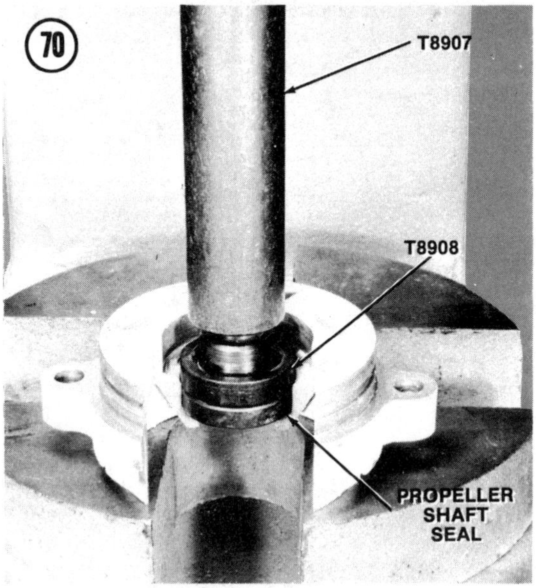

12. Apply grease to sealing lips of propeller shaft seal and install bearing cage assembly on propeller shaft.

13. Lightly tap around edge of bearing cage to seat bearing cage in lower gear housing.

14. Apply anti-seize compound to threads of Allen head cap screws. Secure bearing cage assembly to lower gear housing using same.

15. Install propeller, drive pin, seal, propeller nut, and cotter pin.

Clutch Removal

1. Remove lower unit.

2. Remove the propeller shaft bearing cage assembly.

3. Pull lower shift rod up as far as possible and then pull propeller shaft out of the lower gear housing.

4. Remove yoke from shift pin.

5. Drive out spring pin securing clutch and shift pin to propeller shaft using spring pin punch (Special Tool T8919). Remove shift pin and clutch from propeller shaft.

Clutch Installation

1. Install clutch on propeller shaft aligning spring pin holes with slot in propeller shaft.

2. Install shift pin in propeller shaft aligning hole with spring pin holes in clutch.

3. Drive spring pin through clutch, propeller shaft, and shift pin using spring pin punch (Special Tool T8919).

4. Apply heavy grease to groove in shift pin to hold yoke in position. Install yoke in groove of shift pin.

5. Carefully install propeller shaft assembly in gear housing. Make sure that lower shift rod is up as far as possible and pins on each side of yoke are horizontal. Push propeller shaft assembly in until pins of yoke are aligned in slots of shift arm assembly as shown in **Figure 71**.

6. Install bearing cage.

7. Install lower unit.

Propeller Shaft Removal

1. Remove lower unit.

2. Remove the propeller shaft bearing cage assembly.

6

3. Remove clutch, shift pin, and yoke.
4. Press rear bevel gear and bearings off propeller shaft using guide plate from bearing guide set (Special Tool T8918) as shown in **Figure 72**.
5. Remove bronze bearing from rear bevel gear.

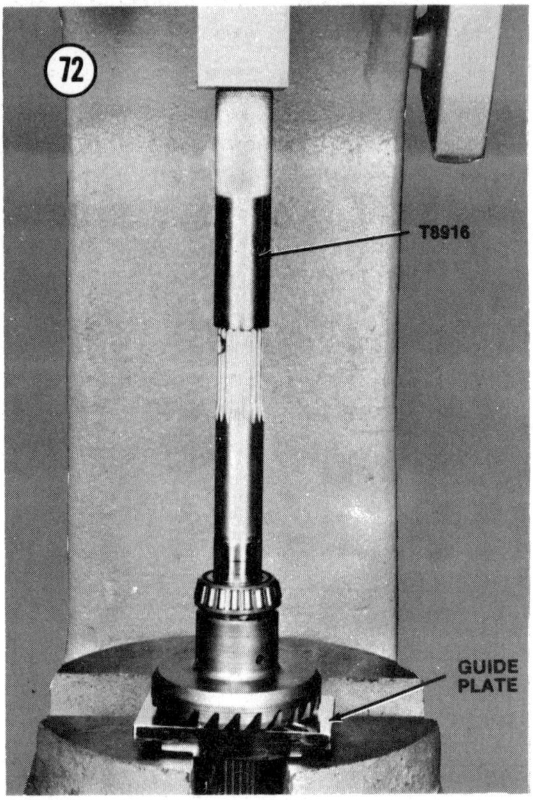

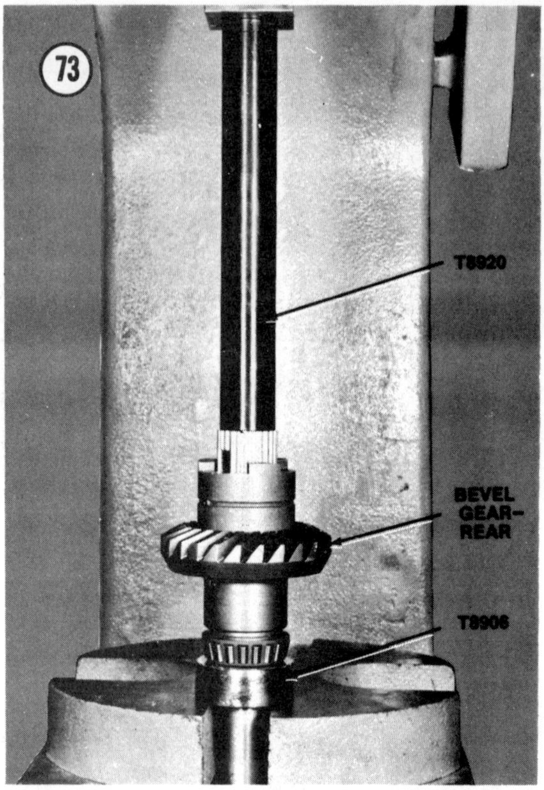

Propeller Shaft Installation

1. Install bronze bearing in bevel gear with flange of bearing on side opposite gear teeth (flange of bearing will be between gear and inner race of roller bearing when roller bearing is pressed on propeller shaft).
2. Slide rear bevel gear thrust washer on propeller shaft.
3. Slide the rear bevel gear assembly on the propeller shaft.
4. Slide roller bearing on propeller shaft with large end of taper toward rear bevel gear. Press bearing on propeller shaft using bearing installer (Special Tool T8906) and drive shaft installer (Special Tool T8920) as shown in **Figure 73**.
5. Press bearing on shaft until it bottoms against bearing flange of rear bevel gear.
6. Check the bevel pinion/rear bevel gear for clearance.
7. Install clutch, shift pin, and yoke.
8. Install propeller shaft bearing cage assembly.
9. Install lower unit.

Front Bevel Gear Removal/Installation

1. Remove lower unit.
2. Separate upper gear housing from lower.
3. Remove propeller shaft.
4. Remove front bevel gear assembly and thrust washer from lower gear housing.
5. Remove front bevel gear bearing cup using cup remover (Special Tool T2995) with bearing guide set (Special Tool T8918) as shown in **Figure 74**.
6. Press bearing cup in lower gear housing using cup installer (Special Tool T8909) with driver handle (Special Tool T8907) and guide plate from bearing guide set (Special Tool T8918) as shown in **Figure 75**.
7. Install forward bevel gear assembly with a 0.059 in. thick front bevel gear spacer. Com-

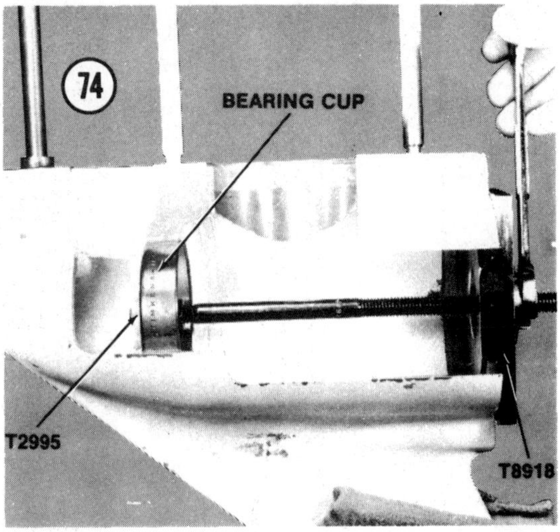

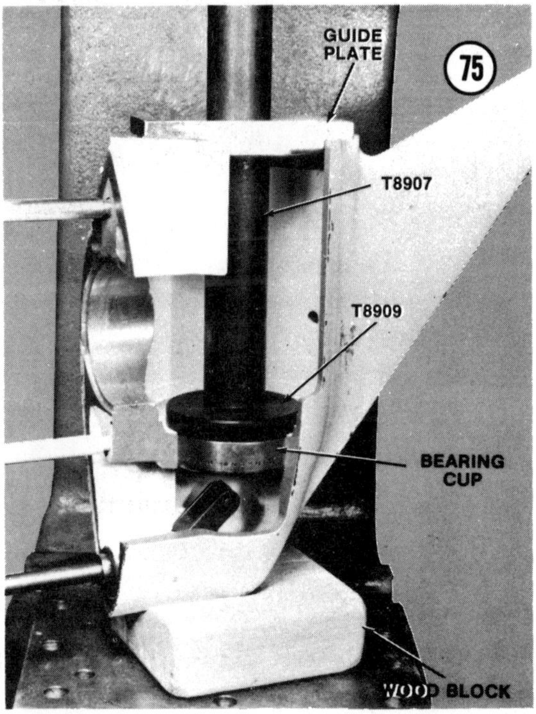

plete lower gear housing assembly. Do not assemble upper gear housing at this time.

8. Check propeller shaft end float.

9. After checking propeller shaft end float, install proper thickness spacer and complete the assembly.

Checking Propeller Shaft End Float

1. Install a 0.059 in. thick spacer on propeller shaft (front bevel gear side).

2. Install propeller shaft in lower gear housing.

3. Install propeller shaft bearing cage on lower gear housing.

> NOTE: *Leave propeller shaft bearing cage seal (large O-ring) off bearing cage for easy installation and removal after checking end float.*

4. Install dial indicator post in one of the bearing cage screw holes and tighten securely. Install hex socket head screw in other screw hole and tighten securely.

5. Install dial indicator (Special Tool T8902 or equivalent) with holder (Special Tool T8901 or equivalent) on post.

6. Preload dial indicator at least ½ turn on indicator needle. Secure indicator to post. Tap indicator shaft with finger to be certain indicator is tightened securely to post.

7. Rotate propeller shaft clockwise and counterclockwise while applying force to seat propeller shaft bearings.

8. Set dial on indicator to align zero with needle.

9. Lift the propeller shaft up and read the total indicated movement of the needle as shown in **Figure 76**. This reading is the total propeller shaft end float. The propeller shaft end float should be 0.005 ± 0.001 in.

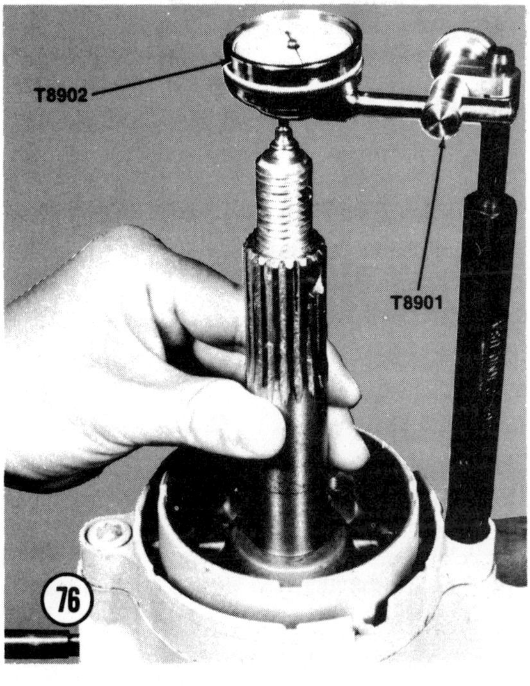

For example:

	Example A	Example B
Total indicated reading	0.017	0.018
End float allowed	—0.005	—0.005
Difference	0.012	0.013
Thickness spacer in gear housing	+0.059	+0.059
Thickness spacer required	0.071	0.072

Shift Arm Removal/Installation

1. Remove lower unit.
2. Remove upper gear housing assembly.
3. Remove propeller shaft assembly.
4. Remove shift rod from shift arm.
5. Remove pivot screw securing shift arm to lower gear housing.
6. Remove shift arm from lower gear housing.
7. Install shift arm in lower gear housing with forked ends in first.
8. Align pivot hole in shift arm with hole in lower gear housing and install pivot screw with new nyltite washer to secure shift arm.
9. Install lower shift rod in shift arm. Bottom threads of lower shift rod in shift arm.
10. Install propeller shaft assembly.
11. Install upper gear housing assembly.
12. Install lower unit.

Lower Gear Housing Removal/Installation

1. Remove lower unit.
2. Remove upper gear housing.
3. Remove propeller shaft assembly.
4. Remove front bevel gear.
5. Remove shift arm.
6. Remove pilot from forward stud hole in lower gear housing.
7. Install pilot in forward stud hole of lower gear housing.
8. Install shift arm in lower gear housing.
9. Install front bevel gear.
10. Install propeller shaft assembly.
11. Install upper gear housing.
12. Install lower unit.

Exhaust Snout Removal/Installation

1. Remove long screw (rear screw) with washer and short screw (forward screw) with lockwasher securing snout to upper gear housing.
2. Remove snout from upper gear housing.
3. Apply Loctite "D" to threads of exhaust snout screws.
4. Install long screw in rear exhaust snout screw hole. Do not tighten securely at this time.
5. Install short screw in forward exhaust snout screw hole. Do not tighten at this time.
6. While looking at engine from rear, move exhaust snout all the way to the left. Then move exhaust snout 1/16 in. back to the right.
7. Hold position of exhaust snout and torque forward screw to 70 in.-lb. and rear to 160 in.-lb.

POWER HEAD (3-CYLINDER ENGINES)

Cylinder Head Removal

1. Remove spark plugs.
2. Remove 14 cylinder head bolts and washers securing cylinder head to cylinder. Remove cylinder head and gasket.
3. Remove thermoswitch (located next to No. 1 spark plug). Remove cylinder head cover and gasket from cylinder head.
4. Remove the thermostat from cavity in the cylinder head.

Cylinder Head Installation

1. Clean all gasket surfaces.

CAUTION

When cleaning gasket surfaces, be careful not to scratch or groove them.

2. Install thermostat in cavity of cylinder head with bypass slot in thermostat positioned up.
3. Install cylinder head cover and new gasket on cylinder head and secure with thermoswitch and 2 screws.
4. Install cylinder head with new head gasket on power head. Secure cylinder head with 14 head bolts and plain washers. First torque all cylinder head bolts to 75 in.-lb. following sequence

shown in **Figure 77**. Then increase torque in increments of 25-50 in.-lb. to specified torque.

> NOTE: *Torque for 5/16-18 thread bolts is 225 ± 5 in.-lb. Torque for 3/8-16 thread bolts is 270 ± 5 in.-lb.*

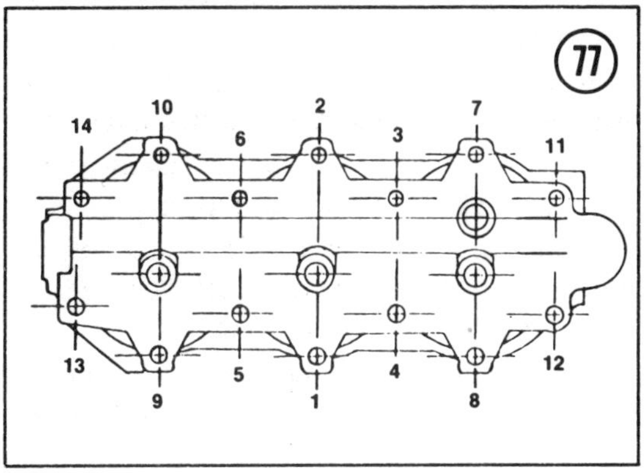

5. Install spark plugs on cylinder head.
6. Run engine for 15 minutes. Allow engine to cool, then retorque cylinder head bolts.

Reed Assembly Removal

1. Disconnect fuel line from bottom carburetor and carburetor intake cover drain hose from carburetor adapter flange.
2. Remove throttle tie bar from throttle shutter arm of carburetors.
3. Disconnect throttle cam link end connector from tower shaft. Remove nuts securing carburetors to carburetor adapter flange.
4. Remove carburetors and intake cover as an assembly from power head.
5. Remove choke solenoid and clamp.
6. Remove screws securing deflector plate and reed plate to power head as shown in **Figure 78**. Remove carburetor adapter flange assembly.
7. Remove stop nut securing throttle cam to carburetor adapter flange. Remove throttle cam assembly.
8. Remove reed plate assemblies and deflector plate from carburetor adapter flange.

Reed Assembly Installation

1. Clean all gasket surfaces, being careful not to scratch or groove them.

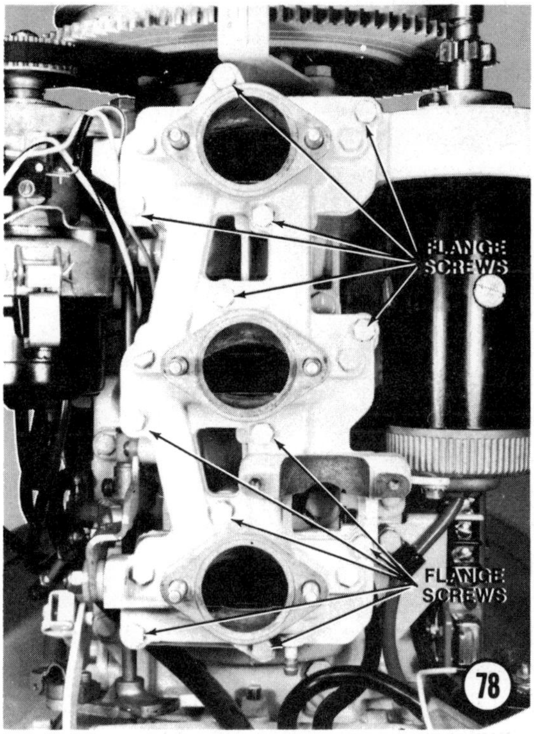

2. Install new gaskets between reed plates and deflector plate. Install new gasket between deflector plate and carburetor adapter flange.
3. Secure reed plate assemblies and deflector plate to carburetor adapter flange.
4. Install throttle cam assembly with nylon washer on each side of carburetor adapter flange stud. Secure throttle cam on stud with stop nut. Tighten stop nut until throttle cam pivots freely on stud, but with no side play.
5. Install carburetor adapter flange on power head and secure with 12 screws as shown in Figure 78.

> NOTE: *The 2 longer screws used are positioned under top carburetor flange and middle carburetor flange.*

6. Install choke solenoid and clamp and secure with 2 screws. Adjust choke solenoid position after carburetors are installed as outlined under *Tune-up*.
7. Install carburetors and intake cover assembly on power head. Insert choke solenoid plunger in solenoid and align carburetors on studs on adapter flange. Secure carburetors to adapter flange with 6 nuts.

8. Install throttle tie bar and secure with retaining clips. Synchronize carburetor shutters as outlined under *Tune-up*.
9. Adjust the throttle pickup as outlined under *Tune-up*.
10. Connect fuel line (fuel pump to bottom carburetor) to fitting on bottom carburetor. Connect drain hose from carburetor intake cover to fitting on carburetor adapter flange.

Reed Removal

1. Remove reed plate assembly.
2. Remove screws securing reed stop and reeds on each side of plate.
3. Remove reed stops and reeds.

Reed Installation

1. Install one 4-petal and one single petal reed set on each side of plate.
2. Position reeds over openings so that they overlap openings by at least 0.040 in.
3. Install reed stops. Secure reeds and stops to plate with 5 screws on each side.
4. Check reed stop openings. Reed stop opening is 0.28 ± 0.010 in.
5. Check reeds for warpage. Reeds are allowed to stand open a maximum of 0.010 in. If reeds are standing open more than 0.010 in., remove and straighten.
6. Install reed stop assembly.

Crankshaft Bearing Cage Removal/Installation

1. Remove flywheel and stator plate.
2. Remove crankshaft bearing cage.
3. Press the crankshaft bearing seal out of the bearing cage.
4. Remove bearing cage seal from groove on top of power head.
5. Clean gasket surfaces on bearing cage and power head.
6. Position crankshaft bearing seal on bore with garter spring toward inside of crankcase. Press seal in bore of bearing cage as shown in **Figure 79**.

7. Install new bearing cage seal (O-ring seal) on bearing cage assembly.
8. Apply a bead of sealant around surface of bearing cage halfway between screw holes and O-ring seal.
9. Install seal protector (Special Tool T8915) on top of crankshaft. Apply grease between lips of crankshaft seal. Install bearing cage assembly on seal protector. Slide bearing cage down crankshaft on power head.
10. Align holes of bearing cage with hole in power head. Apply sealant to threads of bearing cage screws. Install screws to secure bearing cage to power head.
11. Install stator and flywheel.

Throttle Tower Shaft Removal/Installation

1. Remove distributor.
2. Disconnect throttle link from rod end connector stud on tower shaft.
3. Remove screws securing tower shaft to power head and lift tower shaft off.
4. Install tower shaft with bottom end in spacer plate.
5. Align holes in nylon bearings with holes on power head and secure tower shaft with 4 screws.
6. Connect throttle link to tower shaft. Check throttle shutters to see that they are horizontal at wide open throttle. Readjust if necessary.
7. Install distributor.

Power Head Removal

1. Remove rear motor leg cover.
2. Remove 6 elastic stop nuts securing power head to motor leg.
3. Remove fuel pump assembly from transfer port cover.
4. Remove distributor from power head.
5. Remove tower shaft.
6. Remove top elastic stop nut securing upper shift rod to interlock arm.
7. Remove lead wire from choke solenoid.
8. Remove all lead wires from starter relay. Clamp the holding wiring harness at the base of starter relay.
9. Remove battery ground wire from crankcase cover.
10. Remove ground wire from power head.
11. Remove remote electric cable wires from terminal block and clamp.
12. Remove bolts securing spacer plate to motor leg.
13. Lift power head, spacer plate, and exhaust tube from motor leg using hoist and lifting hook (Special Tool T8933 or equivalent) on end of crankshaft.
14. Remove lower cylinder exhaust gasket.
15. Remove screws securing exhaust tube to spacer plate.
16. Remove the elastic stop nuts securing the spacer plate to base of power head and remove the spacer plate.
17. Remove upper cylinder exhaust gasket.

Power Head Installation

1. Clean all gasket surfaces.
2. Apply sealant to both sides of upper cylinder exhaust gasket in area between forward stud holes. Install upper cylinder exhaust gasket on power head.
3. Install spacer plate on upper cylinder exhaust and secure with elastic stop nuts. Torque nuts to 270 in.-lb.
4. Install exhaust tube to spacer plate and secure with 4 screws. Before installing screws, apply anti-seize compound to threads of screws. Torque screws to 70 in.-lb.
5. Install lower cylinder exhaust gasket to top of motor leg aligning holes of gasket with holes in motor leg.
6. Install power head on motor leg and align drive shaft splines with crankshaft.
7. Secure power head to motor leg with 6 screws through spacer plate and 6 stop nuts on studs on power head. Torque bolts and nuts 270 in.-lb.
8. Connect lead wires for remote electric cable to terminal block.
9. Connect ground wire from support plate to exhaust port cover screw (Delta system only).
10. Connect lead wires to starter relay. See *Starter Relay Removal/Installation*.
11. Connect battery cable ground lead to crankcase cover.
12. Connect choke wire to choke solenoid. Hold lead wire to body of solenoid with cable tie, retaining band, or tape.
13. Install elastic stop nut to secure upper shift rod to interlock arm. Check adjustment of interlock as follows.
    a. Set engine in exact NEUTRAL gear position (middle of upper shift rod travel between FORWARD and REVERSE gear position).
    b. Adjust interlock arm position so that top of interlock arm is even with top of neutral stop on tower shaft. Make adjustment by turning stop nut above interlock arm and nut below interlock arm.
14. Install tower shaft.
15. Install distributor.
16. Install fuel pump assembly.
17. Install rear motor leg cover.

6

Short Block Removal/Installation

1. Remove flywheel and stator plate.
2. Remove crankshaft bearing cage.
3. Remove carburetor adapter flange and reed plate assemblies.
4. Remove distributor.
5. Remove tower shaft.
6. Remove fuel pump.
7. Remove C-D unit.
8. Remove cylinder drain covers.

9. Remove transfer port covers.
10. Remove cylinder head.
11. Remove cylinder exhaust port cover, plate, and gaskets.
12. Remove wiring harness.
13. Remove terminal block bracket assembly.
14. Remove rectifier.
15. Remove starter.
16. Remove power head, exhaust tube, and spacer plate.
17. Installation is the reverse of these steps.

Crankshaft Removal/Installation

1. Remove power head.
2. Remove the carburetor, carburetor adapter flanges, and deflector plate assemblies.
3. Remove crankshaft bearing cage assembly.
4. Remove main bearing bolts and crankcase parting line screws.

> NOTE: *As bolts and screws are being removed, note different lengths. Make sketch showing location of each size screw. Also note that 2 top crankcase parting line screws (one on each side) are assembled from the opposite side. Make note on sketch.*

5. Drive dowel pins out as shown in **Figure 80**.

6. Pry crankcase cover from cylinder using large screwdriver at each pry point as shown in **Figure 81**. Lift crankcase cover from cylinder.
7. Remove crankcase parting line seal from groove in cylinder.

8. Remove connecting rod cap screws using 12-point socket (Special Tool T2953 or equivalent) as shown in **Figure 82**. Mark each rod cap showing position in cylinder as rod caps are removed.

9. Remove crankpin needle bearings and cages from crankshaft throws.

> NOTE: *Be sure to group rollers and cages with respective rod cap. Do not mix needles or cages on one rod cap with another.*

10. Lift crankshaft with main bearings from cylinder.
11. Remove snap ring from groove in main bearing as shown in **Figure 83**. Remove center main bearing race and caged rollers.
12. Remove crankcase seal from groove in crankshaft next to main bearing. See Figure 83. Be sure to group all components of each main bearing group together—do not mix.

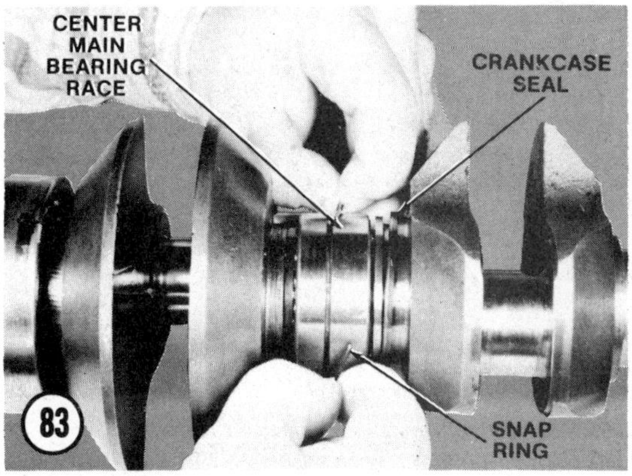

13. Slide lower main bearing with seal off bottom end of crankshaft.

14. To remove crankshaft lower seal, reinstall lower main bearing assembly on end of crankshaft and insert screwdriver between seal and bearing. Twist screwdriver and pry seal out of bearing case as shown in **Figure 84**.

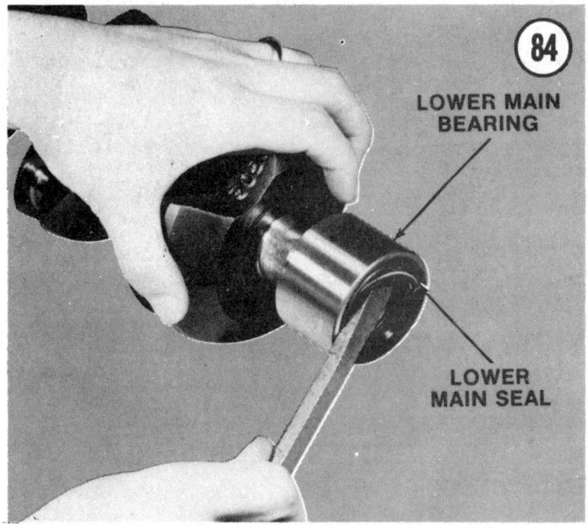

Crankshaft Installation

1. Clean all gasket surfaces and crankcase parting line surfaces.

2. Press seal in lower main bearing case (garter spring out) using seal installer (Special Tool T8925). Press in until tool bottoms on the bearing case.

3. Apply grease between lips of crankshaft lower seal. Install lower main bearing assembly on bottom of crankshaft.

4. Install center main bearings on crankshaft with holes in bearing race between snap ring groove on race and crankcase seal groove on crankshaft. Secure race to crankshaft with snap ring. Do not have gap of snap ring over fracture in main bearing race.

5. Scrape old Loctite off outer diameter of upper main bearing. Clean bearing surface with Locquic. Apply a bead of Loctite retaining compound around outer surface of bearing.

6. Apply grease to crankcase seal groove in crankshaft to retain seal in groove. Install crankcase seal in each groove in crankshaft.

7. Install crankshaft assembly on cylinder. Align large hole of each main bearing in locating pins in cylinder main bearing bores.

8. Examine crankpin needle bearing cages. Note that each cage is notched on one side as shown in **Figure 85**. Notched side is always toward upper main bearing. Install crankpin needle bearing cage half in connecting rod with notched side toward upper main bearing. Apply a light coating of grease on cage half. Install 7 needles in cage half. Pull rod with cage half and needles up and against crankpin throw. Install crankpin needle bearing cage half on crankpin throw with notched side toward upper main bearing. Apply light coating of grease on cage half. Install the remaining 9 needles.

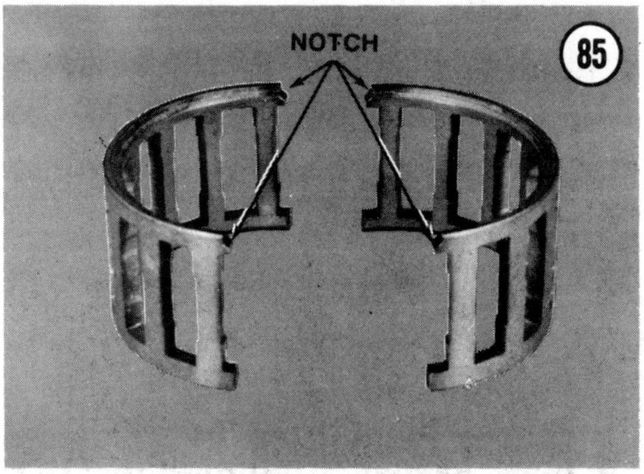

9. Install rod cap over crankpin needle bearing and cage with match mark on rod shank aligned with match mark on rod cap as shown in **Figure 86**. If connecting rod has a sanded surface across fracture joint on screw bosses, torque rod cap screw to 15 in.-lb. maximum. Check for rod cap offset by lightly running a sharp lead pencil across sanded area. If offset is present, pencil will stop at fracture joint. Loosen rod cap

screws. Reset rod cap on connecting rod and re-torque rod cap screws to 15 in.-lb. Recheck for offset. If offset is still present, replace the connecting rod.

10. Torque cap screws to 170 ± 5 in.-lb. using torque wrench and 12-point socket (Special Tool T2953 or equivalent).

11. Follow Steps 8 through 10 for remaining connecting rods.

12. Install new crankcase parting line seal in grooves of cylinder.

13. Apply sealant to areas between cylinders inside of seal groove and areas of both upper and lower main bearings on both sides of seal groove.

14. Install crankcase cover on cylinder. Drive in 2 dowel pins to locate crankcase cover on cylinder. Apply sealant on threads of crankcase bolts. Install bolts as shown in **Figure 87**. Torque bolts to 270 in.-lb. from center of crankcase and outward.

15. Install crankcase parting line screws.

16. Install crankcase bearing cage assembly.

17. Install the carburetors, carburetor adapter flanges, and deflector plate assemblies.

Connecting Rod/Piston Removal

1. Remove cylinder head.
2. Remove crankshaft assembly.

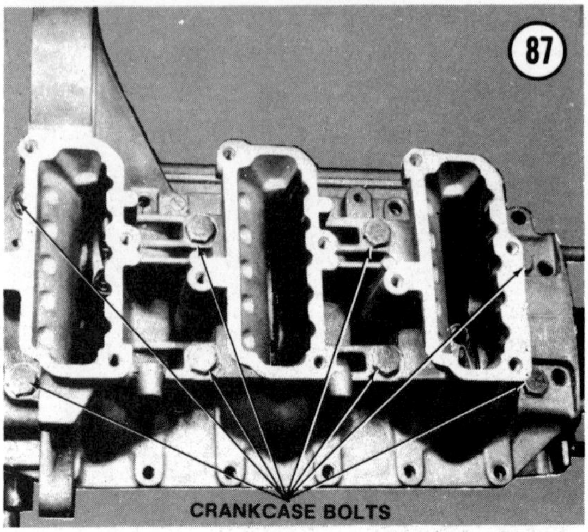

3. Push piston assembly out of cylinder bore.
4. Remove piston rings from piston using piston ring expander (Special Tool T8926 or equivalent) as shown in **Figure 88**.

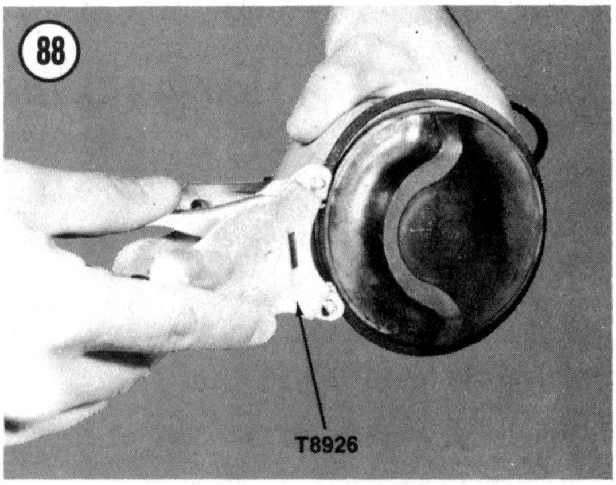

5. Remove piston pin from piston assembly using piston pin tool (Special Tool T2990 or equivalent) as outlined below.

   a. Place piston on pillow block with piston pin aligned with hole in pillow block.
   b. Install stepped end of drive pin in I.D. of piston pin.
   c. Insert end of shim bar marked "295" between large diameter of spacer and needles.

   NOTE: *The shim bar has 2 slots marked "310" and "295". The "310" end is used to install piston pin. The "295" end is used primarily to remove piston pin. In very rare cases, it may be necessary to use the "295" end to install piston pin if the "310" end will not slide in.*

d. Press piston pin out as shown in **Figure 89**.

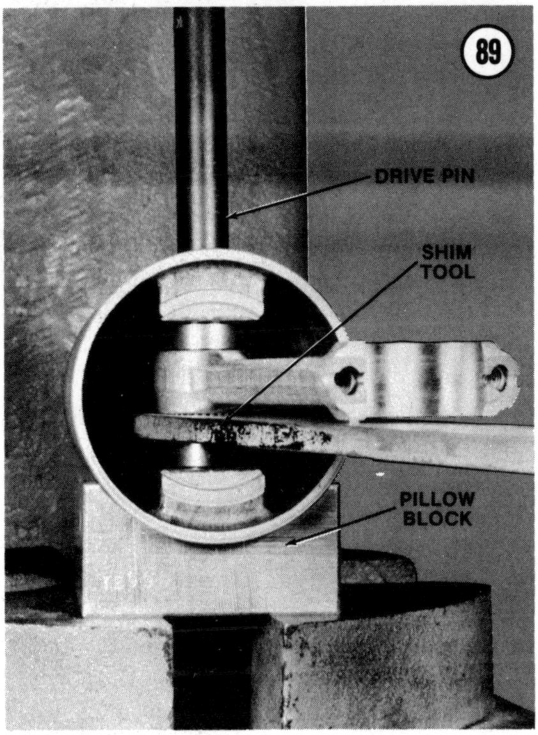

6. Remove connecting rod, piston pin spacers, and needles from piston. Do not lose any needles from connecting rod.

NOTE: *There are 26 needles per bearing set.*

Connecting Rod/Piston Installation

1. Install alignment pin from piston tool set through one side of piston.

2. Install spacer on alignment pin with small diameter end toward inside of piston or toward connecting rod when installed.

3. Install piston pin needle bearings (26 per set) in piston pin bore of connecting rod.

NOTE: *If old needles are used, coat bore of connecting rod with grease to retain needles. Then press needles firmly against bore of connecting rod.*

4. Install connecting rod with needles on alignment pin with match mark on crankpin end of connecting rod toward intake side of piston. See Figure 89. This will position match mark of connecting rod "up" (toward flywheel end of crankshaft).

5. Push alignment pin through connecting rod. Install other spacer with small diameter end toward connecting rod.

6. Push alignment pin through other spacer and in piston pin bore on other side of piston.

7. Install shim bar with end marked "310" between large diameter end of first spacer and connecting rod. See **Figure 90**. Slots on each end of shim tool have a step. This step is clearance for piston pin needles.

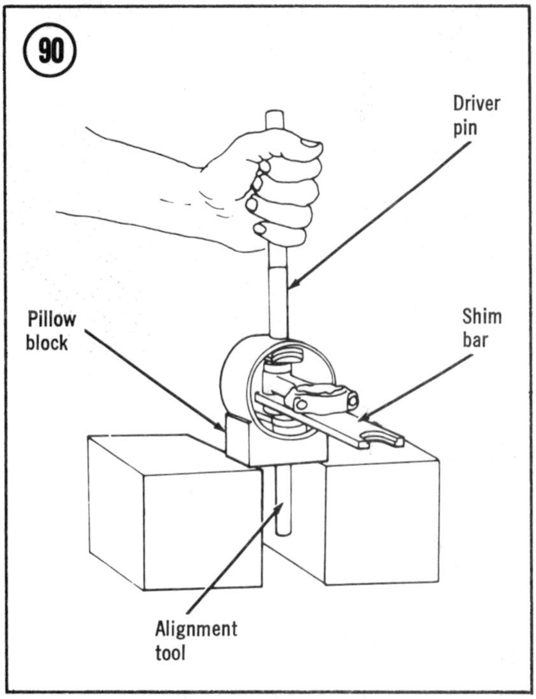

8. Place above assembly on pillow block. Install piston pin on bore of piston. Install driver pin with stepped end in end of piston pin. Press piston pin in bore of piston while holding alignment tool as shown in **Figure 91**. Press piston pin until it is centered in piston.

9. If new piston pin needle bearings were installed, apply a liberal amount of motor oil on them. Connecting rod must slide easily between the 2 spacers.

10. Install piston rings on piston with bevel on piston ring positioned up as shown in **Figure 92**.

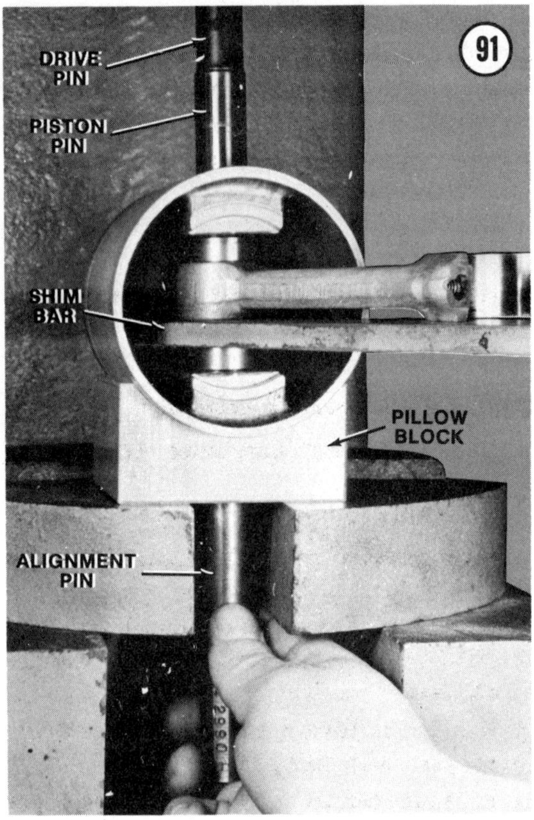

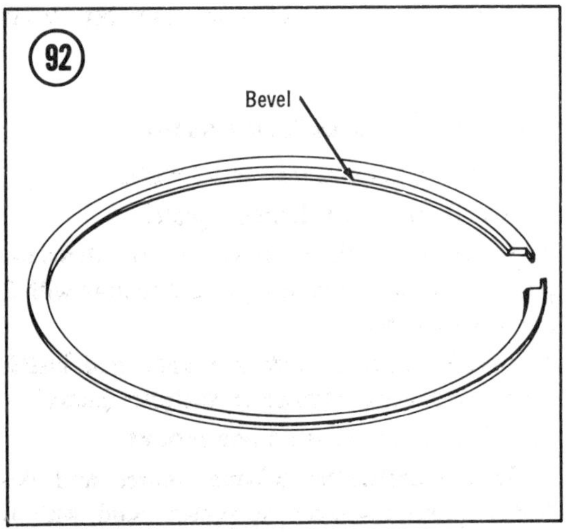

11. Install piston assemblies in cylinder using ring compressor as shown in **Figure 93**. Position pistons in cylinder with intake baffle on piston on intake side of cylinder.

12. Install crankshaft assembly and complete assembly of power head.

13. Install cylinder head.

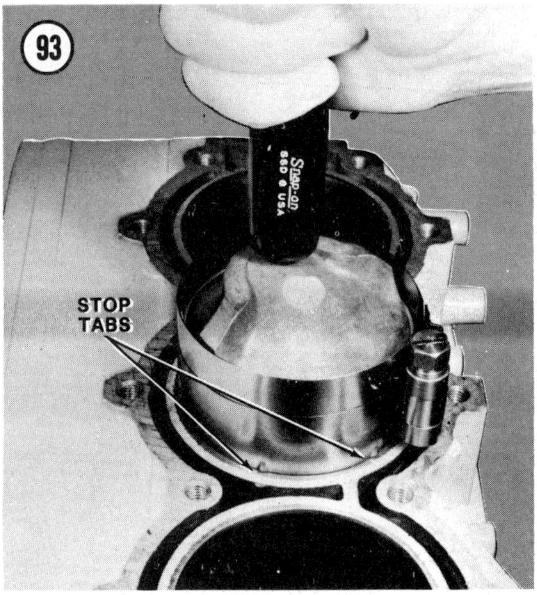

POWER HEAD (4-CYLINDER ENGINES)

Cylinder Head Removal

1. Remove thermostat cover and gasket from cylinder head.

2. Remove the thermostat from cavity in the cylinder head.

3. Remove spark plugs from cylinder head.

4. Remove bolts and washers securing cylinder head to power head. Remove cylinder head and gasket from power head.

Cylinder Head Installation

1. Install thermostat in cylinder head with by-pass slot in thermostat positioned up.

2. Install new gasket and thermostat cover on cylinder head.

> NOTE: *When cleaning gasket surfaces, be careful not to scratch or groove same.*

3. Install cylinder head with new gasket on power head. Secure cylinder head with head bolts and plain washers. First, torque all cylinder head bolts to 75 in.-lb. following sequence as shown in **Figure 94**. Then increase torque in increments of 50 in.-lb. to specified torque.

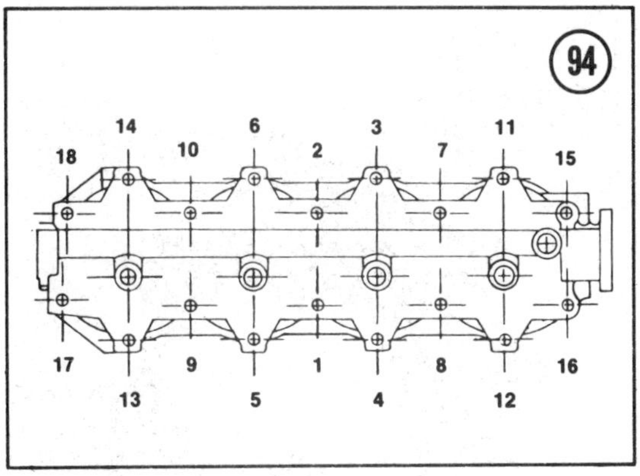

NOTE: *Torque for 5/16-18 thread bolts is 225 ± 5 in.-lb. Torque for 3/8-16 thread bolts is 270 ± 5 in.-lb.*

4. Install spark plugs on head.
5. Run engine for 15 minutes. Allow engine to cool then retorque cylinder head bolts.

Top Reed Assembly Removal

1. Remove the carburetor as outlined under *Carburetor*.
2. Remove choke solenoid with bracket.
3. Disconnect balance tube from carburetor adapter flange.
4. Remove remaining 6 screws securing carburetor adapter flange to power head. Remove both carburetor adapter flange and deflector plate with reed plate assemblies.
5. Separate carburetor adapter flange from deflector plate assembly.
6. Remove each reed plate from deflector plate.
7. Remove the reed plate gasket from the deflector plate.

Top Reed Assembly Installation

1. Clean gasket surfaces on all parts.
2. Install gasket on deflector plate and install reed plate assembly.
3. Secure each reed plate assembly with 2 flat head screws.
4. Install gasket on deflector plate assembly and install carburetor adapter flange.
5. Install adapter flange with deflector plate assembly on power head and connect balance tube to fitting on adapter flange.
6. Secure adapter flange and deflector plate assembly to power head with 6 short screws. Leave lower 2 holes for choke solenoid bracket.
7. Install choke solenoid bracket with choke solenoid on adapter flange and secure with 4 long screws.
8. Install the carburetor as outlined under *Carburetor*.
9. Adjust the choke solenoid as outlined under *Tune-up*.

Bottom Reed Assembly Removal

1. Remove bottom carburetor as outlined under *Carburetor*.
2. Remove choke solenoid bracket.
3. Disconnect balance tube from carburetor adapter flange.
4. Remove elastic stop nut securing throttle cam to carburetor adapter flange. Remove throttle cam and nylon bearings.
5. Remove carburetor adapter flange and deflector plate with reed plate assemblies.
6. Separate carburetor adapter flange from deflector plate.
7. Remove each reed plate assembly from deflector plate.

Bottom Reed Assembly Installation

1. Clean gasket surfaces on all parts.
2. Install gasket on deflector plate.
3. Install reed plate assemblies on deflector plate and secure each reed plate assembly with 2 flat head screws.
4. Install gasket on deflector plate and install carburetor adapter flange on deflector plate.
5. Install above parts on power head.
6. Secure carburetor adapter flange and deflector plate assembly to power head with 6 screws. Leave upper 2 holes for choke solenoid bracket. Connect balance tube to fitting on adapter flange.
7. Install choke solenoid bracket with choke solenoid on adapter flange. Secure with 4 long screws.
8. Install the carburetor as outlined under *Carburetor*.

6

9. Adjust the choke solenoid as outlined under *Tune-up*.

10. Install throttle cam with nylon bearing on each side of cam on stud of carburetor adapter flange and secure with elastic stop nut. Tighten elastic stop nut enough so that throttle cam pivots freely but with no side play.

11. Adjust the throttle pickup as outlined under *Tune-up*.

Reed Removal

1. Remove reed plate assembly.
2. Remove 5 screws securing reed stop and reeds on each side of plate.
3. Remove stops and reeds.

Reed Installation

1. Install one 4-petal and one single petal reed set on each side of plate.
2. Position reeds over plate openings so that reeds overlap openings by at least 0.040 in.
3. Secure reeds and stops to plate with 5 screws on each side of plate.
4. Check reed stop openings. Reed stop opening is 0.28 ± 0.010 in.
5. Check reeds for warpage. Reeds are allowed to stand open a maximum of 0.010 in. If reeds are standing open more than 0.010 in., remove and straighten.
6. Install reed stop assembly.

Crankshaft Bearing Removal/Installation

1. Remove flywheel and stator plate.
2. Remove crankshaft bearing cage assembly.
3. Press the crankshaft bearing seal out of the bearing cage.
4. Remove bearing cage seal from groove on top of power head.
5. Clean gasket surfaces on bearing cage and power head.
6. Position crankshaft bearing seal on bore of crankshaft bearing cage with garter spring toward inside of crankcase. Press seal in bore of bearing cage using seal installer (Special Tool T8903) as shown in **Figure 95**.

95

7. Install new bearing cage seal (O-ring) on bearing cage assembly.
8. Apply a bead of sealant around surface of bearing cage halfway between screw holes and O-ring seal.
9. Install seal protector (Special Tool T8915) on top of crankshaft. Apply grease between lips of crankshaft seal. Install bearing cage assembly on seal protector. Slide bearing cage down crankshaft on power head.
10. Align holes of bearing cage with holes in power head. Apply sealant to threads of bearing cage screws. Install screws to secure bearing cage to power head.
11. Install stator and flywheel.

Throttle Tower Shaft Removal/Installation

1. Remove distributor.
2. Disconnect throttle link from rod end connector stud on tower shaft.
3. Remove screws securing tower shaft to power head and lift off.
4. Install tower shaft with bottom end in spacer plate bearing.
5. Align holes in nylon bearings with holes on power head and secure tower shaft to power head with 4 screws.

6. Connect throttle link to tower shaft. Check throttle shutters to see that they are horizontal at wide open throttle. Readjust if necessary.

7. Install distributor.

Power Head Removal

1. Remove rear motor leg cover.
2. Remove 6 elastic stop nuts securing power head to motor leg.
3. Remove fuel pump assembly from transfer port cover.
4. Remove distributor from power head.
5. Remove tower shaft.
6. Remove top elastic stop nut securing upper shift rod to interlock arm.
7. Remove lead wire from choke solenoid.
8. Remove all lead wires from starter relay and clamp the holding wiring harness at the base of starter relay.
9. Remove battery ground wire from crankcase cover.
10. Remove ground wrie from power head.
11. Remove remote electric cable wires from terminal block and clamp.
12. Remove 6 bolts securing spacer plate to motor leg.
13. Lift power head, spacer plate, and exhaust tube from motor leg using hoist and lifting hook (Special Tool T8933 or equivalent) on end of crankshaft.
14. Remove lower cylinder exhaust gasket.
15. Remove screws securing exhaust tube to spacer plate.
16. Remove elastic stop nuts securing the spacer plate to base of power head and remove the spacer plate.
17. Remove upper cylinder exhaust gasket.

Power Head Installation

1. Clean all gasket surfaces.
2. Apply sealant to both sides of upper cylinder exhaust gasket in area between 2 forward stud holes. Install upper cylinder exhaust gasket on power head.
3. Install spacer plate on upper cylinder exhaust and secure with 4 elastic stop nuts. Torque nuts to 270 in.-lb.
4. Install exhaust tube to spacer plate and secure with 4 screws. Before installing screws, apply anti-seize compound to threads. Torque screws to 70 in.-lb.
5. Install lower cylinder exhaust gasket to top of motor leg. Align holes of gasket with holes in motor leg.
6. Install power head on motor leg. Align driveshaft splines with crankshaft.
7. Secure power head to motor leg with 6 screws through spacer plate and 6 stop nuts on power head studs. Torque bolts and nuts to 270 in.-lb.
8. Connect lead wires of remote electric cable to terminal block.
9. Connect ground lead wire from support plate to exhaust port cover screw (Delta system only).
10. Connect lead wires to starter relay. See *Starter Relay Removal/Installation.*
11. Connect battery cable ground lead to crankcase cover.
12. Connect choke lead wire to choke solenoid. Hold lead wire to body of solenoid with cable tie, retaining band, or tape.
13. Install elastic stop nut to secure upper shift rod to interlock arm. Check adjustment of interlock arm as follows.
    a. Set engine in exact neutral gear position (middle of upper shift rod travel between forward and reverse gear position).
    b. Adjust interlock arm position so that top of interlock arm is even with top of neutral stop on tower shaft. Adjustment is made by turning stop nut above interlock arm and nut below interlock arm.
14. Install tower shaft.
15. Install distributor.
16. Install fuel pump assembly.
17. Install rear motor leg cover.

Short Block Removal/Installation

1. Remove flywheel and stator plate.
2. Remove crankshaft bearing cage.
3. Remove carburetors.

4. Remove carburetor adapter flange and reed plate assemblies.
5. Remove distributor.
6. Remove tower shaft.
7. Remove fuel pump.
8. Remove C-D unit.
9. Remove cylinder drain covers.
10. Remove transfer port covers.
11. Remove cylinder head.
12. Remove cylinder exhaust port cover, plate, and gaskets.
13. Remove wiring harness.
14. Remove terminal block bracket assembly.
15. Remove rectifier.
16. Remove starter.
17. Remove power head, exhaust tube and spacer plate.
18. Installation is the reverse of these steps.

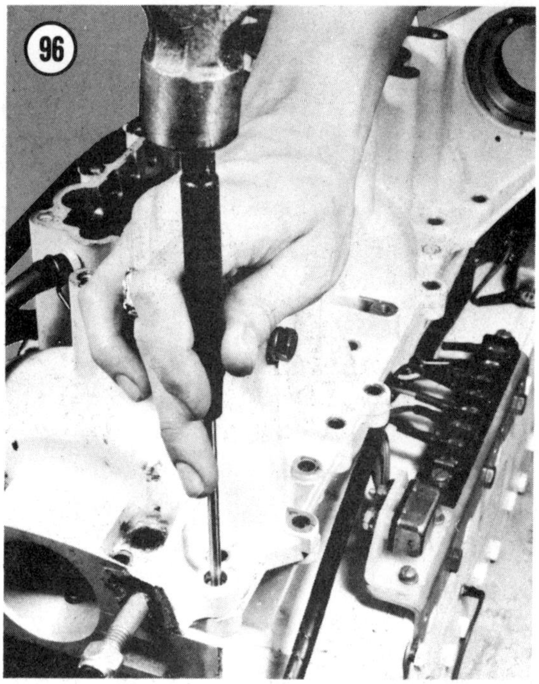

Crankshaft Removal

1. Remove power head.
2. Remove the carburetor, carburetor adapter flanges, and deflector plate assemblies.
3. Remove crankshaft bearing assembly.
4. Remove main bearing bolts and crankcase parting line screw.

> NOTE: *As bolts and screws are being removed, note different lengths. Make sketch showing location of each size screw. Also note that 2 top crankcase parting line screws are assembled from the opposite side. Make note on sketch.*

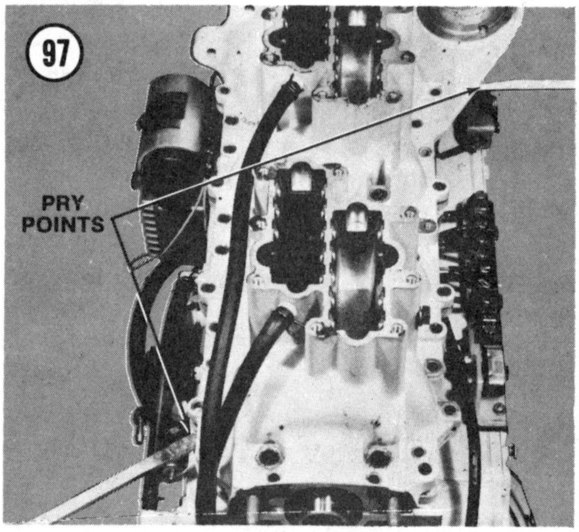

5. Drive dowel pins out as shown in **Figure 96**.
6. Pry crankcase cover from cylinder using large screwdriver at each pry point as shown in **Figure 97**. Lift crankcase cover from cylinder.
7. Remove crankcase parting line seal from groove in cylinder.
8. Remove connecting rod cap screws using 12-point socket (Special Tool T2953 or equivalent) as shown in **Figure 98**. Mark each rod cap showing position in cylinder as rod caps are removed.
9. Remove crank pin needle bearings and cages from crankshaft throws.

> NOTE: *Be sure to group rollers and cages with respective rod cap. Do not at any time mix needles or cages of one rod cap with another.*

10. Lift crankshaft with main bearings from cylinder.
11. Remove snap ring from groove in main bearing as shown in **Figure 99**. Remove center main bearing race and caged rollers.
12. Remove crankcase seal from groove in crankshaft next to main bearing. See Figure 99.

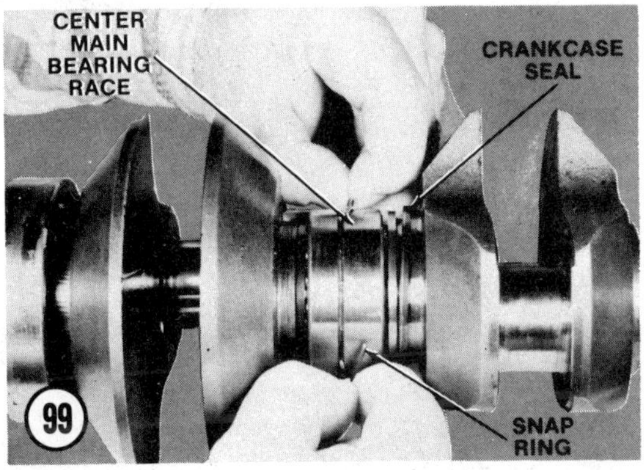

Be sure to group all components of each main bearing group together—do not mix. See **Figure 100**.

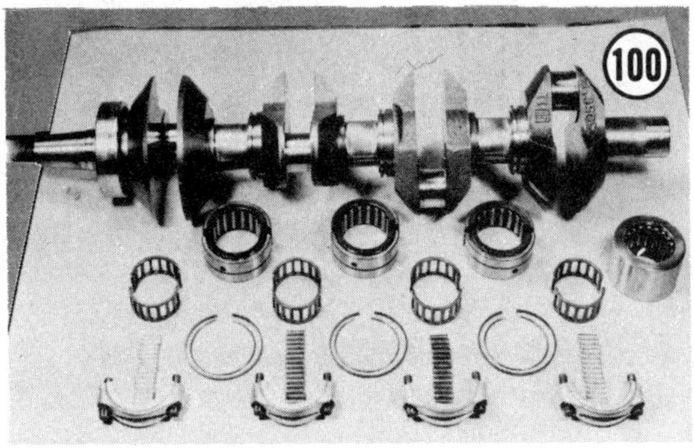

13. Slide lower main bearing with seal off bottom end of crankshaft.

14. To remove crankshaft lower seal, reinstall lower main bearing assembly on end of crankshaft and insert screwdriver between seal and bearing. Twist screwdriver and pry seal out of bearing case as shown in **Figure 101**.

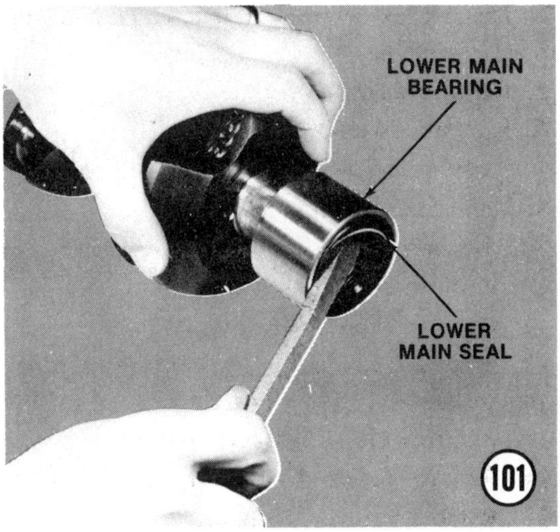

Crankshaft Installation

1. Clean all gasket surfaces and crankcase parting line surfaces.

2. Press seal in lower main bearing case (garter spring out) using seal installer (Special Tool T8925). Press seal in until tool bottoms on bearing case.

3. Apply grease between lips of crankshaft lower seal. Install lower main bearing assembly on bottom of crankshaft.

4. Install center main bearings on crankshaft with holes in bearing race between snap ring groove on race and crankcase seal groove on crankshaft. Secure race to crankshaft with snap ring. Do not have gap of snap ring over fracture in main bearing race.

5. Scrape old Loctite off outer diameter of upper main bearing. Clean bearing surface with Locquic. Apply a bead of Loctite retaining compound around outer surface of bearing.

6. Apply grease to crankcase seal groove in crankshaft to retain seal in groove. Install crankcase seal in each groove in crankshaft.

7. Install crankshaft assembly on cylinder. Align large hole of each main bearing in locating pins in cylinder main bearing bores.

8. Examine crank pin needle bearing cages. Note that each cage is notched on one side as shown in **Figure 102**. Notched side is always toward upper main bearing. Install crank pin needle bearing cage half in connecting rod with notched side towards upper main bearing. Apply

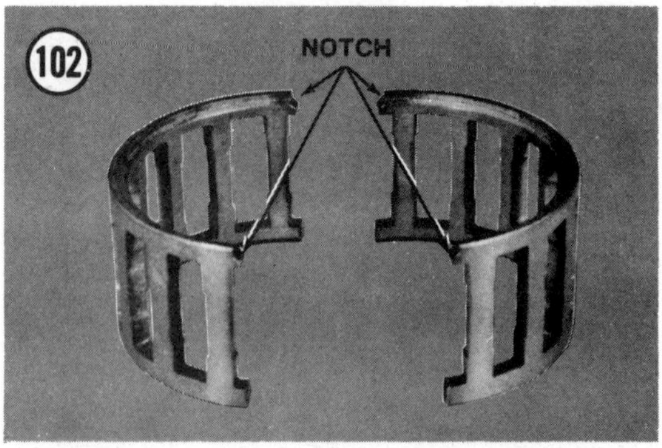

a light coating of grease on cage half. Install 7 needles in cage half. Pull rod with cage half and needles up and against crank pin throw. Install crank pin needle bearing cage half on crank pin throw with notched side toward upper main bearing. Apply light coating of grease on cage half. Install remaining 9 needles.

9. Install rod cap over crank pin needle bearing and cage with match mark on rod shank aligned with match mark on rod cap as shown in **Figure 103**. If connecting rod has a sanded surface across fracture joint on screw bosses, torque rod cap screw to 15 in.-lb. maximum. Check for rod cap offset by lightly running a sharp lead pencil across sanded area. If offset is present, pencil will stop at fracture joint. Loosen rod cap screws. Reset rod cap on connecting rod and retorque rod cap screws to 15 in.-lb. Recheck for offset. If there is offset still present, replace the connecting rod.

10. Torque cap screws to 170±5 in.-lb. using torque wrench and 12-point socket (Special Tool T2953 or equivalent).

11. Follow Steps 8 through 10 for remaining connecting rods.

12. Install new crankcase parting line seal in grooves of cylinder.

13. Apply sealant to areas between cylinders inside of seal groove and areas of both upper and lower main bearings on both sides of seal groove.

14. Install crankcase cover on cylinder. Drive in 2 dowel pins to locate crankcase cover on cylinder. Apply sealant on threads of crankcase bolts. Install bolts as shown in **Figure 104**. Torque bolts to 270 in.-lb. from center of crankcase and outward.

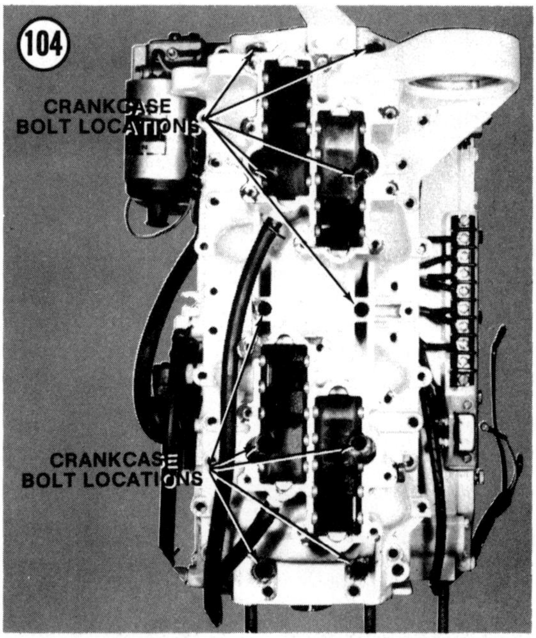

15. Install crankcase parting line screws.

16. Install crankcase bearing cage assembly.

17. Install carburetors, carburetor adapter flanges, and deflector plate assemblies.

18. Install power head.

Connecting Rod/Piston Removal

1. Remove cylinder head.
2. Remove crankshaft assembly.
3. Push piston assembly out of cylinder bore.

4. Remove piston rings from piston using piston ring expander (Special Tool T8926 or equivalent) as shown in **Figure 105**.

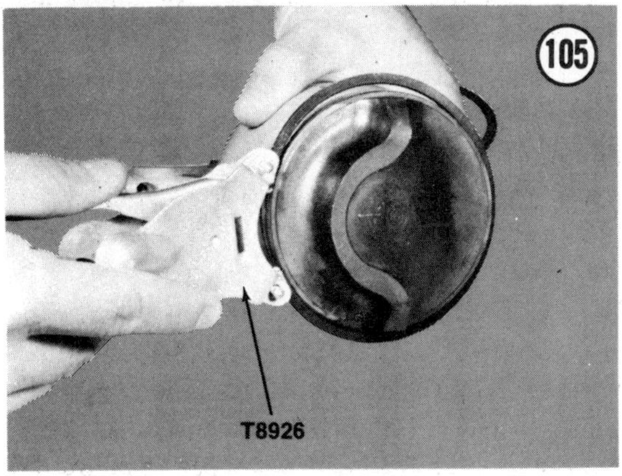

5. Remove piston pin from piston assembly using piston pin tool (Special Tool T2990 or equivalent) as outlined below.

a. Place piston on pillow block with piston pin aligned with hole in pillow block.

b. Install stepped end of drive pin in I.D. of piston pin.

c. Insert end of shim bar marked "295" between large diameter of spacer and needles.

NOTE: *The shim bar has 2 slots which are marked "310" and "295". The "310" end is used to install piston pin. The "295" end is used primarily to remove piston pin. In very rare cases, it may be necessary to use the "295" end to install piston pin if the "310" end will not slide in.*

d. Press piston pin out, shown in **Figure 106**.

6. Remove connecting rod, piston pin spacers, and needles from piston. Do not lose any needles from connecting rod.

NOTE: *There are 26 needles per bearing set.*

Connecting Rod/Piston Installation

1. Install alignment pin from piston tool set through one side of piston.

2. Install spacer on alignment pin with small diameter end toward inside of piston or toward connecting rod when installed.

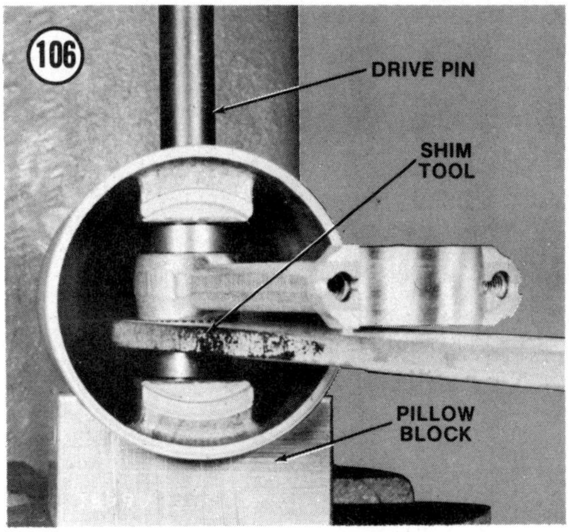

3. Install piston pin needle bearings (26 per set) in piston pin bore of connecting rod.

NOTE: *If old needles are used, coat bore of connecting rod with grease to retain needles. Then press needles firmly against bore of connecting rod.*

4. Install connecting rod with needles on alignment pin with match mark on crankpin end of connecting rod toward intake side of piston. See Figure 106. This will position match mark of connecting rod "up" (toward flywheel end of crankshaft).

5. Push alignment pin through connecting rod. Then install other spacer with small diameter end toward connecting rod.

6. Push alignment through other spacer and in piston pin bore on other side of piston.

7. Install shim bar with end marked "310" between large diameter end of first spacer and connecting rod. See **Figure 107**.

8. Slots on each end of shim tool have a step. This step is clearance for piston pin needles.

9. Place above assembly on pillow block. Install piston pin on bore of piston. Install driver pin with stepped end in end of piston pin. Press piston pin in bore of piston while holding alignment tool as shown in **Figure 108**. Press piston pin until it is centered in piston.

10. If new piston pin needle bearings were installed, apply a liberal amount of motor oil on them. Connecting rod must slide easily between the 2 spacers.

6

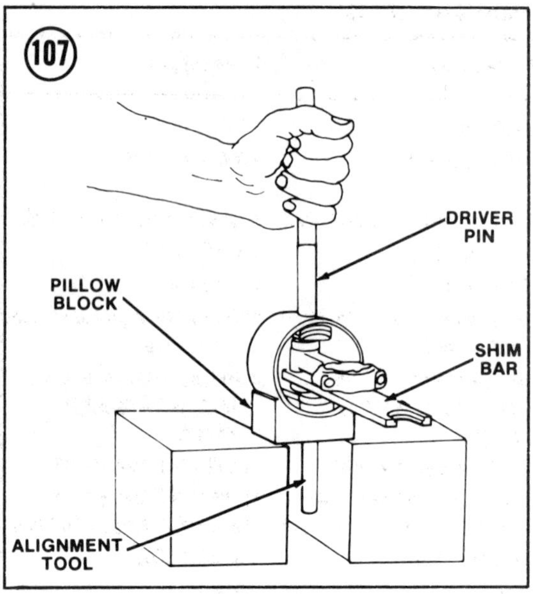

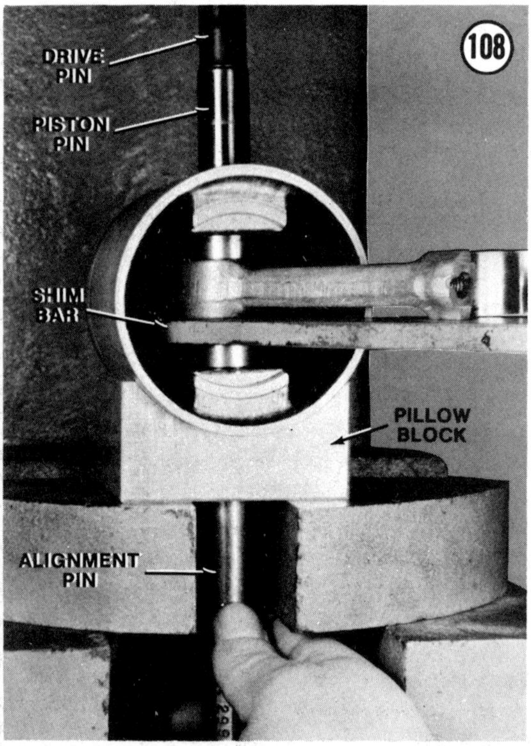

11. Install piston rings on piston with bevel on piston ring positioned up, shown in **Figure 109**.

> NOTE: *On 130 hp and 150 hp models, there are 2 different rings used per piston. The small beveled ring belongs in the bottom ring groove. The large beveled ring belongs in the top ring groove.*

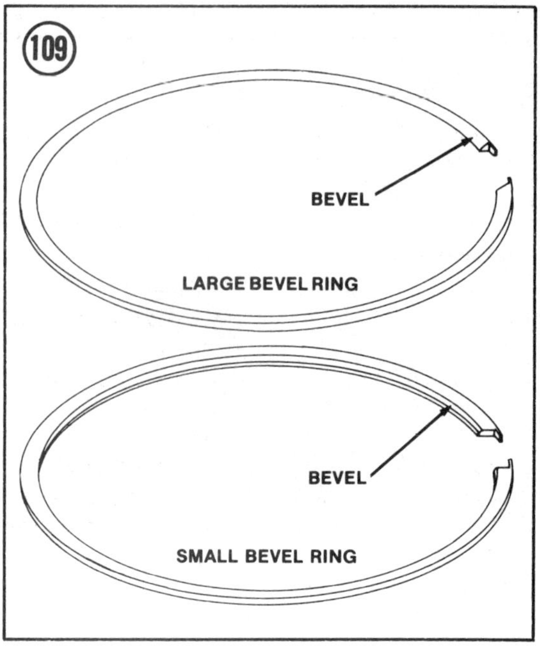

12. Install piston assemblies in cylinder with ring compressor as shown in **Figure 110**. Position pistons in cylinder with piston intake baffle on intake side of cylinder.

13. Install crankshaft assembly and complete assembly of power head.

14. Install cylinder head.

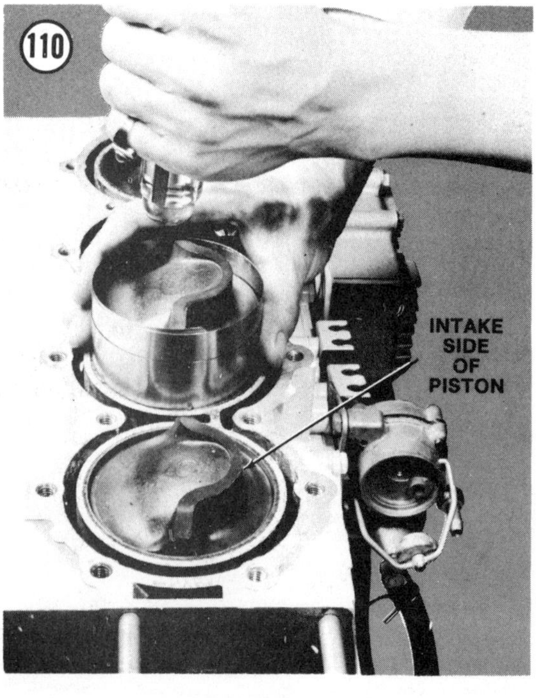

Table 1 ENGINE SPECIFICATIONS (70-135 HP)

	70 Horsepower	75 Horsepower	85 Horsepower
Horsepower, BIA rated @	4,750 rpm	4,750 rpm	5,000 rpm
Recommended operating range	4,400-5,100 rpm	4,400-5,100 rpm	4,500-5,500 rpm
Engine—2-cycle	3-cylinder, firing order—1, 2, 3	3-cylinder, firing order—1, 2, 3	3-cylinder, firing order—1, 2, 3
Bore and stroke	3-5/16 x 2.8 in.	3-5/16 x 2.8 in.	3-5/16 x 2.8 in.
Cubic inch displacement	72.39 cu. in.	72.39 cu. in.	72.39 cu. in.
Cooling	Water cooled displacement type water pump	Water cooled displacement type water pump	Water cooled displacement type water pump
Propeller—standard	Aluminum alloy, 12 in. dia., 15 in. pitch, right-hand rotation	Aluminum alloy, 13 in. dia., 17 in. pitch, right-hand rotation	Aluminum alloy, 13 in. dia., 15 in. pitch, right-hand rotation
Electric system	12 volt—negative ground	12 volt—negative ground	12 volt—negative ground
Alternator—output maximum	10 amps at 4,750 rpm. Alternator cut-in speed 1,000 rpm	10 amps at 4,750 rpm. Alternator cut-in speed 1,000 rpm	10 amps at 5,000 rpm. Alternator cut-in speed 1,000 rpm
Spark plug type	Champion L20V	Champion L20V	Champion L20V
Breaker point gap	0.014 in.	0.014 in.	0.014 in.
Compression average lbs.	130-140 psi	145-155 psi	145-155 psi
*Oil ratio per gallon of gas (break-in)	1/3 pint	1/3 pint	1/3 pint
Oil ratio per gallon of gas (after break-in)	1/6 pint	1/6 pint	1/6 pint

	90 Horsepower	105 Horsepower	120 Horsepower
Horsepower, BIA rated @	5,000 rpm	5,000 rpm	5,250 rpm
Recommended operating range	4,500-5,500 rpm	4,500-5,500 rpm	5,000-5,500 rpm
Engine—2-cycle	3-cylinder, firing order—1, 2, 3	4-cylinder, firing order—1, 3, 2, 4	4-cylinder, firing order—1, 3, 2, 4
Bore and stroke	3-5/16 x 2.8 in.	3-5/16 x 2.8 in.	3-5/16 x 2.8 in.
Cubic inch displacement	72.39 cu. in.	96.55 cu. in.	96.55 cu. in.
Cooling	Water cooled displacement type water pump	Water cooled displacement type water pump	Water cooled displacement type water pump
Propeller—standard	Aluminum alloy, 13 in. dia., 19 in. pitch, right-hand rotation	Aluminum alloy, 13 in. dia., 17 in. pitch, right-hand rotation	Aluminum alloy, 13 in. dia., 17 in. pitch, right-hand rotation
Electric system	12 volt—negative ground	12 volt—negative ground	12 volt—negative ground
Alternator—output maximum	10 amps at 5,000 rpm. Alternator cut-in speed 1,000 rpm	10 amps at 5,000 rpm. Alternator cut-in speed 1,000 rpm	10 amps at 5,250 rpm. Alternator cut-in speed 1,000 rpm
Spark plug type	Champion L20V	Champion L20V	Champion L20V
Breaker point gap	0.014 in.	0.010 in.	0.010 in.
Compression average lbs.	155-165 psi	130-140 psi	145-155 psi
*Oil ratio per gallon of gas (break-in)	1/3 pint	1/3 pint	1/3 pint
Oil ratio per gallon of gas (after break-in)	1/6 pint	1/6 pint	1/6 pint

(continued)

6

Table 1 ENGINE SPECIFICATIONS (continued)

	130 Horsepower	135 Horsepower	135 Horsepower (Racing)
Horsepower, BIA rated @	5 250 rpm	5,000 rpm	5,400 rpm
Recommended operating range	5,000-5,500 rpm	4,500-5,500 rpm	5,200-5,600 rpm
Engine—2-cycle	4-cylinder, firing order—1, 3, 2, 4	4-cylinder, firing order—1, 3, 2, 4	4-cylinder, firing order—1, 3, 2, 4
Bore and stroke	3-5/16 x 2.8 in.	3-3/8 x 2.8 in.	3-5/16 x 2.8 in.
Cubic inch displacement	96.55 cu. in.	99.8 cu. in.	96.55 cu. in.
Cooling	Water cooled displacement type water pump	Water cooled displacement type water pump	Water cooled displacement type water pump
Propeller—standard	Aluminum alloy 13 in. dia., 19 in. pitch, right-hand rotation	Aluminum alloy 13 in. dia., 19 in. pitch, right-hand rotation	Aluminum alloy 13 in. dia., 19 in. pitch, right-hand rotation
Electric system	12 volt—negative ground	12 volt—negative ground	12 volt—negative ground
Alternator—output maximum	10 amps at 5,250 rpm. Alternator cut-in speed 1,000 rpm	10 amps at 5,000 rpm. Alternator cut-in speed 1,000 rpm	10 amps at 5,400 rpm. Alternator cut-in speed 1,000 rpm
Spark plug type	Champion L20V	Champion L20V	Champion L20V
Breaker point gap	0.010 in.	0.010 in.	0.010 in.
Compression average lbs.	155-165 psi	155-165 psi	175-185 psi
*Oil ratio per gallon of gas (break-in)	1/3 pint	1/3 pint	1/3 pint
Oil ratio per gallon of gas (after break-in)	1/6 pint	1/6 pint	1/3 pint

* **Important**—When pistons, piston rings, piston pins, connecting rods, connecting rod bearings, crankshaft or crankshaft bearings are replaced, the break-in oil ratio and procedure for new engines must be used.

Table 2 TORQUE SPECIFICATIONS

	Special Items**			Standard Hardware**	
	70, 75, 85, 90 hp	105, 120, 130, 135 hp	135 (Racing)	Screw Size	Torque
*Cylinder head	270—⅜-16 bolts 225—5/16-18 bolts	270—⅜-16 bolts 225—5/16-18 bolts	225	10 - 24	30
Flywheel	90 ft.-lb.	90 ft.-lb.	90 ft.-lb.	10 - 32	35
Main bearing bolts	270	270	270	12 - 24	45
Connecting rod screws	170	170	170	¼ - 20	70
Nose cone nut (Racing engines)		325	325	5/16 - 18 ⅜ - 16	160 270
Driveshaft nut (Racing engines)		50 ft.-lb.	50 ft.-lb.	Gear housing plug	90 - 115
Propeller shaft nut (Racing engines)		50 ft.-lb.	50 ft.-lb.	Spark plug 14mm	120 - 180

*Torque from center out. Re-torque after engine has been run-in.
**All values in inch-pounds unless otherwise stated.

APPENDIX

WIRING DIAGRAMS

7

WIRING DIAGRAM — 25-30 HP

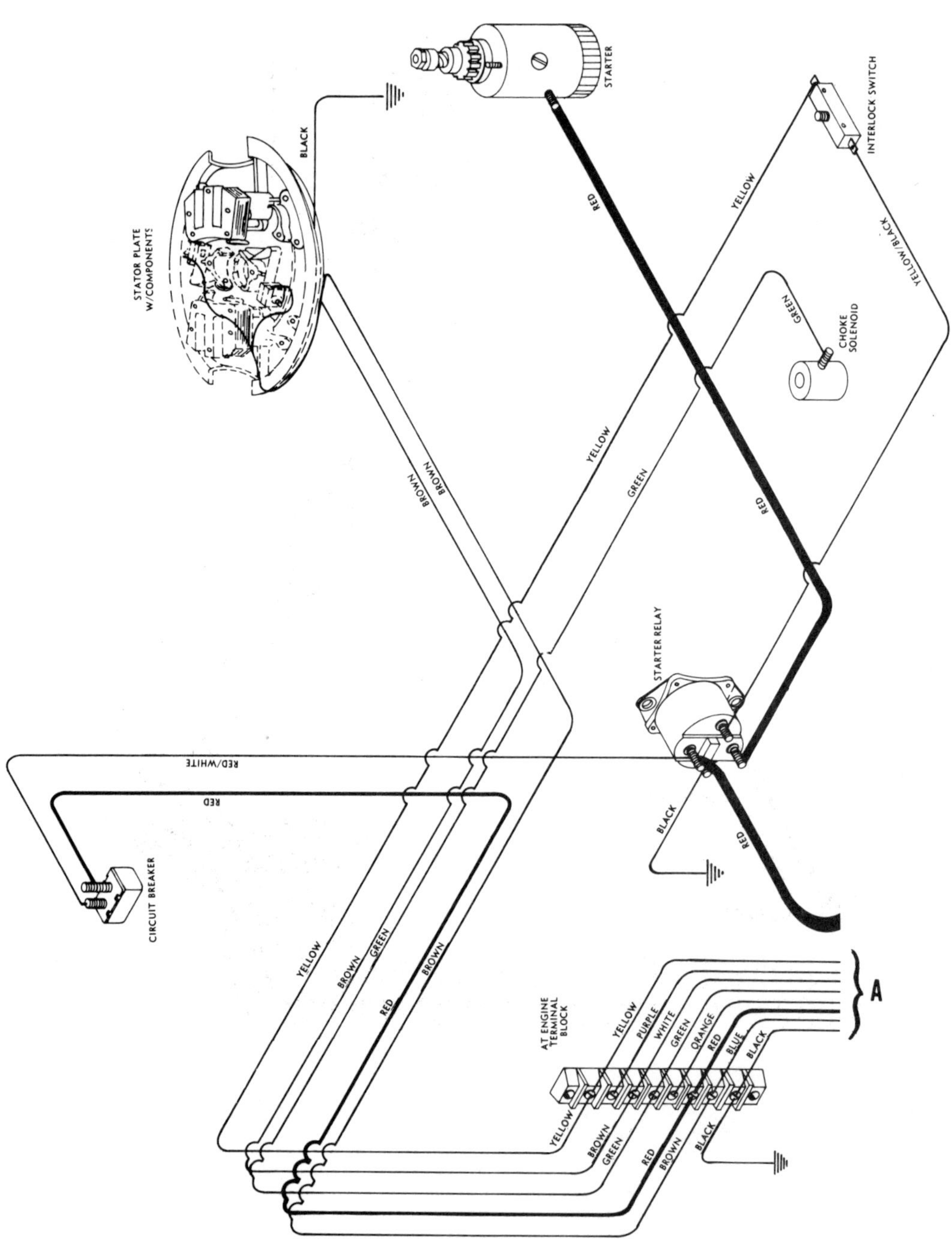

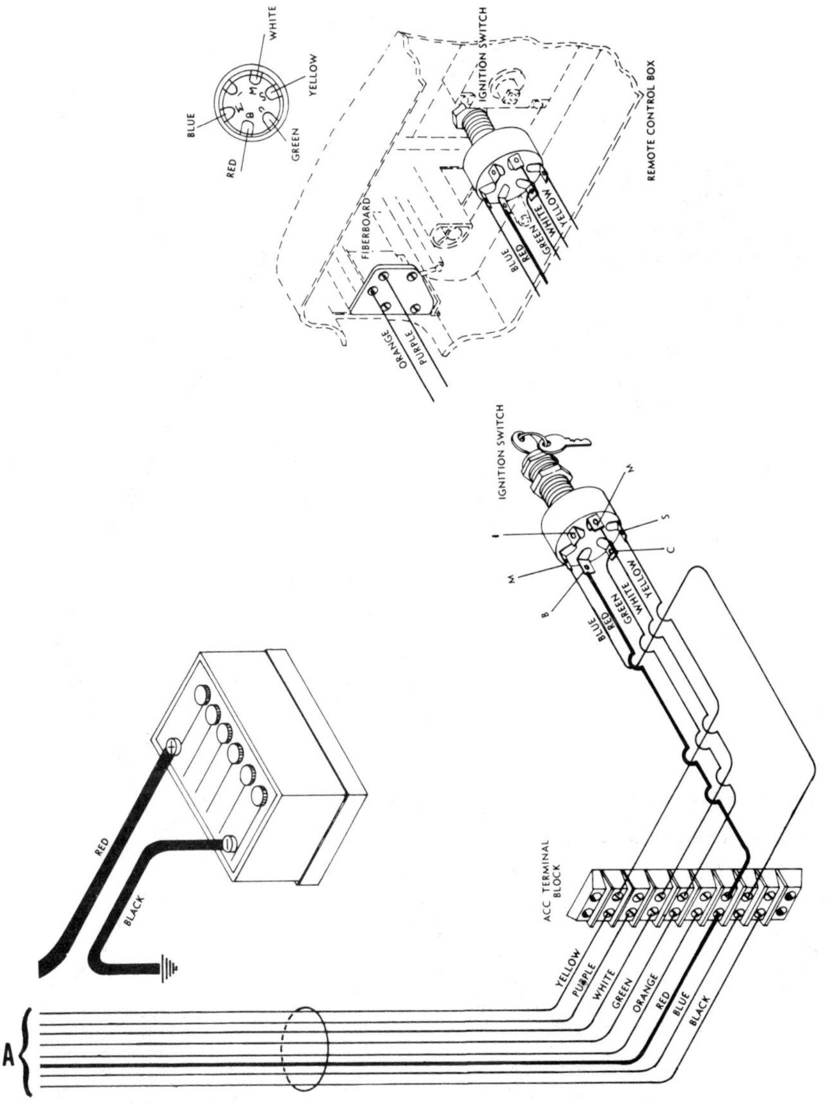
WHITE
YELLOW
GREEN
BLUE
RED
IGNITION SWITCH
REMOTE CONTROL BOX
FIBERBOARD
BLUE
RED
GREEN
WHITE
YELLOW
ORANGE
PURPLE
IGNITION SWITCH
M
S
C
I
M
B
BLUE
RED
GREEN
WHITE
YELLOW
ACC TERMINAL BLOCK
RED
BLACK
YELLOW
PURPLE
WHITE
GREEN
ORANGE
RED
BLUE
BLACK
A

WIRING DIAGRAM — 35, 45, 50, & 55 HP MAGNETO IGNITION

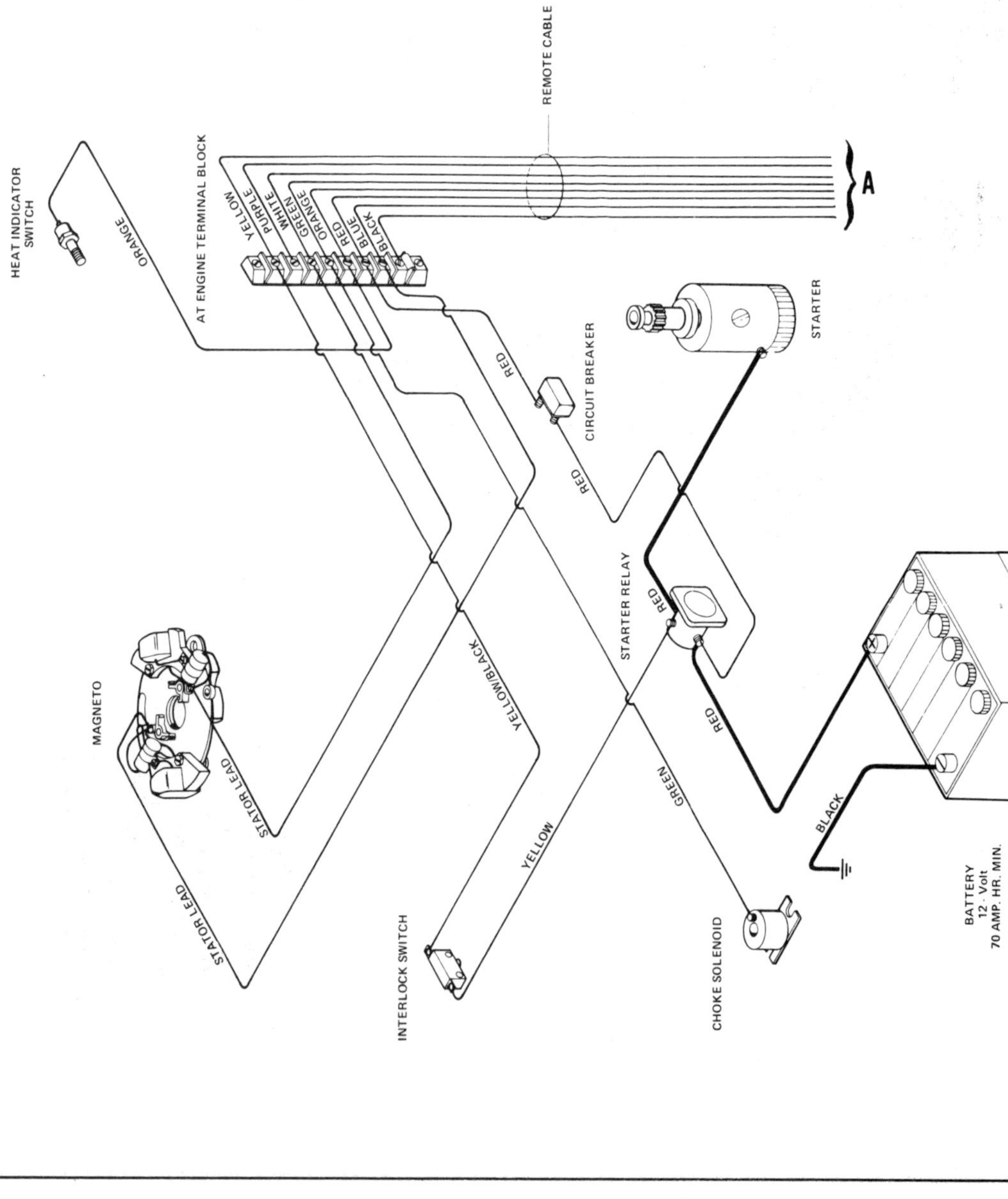

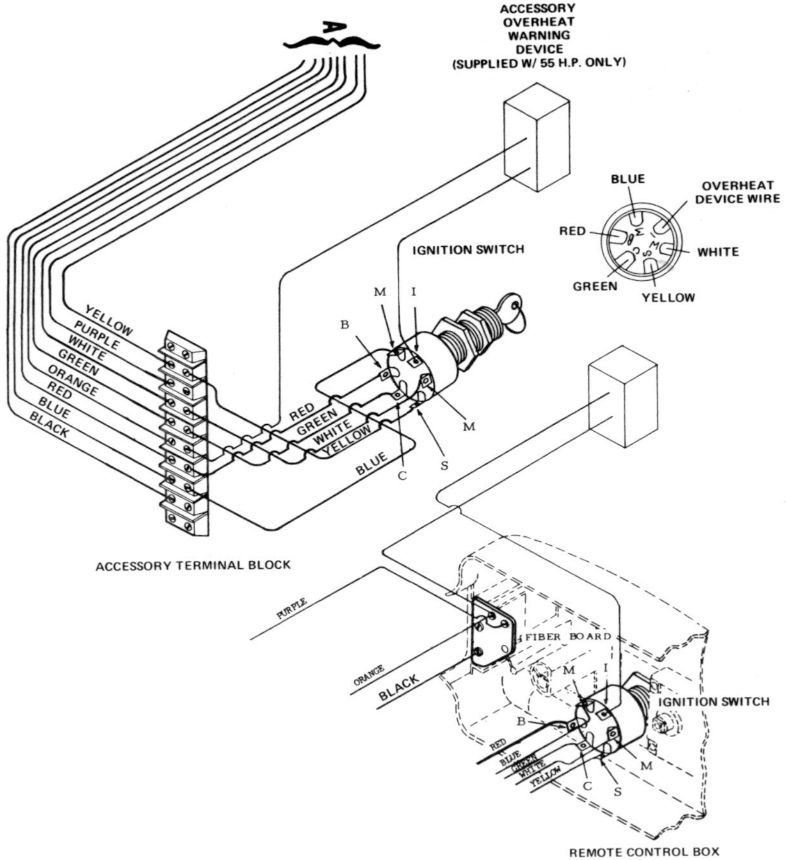

COLOR CODE

White = Tachometer circuit
Red = Battery circuit
Blue = Ignition circuit
Orange = Overheat circuit
Green = Choke circuit
Yellow = Starting circuit
Purple = Not used
Black = Ground return circuit
⏚ = Ground connection

WIRING DIAGRAM — 35, 45, 50, & 55 HP
BATTERY IGNITION WITH ALTERNATOR

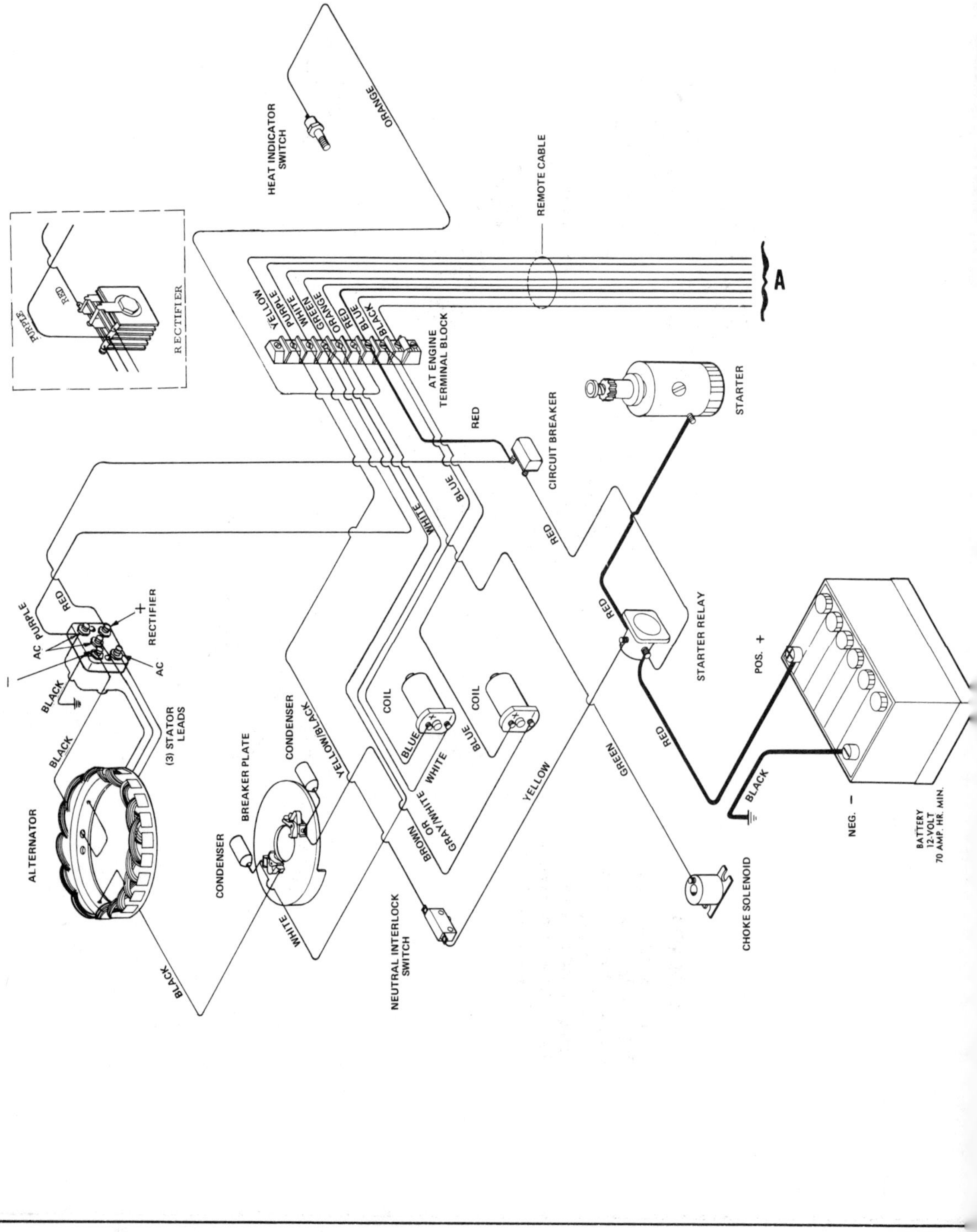

COLOR CODE

White = Tachometer circuit
Red = Battery circuit
Orange = Overheat circuit
Green = Choke circuit
Yellow = Starting circuit
Black = Ground return circuit
⏚ = Ground connection

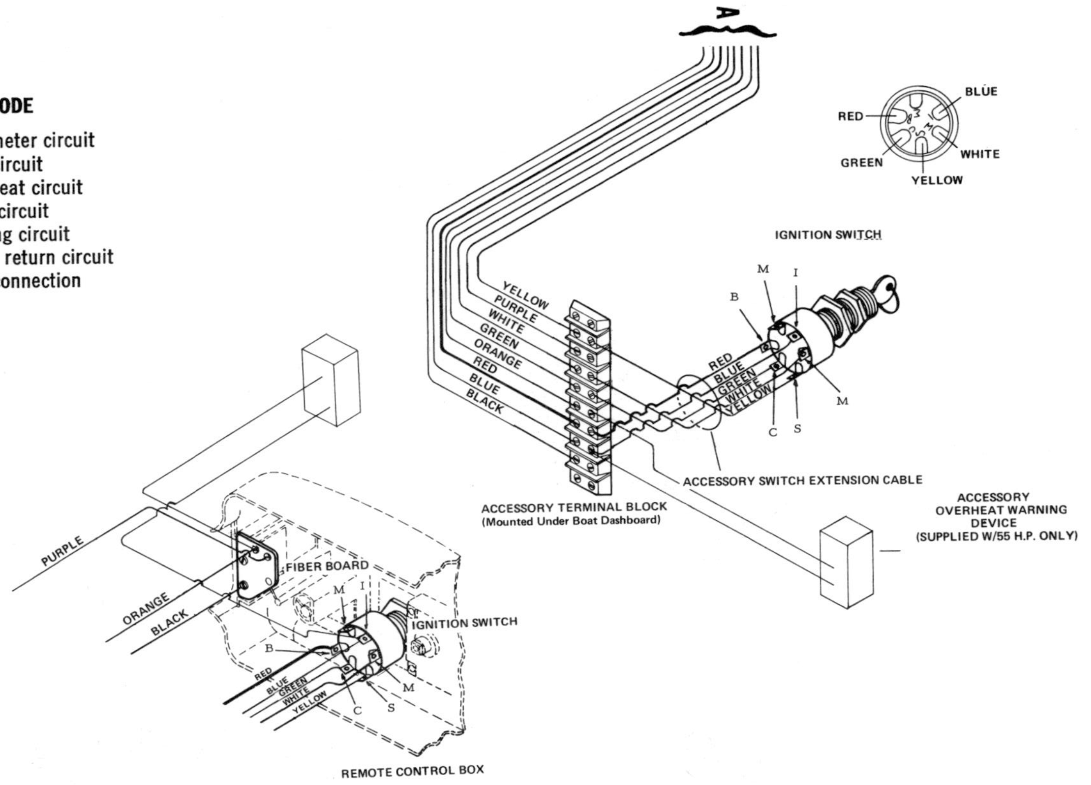

WIRING DIAGRAM — 45 & 55 HP MAGNAPOWER CD IGNITION

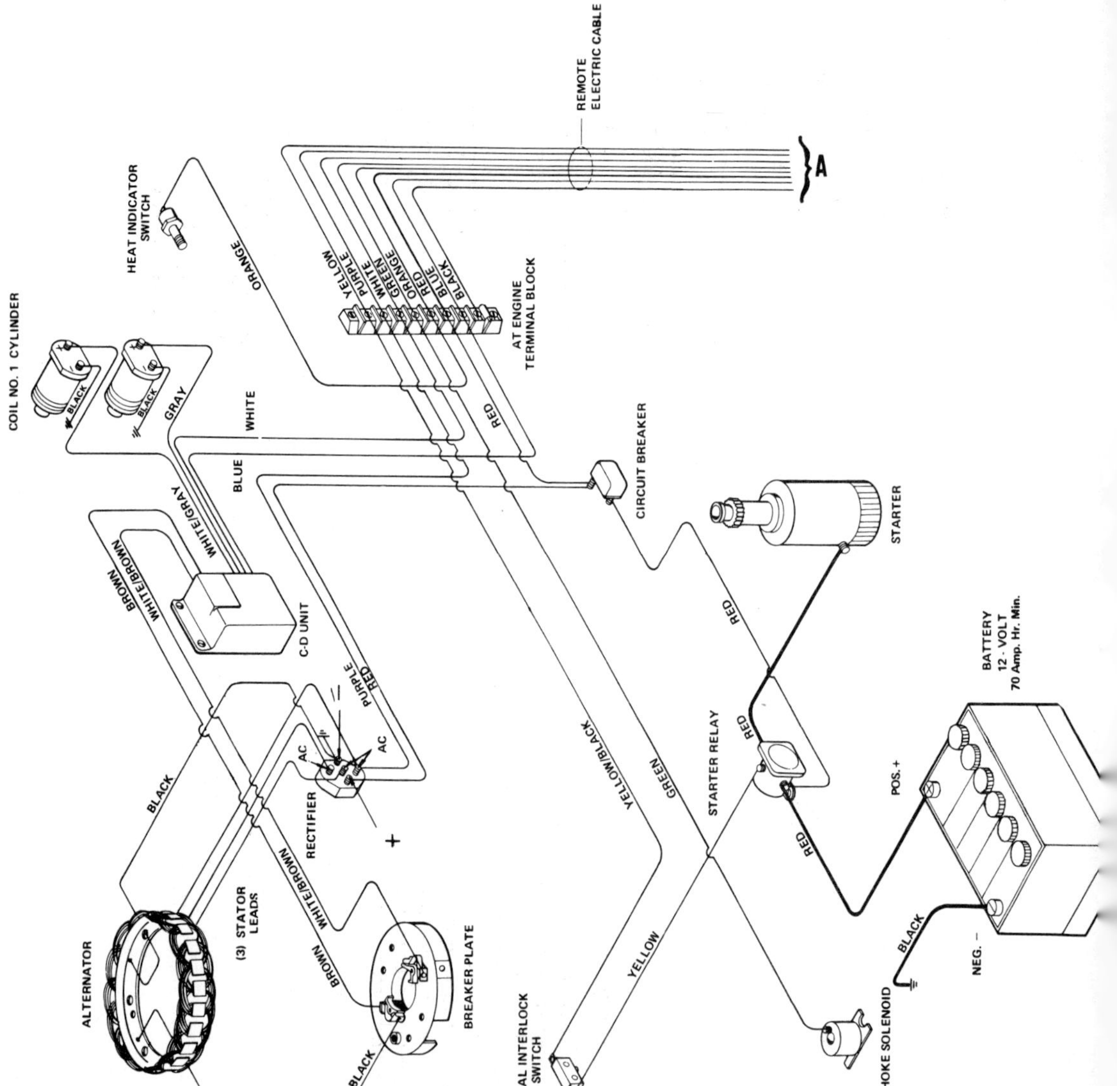

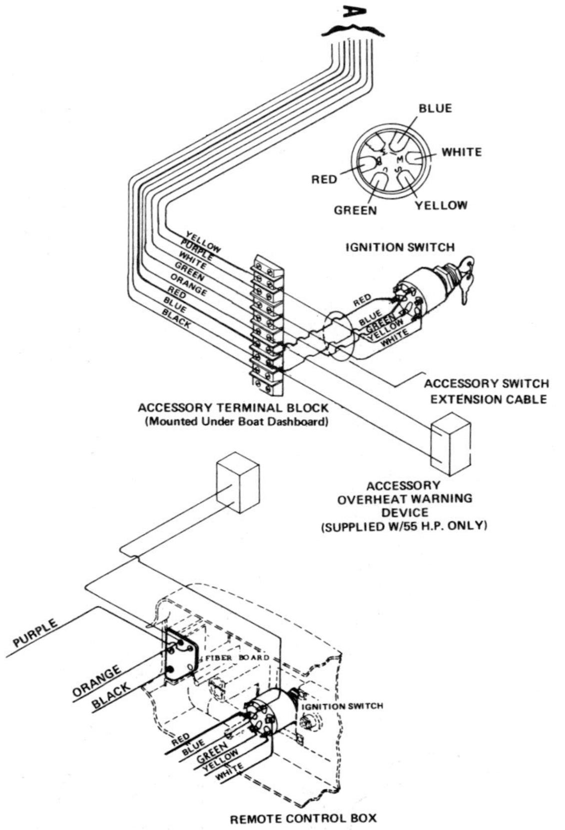

COLOR CODE

White = Tachometer circuit
Red = Battery circuit
Blue = Ignition circuit
Orange = Overheat circuit
Green = Choke circuit
Yellow = Starting circuit
Purple = Charge indicator circuit
Black = Ground return circuit
⏚ = Ground connection

WIRING DIAGRAM — 75-105 HP
BATTERY IGNITION WITH ALTERNATOR

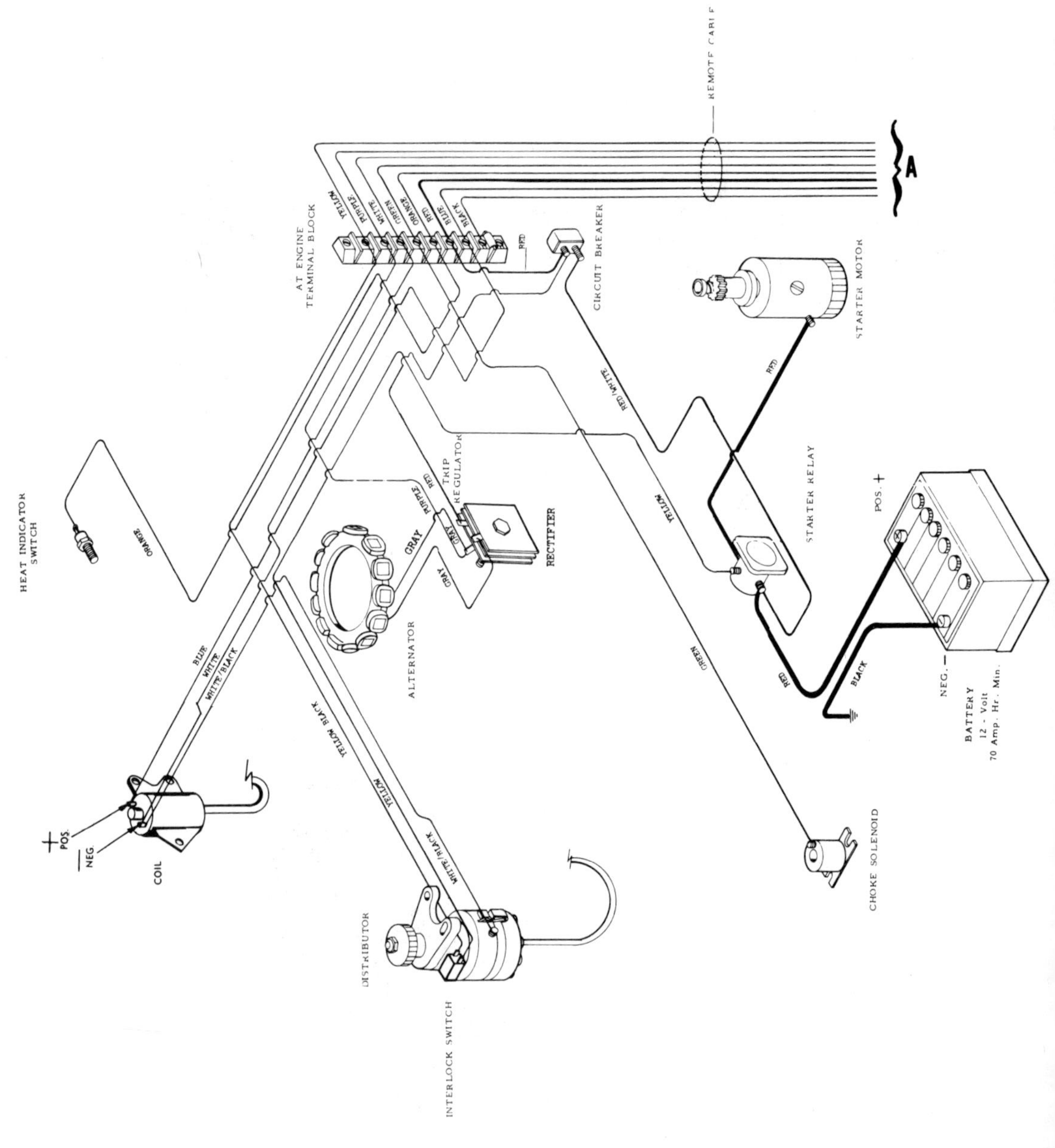

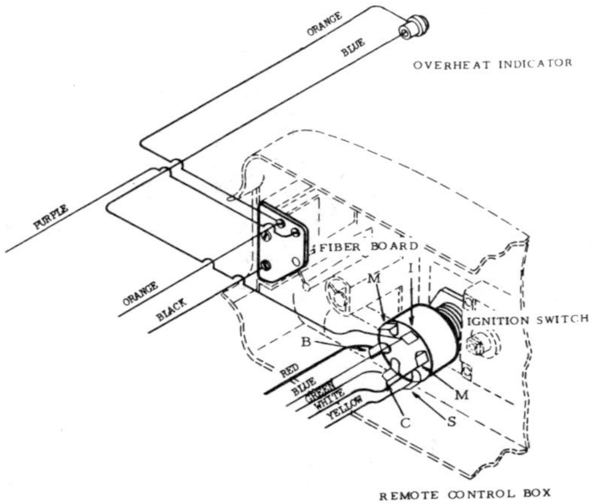

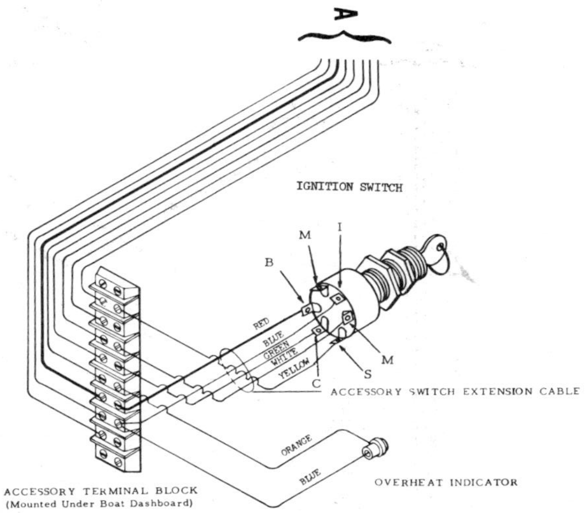

COLOR CODE

White = Tachometer circuit
Red = Battery circuit
Blue = Ignition circuit
Orange = Overheat circuit
Green = Choke circuit
Yellow = Starting circuit
Purple = Charge indicator circuit
Black = Ground return circuit
⏚ = Ground connection

7

WIRING DIAGRAM — 70, 75, 85, 105, 120 & 135 HP MAGNAPOWER CD IGNITION

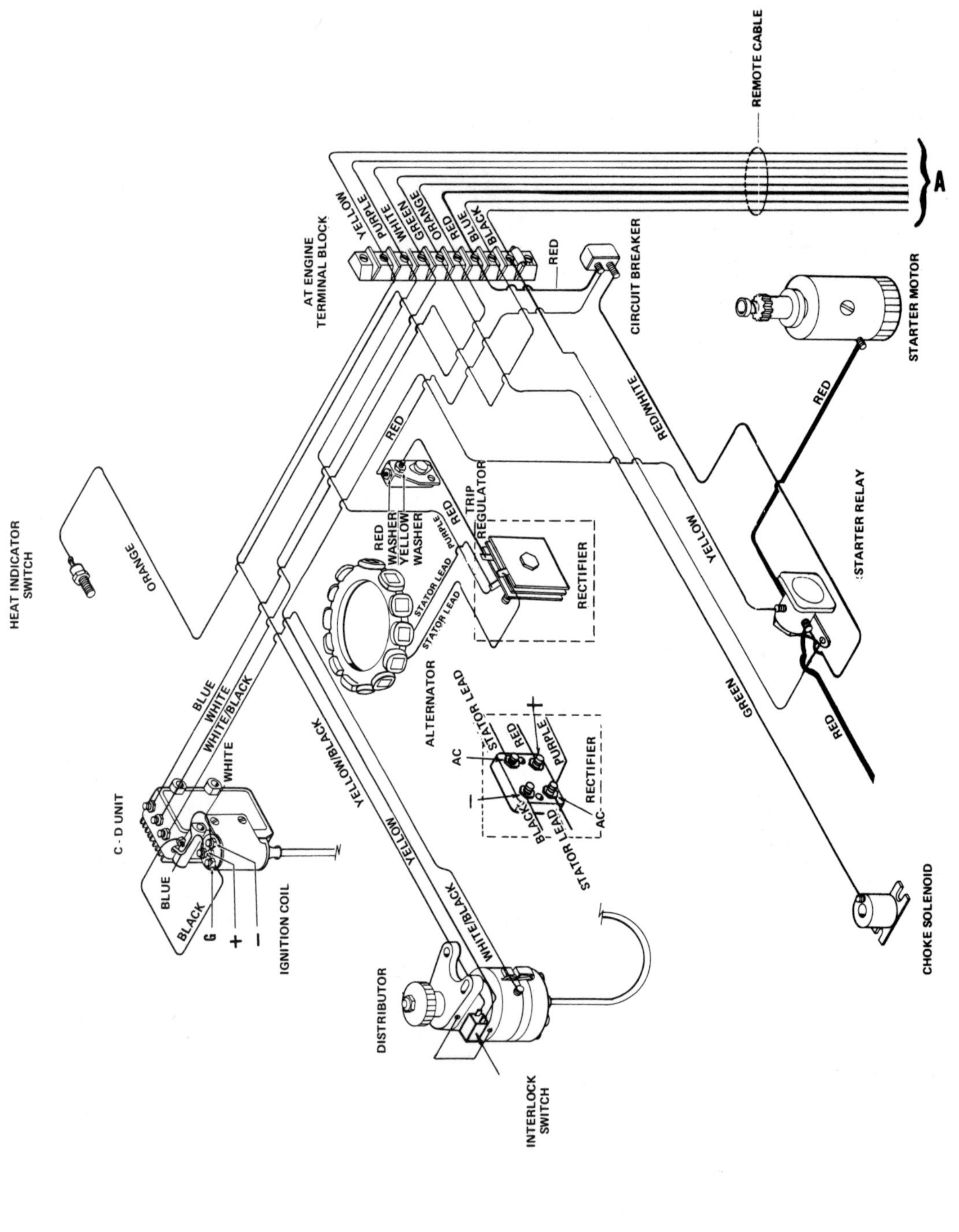

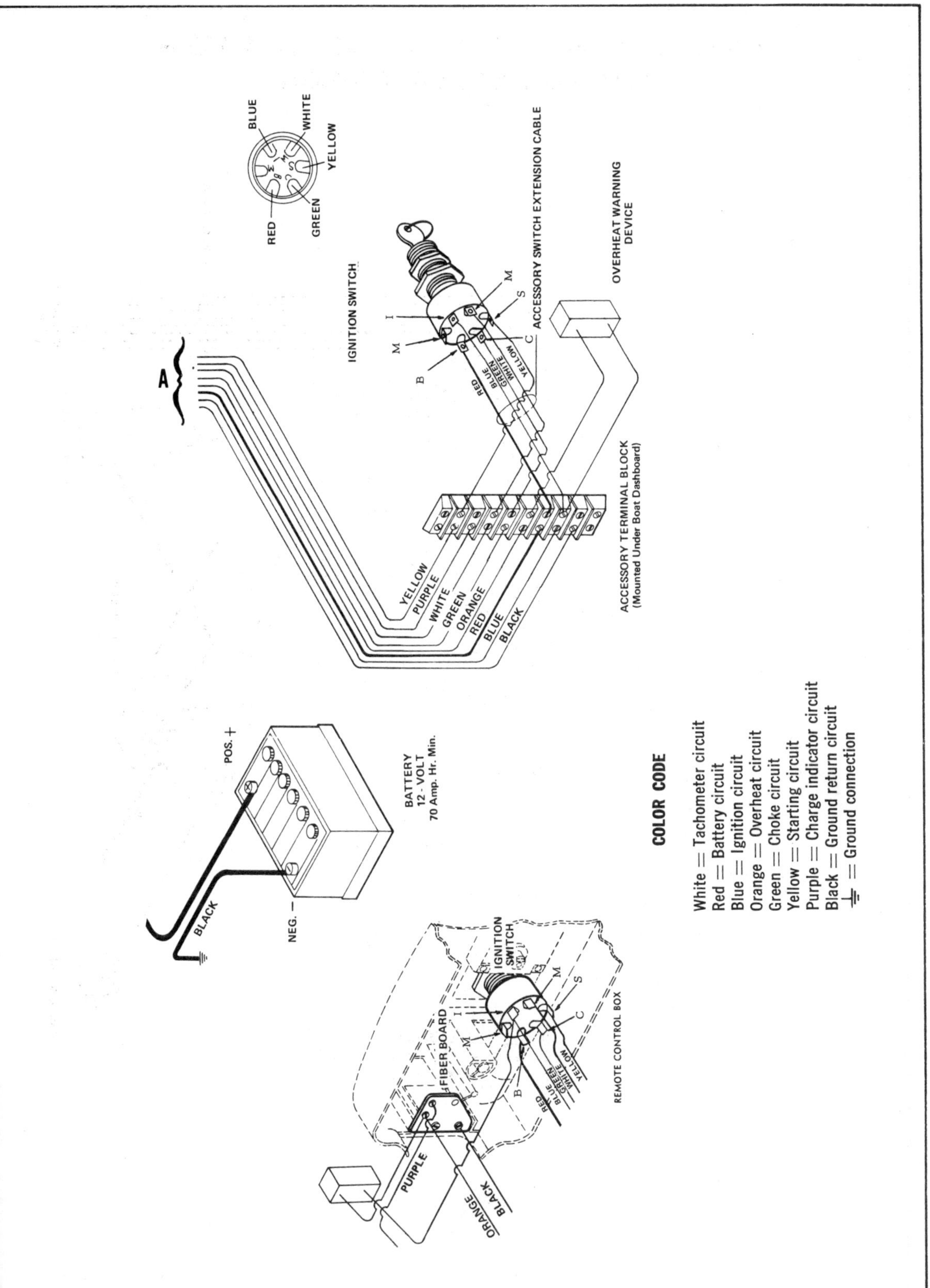

BLUE
WHITE
YELLOW
RED
GREEN
IGNITION SWITCH
ACCESSORY SWITCH EXTENSION CABLE
OVERHEAT WARNING DEVICE
A
I
M
S
M
B
C
RED
BLUE
GREEN
WHITE
YELLOW
YELLOW
PURPLE
WHITE
GREEN
ORANGE
RED
BLUE
BLACK
ACCESSORY TERMINAL BLOCK
(Mounted Under Boat Dashboard)
POS. +
NEG. −
BLACK
BATTERY
12 - VOLT
70 Amp. Hr. Min.
COLOR CODE
White = Tachometer circuit
Red = Battery circuit
Blue = Ignition circuit
Orange = Overheat circuit
Green = Choke circuit
Yellow = Starting circuit
Purple = Charge indicator circuit
Black = Ground return circuit
⏚ = Ground connection
IGNITION SWITCH
FIBER BOARD
REMOTE CONTROL BOX
PURPLE
ORANGE
BLACK

WIRING DIAGRAM — 70, 85, 105, 120, 130, 135, & 150 MAGNAPOWER CD IGNITION

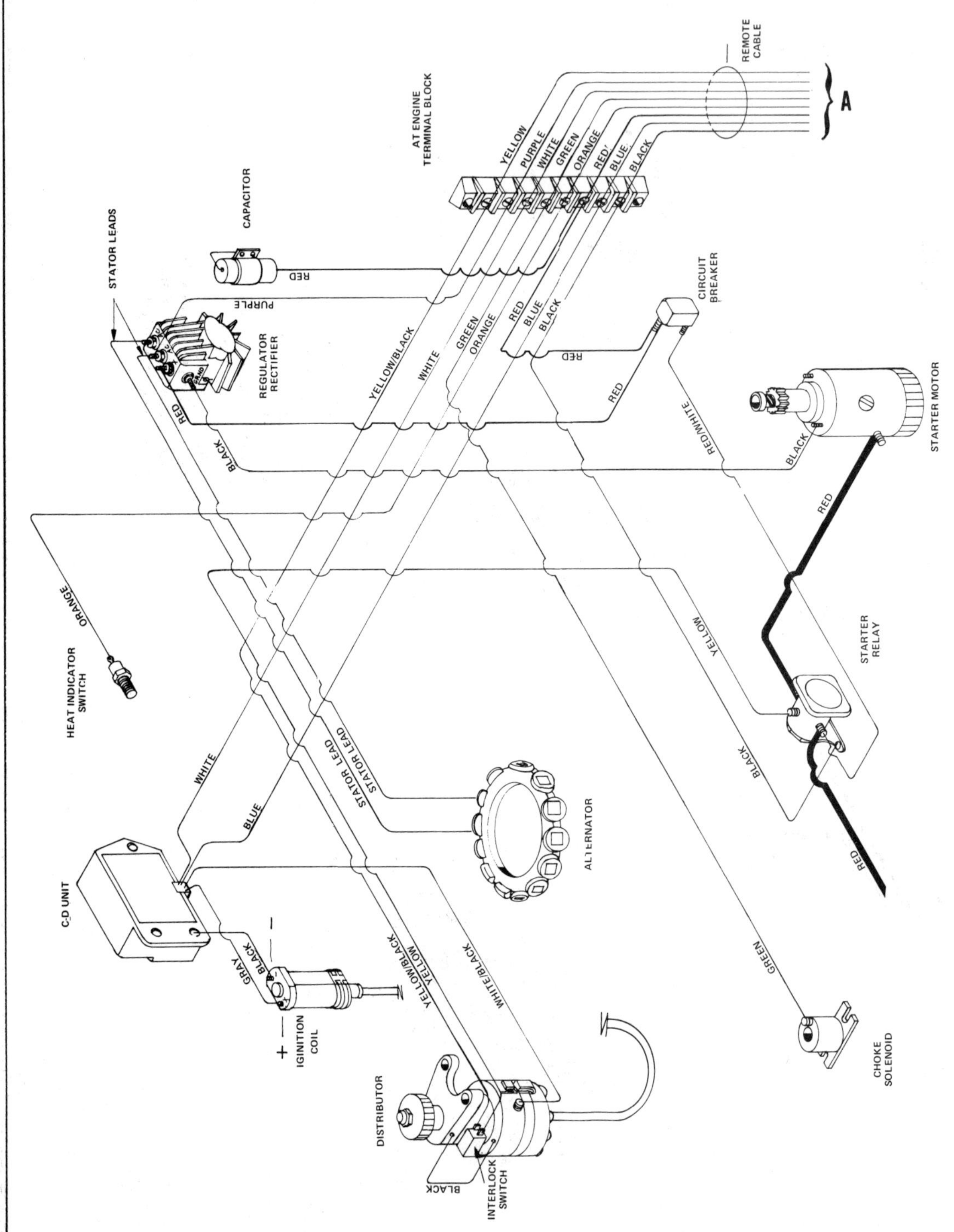

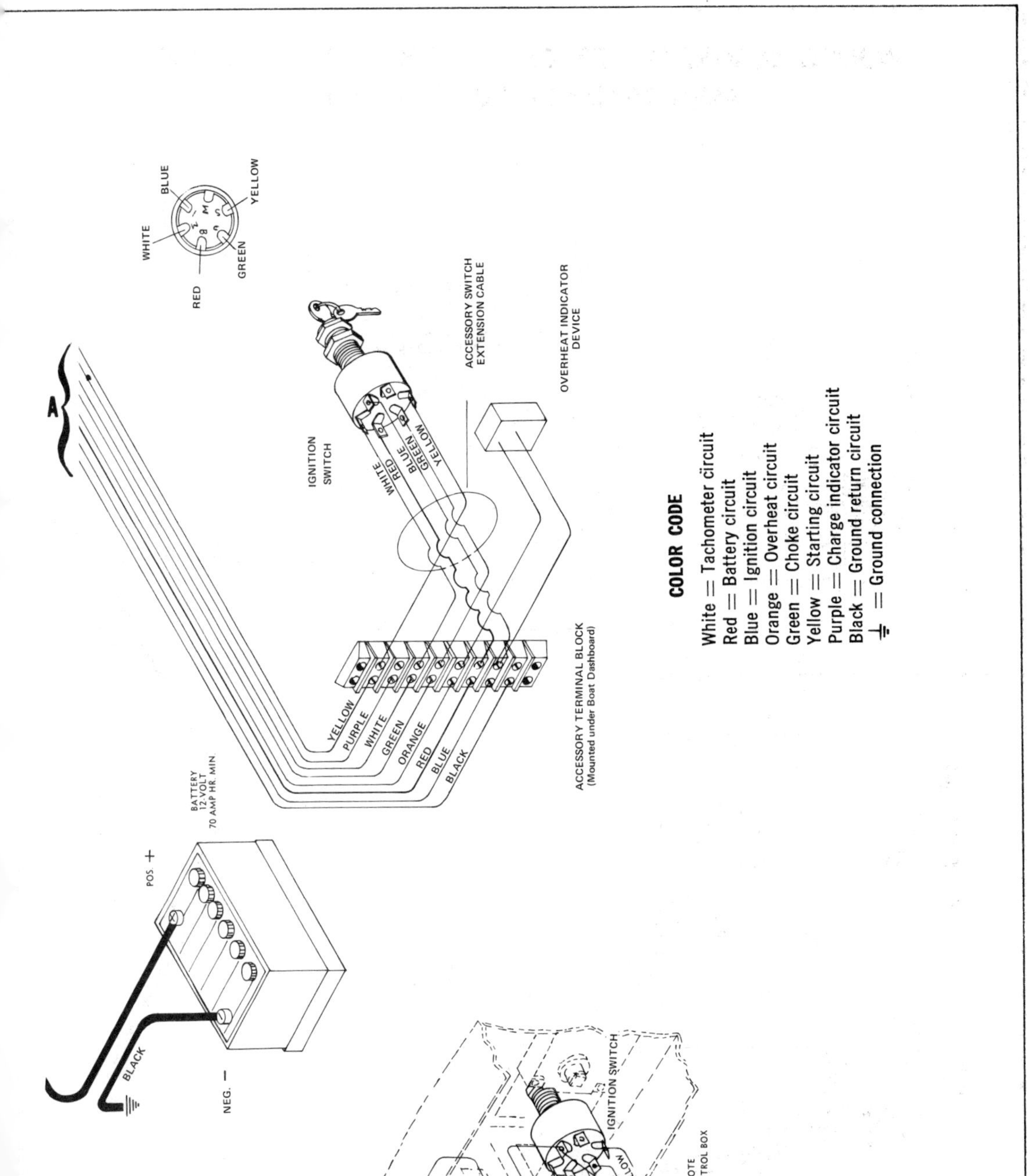
A
IGNITION SWITCH
WHITE
RED
BLUE
GREEN
YELLOW
ACCESSORY SWITCH EXTENSION CABLE
OVERHEAT INDICATOR DEVICE
ACCESSORY TERMINAL BLOCK (Mounted under Boat Dashboard)
YELLOW
PURPLE
WHITE
GREEN
ORANGE
RED
BLUE
BLACK
BATTERY 12-VOLT 70 AMP HR. MIN
POS. +
NEG. –
BLACK
REMOTE CONTROL BOX
IGNITION SWITCH
FIBER BOARD
ORANGE
PURPLE
BLACK
COLOR CODE
White = Tachometer circuit
Red = Battery circuit
Blue = Ignition circuit
Orange = Overheat circuit
Green = Choke circuit
Yellow = Starting circuit
Purple = Charge indicator circuit
Black = Ground return circuit
⏚ = Ground connection

7

SUPPLEMENT

1976-1979 SERVICE INFORMATION

The following supplement provides procedures unique to the 1976 and later Chrysler outboard motors from 25 to 140 horsepower. All other service procedures are identical to earlier models.

The chapter headings in this supplement correspond to those in the main portion of this book. If a change is not included in the supplement, there are no changes affecting the 1976 and later models.

CHAPTER SIX

OUTBOARD MOTORS (70 TO 140 HP)

This chapter includes only information for 1976 and later models that is different from that found in Chapter Six for earlier models.

TIMING

Breakerless Models

1. Disconnect battery cables from battery terminals.

2. Remove all spark plugs from cylinder head.

3. Screw the barrel of special timing tool J2937-1 completely into the top cylinder spark plug hole.

4. Insert the rod portion of the timing tool into the barrel with the 2 marks identified as "25 through 55 H.P." toward the outside. Hold the rod tightly against the piston and turn the crankshaft in the direction of engine rotation to locate top dead center (TDC). This is the point at which the piston is closest to the cylinder head (and the point where the marks on the rod extend the furthest away from the barrel, as shown in **Figure 1**).

5. Screw the timing tool barrel in or out as needed until the inside line of the timing rod is in alignment with the edge of the barrel. Refer to **Figure 1**.

6. With your finger, apply light pressure to the end of the rod and turn the crankshaft clockwise in the direction of engine rotation until the outer line of the rod lines up with the edge of the barrel (**Figure 2**).

> NOTE: *The rod will go completely into the barrel of the timing tool. Hold your finger over the barrel hole until the rod comes back out. (If you remove your finger, the rod will shoot out of the barrel on the compression stroke.) Check to find the location of the outer line in relationship to the end of the barrel as the rod comes out. If the outer line goes beyond the edge of the barrel, the engine must be rotated clockwise again. The piston is now positioned at 32° before top dead center* (BTDC). *See* **Figure 2**.

1

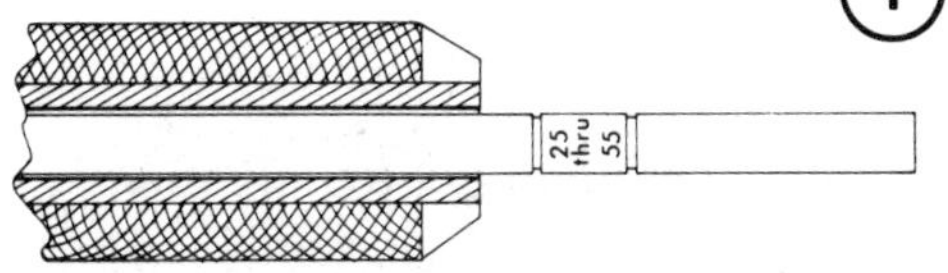

Establishing top dead center

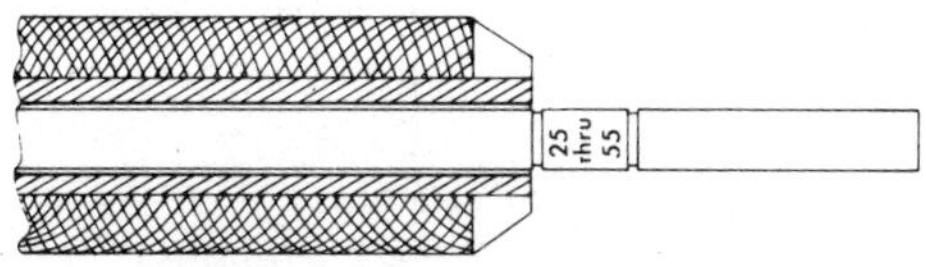

Aligning barrel to tool with mark on rod

2

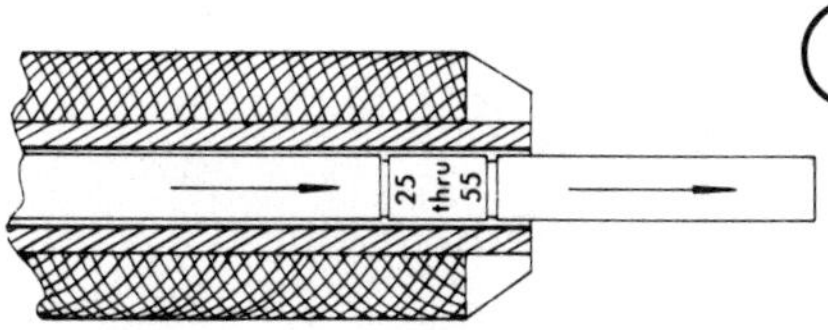

Approaching 32° before top dead center

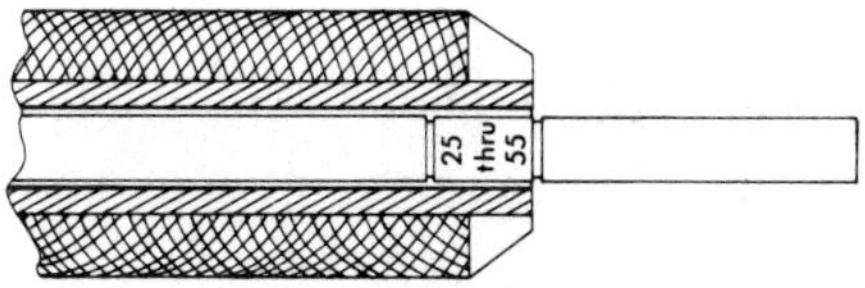

32° before top dead center

7. Check the decal on the flywheel ring gear. The 32° BTDC mark on the decal must be lined up with the index marks on the timing pointer. If the marks are not aligned, adjust the timing pointer.

8. Remove timing tool from the cylinder head.

9. Turn the flywheel to align the TDC (top dead center) mark on the decal with the index mark on timing pointer. Turn the distributor pulley to match the index mark on the pulley, with the outside diameter of the flywheel (**Figure 3**).

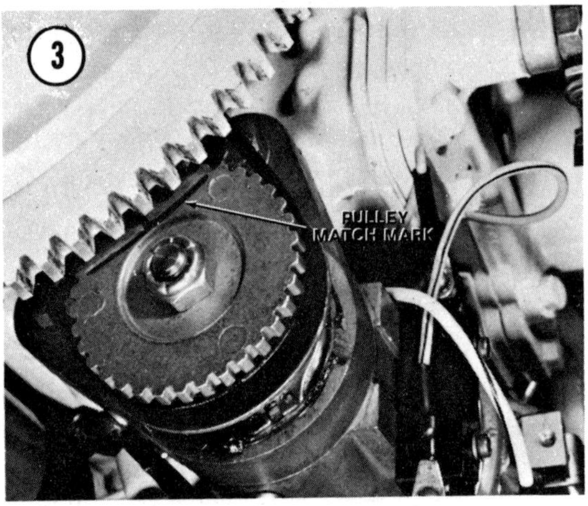

10. Install the distributor belt over the pulley and adjust the distributor belt tension (**Figure 4**). This is best accomplished by positioning the tip of a 0.008 in. thickness feeler gauge against the middle of the belt length and pushing against the belt until the feeler gauge bends without further movement of the belt. The belt should deflect 3/16-1/4 in. for proper tension. If it deflects more than 1/4 in., a variation of timing will occur; if it deflects less than 3/16 in., towershaft linkage binding and/or excessive towershaft bearing wear could occur.

11. Adjust the distributor control rod until the distance between the nylon swivels is ⅜-½ in. See **Figure 5**.

12. Connect a timing light to the No. 1 cylinder spark plug lead wire. Start the engine and accelerate to WOT (wide open throttle). The 32° mark on the decal should be in alignment with the index mark on the timing pointer. If not, retard the engine and shut engine off.

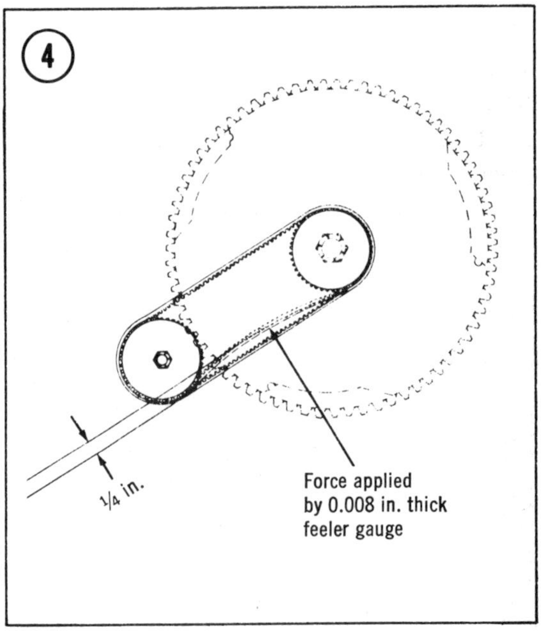

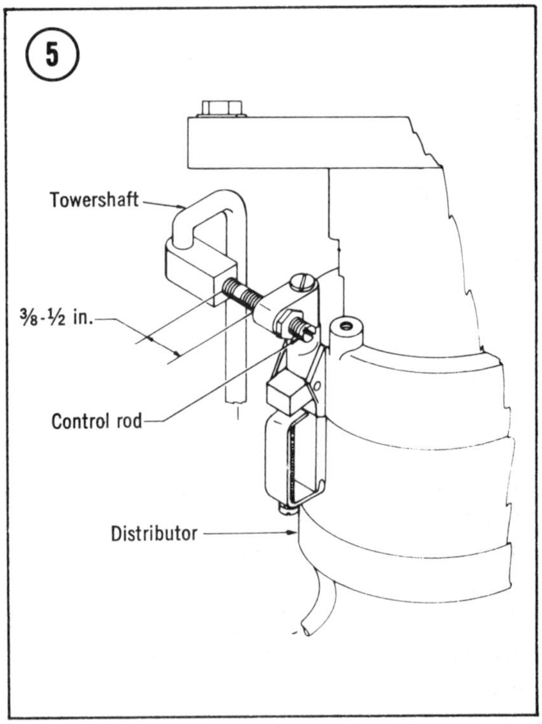

13. Adjust the control rod between the towershaft and distributor. Refer to **Figure 5**. Start the engine again and check the timing at WOT. If necessary, repeat Step 12, preceding, until the 32° mark on the flywheel is in alignment with the idex mark on the timing pointer.

Magnapower II

1. Perform Steps 1-8 under *Breakerless Models,* preceding.

2. Rough set the control rod to ⅝ in. (**Figure 6**).

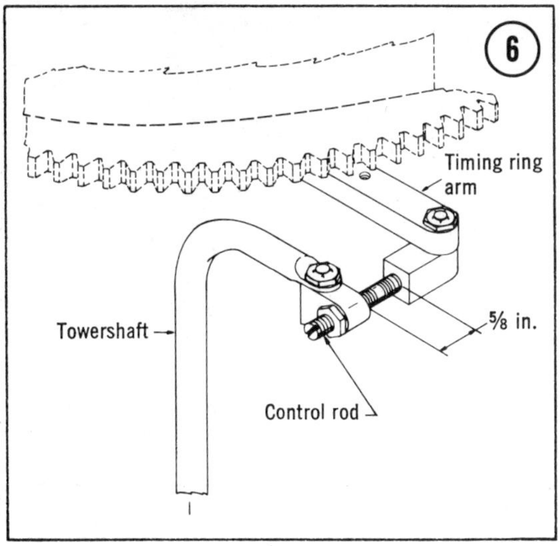

3. Connect a timing light to the No. 1 cylinder spark plug lead wire. The engine must be at the full retard position. Crank the engine over (with engine in test tank or on the water). The timing must be quite close (the TDC mark on the decal in relationship to the timing pointer index mark). If it is not close (or within 3° of the index mark), recheck timing as outlined under Steps 2-7 under *Breakerless Models* in the preceding section.

4. Start engine and accelerate to WOT (wide open throttle), or a minimum of 4,500 rpm. The 32° mark on the decal should align with the timing pointer index mark. If it does not, retard and shut off the engine. Adjust the link between the towershaft and timing ring (refer to **Figure 6**) until the 32° mark on the decal aligns with the timing pointer index mark.

> NOTE: *To advance the timing, turn the link counterclockwise (as viewed from the front of the engine); to retard timing, turn link clockwise. See* **Figure 6**.

> CAUTION
> *Do not adjust link while engine is running.*

3-CYLINDER IGNITION (BREAKERLESS)

Distributor Belt Removal/Installation

1. Loosen 2 bolts holding distributor to powerhead. Slip distributor belt off pulley.

2. Remove the flywheel. Refer to Chapter Six, *Flywheel, Removal,* in the front of this manual, for the procedure.

3. Remove distributor belt.

4. To install distributor belt, reverse preceding steps. Refer to Chapter Six, *Flywheel, Installation,* in the front of this manual, for the procedure.

Distributor Cap Replacement

1. Loosen screws on distributor retaining clips and remove distributor cap assembly from distributor.

2. Disconnect high tension lead wire from coil.

3. Remove spark plug lead wires from spark plugs and retaining clips.

4. Remove distributor cap assembly from engine.

5. Remove screws on distributor cover and pull cover with lead wires from cap.

6. Pull seal away from cover and pull lead wires from seal. Pull lead wires from cover.

7. Insert lead wires through cap cover and through seal. Align screw holes (cover to cap) and vent hole in cover with vent screen in seal. Allow at least one inch of lead wire to extend through cap seal as shown in **Figure 7**.

8. Insert lead wire ends in distributor cap against pointed contacts. Align screw holes (distributor cover to cap) and vent holes.

9. Draw distributor cover against cap using 2 screws and tighten until screws bottom.

10. Check lead wire continuity with a test light (special tool T2938-1 or equivalent) as shown in **Figure 8**. If test light does not light for any specific wire, remove distributor cover and repeat Steps 1-4.

11. Install distributor cap on distributor. Align hole in cap wall with locating pin in distributor housing. Secure cap assembly to distributor with retaining clips.

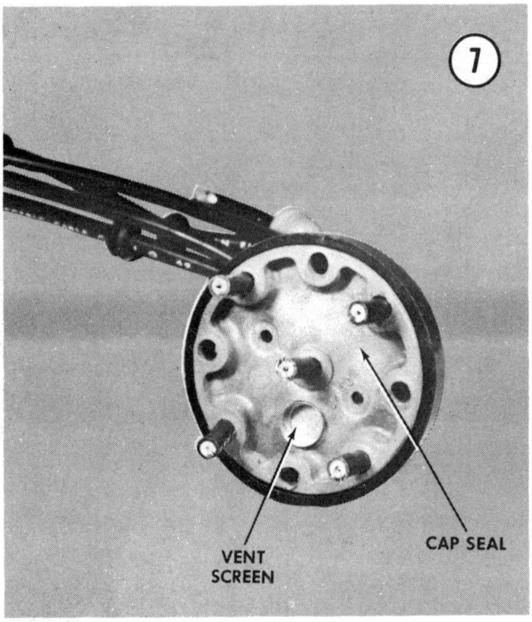

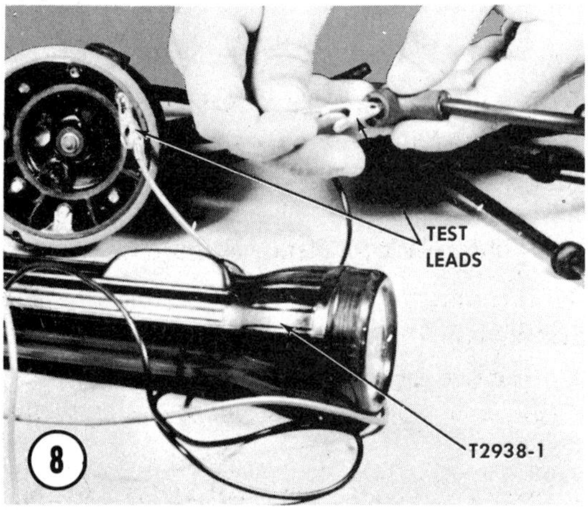

12. Route center lead wire from cap assembly to coil and insert lead wire end firmly in coil. Push boot over end of coil.

13. Route spark plug lead wires to respective spark plugs. See **Figure 9** for identification of lead wires.

Distributor Pulley and Shaft Removal

1. Disconnect white/black striped lead and blue lead from stud terminals on distributor housing.

2. Remove distributor cap assembly from distributor after loosening screws on retaining clip.

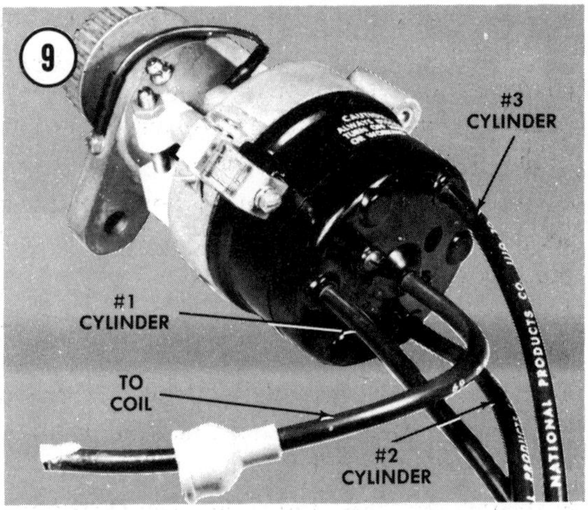

3. Remove 2 bolts holding distributor bracket to powerhead, then remove distributor.

4. Clamp distributor pulley in a vise (use light pressure and protective vise jaws). Remove stop nut from distributor shaft and pull distributor from pulley.

5. Remove spacer, and large and small washers from pulley end of distributor shaft. Pull distributor shaft from distributor housing and remove the bronze spacer. See **Figure 10**.

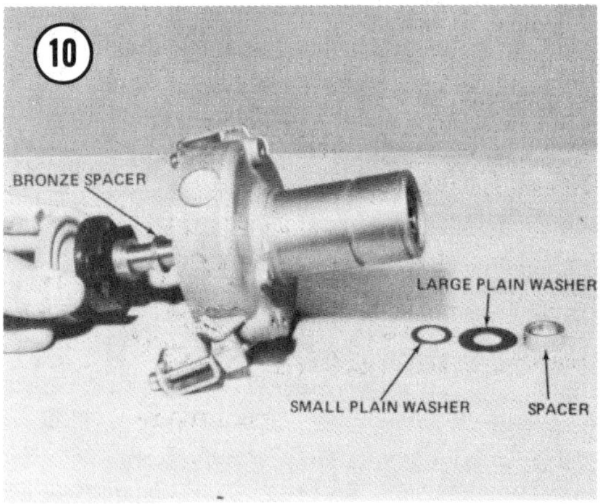

Distributor Pulley and Shaft Installation

1. Install bronze spacer on distributor shaft.

2. Install distributor shaft in distributor housing until bronze spacer on shaft bottoms against distributor housing.

3. Install small plain washer, large plain washer, and spacer on pulley end of distributor shaft.

4. Install Woodruff key in slot on pulley end of distributor shaft. Install pulley on end of shaft. Clamp the distributor pulley in a vise (use protective vise jaws). Install the stop nut on the end of the shaft and tighten securely.

5. Install the distributor on the powerhead and secure with 2 bolts (but do not tighten these 2 bolts securely at this time).

6. Install distributor cap assembly and secure with retainers.

7. Connect the white/black striped lead and blue lead to stud terminals on distributor housing and secure with lockwasher and hex nut.

8. Install the distributor belt. See *Distributor Belt Removal/Installation* in this section.

Preamplifier Removal/Installation

1. Disconnect battery leads from battery terminals.

2. Remove distributor shaft. See *Distributor Pulley and Shaft Removal* in the preceding section.

3. Remove preamplifier leads from terminals on distributor housing (**Figure 11**).

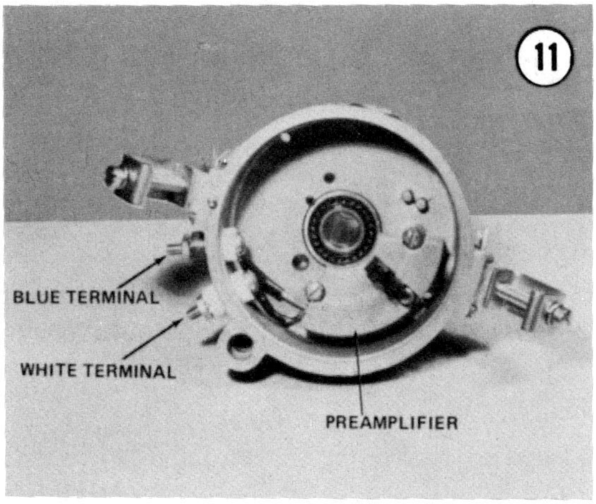

4. Remove 2 screws and lockwashers holding preamplifier to distributor housing and remove preamplifier.

5. To install preamplifier, install it on the distributor housing and secure with 2 screws and lockwashers (**Figure 12**).

6. Connect preamplifier leads to terminals on distributor housing. Refer to **Figure 11**.

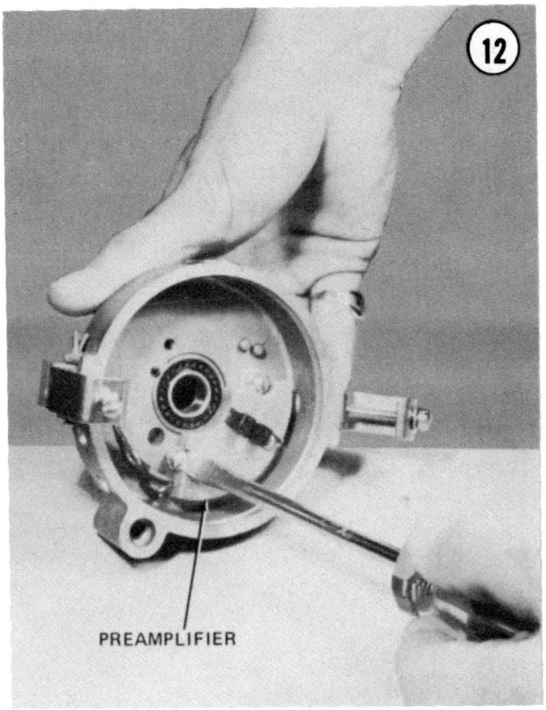

7. Install distributor shaft. Refer to *Distributor Pulley and Shaft Installation* in this section.

8. Connect battery leads to battery terminals.

Distributor Bracket Removal/Installation

1. Disconnect battery leads from battery terminals.

2. Remove distributor pulley and shaft. See *Distributor Pulley and Shaft Removal* in this section.

3. Remove screw and lockwasher holding ground lead to distributor bracket.

4. Remove retaining ring with retaining ring pliers (special tool T1082 or equivalent) as shown in **Figure 13**. Slide the distributor bracket and thrust washer off the distributor housing.

5. Remove shims (if any) from distributor housing.

6. To install the bracket, proceed as follows:

   a. Install distributor bracket on distributor housing.

   b. Install thrust washer and retaining ring to hold distributor bracket to housing.

   c. Use a feeler gauge (special tool T8930-1 or equivalent), as shown in **Figure 14**, to

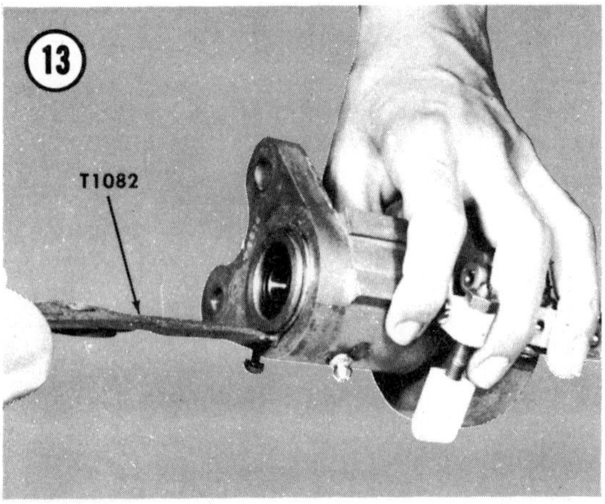

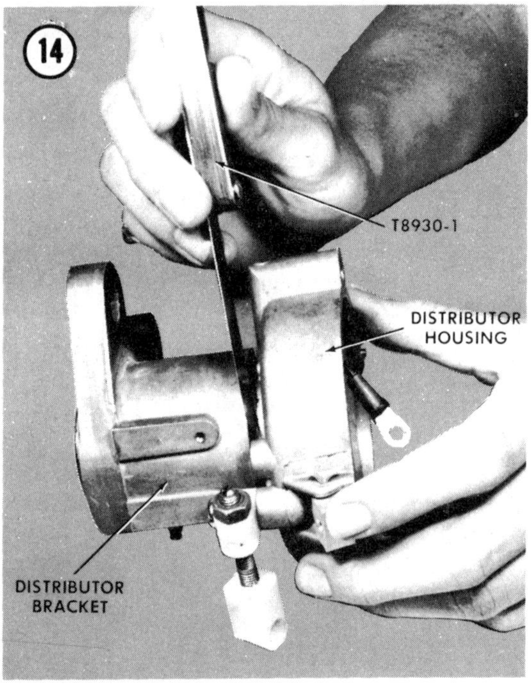

determine clearance between distributor housing and distributor bracket. The clearance must not be more than 0.005 in., or less than 0.001 in.

d. If shims are needed, remove retaining ring, thrust washer, and bracket and add necessary shims. Reinstall distributor bracket on housing and secure with retaining ring.

e. Install screw and lockwasher to hold ground lead to distributor bracket.

7. Install distributor pulley and shaft. Refer to *Distributor Pulley and Shaft Installation* in this section.

8. Connect battery leads to battery terminals.

Distributor Housing Removal/Installation

1. Remove distributor bracket (refer to *Distributor Bracket Removal/Installation* in this section), and pulley and shaft (refer to *Distributor Pulley and Shaft Removal* in this section).

2. Remove preamplifier. See *Preamplifier Removal/Installation* in this section.

3. Remove terminal screw posts and insulators from distributor housing.

4. Remove distributor control rod link assembly by removing screw holding it to the distributor housing (**Figure 15**).

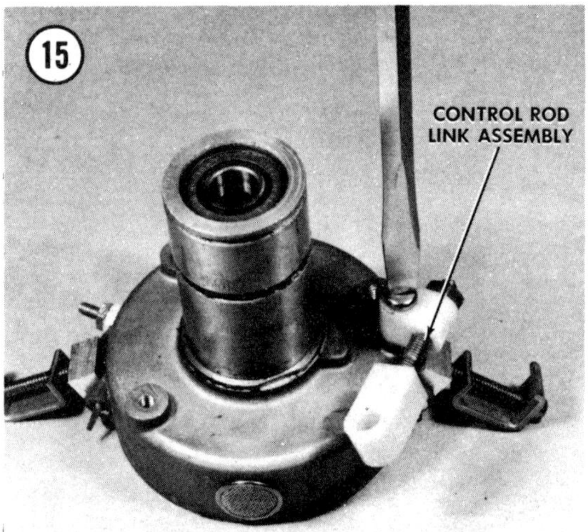

5. Remove ground wire from housing by removing screw and lockwasher holding it to the housing.

6. To install the distributor housing, reverse Steps 1-4.

7. Install ground lead to distributor housing with screw and lockwasher.

4-CYLINDER IGNITION (MAGNAPOWER II)

Interlock Switch Removal/Installation

1. Remove 2 screws and lockwashers holding lead wires to each end of interlock switch.

2. Remove 2 screws and plain washers holding interlock switch to interlock mounting bracket, and remove switch (**Figure 16**).

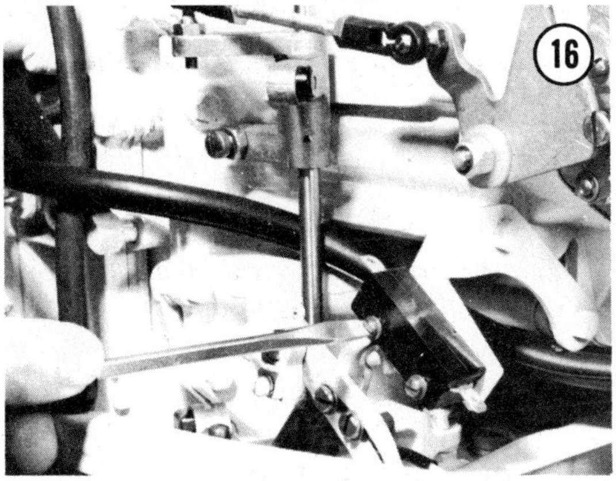

3. Install the interlock switch on the interlock switch bracket with white button facing down. Secure in place with 2 screws and plain washers.

4. Install lead wires to terminals on each end of interlock switch and hold in place with 2 screws and lockwashers (**Figure 17**).

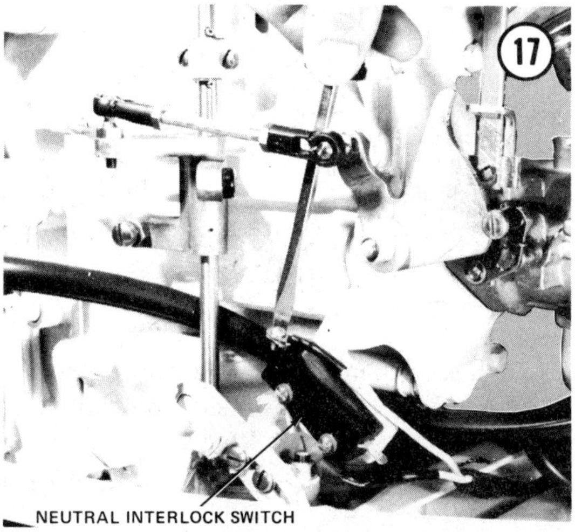

5. Adjust interlock cam. Refer to Chapter Six, *Tune-up, Neutral Interlock Switch Cam (Shift Arm) Adjustment* section, in the front of this manual.

Choke Solenoid Removal/Installation

1. Remove ty-rap holding green lead to choke solenoid.

2. Remove hex nut and lockwasher holding green lead to terminal post on choke solenoid.

3. Remove 2 hex head screws and clamp holding choke solenoid to bracket. Remove choke solenoid from engine by pulling it from the choke solenoid plunger (**Figure 18**).

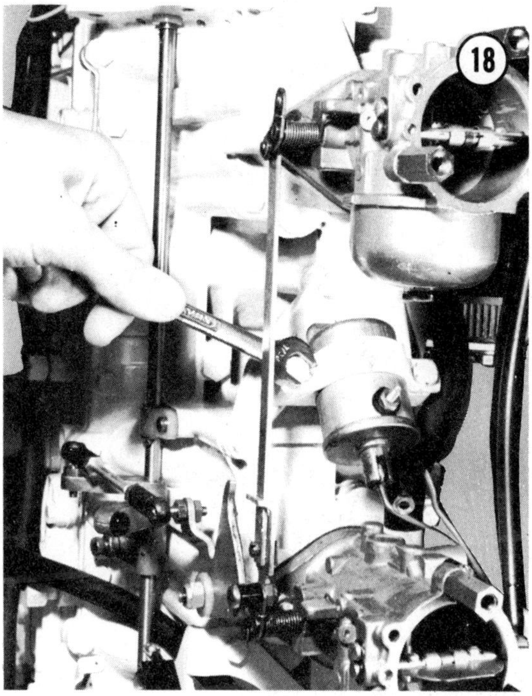

4. Install the choke plunger in the choke solenoid and install solenoid on bracket with terminal post at approximately 2 o'clock position.

5. Install the solenoid clamp and secure with 2 screws. Do not tighten at this time.

6. Adjust the choke solenoid position in the bracket. Refer to Chapter Six, *Tune-up, Synchronizing Choke Shutters (4-Cylinder Engines)*, in the front of this manual.

7. Connect the green lead wire to terminal post on solenoid and secure with lockwasher and hex nut.

8. Install ty-rap around solenoid and over wire to secure wire to body of solenoid.

Starter Solenoid Relay Removal/Installation

1. Disconnect battery leads from battery terminals.

2. Remove nut holding positive (+) battery lead wire (black with red end) and small (red/white stripe) lead wire to forward stud terminal of starter relay. Remove both leads (**Figure 19**).

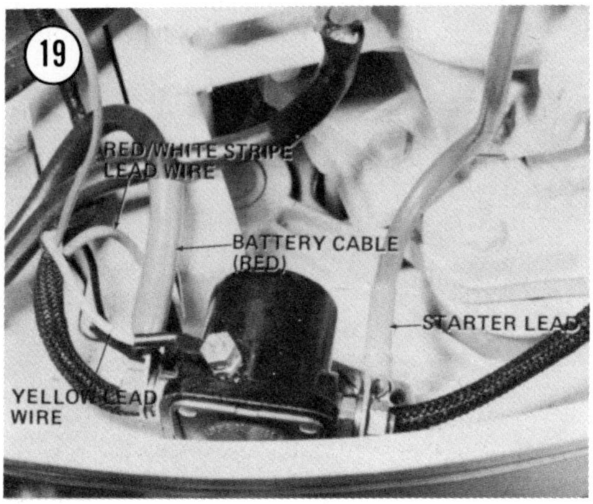

3. Remove nut holding yellow lead wire to top stud terminal on starter relay. Remove lead wire. See **Figure 19**.

4. Remove nut holding red lead wire (relay to starter motor) to rear stud terminal of starter relay. Remove lead wire. See **Figure 19**.

5. Remove rear mounting screw and lockwasher holding starter relay to support plate.

6. Remove forward mounting screw, wiring harness clamp, and ground lead securing starter relay to support plate. Remove starter relay.

7. To install the starter relay, position it on the bosses in the support plate and install rear mounting screw and lockwasher. Tighten securely.

8. Install the forward mounting screw, ground lead (from wiring harness), and wiring harness clamp. Tighten securely (**Figure 20**).

9. Install red/white stripe lead wire, lockwasher, and positive (+) battery lead on forward stud terminal on starter relay. Install hex nut and tighten securely.

10. Install lockwasher and yellow lead wire on the top stud terminal of the starter relay. Install hex nut and tighten securely.

11. Install lockwasher and red starter lead to the rear stud terminal on the starter relay. Install hex nut and tighten securely.

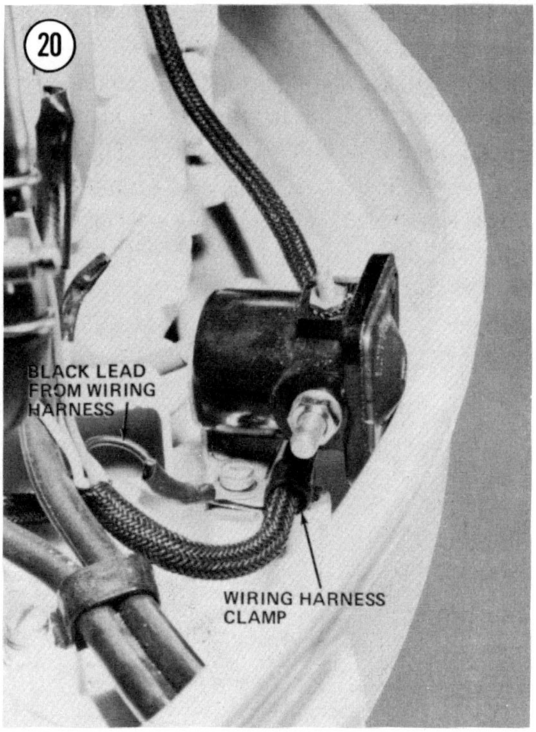

12. Connect the battery leads to the battery terminals.

Circuit Breaker Removal/Installation

1. Disconnect the battery leads from battery terminals.

2. Loosen 2 screws and plain washers holding circuit breaker bracket to terminal block bracket. Remove circuit breaker and bracket (**Figure 21**).

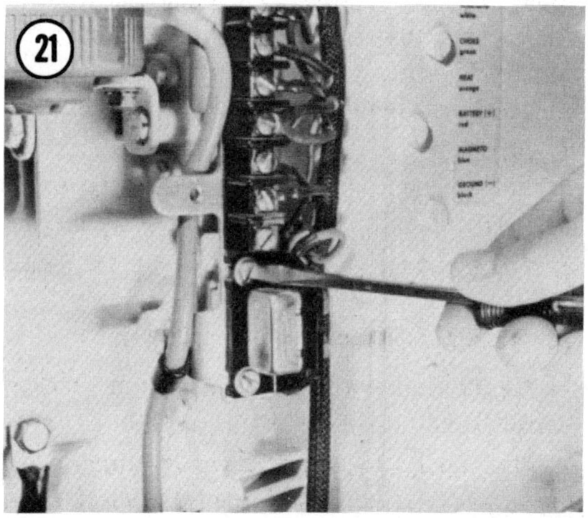

3. Remove hex nut, lead wire, and lockwasher from terminals of circuit breaker.

4. Remove hex nuts holding circuit breaker to bracket. Separate circuit breaker from bracket.

5. To install the circuit breaker on the bracket, position it so that the long stud terminal faces down when bracket is installed on engine. Secure circuit breaker to bracket with hex nuts (**Figure 22**).

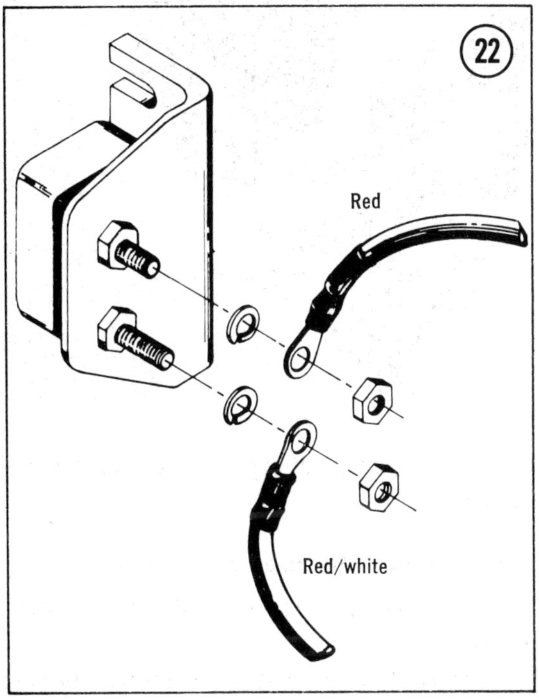

6. Install circuit breaker assembly on terminal block bracket and secure with 2 screws and plain washers (**Figure 22**). Then install lockwasher and red lead to top (short) stud terminal of circuit breaker and secure with hex nut. Refer to **Figure 22**.

7. Install lockwasher with red/white stripe lead to the long (bottom) stud terminal of the circuit breaker. Install hex nut and tighten securely.

8. Connect battery leads to battery terminals.

Terminal Block Removal/Installation

1. Disconnect battery leads from battery terminals.

2. Disconnect lead wires from terminal block, then remove 2 screws holding terminal block to terminal block bracket. Remove the terminal block.

3. To install the terminal block, position it on the terminal block bracket and install 2 screws securely.

4. Connect lead wires to terminal block (**Figure 23**).

5. Connect battery leads to battery terminals.

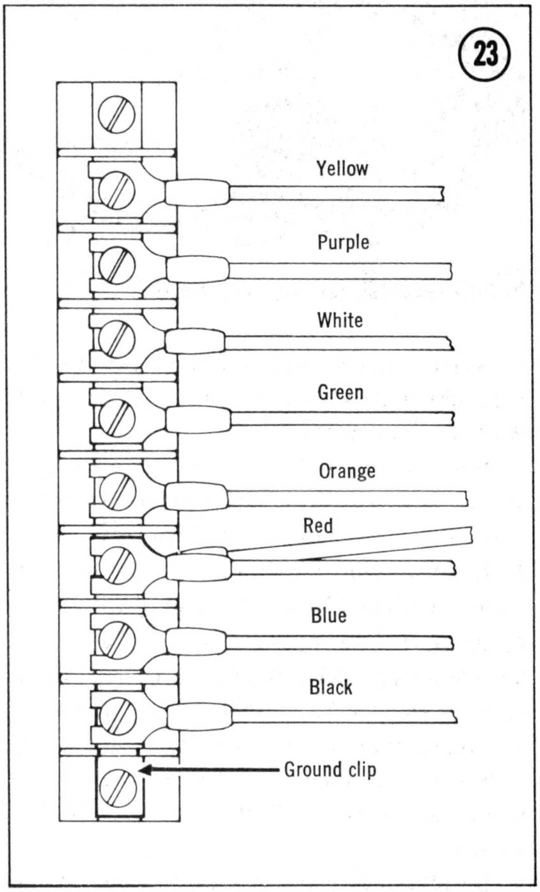

Ignition Coil Removal/Installation

1. Disconnect battery leads from battery terminals.

2. Disconnect primary lead wire (coil to spark plug) from top of coil by removing boot and pulling lead from coil.

3. Remove 3 screws and plain washers holding coil to cylinder head cover. Remove the coil (**Figure 24**).

4. Remove nuts, lockwashers, and lead wires from bottom of coil. Remove coil.

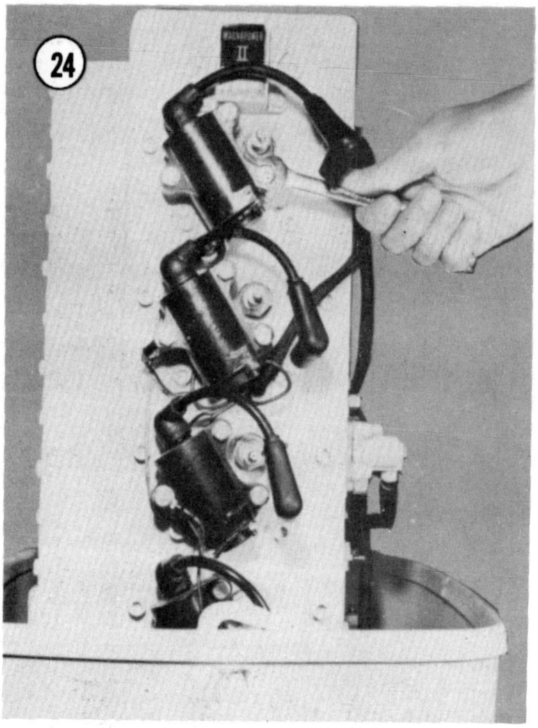

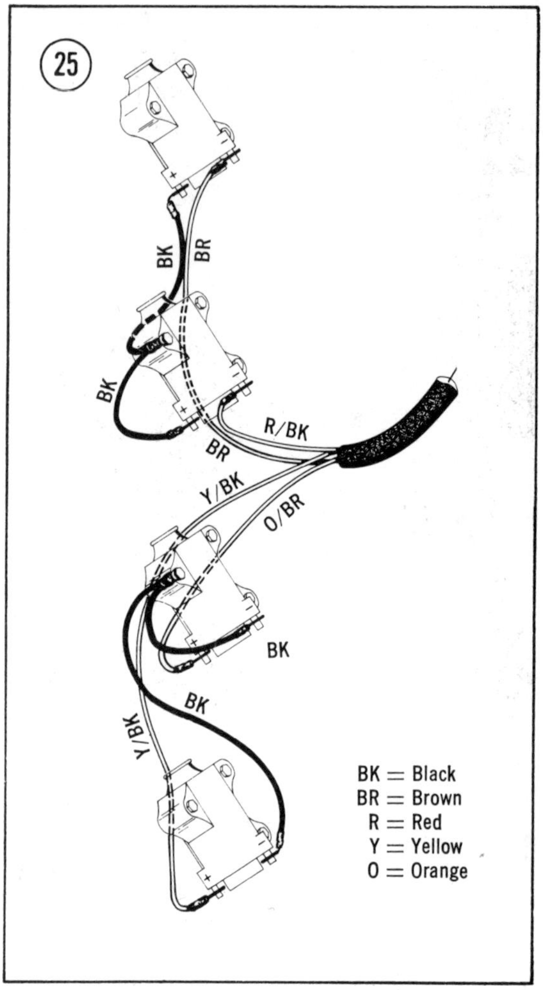

5. To install the coil, connect lead wires to ignition coil terminals and install lockwashers and hex nuts. Tighten securely (**Figure 25**). Then install ignition coil on cylinder head cover and secure with 3 screws and plain washers. Torque screws to 70 in.-lb.

6. Connect the high tension lead wire from the spark plug to the coil by pushing it into the coil, then pushing boot in place on coil end.

Thermoswitch Removal/Installation

1. Remove hex nut, lead wire, and lockwasher from stud terminal on thermoswicth.

2. Remove top ignition coil. See *Ignition Coil Removal/Installation* in this section.

3. Remove thermoswitch from cylinder head cover as shown in **Figure 26**.

4. To install the thermoswitch, position it on the cylinder head cover, install lockwasher, lead wire, and hex nut to terminal, and tighten securely.

5. Install ignition coil. Refer to *Ignition Coil Removal/Installation* in this section.

C-D Module Timing Ring Retainer Removal/Installation

1. Disconnect battery leads from battery terminals.

2. Remove flywheel. Refer to Chapter Six, *Flywheel, Removal,* in the front of this manual for the procedure.

3. Remove 4 stop nuts, timing ring retainer, and 4 bowed washers holding timing ring retainer to studs. Remove timing ring retainer (**Figure 27**).

4. Remove 5 screws holding C-D module to bearing cage. Remove C-D module from engine (**Figure 28**).

5. To install the C-D module and timing ring retainer, place the C-D module on the bearing cage and install 2 studs. Tighten securely.

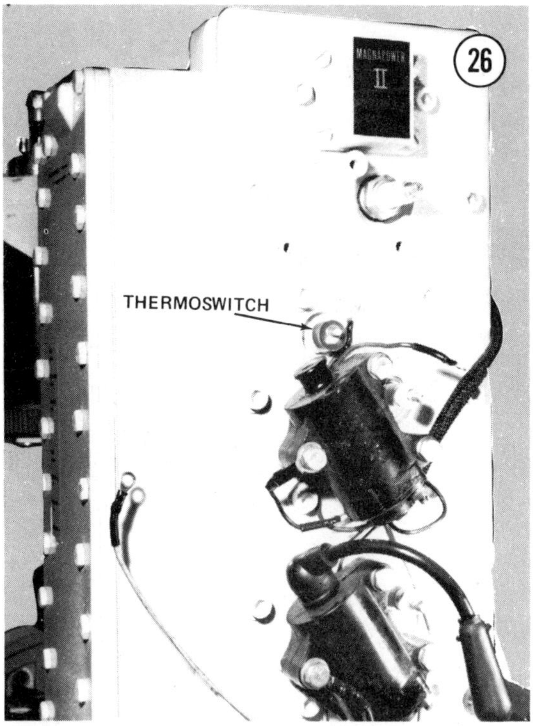

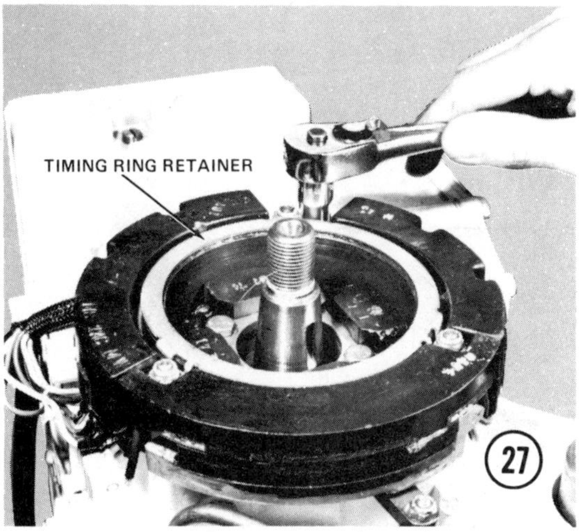

NOTE: *Push in on module to seat it properly against the bearing cage, when tightening mounting studs.*

6. Install screws, lead wires, and lockwasher to C-D module and tighten securely. Refer to **Figure 29** for proper lead wire connection.

7. Install 4 bowed washers, timing ring retainer, and 4 stop nuts. Tighten nuts down evenly onto a 0.003 in. feeler gauge blade placed between

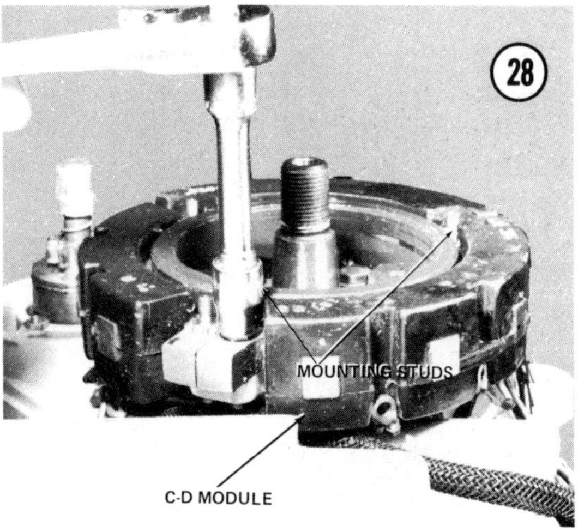

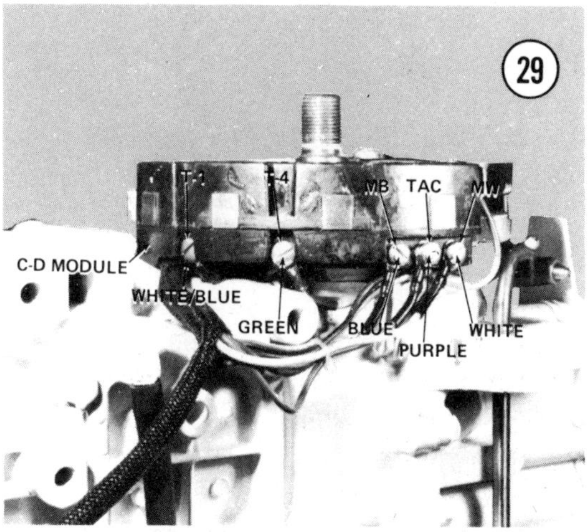

the retainer and timing ring at the retainer legs. There should be some drag on the feeler gauge. See **Figure 30**.

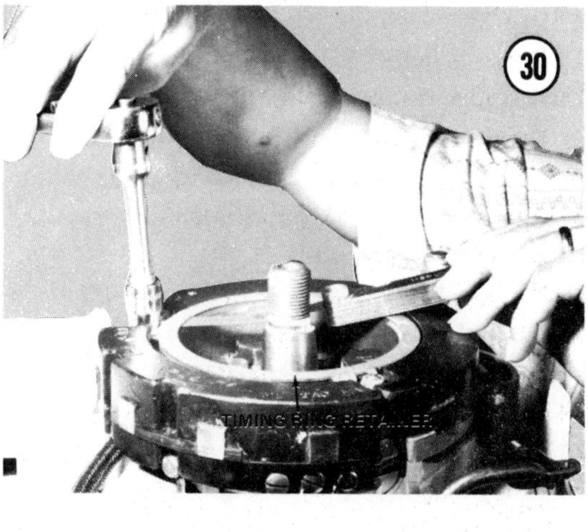

8

8. Check friction of timing ring by rotating it, using a spring scale attached to the outside hole of the pivot arm (towershaft disconnected). The reading should be 3-5 lb. Readjust stop nuts evenly (but no more than 1/8 turn to get proper friction). Refer to **Figure 31**.

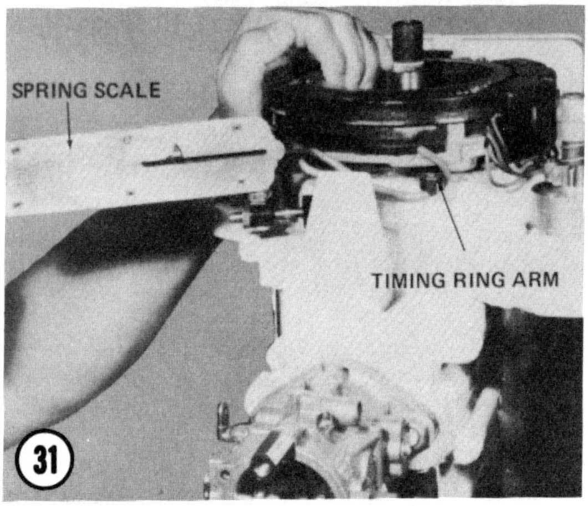

9. Install flywheel. Refer to Chapter Six, *Flywheel, Installation,* in the front of this manual, for the procedure.

10. Connect battery leads to battery terminals.

Alternator Stator Module Removal/Installation

1. Disconnect battery leads from battery terminals.

2. Remove flywheel. Refer to *Flywheel, Removal,* Chapter Six in the front of this manual, for the procedure.

3. Remove 2 screws and lockwashers holding lead wires to alternator stator module.

4. Remove timing ring retainer. Refer to *C-D Module Timing Ring Retainer Removal/Installation* in this section.

5. Remove 2 studs holding alternator stator module to bearing cage, then remove module from engine (**Figure 32**).

6. To install the alternator stator module, place it on the bearing cage and install 2 studs. Tighten securely.

> NOTE: *Push in on module to seat it properly against the bearing cage when tightening mounting studs.*

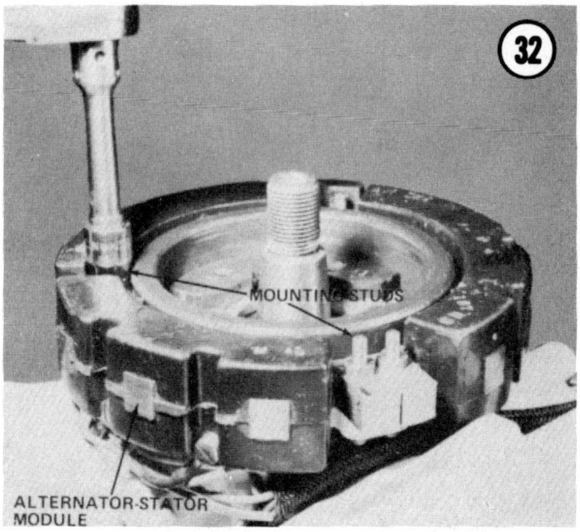

7. Install 2 screws, lead wires, and lockwashers to alternator stator module. Tighten securely. Refer to **Figure 33** for proper lead connection.

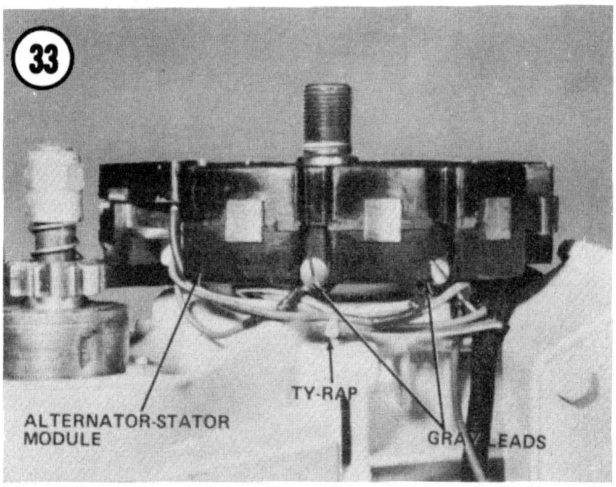

8. Install timing ring retainer. Refer to *C-D Module Timing Ring Retainer Removal/Installation* in this section.

9. Install flywheel. Refer to *Flywheel, Installation,* in Chapter Six, in the front of this manual, for the procedure.

10. Connect battery leads to battery terminals.

Capacitor Module Removal/Installation

1. Disconnect battery leads from battery terminals.

2. Remove flywheel. Refer to *Flywheel, Removal,* in Chapter Six in the front of this manual, for the procedure.

3. Remove timing ring retainer. Refer to *C-D Module Timing Ring Retainer Removal/Installation* in this section.

4. Remove 2 screws and lockwashers holding capacitor leads to C-D module.

5. Remove 2 studs holding capacitor module to bearing cage. Remove capacitor (**Figure 34**).

6. To install capacitor module, place it on the bearing cage, install 2 studs, and tighten securely.

> NOTE: *When tightening mounting studs, push in on module to seat it properly.*

7. Install 2 screws, lead wires, and lockwashers holding capacitor leads to C-D module (**Figure 35**).

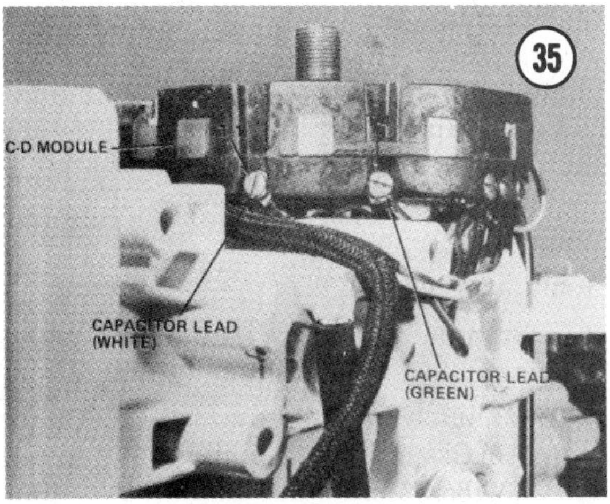

8. Install timing ring retainer. Refer to *C-D Module Timing Ring Retainer Removal/Installation* in this section.

9. Install flywheel. Refer to *Flywheel, Installation,* Chapter Six, in the front of this manual, for the procedure.

10. Connect battery leads to battery terminals.

Regulator-Rectifier Module Removal/Installation

1. Disconnect battery leads from battery terminals.

2. Remove flywheel. Refer to *Flywheel Removal,* Chapter Six in the front of this manual, for the procedure.

3. Remove capacitor module. Refer to *Capacitor Module Removal/Installation* in this section.

4. Remove 2 screws and lockwashers holding regulator-rectifier leads to alternator module. Remove one screw holding regulator-rectifier lead to terminal block.

5. Remove 2 screws and lockwashers holding regulator-rectifier to bearing cage. Remove regulator-rectifier (**Figure 36**).

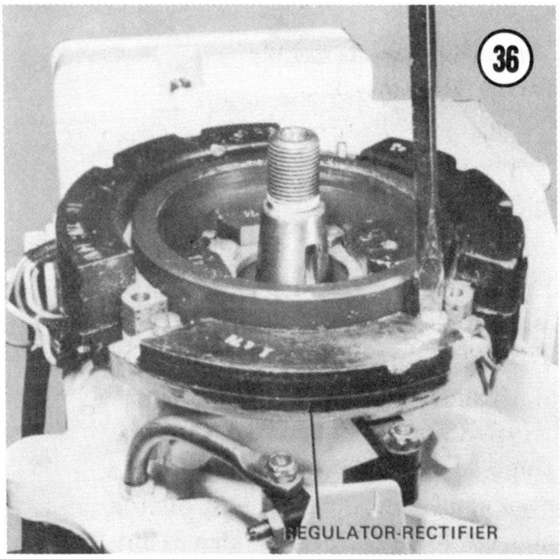

6. To install the regulator-rectifier, position it on the bearing cage and secure with 2 screws and lockwashers.

> NOTE: *Push in on module to seat it properly when tightening mounting screws.*

7. Install 2 screws and lockwashers to secure the regulator-rectifier leads to alternator module (**Figure 37**). Install one screw to hold the red regulator-rectifier lead to the terminal block.

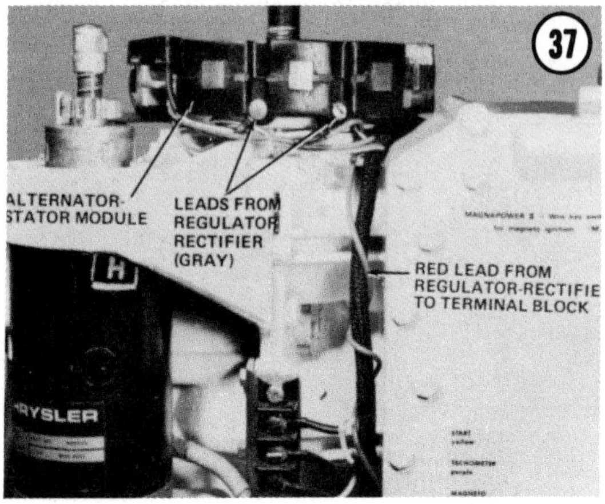

8. Install capacitor module. Refer to *Capacitor Module Removal/Installation* in this section.

9. Install flywheel. Refer to *Flywheel, Installation,* Chapter Six in the front of this manual, for the procedure.

10. Connect battery leads to battery terminals.

Trigger Module Removal/Installation

1. Disconnect battery leads from battery terminals.

2. Remove flywheel. Refer to *Flywheel, Removal,* Chapter Six in the front of this manual, for the procedure.

3. Remove 8 screws and lockwashers holding lead wires to trigger modules.

4. Remove 4 screws holding trigger assembly to bearing cage (**Figure 38**). Remove trigger assembly from bearing cage.

5. Remove trigger module from mounting plate (bend the metal clip down and slide the module from the plate as shown in **Figure 39**).

6. To install the trigger module, place it on the mounting plate with the terminals facing upward. Secure it by bending metal clip down. Refer to **Figure 39**.

7. Place the trigger assembly on bearing cage (with terminals facing upward) and install 4 screws (tighten securely). Then install 8 screws, lockwashers, and lead wires on trigger modules as shown in **Figure 40**.

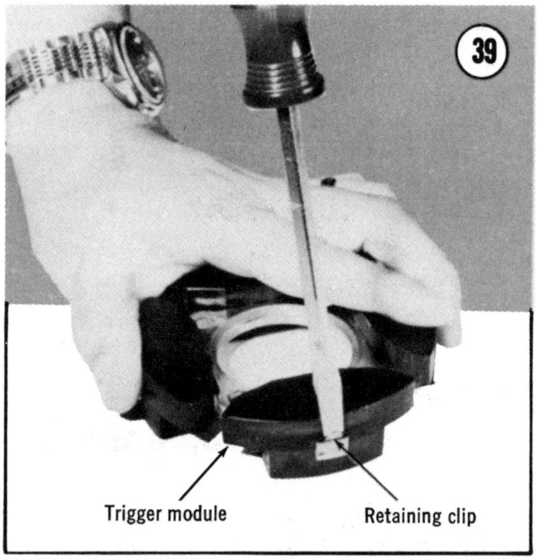

8. Install flywheel. Refer to Chapter Six, *Flywheel, Installation,* in the front of this manual, for the procedure.

9. Connect battery leads to battery terminals.

Timing Ring Removal/Installation

1. Remove flywheel. Refer to Chapter Six, *Flywheel, Removal,* in the front of this manual, for the procedure.

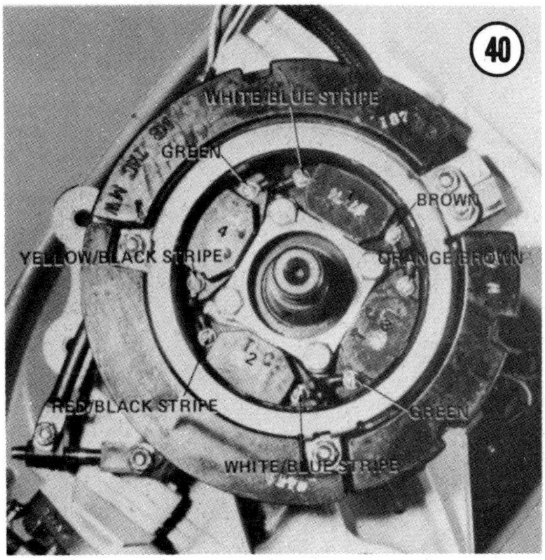

2. Remove screw, stop nut, and bowed washer holding spark control link to the timing ring arm (**Figure 41**).

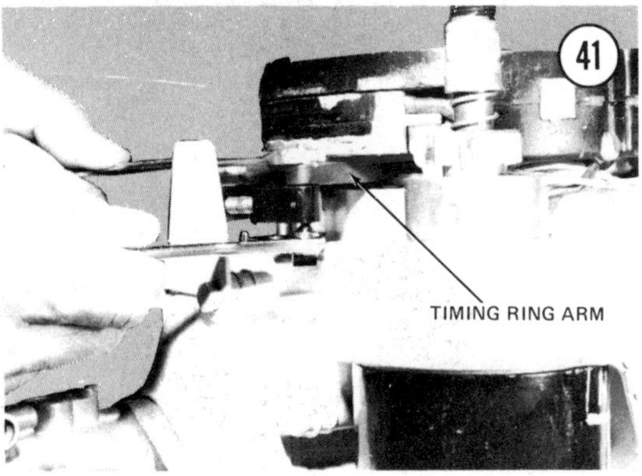

3. Remove trigger module assembly. Refer to *Trigger Module Removal/Installation* in this section.

4. Remove regulator-rectifier module. Refer to *Regulator-Rectifier Module Removal/Installation* in this section.

5. To install the timing ring, apply grease to the bearing cage and lay the timing ring in the bearing cage with timing ring arm to the port side (**Figure 42**).

6. Apply grease (special tool T2961 or equivalent) to timing ring retainer. Install timing ring retainer. Refer to *C-D Module Timing Ring Retainer Removal/Installation* in this section.

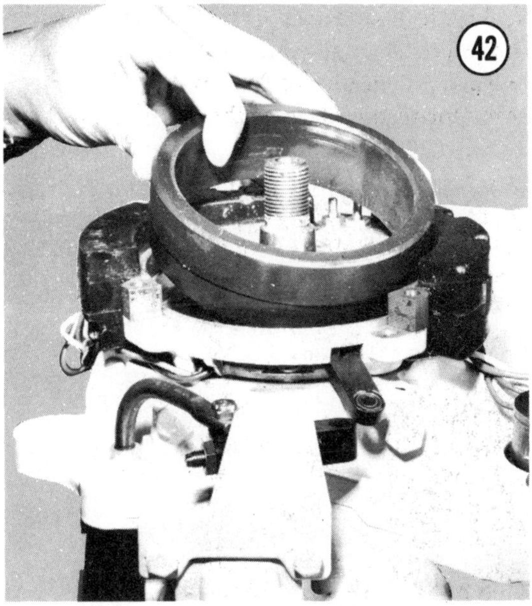

7. Install trigger module assembly. Refer to *Trigger Module Removal/Installation* in this section.

8. Install screw, stop nut, and bowed washer holding spark control link to the timing ring arm. Refer to **Figure 41**.

9. Install flywheel. See *Flywheel, Installation,* Chapter Six in the front of this manual, for the procedure.

Wiring Harness Removal/Installation

1. Disconnect battery leads from battery terminals.

2. Remove flywheel. Refer to Chapter Six, *Flywheel, Removal,* in the front of this manual, for the procedure.

3. Remove lead wires from interlock switch terminals.

4. Remove green lead from choke solenoid terminal.

5. Remove lead wires from starter relay. See *Starter Solenoid (Relay) Removal/Installation* in this section.

6. Disconnect lead wires from circuit breaker. Refer to *Circuit Breaker Removal/Installation* in this section.

7. Disconnect lead wires from terminal block; remove lead wires from ignition coils (refer to

Ignition Coil Removal/Installation in this section); remove orange lead from stud terminal on thermoswitch.

8. Remove 8 lead wires from C-D module. Refer to *C-D Module Timing Ring Retainer Removal/Installation* in this section. Remove the wiring harness.

> NOTE: *The C-D module must be removed to allow clearance for removal of wiring harness. Refer to* **Figure 43**.

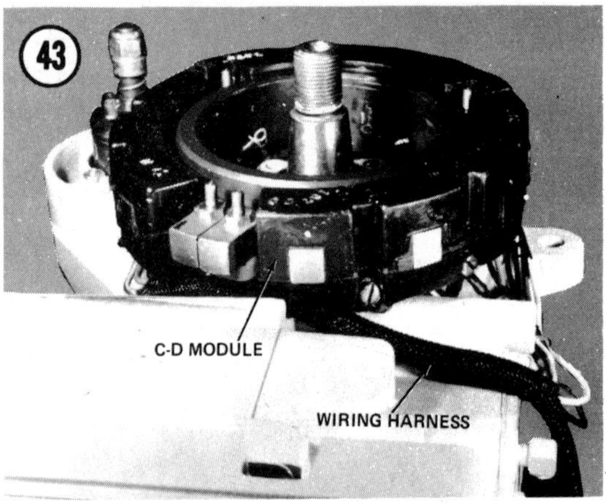

9. To install the wiring harness, connect the leadwires to the terminal block and breaker. Refer to **Figures 22 and 23**.

10. Route the wiring harness down and toward front of engine. Secure wiring harness to forward mounting boss of starter relay with clamp. Connect leads to starter relay (**Figure 20**).

11. Connect the green lead to terminal stud on choke solenoid. Install lockwasher and hex nut and tighten securely.

12. Route the remaining yellow leads under carburetor toward starboard side of engine. Connect leads to interlock switch terminals.

13. Route wiring harness up and over cylinder (**Figure 44**). At first break-out from terminal block, route the orange/brown stripe and brown wires through rear hole (port side) in bearing cage. Connect the orange/brown wire to No. 3 trigger coil rear terminal—connect brown wire to No. 1 trigger coil terminal, port side. Route the green and white/blue stripe wire to the front hole (port side) in bearing cage—connect green wire to forward terminal of No. 3 trigger coil—

connect white/blue stripe wire to port side terminal, No. 2 trigger coil. From the second break-out in wiring harness from terminal block, route yellow/black and red/black stripe wires to front hole in bearing cage (starboard side). Connect the red/black stripe wire to the No. 2 trigger coil starboard side terminal. Connect the yellow/black stripe wire to front terminal of trigger coil No. 4. The 2 short double jumper wires (white/blue stripe and green wires) go in rear hole of bearing cage (starboard); the green wires go to the rear terminal of trigger No. 4—white/blue stripe wire goes to starboard side of trigger coil No. 4.

14. Install C-D module and connect lead wires as outlined in *C-D Module Timing Ring Retainer Removal/Installation* in this section. Install ty-rap around lead wires from harness to C-D module.

> NOTE: *Route wires around the flywheel in a downward fashion and away from flywheel, in order to prevent rubbing on flywheel.*

15. Connect lead wires to ignition coils (**Figure 25**); connect orange lead to stud terminal on thermoswitch and secure with lockwasher and hex nut.

16. Install flywheel. Refer to Chapter Six, *Flywheel, Installation,* in the front of this manual, for the procedure.

17. Connect battery leads to battery terminals.

INDEX

8

NOTES

NOTES

MAINTENANCE LOG

DATE	TYPE OF SERVICE	COST	REMARKS

Do-It-Yourself Boat Maintenance

The world's largest publisher of automotive and motorcycle manuals now offers a complete line of maintenance and tune-up handbooks for owners of sailboats, powerboats, outboard motors, stern drive units, and small inboard engines.

Each title features step-by-step procedures for maintaining and repairing the hull, fittings, interior, electrical systems, plumbing, galley equipment, and the countless other items that keep boat owners busy.

As in all Clymer handbooks, the expert text and detailed photos and illustrations will put money-saving maintenance well within the reach of anyone reasonably handy with tools.

The titles listed below are available through your local bookstore, marine outlet, or postpaid direct from Clymer Publications.

SAILBOAT MAINTENANCE	(B600)	$9.00
POWERBOAT MAINTENANCE	(B620)	$9.00
BRITISH SEAGULL OUTBOARDS, 1.5 TO 6 HP	(B660)	$8.00
CHRYSLER OUTBOARDS, 3.5 TO 20 HP, 1966-1977	(B655)	$8.00
CHRYSLER OUTBOARDS, 25 TO 135 HP, 1966-1977	(B657)	$8.00
EVINRUDE OUTBOARDS, 1.5 TO 33 HP, 1965-1977	(B644)	$8.00
EVINRUDE OUTBOARDS, 40 TO 140 HP, 1965-1977	(B647)	$8.00
JOHNSON OUTBOARDS, 1.5 TO 33 HP, 1965-1977	(B663)	$8.00
JOHNSON OUTBOARDS, 40 TO 140 HP, 1965-1977	(B665)	$8.00
MERCURY OUTBOARDS, 4 TO 40 HP, 1964-1977	(B650)	$8.00
MERCURY OUTBOARDS, 50 TO 150 HP, 1964-1977	(B653)	$8.00
SAILBOAT AUXILIARY ENGINES (Atomic, Chrysler, Ford, Perkins, Pisces, Volvo-Penta, Westerbeke, and Yanmar)	(B610)	$9.00
STERN DRIVE UNITS (OMC, MerCruiser, Volvo, Stern-Powr, Berkeley, and Jacuzzi)	(B641)	$9.00

CLYMER PUBLICATIONS

12860 MUSCATINE STREET • P.O. BOX 20 • ARLETA, CALIFORNIA 91331